I0824367

Art from the Garden

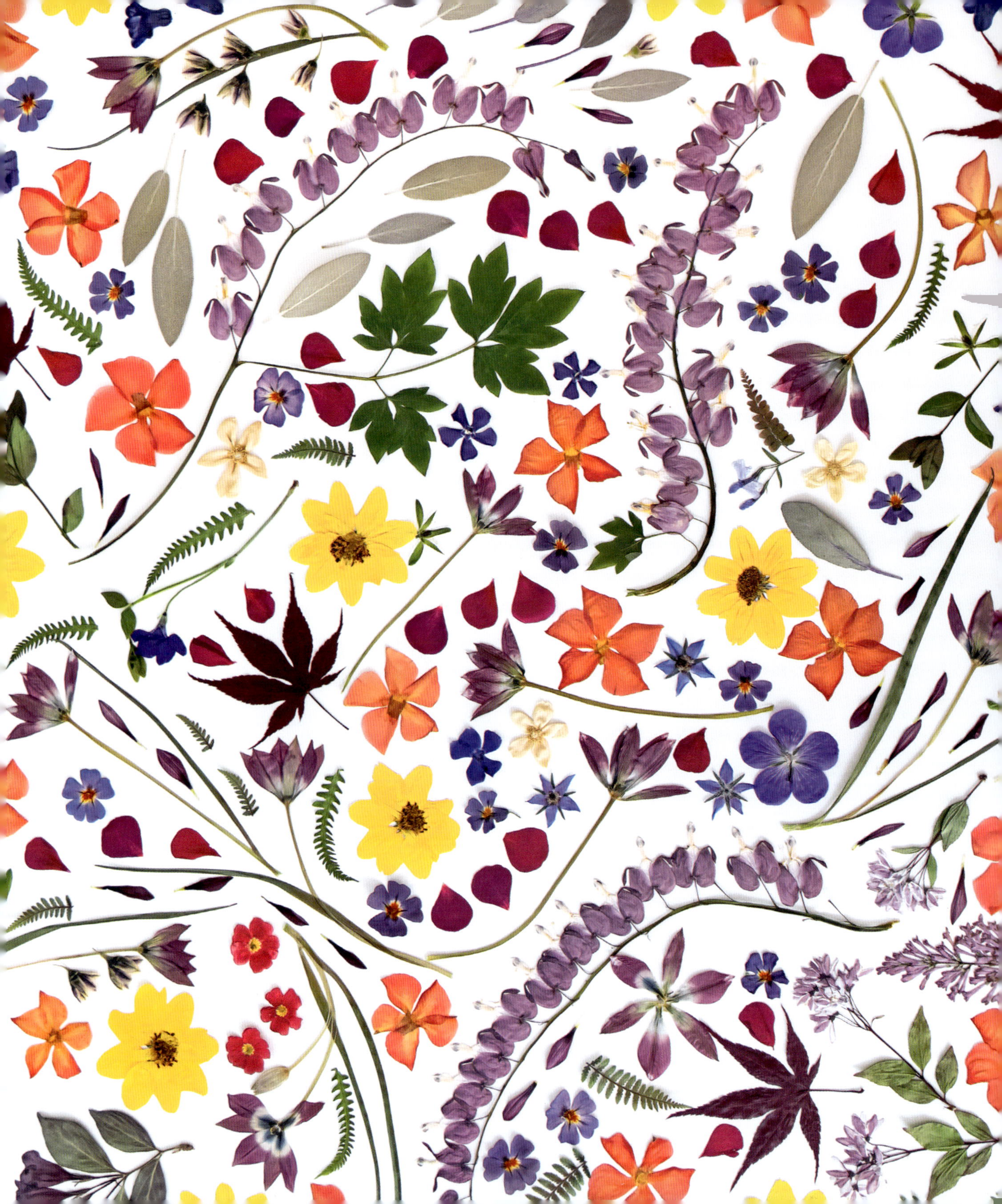

Art from the Garden

CREATE 25 BEAUTIFUL BOTANICAL PROJECTS

Kerry Michaels

Liz Micheels, Art and Design Consultant

Timber Press
Portland, OR

All photos are by the author.

Timber Press
Workman Publishing
Hachette Book Group, Inc.
1290 Avenue of the Americas
New York, New York 10104
timberpress.com

Timber Press is an imprint of Workman Publishing, a division of Hachette Book Group, Inc. The Timber Press name and logo are registered trademarks of Hachette Book Group, Inc.

Printed in Dongguan, China (TLF), on responsibly sourced paper

Text design by Hillary Caudle and Sara Isasi
Cover design by Sara Isasi

ISBN 978-1-64326-417-2

A catalog record for this book is available from the Library of Congress.

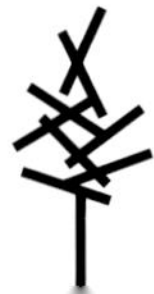

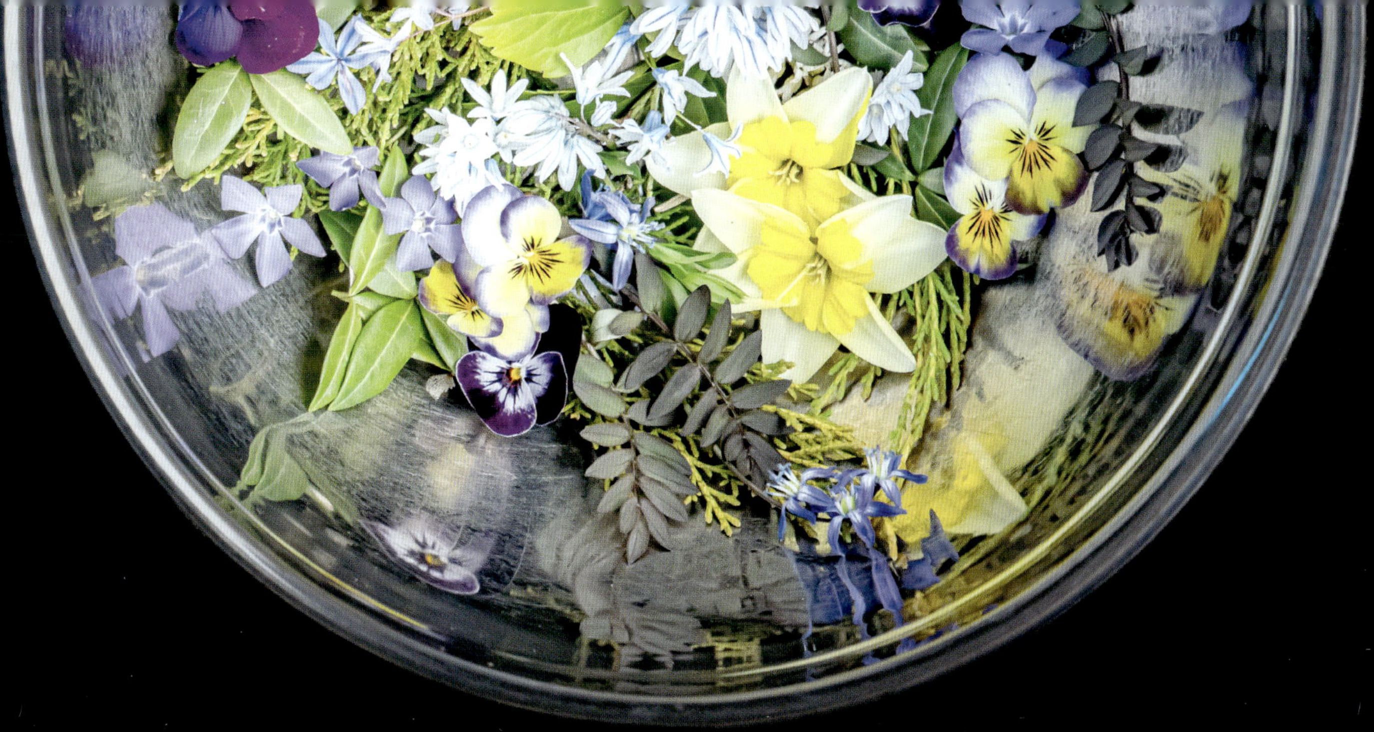

For Brett, Ethan, and Maya
—KM

For David, Graham, and Erik
—LM

And for our Moms

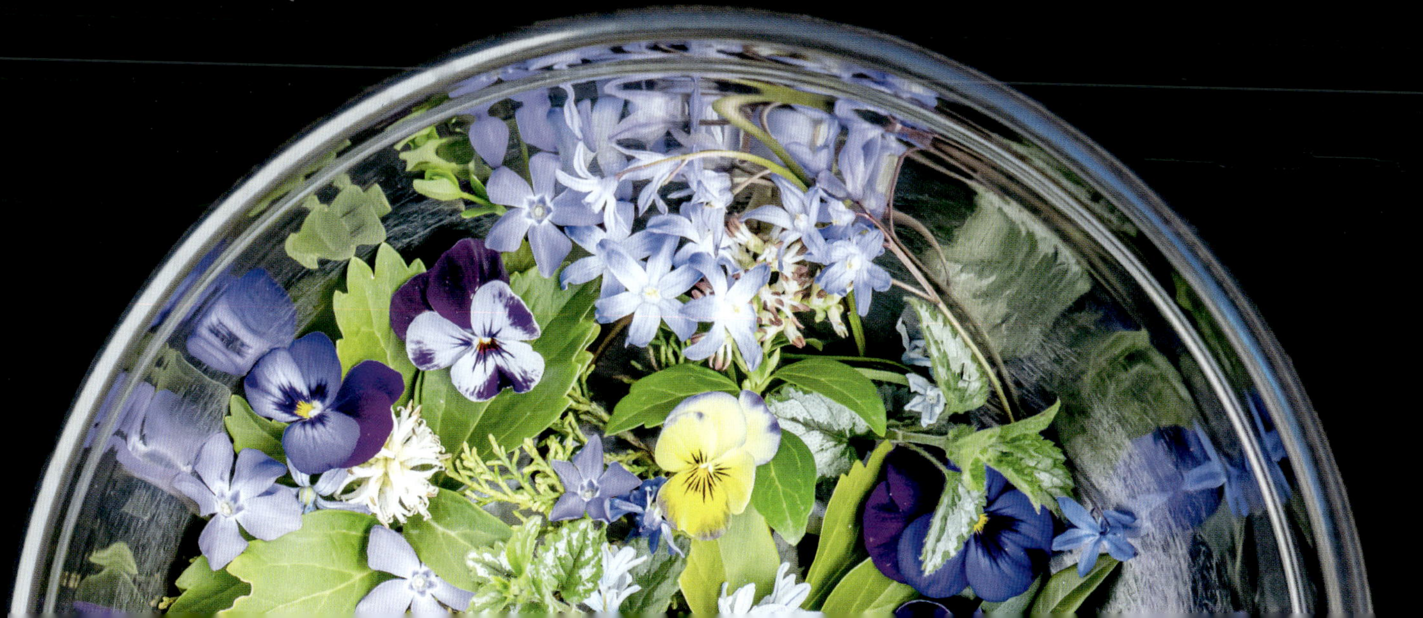

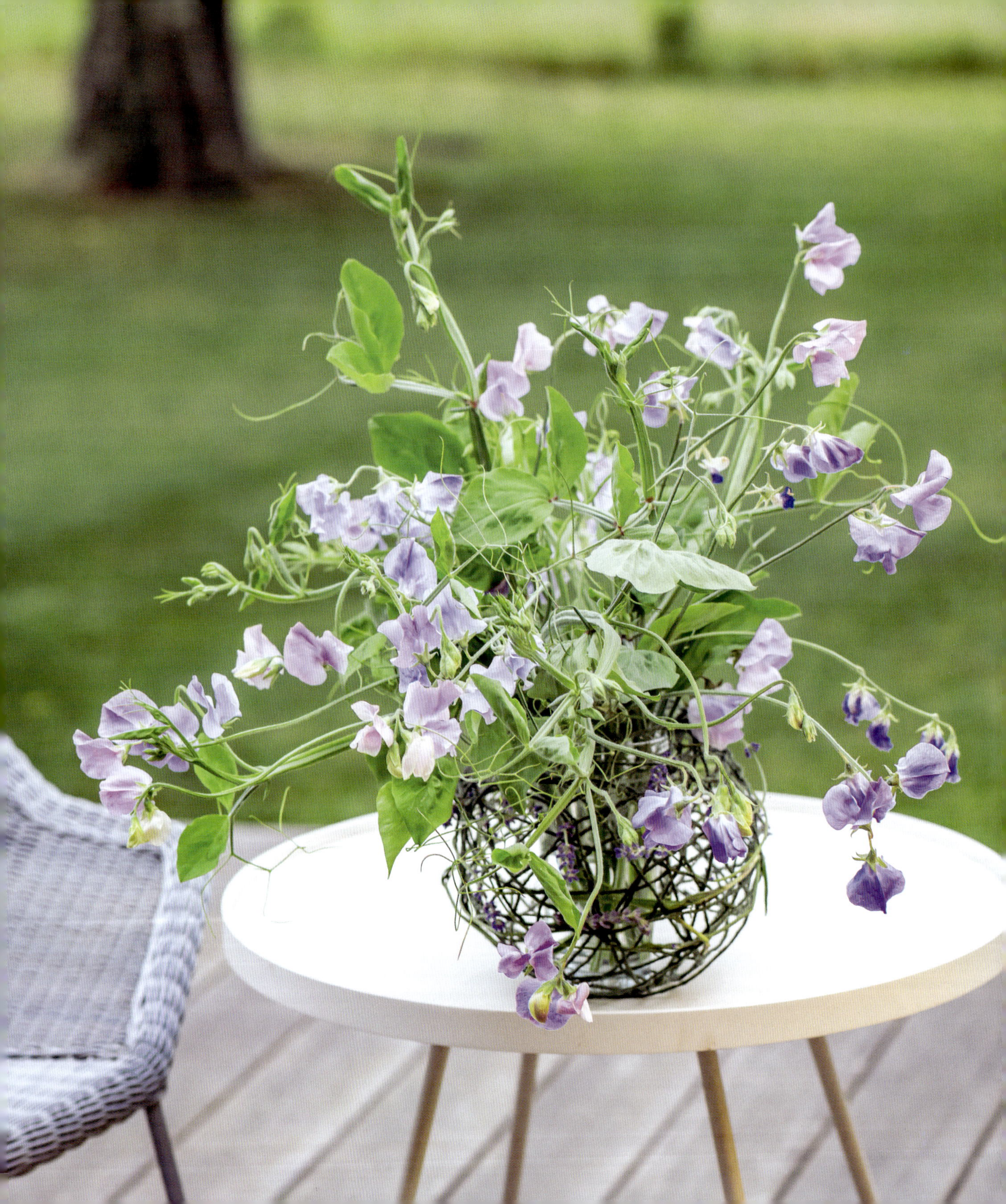

Contents

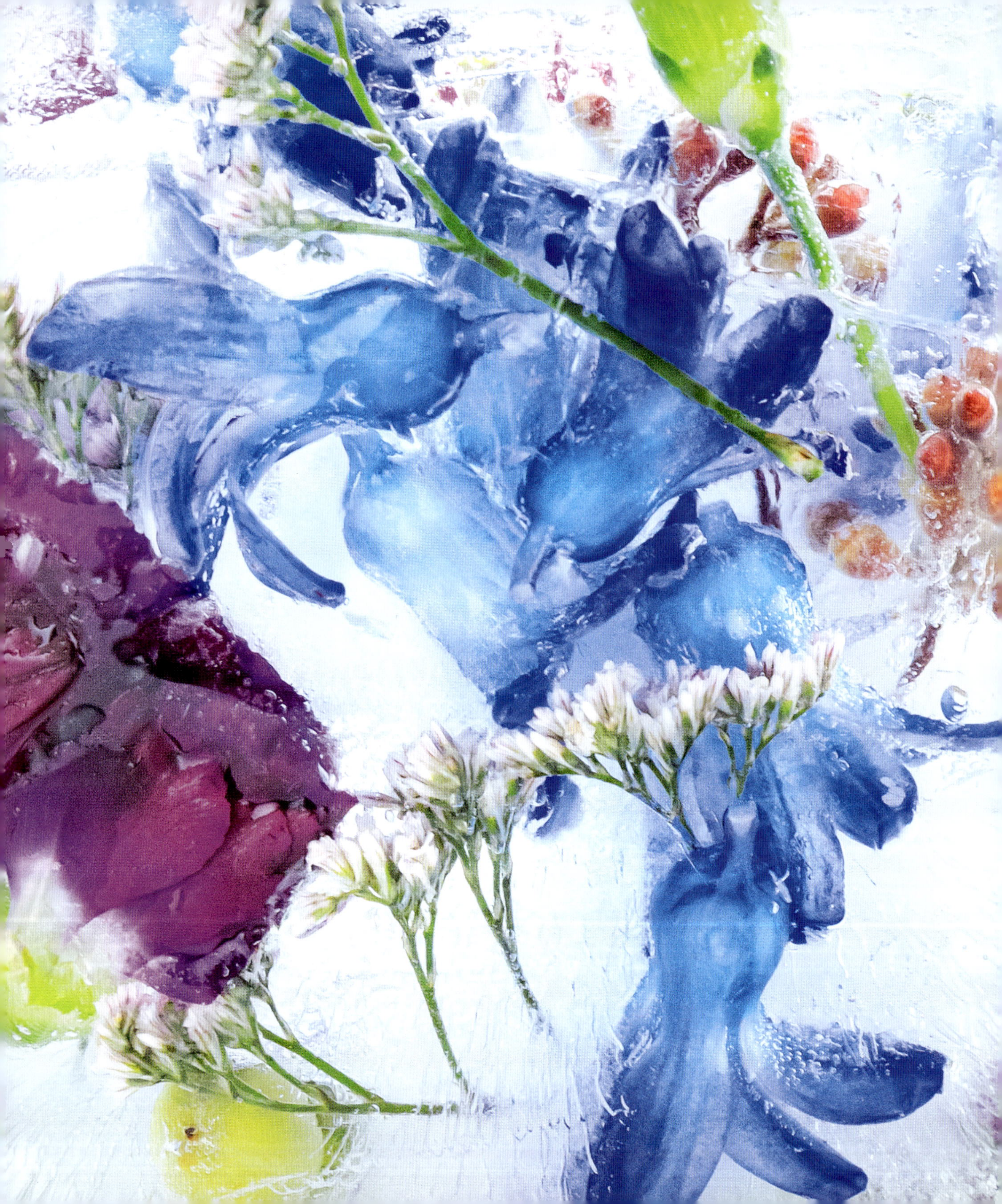

Introduction

Practicing an art, no matter how well or badly, is a way to make your soul grow for heaven's sake. Sing in the shower. Dance to the radio. Tell stories. Write a poem to a friend, even a lousy poem. Do it as well as you possibly can. You will get an enormous reward. You will have created something.

—Kurt Vonnegut,
A Man Without a Country

When I moved from Manhattan to the coast of Maine in 2001, with my husband and our two toddlers, I was woefully unprepared. I couldn't cook, and I certainly didn't garden. In fact, I was a certified houseplant slayer. While I thought plants were beautiful and loved flowers, I had no idea how to keep them alive.

After living in an apartment for most of my adulthood, the requirements of rural(ish) life were hard to reconcile and difficult to master. I could just barely keep my head above domestic waters. And professionally, as a writer and filmmaker, finding a job in Maine proved daunting.

When I saw an ad on Craigslist for a job creating a website on container gardening, I thought, "Well, I've written about so many topics about which I know absolutely nothing, from serial killers to infrastructure to country decorating, why not gardening?" I got the job and wrote articles, shot photos, and posted a daily blog chronicling my successes and failures in container gardening. For the eight years I had the job, each summer I would grow close to a hundred containers and over time learned how to do it fairly successfully. I also learned that to grow plants you have to pay attention, and that by paying attention you can experience wild joy.

And then there's the beauty. The beauty of growing things—flowers, grasses, trees, and leaves. Even weeds can be a wonder. Whether you have grown them yourself, foraged them from your backyard or someone else's, or even bought them at a store, there is so much that can be done by taking these natural elements and trying to maintain their essence—or soul, if you will—while creating art.

I believe in the transformative power of art—making art, looking at art, experiencing it in any way possible. For me, the confluence of art and nature is particularly fascinating and powerful. Hence this book.

The projects here are chosen because they are accessible. They are not a blueprint to get you to a precise outcome but are meant as inspiration to pursue your own vision. You won't need a whole lot of equipment, though some projects are more involved than others. In just a few hours, it is possible to create something that you will, hopefully, be proud of. Though some projects will take longer, many can be completed in an afternoon. But there is a caveat: As with any art or craft, mastery is never easy. It can take years, decades, or even a lifetime to truly understand and become comfortable with processes. Take cyanotypes (also called sun prints). Even small children can use this technique to create gorgeous prints, worthy of framing. But there are also artists who dedicate their lives to the nuances of this process and will blow your mind with the beauty and sophistication of their work.

While there will always be a debate about the difference between art and craft, for the purposes of this book, I will use the words interchangeably, as I think the distinction is mostly academic. There is craft in art and art in craft, so let's consider them equal. I would even posit that perhaps they are both essential to what makes us human.

So please, take these projects as a place to start. Try the processes that appeal to you and run with them. Push the limits of the materials, and don't be afraid to fail, as failure is almost a guarantee when trying a new medium. And if you do fail, try again and again and again. Chances are it will get easier with each attempt, and even if for some reason it doesn't, I can almost guarantee that you will learn something with each try.

I have created many, many hideously ugly projects and will continue to do so. Because just as in learning to garden you have to kill plants, when making art you have to fail and fail spectacularly. While that part isn't necessarily fun, it can also lead you to places in your creative practice and process that you would not have reached otherwise.

Although failure is part of the learning process, so is joy, and thankfully, most days the joy outweighs frustration by miles. These projects are really about joy. I find almost every phase of these projects joyful. Whether it's the adventure of collecting materials, the sensuous squishing of ink, or watching a gloriously blue sun exposure emerge from a water bath, I experience a deep and profound happiness. To see natural materials transformed into art is an alchemy that is magical.

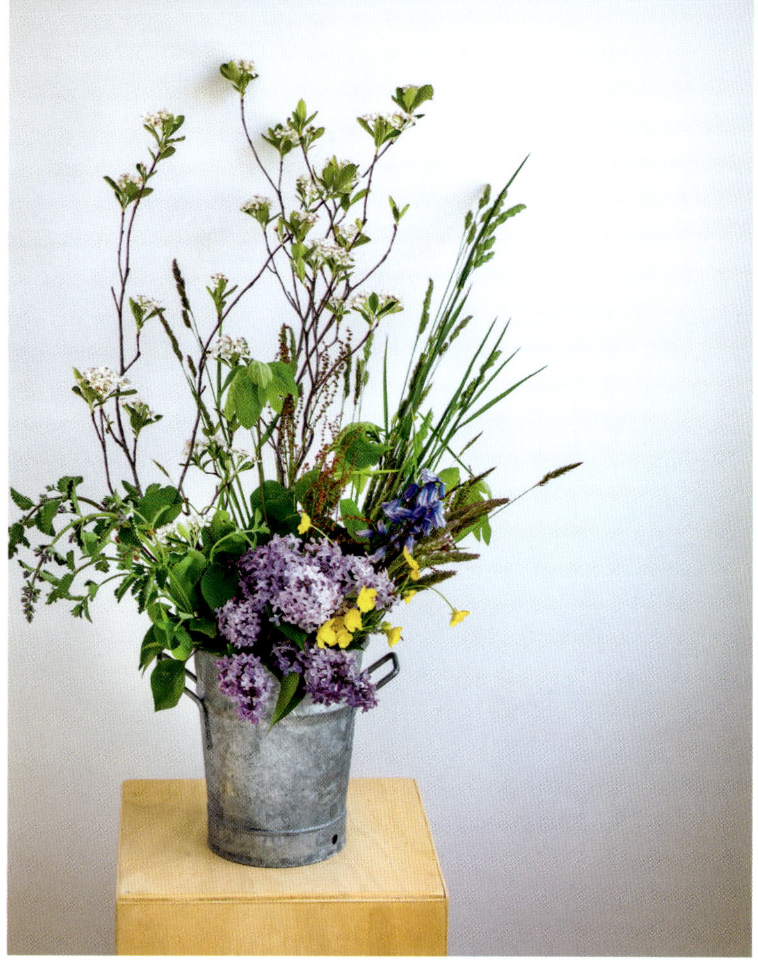

Foraging and Collecting Botanicals

One of my favorite parts of making botanical art is the foraging and collecting, which I have come to think of as an art in itself. I've also found it a meditation—and honestly, it has changed how I see and move through the world. I have realized that there is looking and then there is seeing. What I mean is this: When I started searching for fall leaves, I went out to the woods and looked around, scanning for the autumn-defining oranges, scarlets, and ochers. All I saw was insect-eaten, wind-whipped, brown, curled leaves. Disappointed, I stood there and wondered (and worried) what I was going to do, because I needed those leaves to complete a project. Then I noticed a dusty pink compound leaf at about knee level. It was a wild blackberry leaf, and it was perfect—a little prickly, but I found that I could get rid of the thorns with a thumbnail. I then saw that some of the surrounding blackberry leaves had a lime green and dusty rose striped pattern. Beautiful. Not New England's luminous yellows or maple reds. No, but these leaves were delicate, subtle, and gorgeous. Over time I began to see the woods in a different way—even when not foraging. I started noticing and appreciating individual leaves—their shapes, their colors, and their spatial relationship to each other, and feeling such pleasure from this seeing.

Looking for rocks and stones has also been a revelation. There are so many characteristics that make a rock special and useful. I never really noticed rocks before, but now, as I search for smooth rocks with a pleasing color and shape, I see interesting rocks everywhere. And when I take the time to look at them, it is simultaneously energizing and calming. When I am completely focused on observing and seeing, the wider scenery drops away as my eyes sweep and then focus on just a leaf, rock, or flower. Finding that (almost) perfect, unblemished, symmetrical blossom or pleasantly formed stone is enormously satisfying. Perhaps we are even biologically hardwired for that surge of joy, because historically finding the best fruit or edible plant would have had huge consequences for keeping the family fed and healthy.

Most people will tell you to forage or collect in the early morning, which is considered the optimal time. But I say do it whenever you can fit it into your life. Also, in the early morning, plants are often soaking with dew, which isn't great if you are drying them. I like to at least wait until the sun has dried them off a bit. And although some leaves and flowers will wilt practically the moment you pick them no matter the time of day, most will be fine if you get them into water as soon as possible and use them while they are still fresh.

When collecting botanicals, my favorite receptacle is an old, lightweight mesh colander. I have also used trays, bowls, plastic containers, and, in a pinch, my shirt as a collection vessel, so anything that works for you or that you have on hand is fine. Just try to keep delicate botanicals relatively flat and separated so they don't get tangled, folded, or broken, although this is often easier said than done.

The following list of tips for ethical foraging may seem obvious, but bear with me ...

- When you collect wild things, make sure you know that they are common and not something rare or scarce that needs protecting. There are several great apps that will help you instantly identify plants. These are invaluable tools to have on your phone.

- Only pick what you need, and be sure to leave lots behind. Some people use the "rule of twenty." If there is a large swath of even common plants, take only one in twenty so that you don't damage the colony.

- Never pick from someone's garden, even if you know them, without permission. That said, I have left messages with my phone number in neighbors' mailboxes asking if I can pick a sprig or a few flowers that they have in abundance. Most of the time the answer is yes. It never fails to delight me how generous gardeners are.

- Do not collect in public parks or gardens—not even one leaf. Unless it is explicitly permitted, just don't.

- Pick carefully. Use sharp, clean scissors or garden clippers. And unless you want the entire plant with roots, just cut the part of the plant you need. Also, don't carelessly tread on or smush plants on your way to the chosen one.

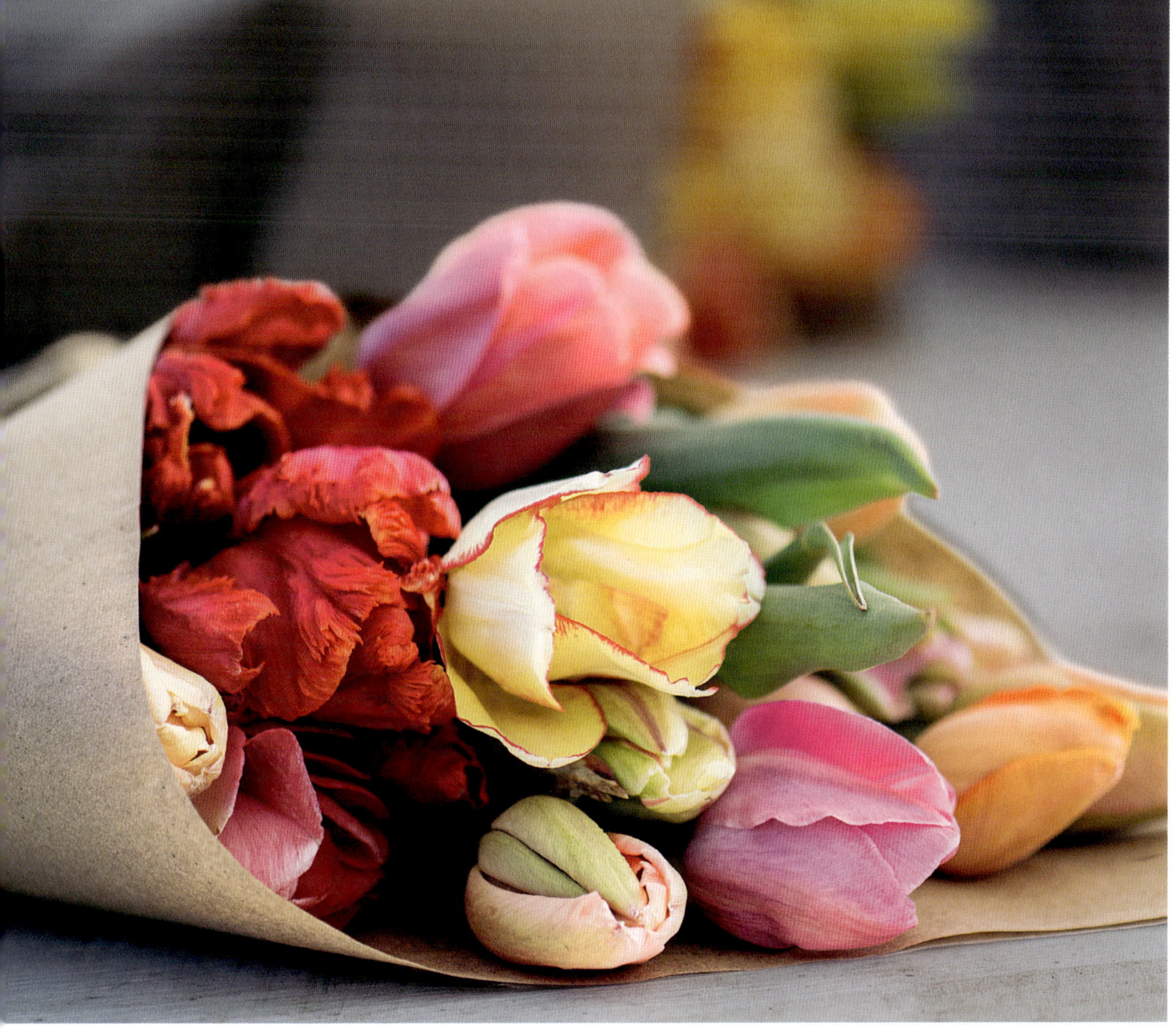

If You Don't Have a Garden or Backyard

If you don't have a garden or backyard, you can still do every project in this book. The most gorgeous blooms can be found at farm stands and farmers' markets. Flowers and foliage are available in supermarkets, nurseries, even big-box stores. But keep in mind that locally grown, independent grower/sellers often have the freshest and most splendid flowers, and by buying from them you are supporting the local economy.

And don't overlook weeds. Some weeds will give even the most refined plants a run for their beauty. It amazes me what beauty can be found in parking lots and by roadsides.

And while there is enormous satisfaction in doing every step in each project in this book—from the gathering and foraging through the creation—it is possible to skip ahead and buy dried botanicals from local flower farmers or online.

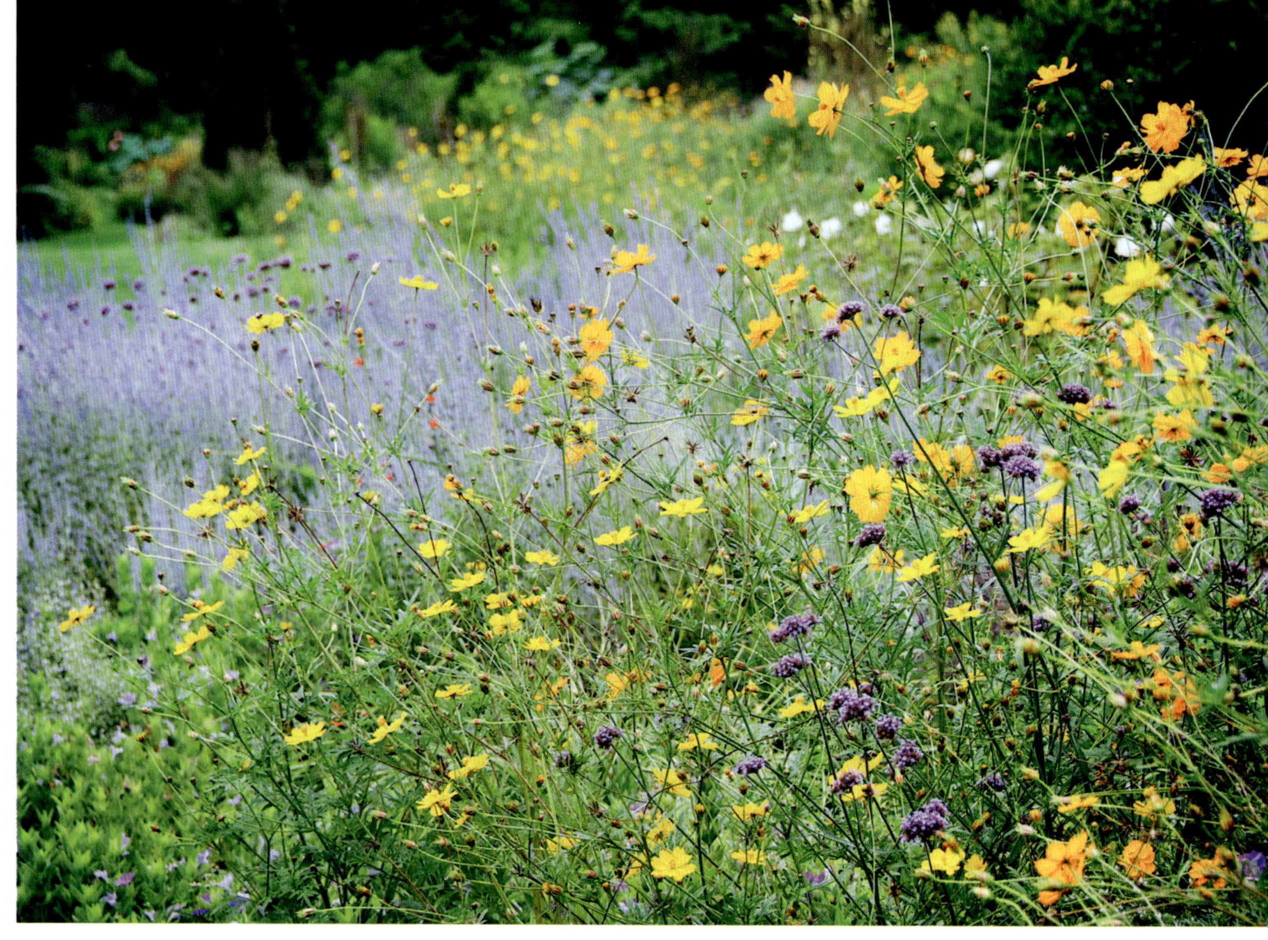

Some Thoughts on Gardening

In the interest of honesty, I will admit to having a love-hate relationship with gardening. In spring I am in love because it is the season of hope and optimism. Spring is about the garden you have in your dreams—the one where there are no weeds, your tomatoes will all ripen into perfect globes of edible sunshine, and your flawless dahlias will bloom with abandon. There is no blight, no earwig infestation, and no random plant death.

In spring I love cleaning out the same garden beds that I have tended for more than twenty-five years. I buy plants and seeds with unbridled gluttony (always exceeding my budget), and I plant way too many containers, but the happiness it brings me is luminous. I have a few weeks of total bliss (and exhaustion), and then comes the maintenance phase . . . which is where things start to fall apart.

All those containers need to be watered. Sometimes every day, if rain is scarce. Sometimes even twice a day, if the weather is hot and sunny. Then the bugs come: tomato hornworms, earwigs, lily leaf beetles, and mosquitoes, to name just a few. My tomatoes get blight or wilt, and the lettuce starts to bolt. And then there are the weeds. I recently ran into a neighbor who said that she loves weeding—that it is her therapy. My first thought was envy. My second thought was incredulity. I wish I loved to weed. I can weed happily for a bit, but not for the marathon it would take to clear my gardens of their weeds. Despite my best efforts, the weeds, as gardeners know all too well, are champions at defeating all attempts to control them. I admire their tenacity but hate their rapacity.

Given these struggles, you may well ask why garden at all. When I was asked to write to a group of urban high school students who were going to start a garden, I thought long and hard about *why* I garden, and this is what I came up with.

LETTER TO NEW GARDENERS

I hear you are going to start a garden. Congratulations. When you start a garden, you are also starting an adventure. And like all good adventures, it is a journey where you begin in one place and sometimes end up where you expected, and sometimes you end up someplace very different than you thought you would. Starting a garden is an act of faith and joy, and to be honest, a bit of an act of insanity.

Let me explain. Gardening isn't easy. If anyone tells you there is a foolproof method, plant, or fertilizer, well then, they are the fool. There are no guarantees with gardening—you can do everything perfectly and still fail. The good news is that you can also make lots of mistakes and still succeed.

When you garden, you depend on the weather, which means you are gambling. Mother Nature can be a witch. She can hurl down too much rain, droughts that will make you weep, and winds that will shred your tender plants. Sometimes she even sends a plague of locusts. That said, she can also dole out a perfect gentle rain that will water your seedlings just the right amount and feed your soul. She can provide the sunlight that will dazzle your eyes and delight your tomato plants. In a word, she is unpredictable.

Gardening is hard work. There is no getting around it. You will sweat and get dirty, sore, and tired. Gardening is also a commitment. If you forget to water something or want to take a long break away from your garden in the middle of the growing season, chances are your plants will die and your garden won't thrive. It's that simple.

"Then why garden?" you might ask. There are, of course, the practical reasons. As Ron Finley, a gardener from South Central Los Angeles says, "Growing food is like printing money." It truly can be. You can buy a packet of seeds for a few dollars and get a ridiculous return on your money. Fancy greens sell in stores for huge amounts, yet they only cost pennies to grow. Do you like lettuce and cucumbers? You can grow pounds and pounds of them, and they will be the best you have ever

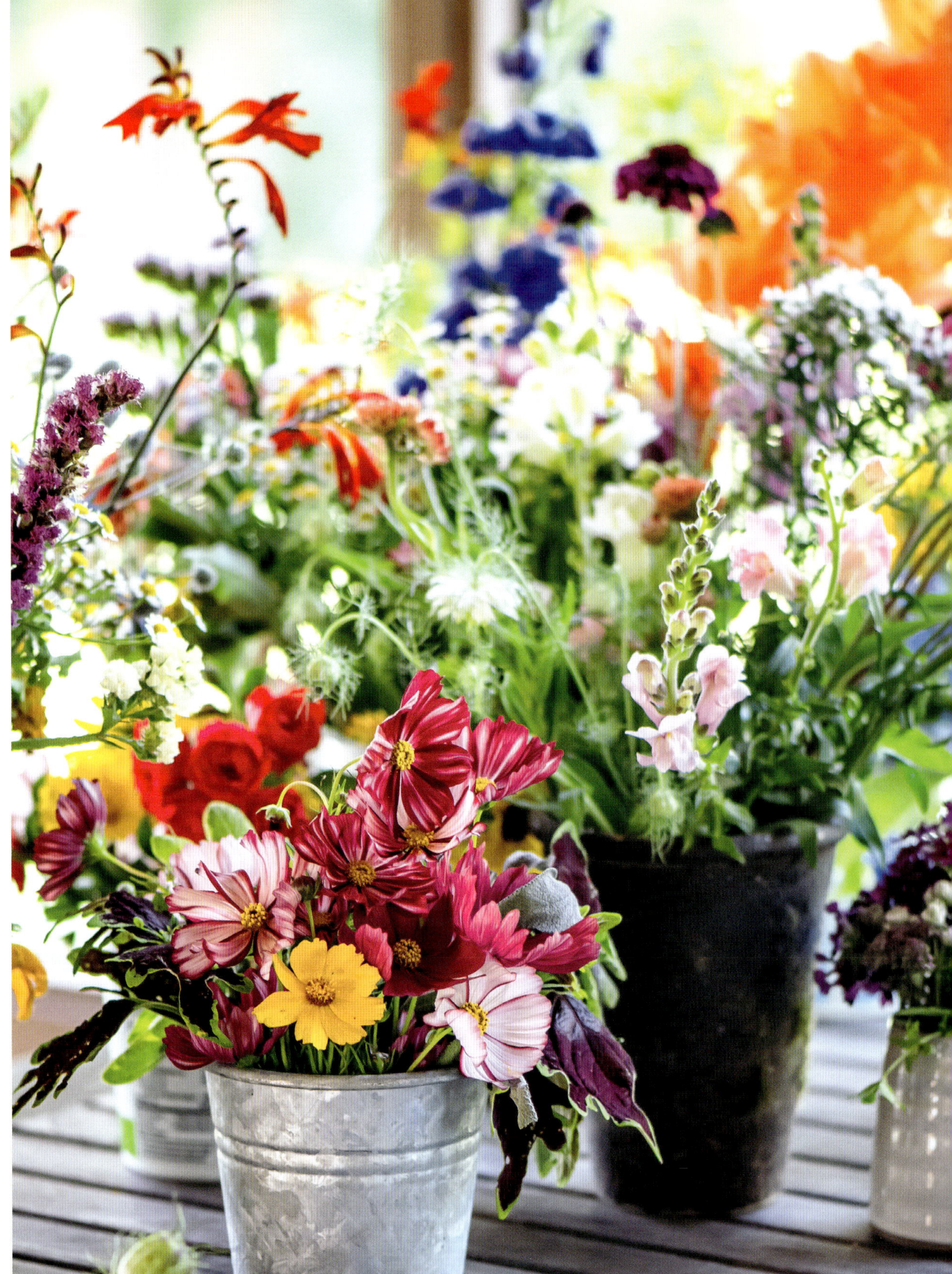

tasted. Peppers and potatoes? You can grow buckets full and have them to eat without ever going to the store. Don't like peas? You might when they are just picked. And flowers? Picking a bouquet of blooms you have grown can offer a kind of bliss that is rare and precious.

People aren't born with green thumbs. That is a ridiculous myth. People who are good gardeners pay attention. They have learned what plants need and they give it to them. Anyone can be a good or even a great gardener. It is truly an equal opportunity endeavor, because you know what? Plants don't care who you are. They don't care about your past and they don't care about your future. They don't care what your issues are or if you are rich, poor, or pretty. They only care that you are present and will care for them.

I garden for all these reasons, but here's really why I garden. It's one of the few things I do where I get to help create small miracles. I plant a tiny, dry tomato seed. It germinates and turns into a fragile seedling. With a combination of effort, patience, and good luck, it turns into a huge, sprawling plant and starts to flower. The bees and pollinators do their thing, and tiny tomatoes appear. They grow and ripen, and when I pick them off the vine and eat them, it feels like I am eating magic. It seems impossible that the seed at the start of the season became this juicy, spectacularly delicious tomato that I get to eat.

And here's some advice. You will kill plants. Even the best gardeners in the world kill plants … and that's fine. The good news is that if you pay attention, you will learn from killing plants. Maybe you overwatered a plant and it keeled over dead, or maybe you forgot to water it enough. Maybe next time you will do it right. Or it might take a few tries, but one day, more of your plants will survive than die, and that feels great.

Gardening is a something you have to learn—it is not something you are born knowing or can instantly master. It requires knowledge and experience, which you can and will get with time, and practice. You can also ask for help. I have found that gardeners are some of the most generous people in the world. Ask them questions, and most of the time they will either give you answers or help you find them. If there is no one around to ask, look it up online or in books. There are huge resources of knowledge available to you for free.

Gardening isn't going to be for everyone, but for those who embrace it, it can change your life; give you something to be proud of; and, who knows—in the end, you might even like eating kale.

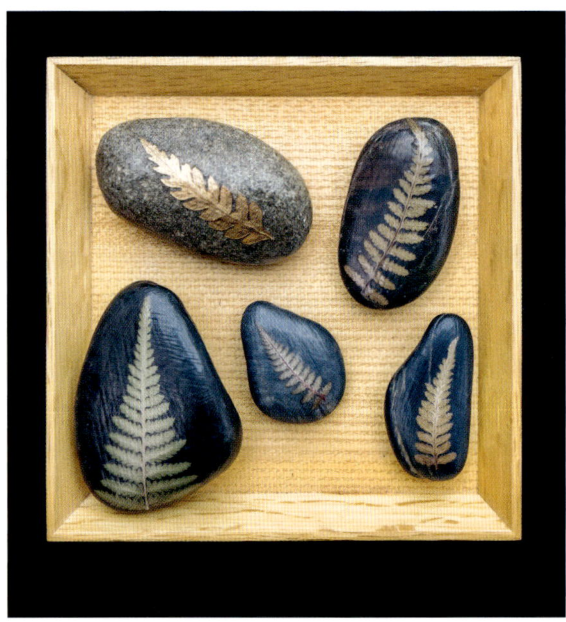

Embracing Wabi Sabi

According to Andrew Juniper in the book *Wabi Sabi: The Japanese Art of Impermanence,* wabi sabi art is "built on the precepts of simplicity, humility, restraint, naturalness, joy, and melancholy as well as the defining element of impermanence."

Wabi sabi, in popular culture, has also come to mean the celebration of imperfection, and I'm totally on board with that concept. The projects in this book don't aim at perfection, they aim for joy, both in the making and the keeping or gifting of them. Imperfection is a given, and the final products will fall somewhere on the spectrum of impermanence.

Your pieces will all have imperfections, but keep in mind that a fault in a piece can be celebrated and transformed into an asset. For example, when I was making the hydrangea bowl on page 149, some of the flowers, once dried, turned an unpleasant brown. I looked at the bowl and considered pitching it, but instead decided to use some gold paint on the brown bits. I was delighted to discover that gold paint can hide a multitude of sins, and that adding that bit of bling enhanced the finished bowl.

Many projects in this book use dried botanicals, and even if those botanicals are preserved in wax, or dried and glued, or sprayed with a preservative, they will fade and change over time. The good news is that there can still be beauty in the more muted colors that evolve, and dried botanicals can have surprising longevity. Dried flowers found in a two-thousand-year-old Roman tomb in Egypt were still intact. There are countless examples of centuries-old framed botanicals in museums and homes that remain stunning, even after their vividness has waned.

So I encourage you to embrace wabi sabi and accept, work with, and, when possible, celebrate the inevitable mistakes and imperfections.

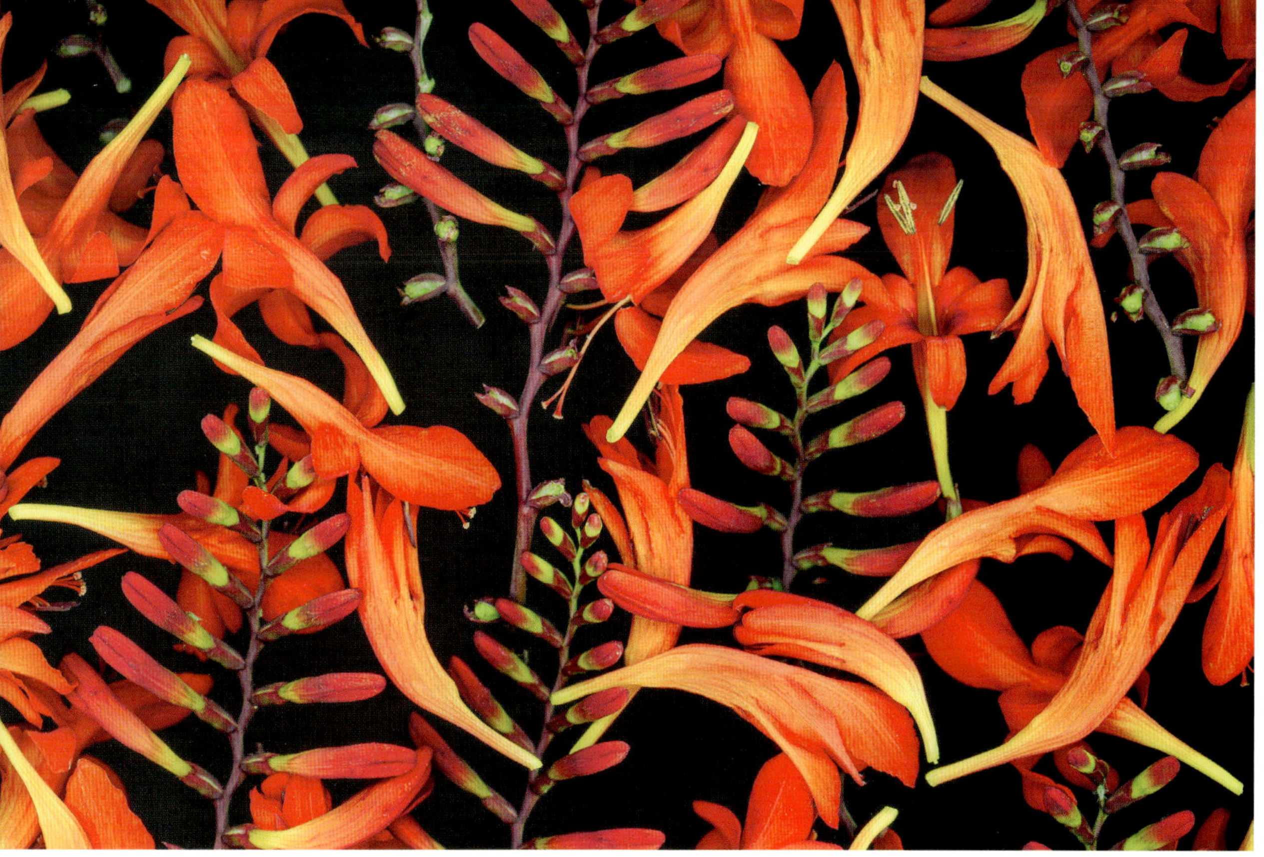

Fear: A Digression

Let's talk about fear for a minute. I'm not going too far out on a limb to say that there is a lot of fear and shame, or fear of shame, when it comes to making art. Ironically, those feelings may be part of what makes it worth doing. To make art, you have to reach and stretch your mind, body, and emotions—in essence, you must grow. Sometimes a piece or process will come easily, but sometimes it will be hard, and, over time, failure is all but guaranteed. On the other hand, if we always succeeded, there wouldn't be much value or pleasure in the successes. To make matters more complex, success in art is totally debatable and completely subjective.

Many of us have an inner critic sitting on our shoulders waiting for us to try something new. For some people, that critic is a vicious little monster who will whisper in your ear how inadequate, incompetent, untalented, and flat-out worthless you are. A critic who will ask, "Who do you think you are that you can make something beautiful or worthwhile?" A voice that will delight in proclaiming, "You are not an artist; you can't make art."

That critic isn't doing anyone any good. While it is important to realistically evaluate and assess your work, free-floating negativity can be a dagger in the heart of creativity. In attempting any creative endeavor, chances are you will need to develop strategies to shut your critic into a mental locked box so that you can go about making your art.

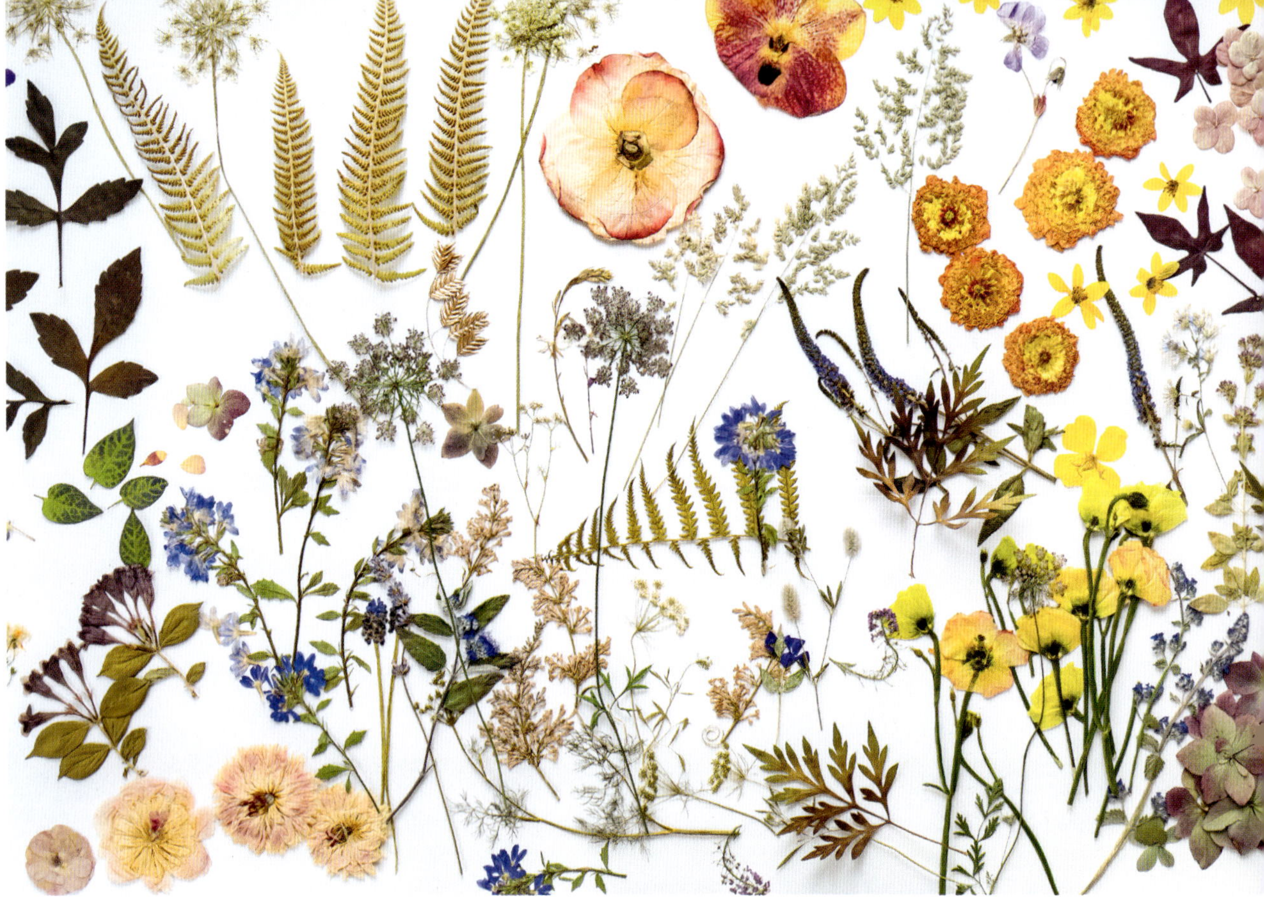

My mother was a wise woman who said many life-changing things, but one of the most helpful was the suggestion that when you are struggling to do something hard or frightening, you should ask yourself, What would you do if you were the most secure person in the world? This question helps tease complex emotions apart, highlighting the insecurities that may be causing anguish, hindering or even stopping you altogether. But the good news is that sometimes just by naming the shame or fear and exposing it to the light, it either evaporates or diminishes to a point where you can wrestle it into submission long enough to proceed through the emotional weeds and do what you want to do. And if that fails, sometimes it's just best to quit for the day, have a stiff drink, and wrestle the demon tomorrow.

Drying Botanicals

I believe in the transformative powers of drying flowers—both on the dryer and the dryee. I'm not being hyperbolic. Drying flowers is one of the easiest, most gratifying projects you can do. It can change how you garden and how you walk through the natural world. Not kidding. Part of the revelation to me was taking a three-dimensional flower and flattening it into two dimensions. Suddenly, the negative space around the flower and leaves popped out. It transformed from a sculptural object to a graphic one, which was visually exciting.

Also, while dried flowers are still somewhat ephemeral—they will change color and fade over time—drying allows you to capture a moment in time and prolong its beauty. Often when I open a flower press, I am stunned by how striking even random placings look and how differently alive —balletic almost—the flowers and foliage can appear, even though they are technically dead.

Although there are many ways to dry botanicals, I primarily use three. The first is in a traditional flower press, made of boards with long bolts and wing nuts, that allows you to sandwich botanicals between layers of paper and dry under pressure. It takes anywhere from a few days to a few weeks for the plant material to dry this way, depending on the air temperature and humidity as well as the moisture content of the leaves and flowers. For the second method, I use a microwave to blast the moisture out of the botanicals. Instead of days and weeks, this can take seconds.

My preferred way to dry flowers is a hybrid of the two methods: first drying in the microwave and then finishing them off in a traditional press, or simply pressing them between layers of paper under the weight of heavy books. I find this is a great way to work and is the most successful and time efficient.

However, some botanicals are too large for the microwave and my traditional presses, so I also have two large, flat boards that I use for drying oversized botanicals—making what is essentially a traditional flower press without the nuts and bolts. I simply place one large board on the bottom and then make layers, sandwiching cardboard, paper, and flowers, as I would with a traditional flower press. Then I place the other board on top. Instead of using screws to create pressure, I stack heavy tiles, large books, and even rocks on top.

Yet another, and perhaps the easiest, way to dry botanicals is to simply press them between the pages of a book. However, be aware, that the pages can get stained. Also, I often forget where I've stashed my botanicals and only find them when I pull something out to read and, like a kaleidoscope of butterflies, the flowers flutter to the floor.

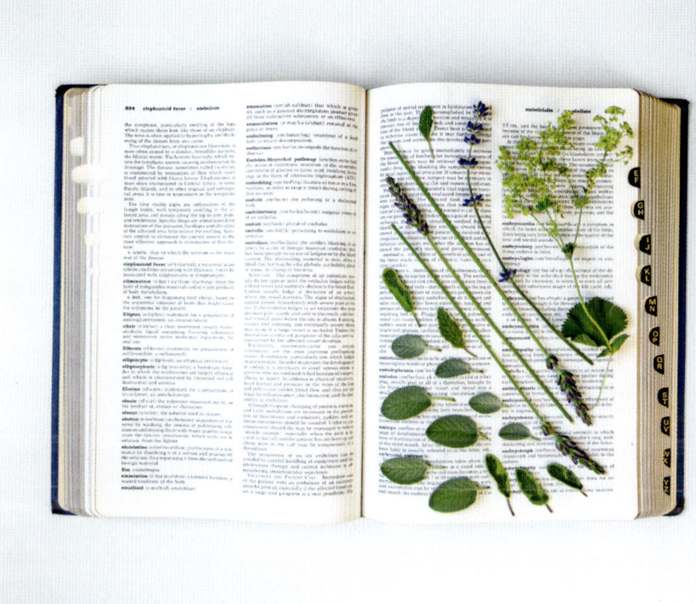

Whatever method you use, once your flowers and leaves are dry, you will want to store them flat and in a place that is as dry as possible. I use plastic bins and separate the layers with copier paper, adding little silica gel bags (the kind that sometimes come in packages) in with the flowers to help absorb moisture.

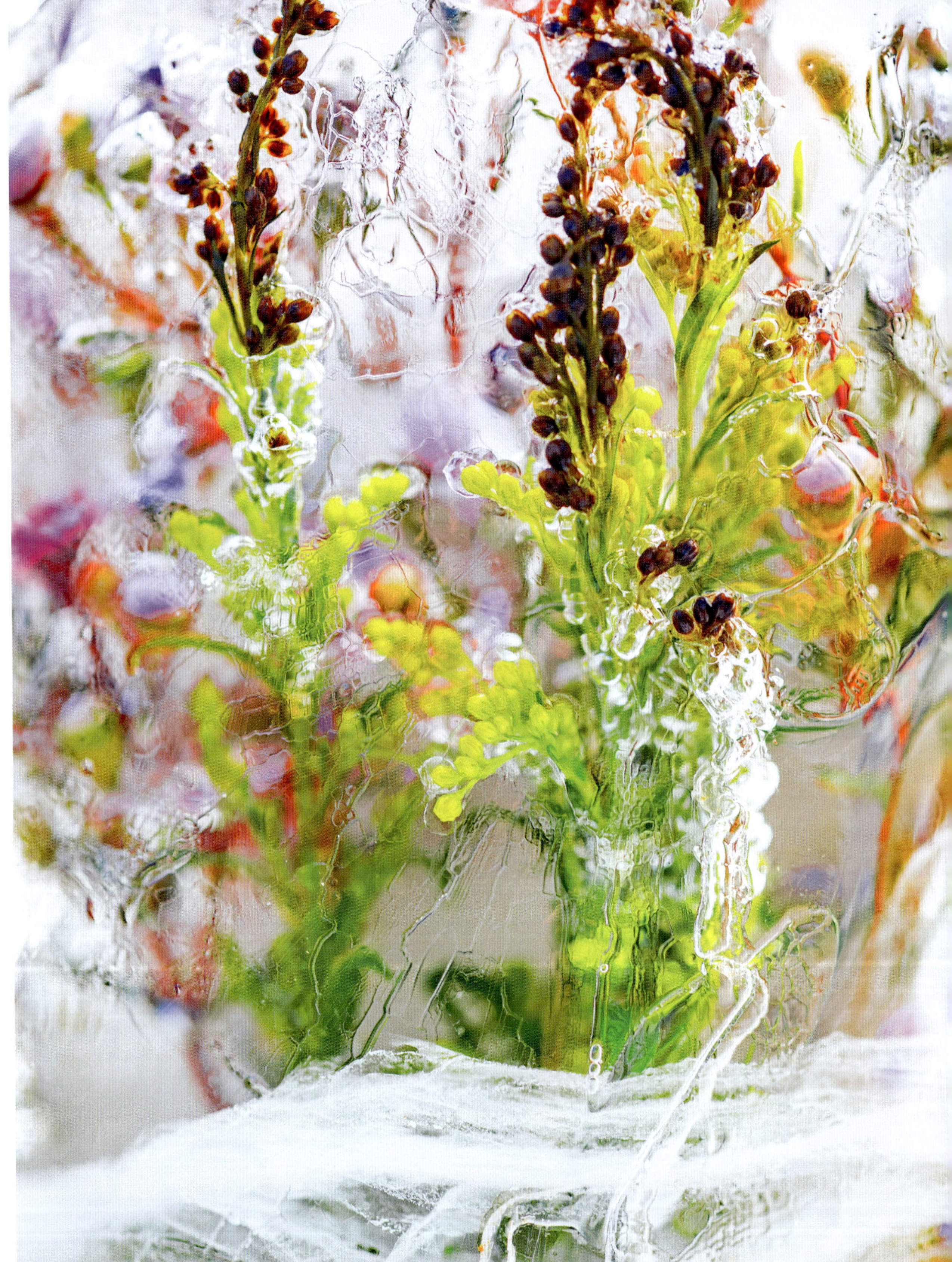

Thoughts on Photography

I started doing photography as a child, before the advent of digital imagery. My father was a pretty good amateur photographer, and he had an old Nikon camera that seemed magical to me. Allowing me to hold it and take a picture was a rare treat he doled out on the most special of occasions. I still remember the resonant and superbly satisfying click of the shutter.

Fast-forward to my short career as a video cameraperson, morphing into a documentary researcher, and then becoming a television writer/producer. During that time, I largely gave up still photography. It wasn't until the advent of the iPhone that I dove back into it headfirst. I rediscovered my love of seeing the world framed—an experience that still completely thrills me. And as so many people have discovered, the old axiom that "the best camera is the one you have with you" often means your phone.

Photography is all about light. You can have the most advanced camera equipment in the world and if your light isn't right, the chances for a good photograph are diminished. You might think that a bright and sunny day would offer the perfect light, but give me an overcast day and I'm in heaven. The diffused light of a cloudy day softens the shadows and makes colors pop.

The good news is even on a glaringly sunny day, if you shoot soon after sunrise or just before sunset you can find some sweet, warm light. The other way to deal with too much light is to modify it, and there are several ways to do this. If you are shooting in bright light, and you have the option, you can move your subject into the shade. You can also create shade. This can be as simple as moving your body (or whatever else you have on hand) to block the sun. If I'm shooting something small, I will sometimes use my large sun hat to create a shadow.

Another option is to buy a pop-up combination diffuser/reflector—perhaps my most-used photo accessory. These light modifiers come in many shapes and sizes and don't have to be expensive. If your light is too harsh, using the diffuser can soften it. If you need more light, use the reflector to bounce light onto your subject. You can use a white sheet or cloth to block direct sunlight from a window, either by attaching it with painter's tape or by draping it on a tension rod if you don't already have something to hang the cloth from.

As for cameras, phones are fantastic, but if you are serious about photography, a higher-quality camera may be a good investment. Whatever you use to capture images, it's worthwhile to dive into learning how to use your specific model.

I'm largely a self-taught photographer and cannot stand reading manuals. Fortunately, there are video courses that will teach you what you need to know for almost any camera or phone you might have. My cameras are much more complicated and sophisticated than I am, and I only use a small number of the vast array of tools with which they come equipped. I used to feel a little ashamed that I didn't know more about the technical side of photography until I was talking to a well-known nature photographer whose luminous images awed me. She said, with acute embarrassment, that she too knew very little about the technical aspects of photography. She didn't care much about equipment or the minutiae of photography, she just cared about knowing enough to get the images she wanted. I loved her message. Learn what you need to know, experiment and increase your knowledge over time.

I also advocate for photographing however you choose. Ignore conventional wisdom if it doesn't work for you. If you are having fun and are happy with your photos, that is all that matters. I often flaunt the maxim that you should use a tripod whenever possible. I hate tripods and am willing to sacrifice a bit of sharpness for the freedom to dance with my camera. That said, sometimes in very low light, a tripod is a godsend.

Photo Editing

When it comes to photography, a frequently overlooked part of getting the images you want is photo editing—which is often the step that can take a mediocre image and make it sing.

Photographing and recording the world have become central to so many people's lives and identities. The statistics are staggering: an estimated 3.8 billion photos a day are taken, approximately 95 million of which are uploaded onto Instagram. Not to be snarky, but many of them could be immeasurably improved by some editing. You can think of it like adding salt to food—the food is edible without the salt, but the flavor will be intensified and taste so much better if you add the right amount.

You can spend hours editing a single photo (as I often do), but you can also greatly improve an image in less than a minute. Even if you simply hit the enhance button (represented by a wand icon), which applies automatic adjustments, your photo will usually look better in an instant. By experimenting with photo editing, not only will your photos improve, but as you become more aware of framing, contrast, and exposure in your editing, you can learn how to take better pictures.

Luckily today most phones and computers come with free, basic photo editing software. There are amazing YouTube tutorials that can get you up and running quickly. There are also a gazillion photo editing apps that are fun and worth experimenting with.

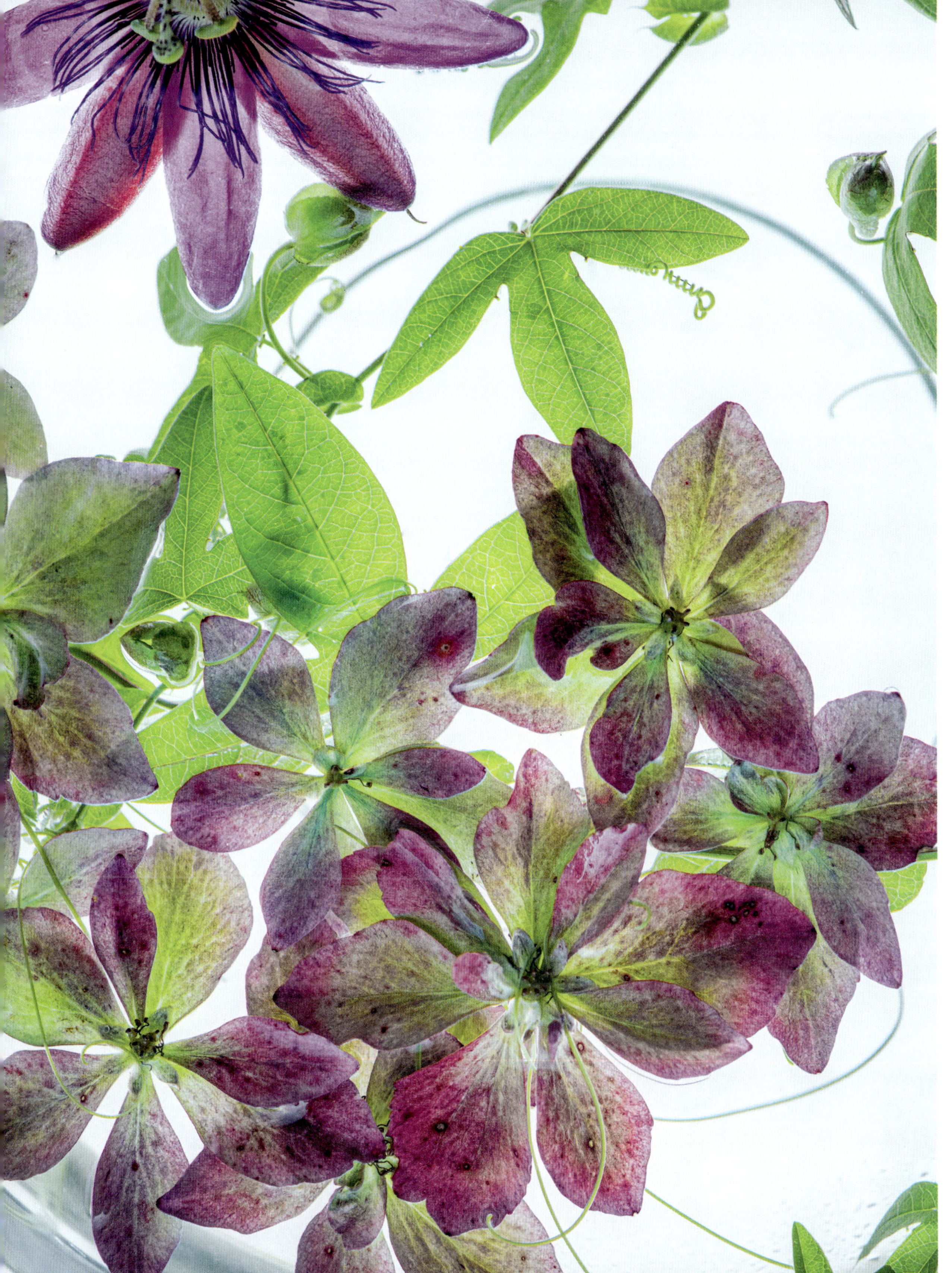

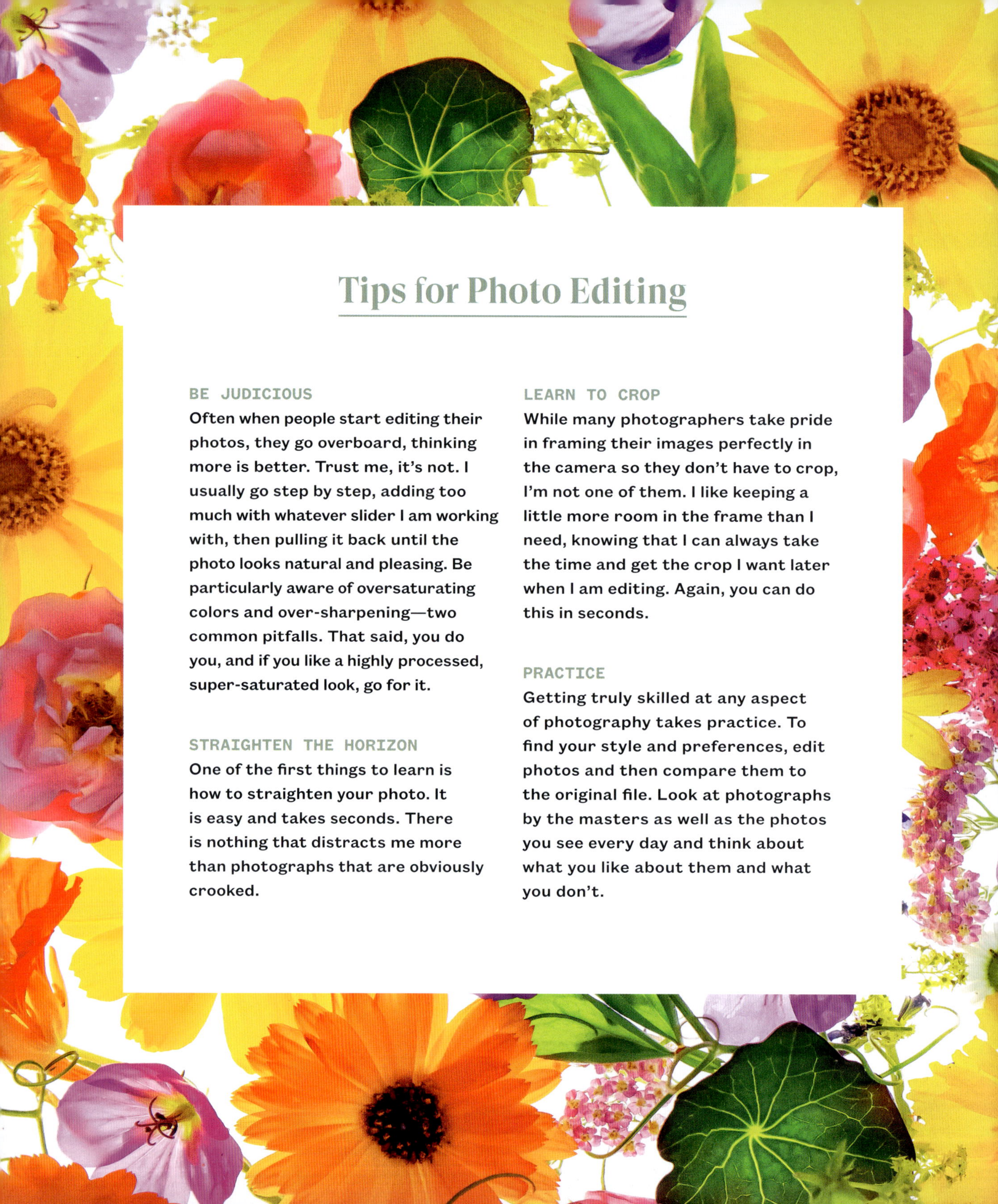

Tips for Photo Editing

BE JUDICIOUS

Often when people start editing their photos, they go overboard, thinking more is better. Trust me, it's not. I usually go step by step, adding too much with whatever slider I am working with, then pulling it back until the photo looks natural and pleasing. Be particularly aware of oversaturating colors and over-sharpening—two common pitfalls. That said, you do you, and if you like a highly processed, super-saturated look, go for it.

STRAIGHTEN THE HORIZON

One of the first things to learn is how to straighten your photo. It is easy and takes seconds. There is nothing that distracts me more than photographs that are obviously crooked.

LEARN TO CROP

While many photographers take pride in framing their images perfectly in the camera so they don't have to crop, I'm not one of them. I like keeping a little more room in the frame than I need, knowing that I can always take the time and get the crop I want later when I am editing. Again, you can do this in seconds.

PRACTICE

Getting truly skilled at any aspect of photography takes practice. To find your style and preferences, edit photos and then compare them to the original file. Look at photographs by the masters as well as the photos you see every day and think about what you like about them and what you don't.

Equipment and Workspace

If you have the room for a dedicated art workspace, that is amazing. If not, a stable table or kitchen counter can be the perfect work area. Some projects are messier than others, and for those, being near a sink can be a bonus, and a cheap plastic tablecloth can be a great reusable surface to work on. The following is a list of helpful tools to have in general. Some projects will need more specific materials, but investing in the following basics is worthwhile for general art/craft making.

GLUES

Who knew there were so many kinds of glue! Decoupage glue, white multipurpose liquid PVA glue, rubber cement, spray adhesive, as well as hot glue, to name a few. If I had to choose one glue to buy for these projects, it would undoubtably be Mod Podge, which is a decoupage glue. Though there are many other brands, this is the one I use. You could even say I have a crush on Mod Podge and have come to think of it as a kind of magic elixir. It is a combination water-based glue, sealer, and finish. It dries fast and almost clear. And there are about a million kinds of Mod Podge. I like the matte finish for most things. Super matte is great too, although it is thicker and can be trickier to use. There is also a pump spray version of Mod Podge, which is not as toxic as spray adhesives and is good for gluing lacy things that would disintegrate if you tried to apply glue with a brush.

The downside of Mod Podge is that it is expensive, and some of the formulas are not archival (meaning that over time they may discolor and won't last as long as an archival glue). Another option is liquid PVA glue—think Elmer's or school glue. Liquid PVA glue can be used as is for gluing or can be watered down for decoupaging. The difference is that liquid PVA glues do not have the finishing and sealing properties of Mod Podge. Also, not all PVA glues are archival. Both Mod Podge and liquid PVA glues are easy to clean up with water.

Another adhesive that I use sparingly and cautiously is an aerosol spray adhesive. It's the best way to apply a super-thin, even coat of very sticky, fast-drying glue on large, delicate, and translucent blooms, but it is toxic if inhaled, is highly flammable, and can cause skin irritation.

GLUE GUN

I love my glue gun. It is small, inexpensive, unfussy, and works remarkably well. The advantage of using a glue gun is that the glue dries super-fast—in fifteen to thirty seconds. This is a huge plus if you need to hold something in place until it sticks. I have tried both corded and cordless glue guns and, surprisingly, I found that a corded glue gun works better. The cordless I tried, although well reviewed just about everywhere, just didn't hold the heat long enough for some projects. While I have not done an exhaustive study, I found that my small, corded glue gun that uses mini glue sticks works perfectly for me. It heats up quickly and stays hot. If you are new to hot gluing, I would recommend practicing on scraps before using the gun on a project. It's more challenging than it would seem to pull the trigger and put just a small dot of glue exactly and only where you want it.

SCISSORS AND CLIPPERS

I have waaay too many garden clippers and scissors, from tiny children's scissors to giant loppers, most in a pathetic state of disrepair. However, I do have a few favorites. If I had to choose only three (god forbid), I would have a sharp, good pair of full-sized scissors; a pair of super-sharp small scissors; and a pair of hefty garden clippers for cutting thick stems or branches.

TWEEZERS

If you are working with dried flowers, you will want tweezers. I have a fabulous set of five pairs, all around the same size, but some are offset, some sharp, and a few blunt. I use them all and love having extras because I often misplace them, so having spares is a great thing. I also have a set of super-long tweezers particularly useful for photography, as they allow me to easily move things around in a shot.

ALSO USEFUL TO KEEP ON HAND

- Painter's tape
- Masking tape
- Cotton swabs
- Toothpicks
- Wooden skewers
- Paper towels
- Baby wipes
- Aluminum foil
- Parchment paper
- Freezer paper or waxed paper
- Foam brushes
- Bristle brushes
- Brush cleaner

A Note about Collaboration

This book was the product of a yearlong collaboration with my friend Liz, whom I have known since I was born. Our mothers were close friends, and we grew up down the street from each other. We know the deep history of each other's lives and families. I am so grateful that she agreed to come on the journey of creating this book with me.

Almost every piece of art created in the how-to sections of this book was produced collaboratively and with great happiness. Even our failures and mistakes were entertaining because they were shared and often resulted in uncontrollable laughter. Liz's talent, eye, taste, and sense of design are masterful. I am thankful that we could share in this adventure.

While making art can be satisfying as a solitary pursuit, it can also be great to work on projects alongside others. I have several friends who are part of art groups that meet regularly to create together. This can be beneficial not only socially; it can also be an easier way to collect and share materials and to learn from others' experiences and challenges—and perhaps drink some good wine.

I have been a member of a small photographers' group for several years. While we don't work together—and in fact most often meet from different states via computer—we share our projects, resources, and techniques, and sometimes we just bitch. The support of this group has not only made my photography better, it has also made me feel a part of a community.

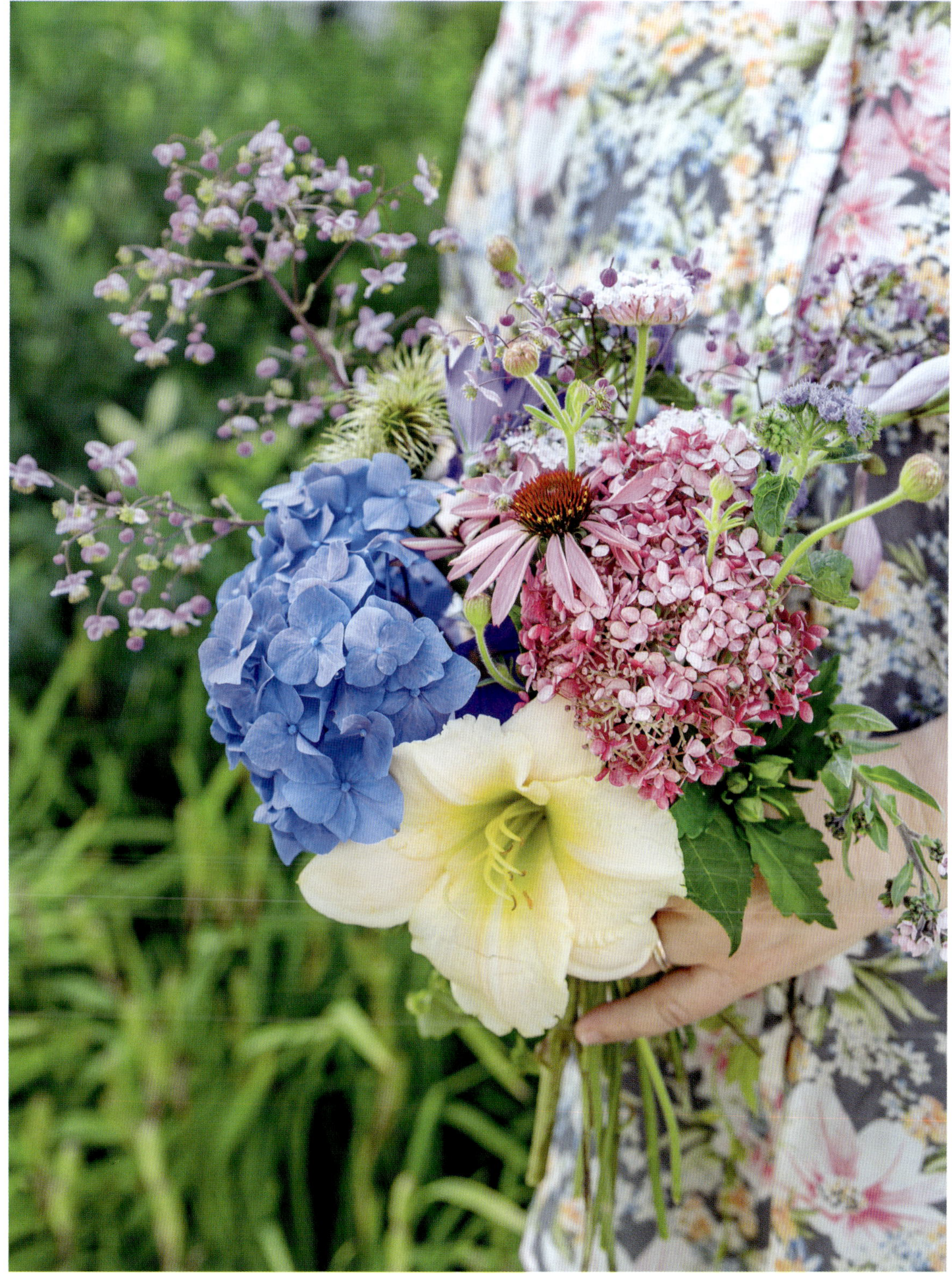

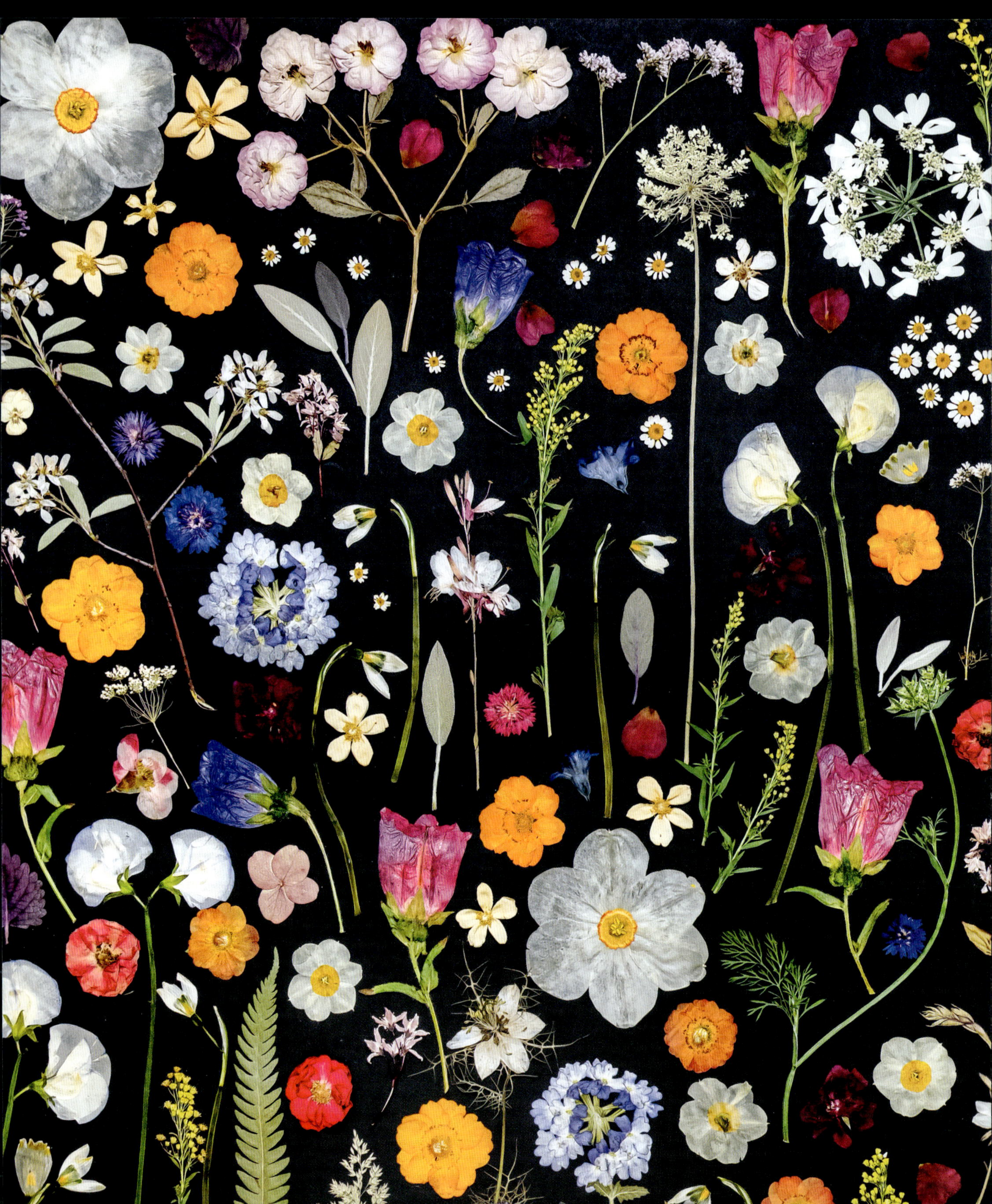

DRIED BOTANICALS

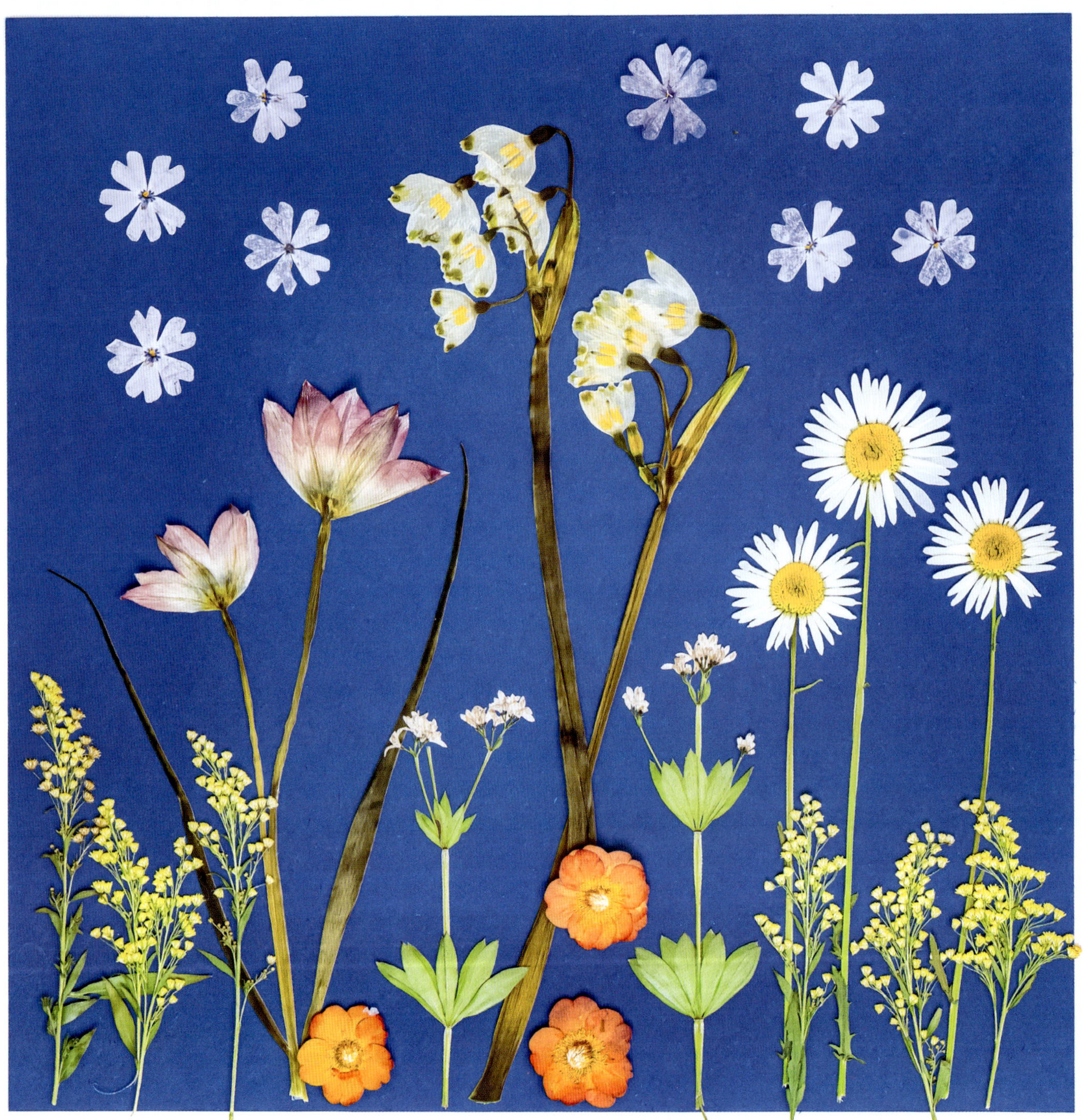

WHAT YOU NEED

- Botanicals
- Microwave press or heavy microwavable baking dish and newsprint
- Scissors
- Microwave
- Tweezers (optional)
- Sharp knife (optional)

1

Microwave Botanical Pressing

I am a big fan of instant gratification, and while microwaving botanicals isn't quite instant, it exponentially speeds up the otherwise long process of using a conventional flower press alone. What would take weeks in a conventional press can be sped up, depending on your botanicals, to a few minutes. I have also found that microwaving will partially dry juicy flowers, like tulips and hellebores, that tend to go moldy in a traditional flower press. The method I most often use is a hybrid of old and new. I first use the microwave to blast most of the moisture out of botanicals, and then put them in a conventional press to finish slowly and completely drying. However, leaves and many flowers (that aren't too moist, like violas and pansies) can be dried successfully by using just the microwave.

There are several different brands of microwave presses, and some can be absurdly pricey. The good news is that the pricey ones don't necessarily work any better than the cheapest. Most microwave presses have a layer of heavy plastic with holes that let the steam escape; two layers of thick wool felt; and then two thinner layers of lightweight cotton fabric. Plastic clips snap on to fasten all the layers together, compressing the botanicals. To use the press, you sandwich the flowers or leaves between the layers of wool felt and the layers of cotton. The challenging part is that some flowers stick to the cotton layer and you have to use some finesse to peel them off.

If you don't want to invest in a microwave press or want to press botanicals that are too large to fit in the relatively small drying area of the presses, you can sandwich your botanicals between thick layers of newsprint, put a heavy microwavable baking dish on top, and zap away.

Be very careful when botanical microwaving, especially if using a press. I have learned from experience that the felt can easily go up in flames. To help prevent this, check your felt and fabric before adding the botanicals; if the felt and fabric are dry, lightly moisten them, then zap them for ten seconds. After that you can sandwich the plant material. Every microwave is different so you will need to experiment, but I have found that fifty-five seconds on a high setting is the most successful timing for my old microwave. It threads the needle of drying and flattening even juicy flowers enough to successfully transfer them to a traditional press, while not risking burning down the house.

Store your finished pressed botanicals somewhere dry, where they can lie flat. I put them on sheets of copy paper in closed plastic boxes. To absorb moisture, I add packets of silica gel desiccant that often come with electronics.

Another cautionary note: I have found microwaving flowers to be completely addictive, as well as a superior method of procrastination.

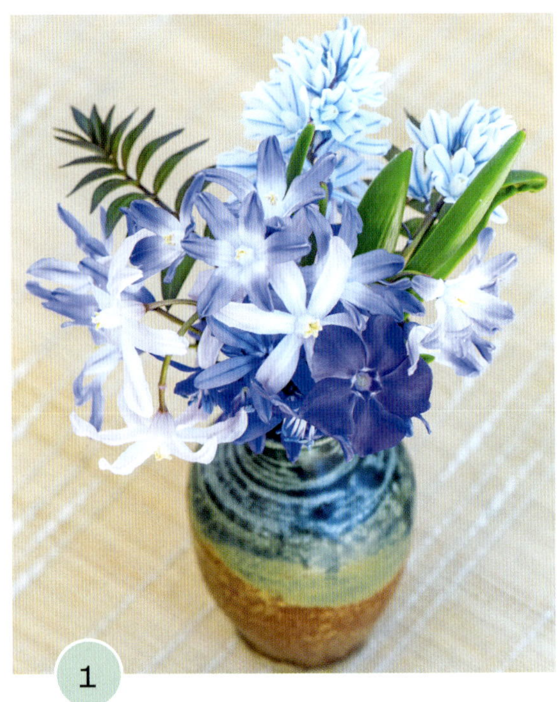

1

Select the Botanicals

I am often surprised by how botanicals turn out when dried. Some that I think will be gorgeous turn into mush or fade into a sickly brown (I'm looking at you, magnolias). Others that I don't expect to work at all turn out to be stunning (thank you, azaleas). The surprise is part of the adventure. A general rule: The flatter the flower, the easier it is to dry. Many people deconstruct and then reconstruct fat flowers by pulling off the petals, drying them separately, and reconstructing them after they are dry. I'm way too lazy to do that. Some botanicals will wilt a nanosecond after you pick them and others will last longer; either way, you will want to microwave them while they are fresh. You can also put cuttings in vases of water until you're ready to pluck off the parts you want to microwave. Just make sure to wipe off any moisture before placing them in the press.

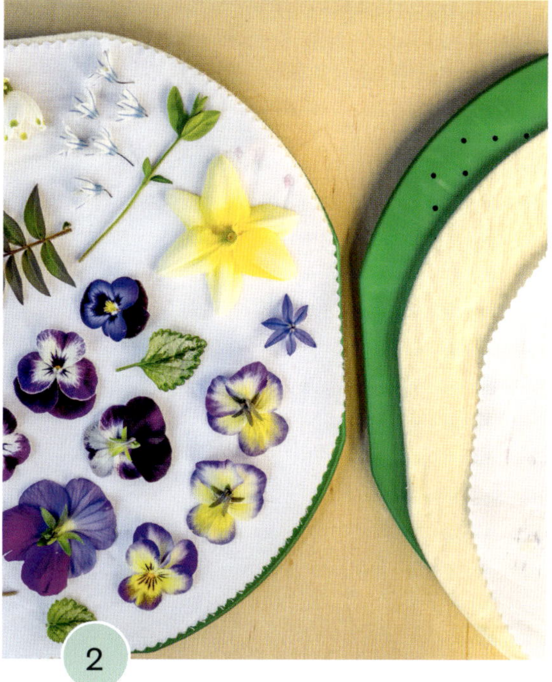

2

Ready the Press

Open your press and place a felt pad on top of the plastic and then a cotton pad on top of the felt. Place the botanicals on top of the cotton layer, separating them enough that they won't touch. Keep in mind that blossoms can spread as they flatten. (Alternatively, place the botanicals on newsprint if you will be using a glass baking dish.) Try different ways of placing your flowers: facedown, faceup, and sideways. Curve the stems or leave them straight. It is often a surprise which works best. Snip off any excess stems or foliage, while being careful to leave the botanical intact.

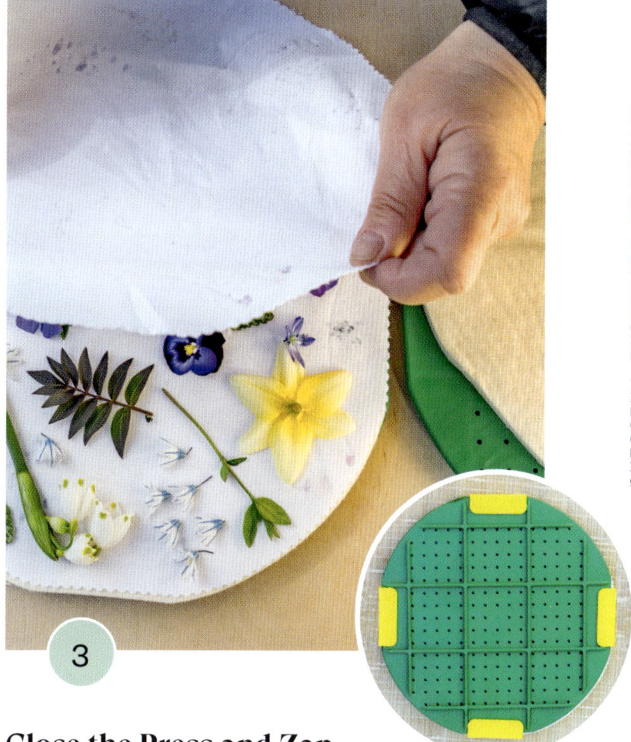

3

Close the Press and Zap

Making sure everything is smooth and flat, place the second cotton layer on top of the botanicals, then the second felt pad on top of the cotton, followed by the plastic plate. Fasten shut. You may have to apply some pressure to get the press to close if you are squashing thick flowers. Carefully align the press or you won't be able to clip it closed. (If using a glass baking dish, place another layer of newsprint over the botanicals, then put the dish on top.) Microwave for 15 seconds to 1 minute, depending on your microwave. To find your microwave's sweet spot, try 15-second bursts at first, checking the flowers for moisture after each burst, until they feel papery and dry. When drying juicy flowers (like tulips, daffodils, or hellebores), I take them out of the press when they are still damp and flexible, finishing them off in a conventional flower press.

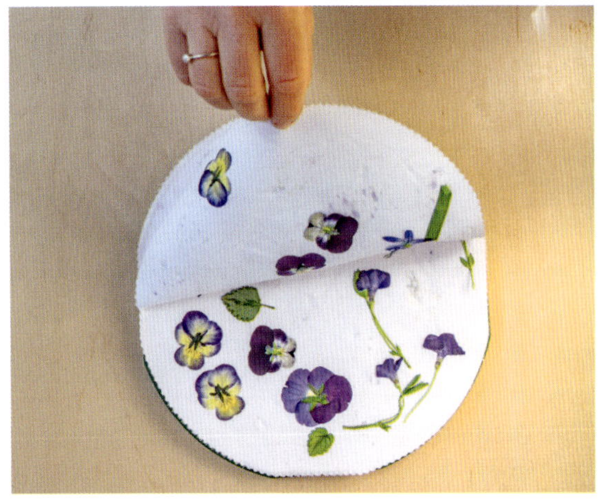

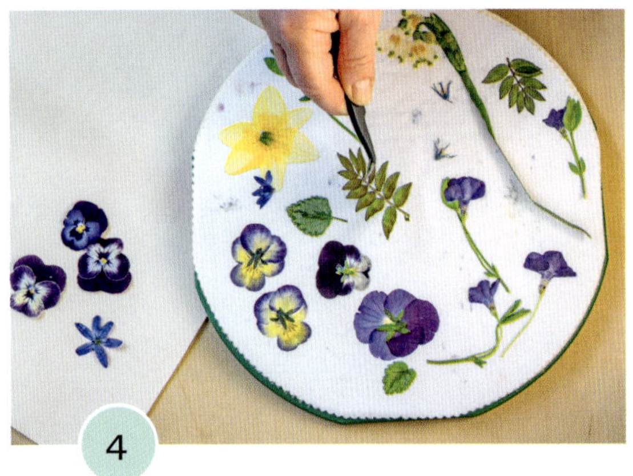

4

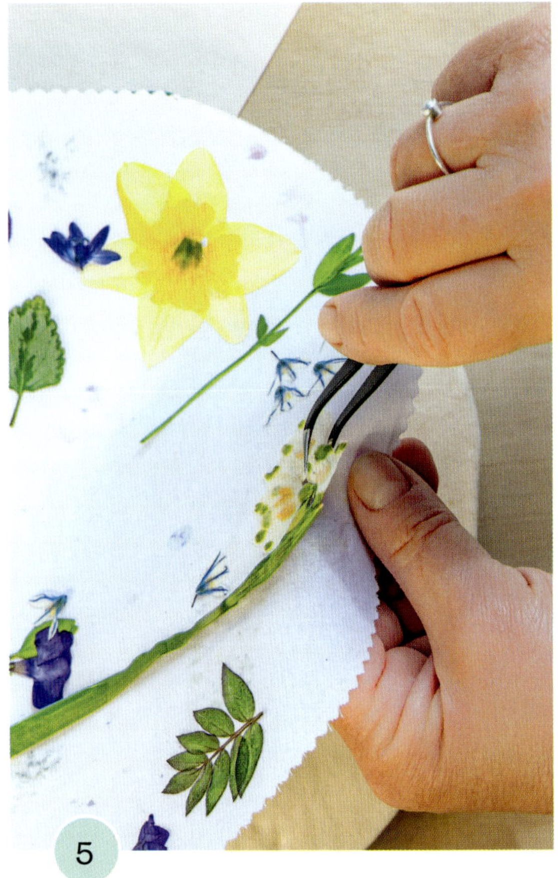

5

Free the Botanicals

Let the press cool down for a few minutes. Open it and carefully peel the top layer of felt then the cotton layer (or the newsprint) from the botanicals. This can be a challenge, as the flowers will sometimes stick and tear if not very carefully peeled off. You can use tweezers or a sharp knife to help peel off fragile blossoms. Bending the fabric away from the edge of a stuck botanical can also help free it.

Assess Dryness

At this point, if your flowers are papery and feel completely dry, you can store them or use them. If they still feel moist and flexible, you can try a few more seconds in the microwave, finish drying them in a conventional press, or simply sandwich them between pieces of paper or newsprint and press under flat weights (books, or boards with weights on top) for a few days to a week. Juicy flowers may take a few weeks to fully dry.

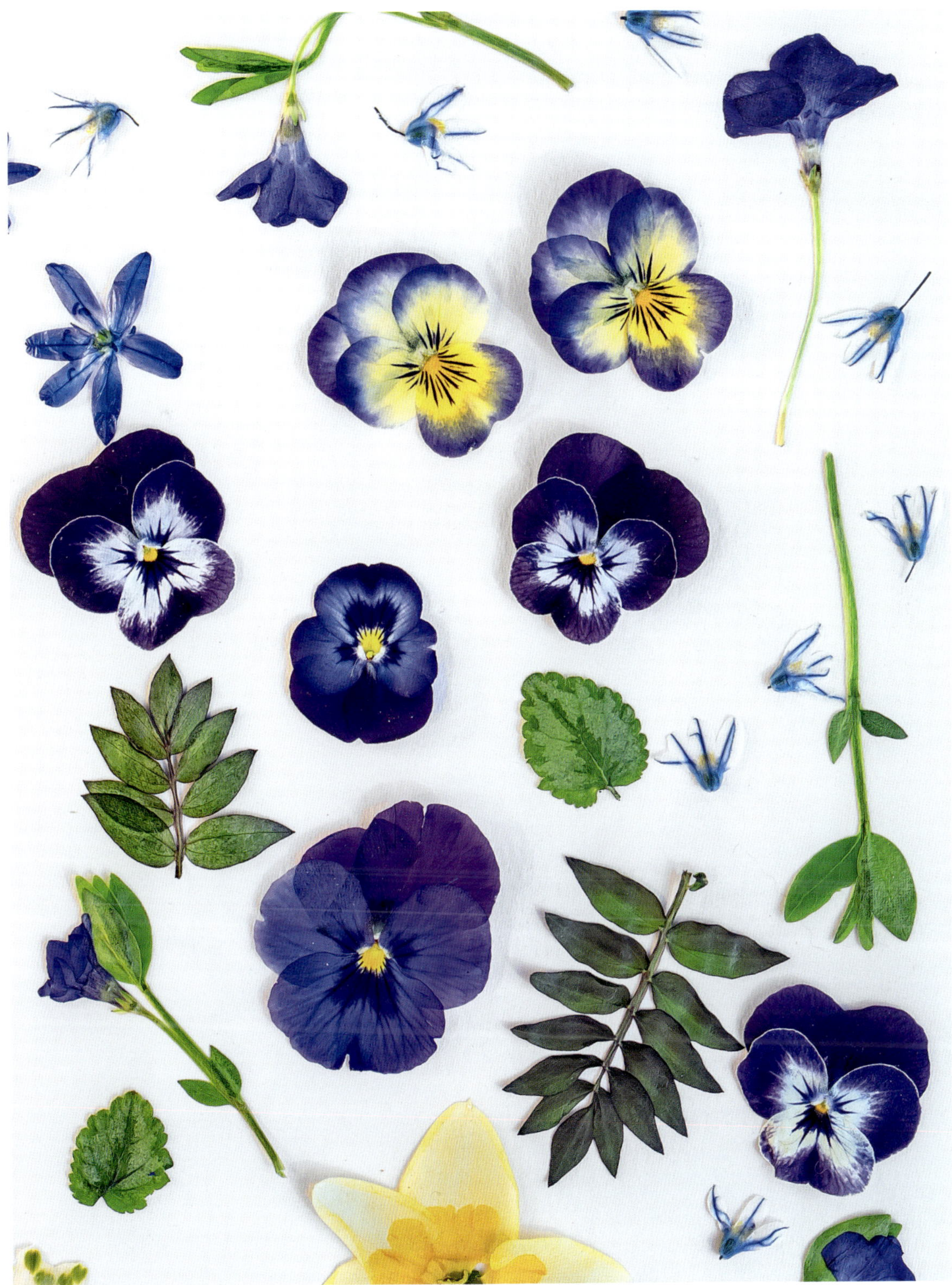

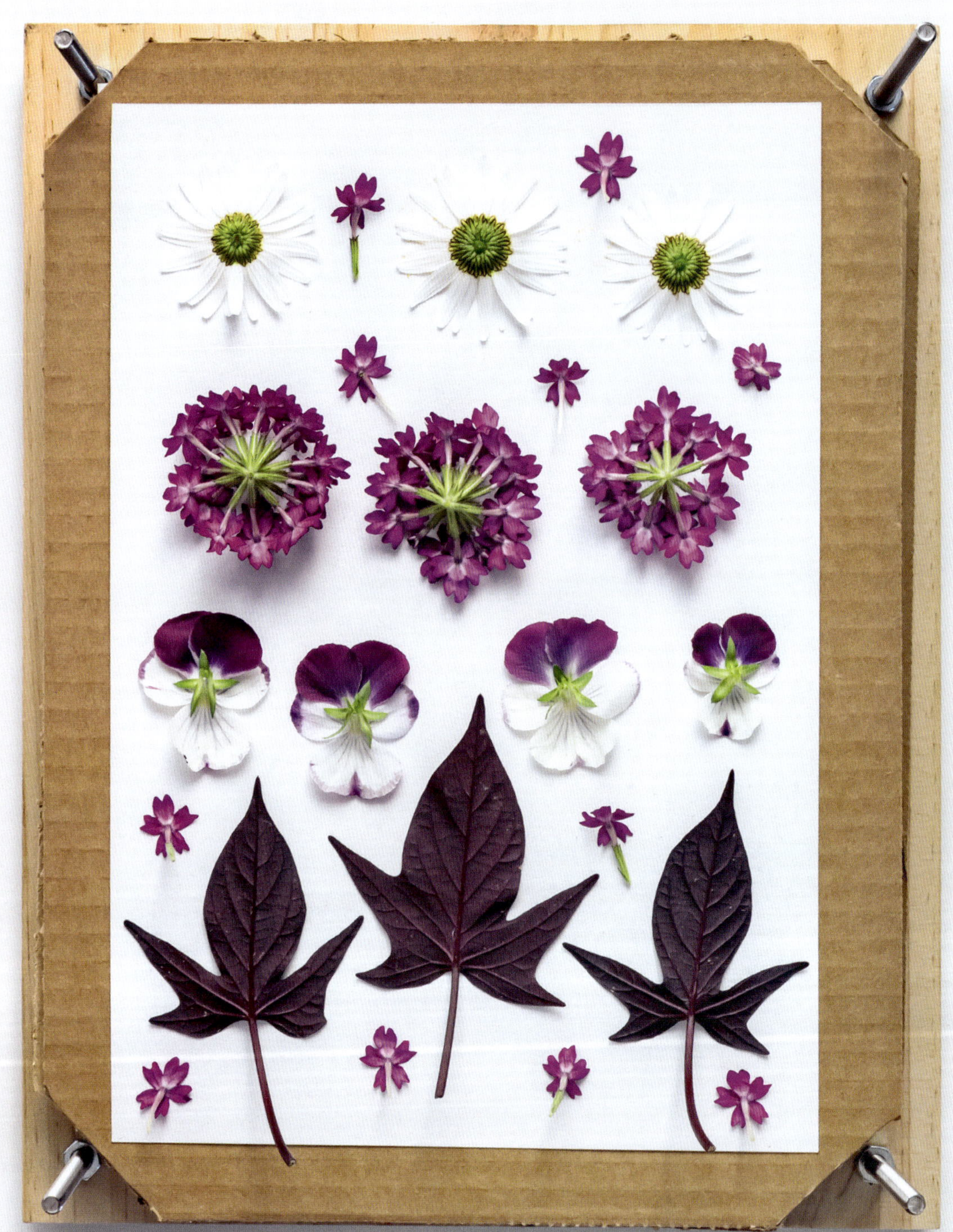

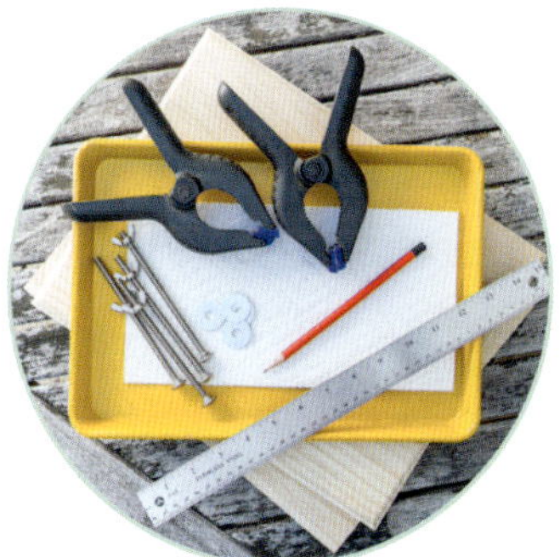

WHAT YOU NEED

- Pencil
- Ruler
- 2 finished wooden boards (each 9 by 12 by ½ inch or 11 by 14 by ¾ inch)
- Clamps
- Electric drill
- Drill bit (size determined by bolt size)
- 4 (6-inch) bolts
- 4 jam nuts (optional)
- Piece of cardboard slightly smaller than the boards
- 4 washers
- 4 wing nuts
- Dried botanicals, decoupage glue, paint, or other decorative materials (optional)

2

DIY Traditional Flower Press

Let me start by saying that I'm not skilled with power tools, and woodworking is not my happy place. But I am fairly cheap by nature, and traditional flower presses tend to be expensive and too small. With those things in mind, I took to the internet and found about a million videos for DIYing a traditional flower press. They made it look easy. I bought two finished wooden panels, bolts, wing nuts, and washers; got out my drill; and took a whack at it. While the resulting press isn't perfect, it works well.

That said, if you don't have a drill or, like me, you're lazy, there's another great way to make a flower press. Simply take two wooden boards, skip the bolts, and fill the press as you would one that is bolted together, but instead of adding pressure by tightening nuts and bolts, put weights (books, bricks, rocks—anything heavy) on top of it. Another advantage to this basic setup, besides instant flower press gratification, is that you can more easily and quickly check how your botanicals are drying and add layers of botanicals; you don't have to unscrew and take the whole thing apart.

On the other hand, one of the biggest advantages to using a bolted press is that you can fill it up to the top without having to worry about it getting wobbly or tipping over. You can also easily move a bolted press around once it is closed and keep adding pressure by tightening the wing nuts as the botanicals dry and shrink. If you really get into drying flowers, it's nice to have several presses of different sizes and types going at once.

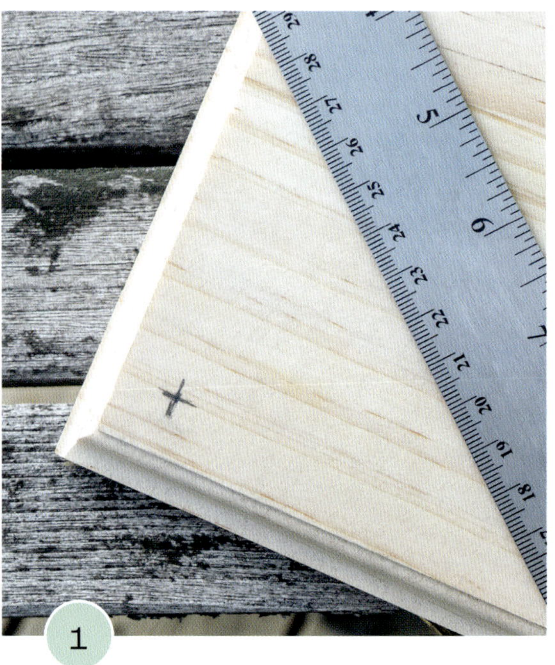

1

Mark the First Board

With a pencil and ruler, mark a hole about an inch from the edge of one board at all four corners. This measurement doesn't have to be terribly precise.

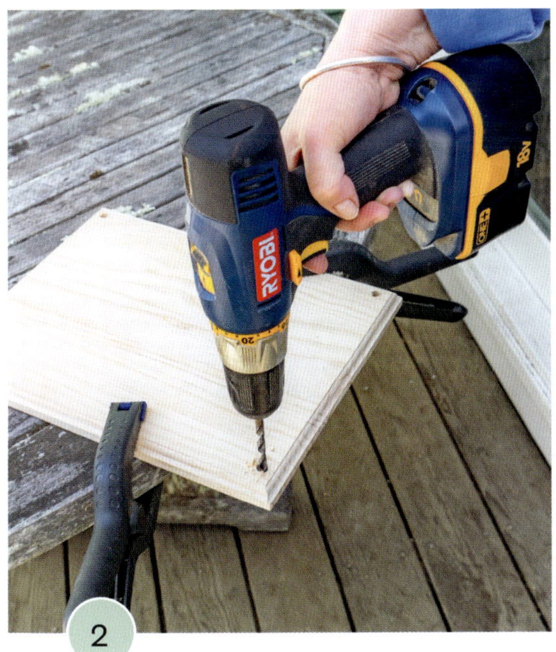

2

Drill Holes

Clamp the board to a stable surface and drill the holes, keeping in mind that the most important thing is for the drill bit to be perpendicular to the board so each bolt will ultimately go in straight.

(Alternatively, you can clamp the two boards together and drill through both at once. If you choose this approach, however, be aware that it can be a challenge to keep the boards from slipping and becoming misaligned. Unclamp the two boards after drilling and skip to step 4.)

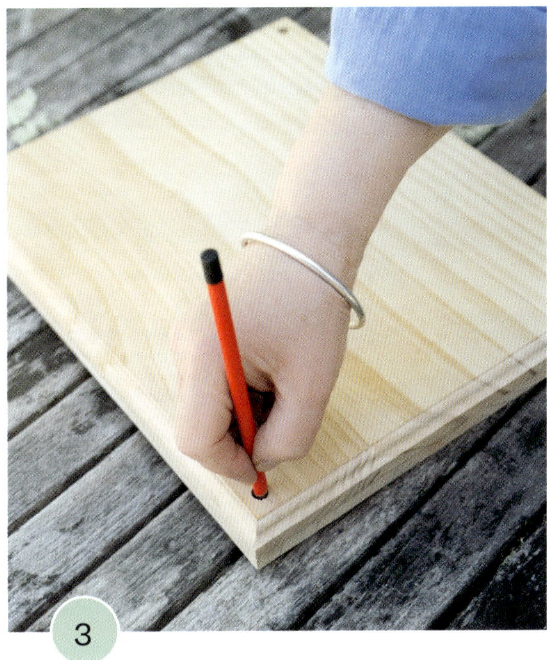

3

Mark and Drill the Second Board

Align the edges of the two boards with the drilled piece on top. Mark the second board by putting a pencil through the centers of the holes of the first board. Separate the boards and drill the second board. Test the fit of the bolts. You might want to make the holes on the top board a little larger than those of the bottom board; this will make it easier to place the top board over the bolts when you are ready to close the press.

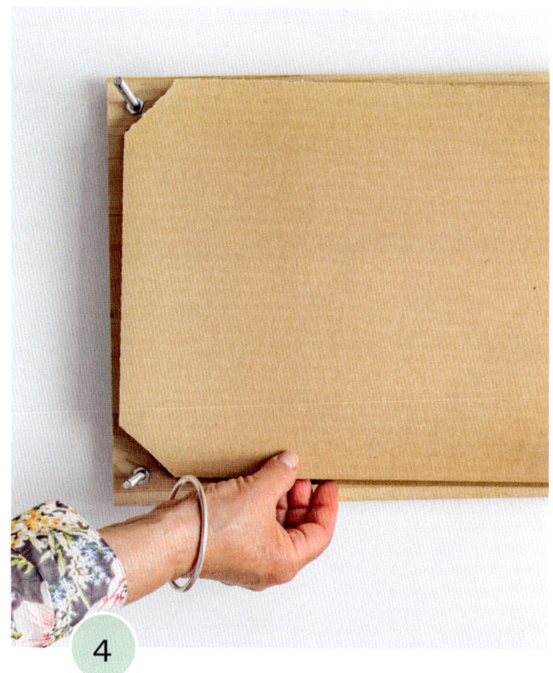

4

Place the Bolts

Thread the four bolts up through the bottom board. Optionally (though I highly recommend this to minimize the frustration of the bolts falling out any time you pick up your open press), screw a small jam nut onto each bolt and tighten it to the board.

Place a layer or two of cardboard on top of the wood to help cushion the botanicals when you fill your press.

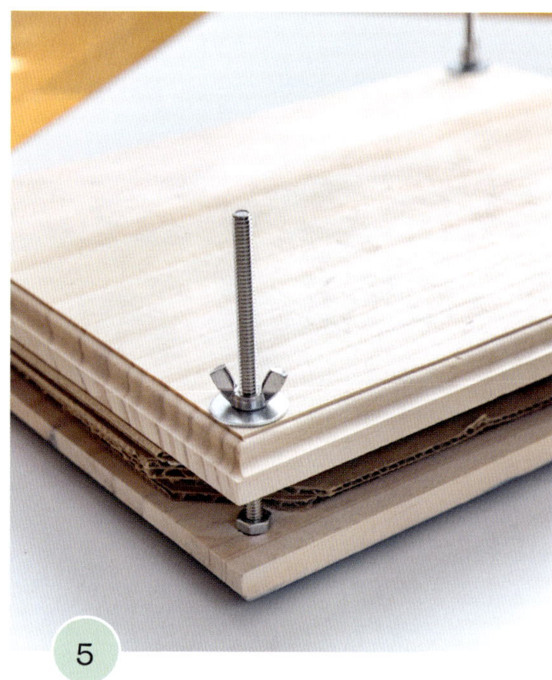

5

Close the Press

Before filling the press, make sure the holes are aligned. Keeping the top board as level as possible, slide it onto the bolts. This can be a bit fiddly, and if it is too difficult because the holes in the top board don't perfectly align with the bolts, you can always make the top holes bigger. Once you have successfully placed the top board on the bolts, slide the washers on the bolts and screw on the wing nuts.

6 

Decorate Your Press

You can zhuzh up your press by decoupaging dried flowers onto it, or by stamping, painting, or cyanotyping the wood.

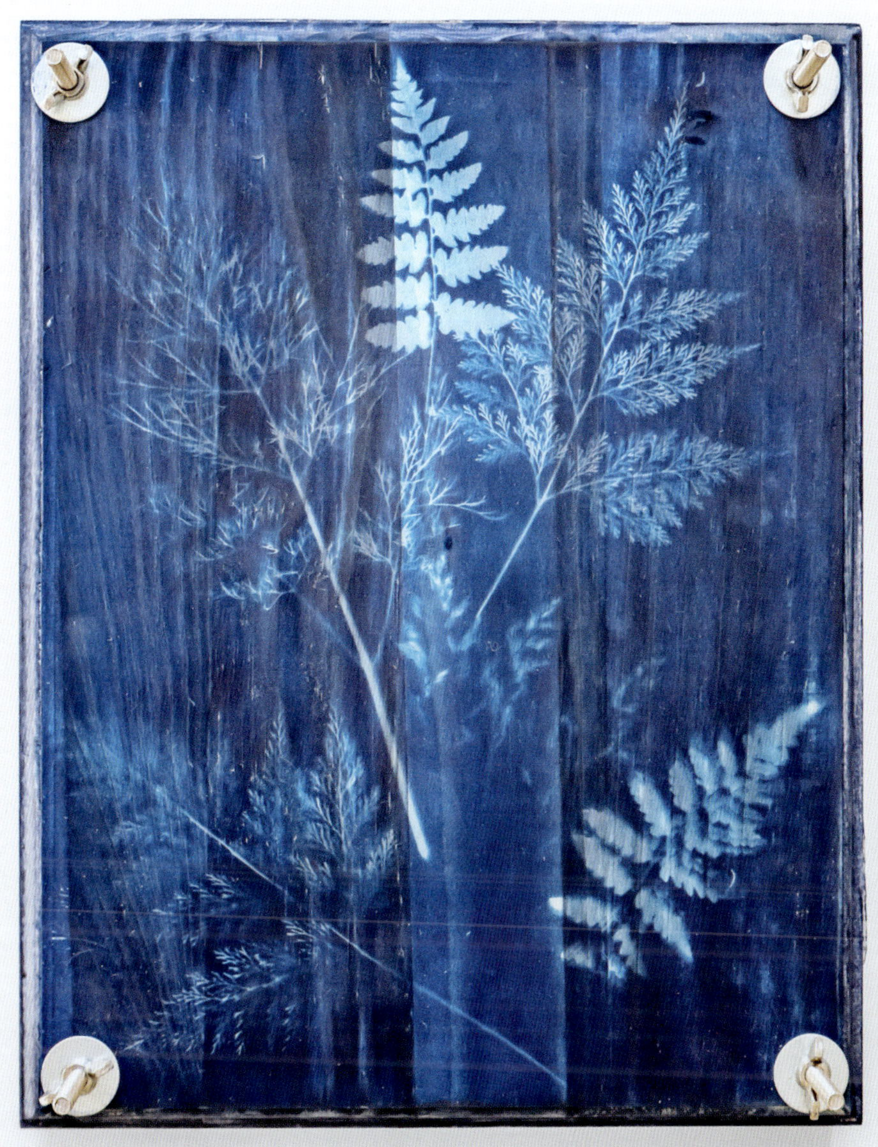

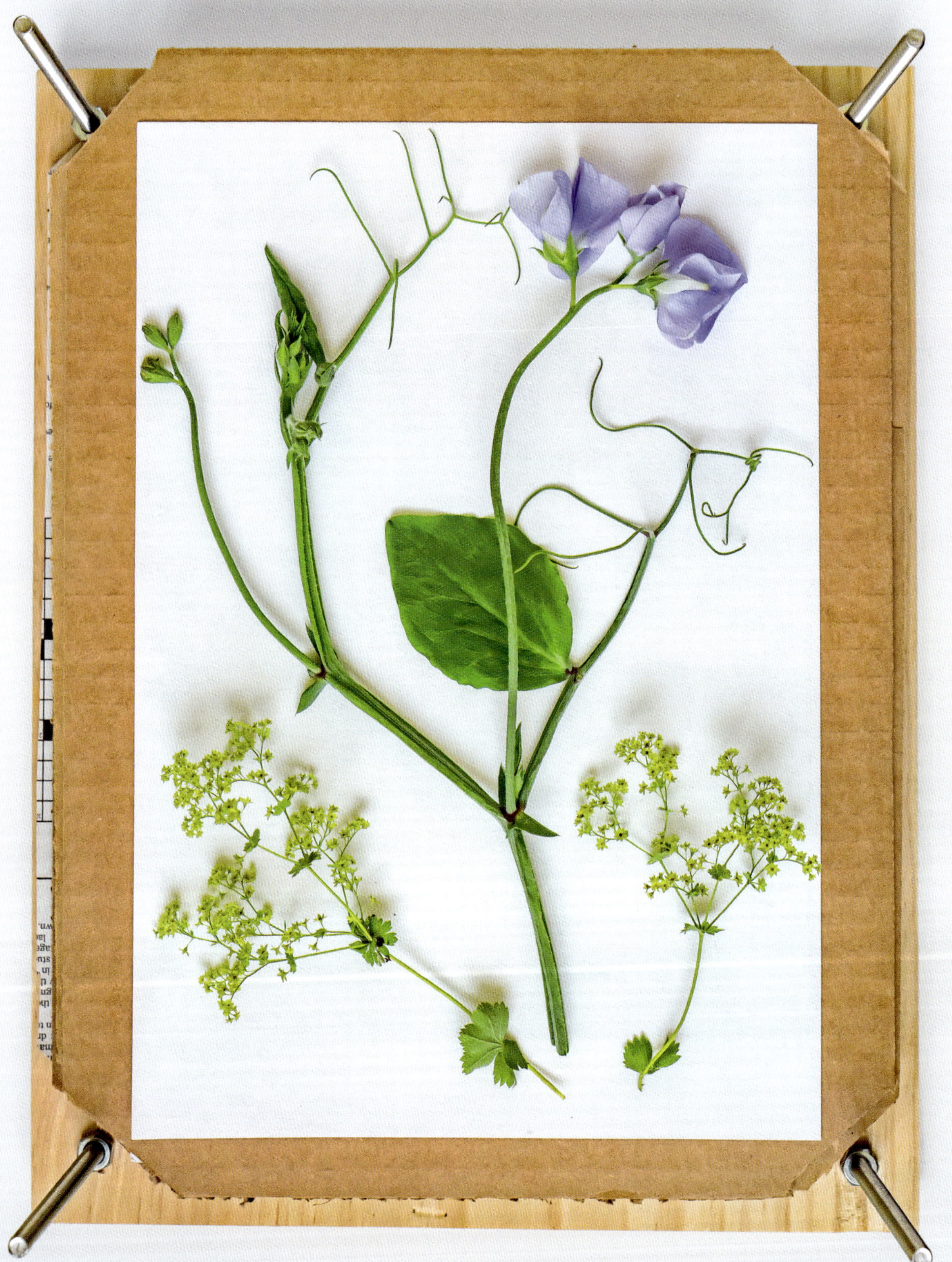

WHAT YOU NEED

- Botanicals
- Flower press or 2 smooth, flat boards
- Cardboard
- Paper

3

Traditional Botanical Pressing

There is something uniquely satisfying about drying botanicals in a traditional press. When you consider how long people have been using presses, you can imagine all the different hands—all shapes, sizes, and colors—that have carefully collected and preserved flowers and botanicals in this way over millennia.

While the ancient Greeks and Romans dried flowers for medicinal, culinary, and decorative uses, the Japanese in the sixteenth century are credited with elevating dried flowers into an art form. Jump forward two hundred years to Victorian England, where the influence of increased trade with Asia started a flower-drying craze.

Fast-forward another two hundred years to the present, and there is an explosion in the popularity of pressing and creating with dried botanicals, as witnessed on Instagram and other social media sites, with just a few common materials.

That said, using a traditional press has a learning curve and requires experimentation and patience. Drying time will depend on many variables, including the amount of heat and humidity in your space, how juicy and thick your botanicals are, and the types of layers (paper and cardboard) used to absorb moisture. The good news is that this is a very low cost and easy way to dry botanicals, and chances are your successes will outnumber your failures.

Currently I'm experimenting with putting the filled and closed flower press into a food dehydrator set at the lowest temperature, which can speed up the drying process from weeks to days. As far as I can tell, it is a success. There is less opportunity for mold to form, the flowers maintain their colors and texture, and I'm exceedingly happy not to have to wait as long.

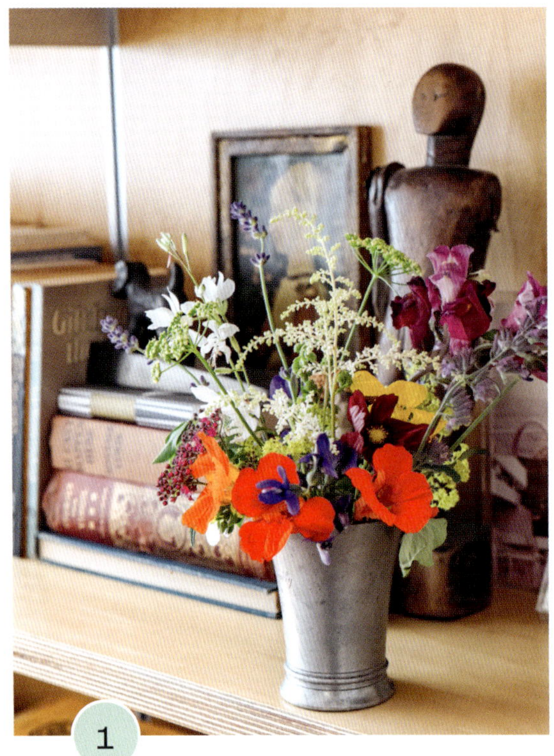

1

2

Select the Botanicals

One of the beauties of drying in a traditional press is how often you will be surprised. So experiment, push the limits, and have fun. Generally, the flatter and more robust your botanical is to start with, the greater your chances of success. Leaves and ferns dry quickly and easily. Pansies, daisies, love-in-the-mist, forget-me-nots, and cosmos are also great starter botanicals. Flowers like dahlias and peonies are riskier. You may want to microwave those thicker blossoms first, which will partially zap the moisture out, then press them. Whatever botanicals you use, check that there is no residual moisture on the botanicals. If there is, gently wipe it off.

Load the Press

Begin by placing a layer or two of cardboard on the bottom of the press. Set a layer of paper on top of the cardboard, then your botanicals, then another layer of paper, and then a final layer of cardboard. Some people swear by copier paper, others blotter paper, still others newsprint. If your budget is unlimited, go for the luxurious blotter paper; it can be expensive but is more absorbent than other paper. But copier paper or newsprint will work fine. One caveat with newsprint is that the ink may transfer, so use it as an absorbent layer and place a piece of blank paper in contact with the botanicals.

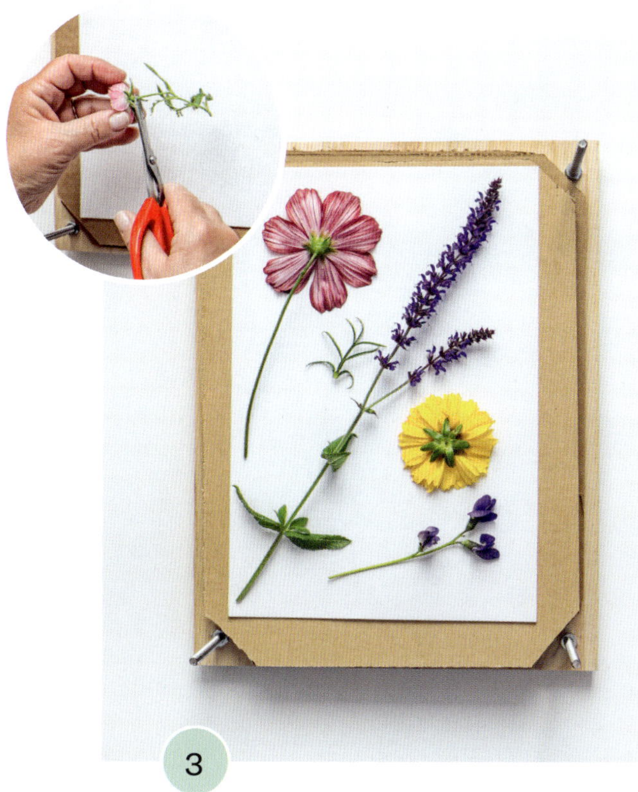

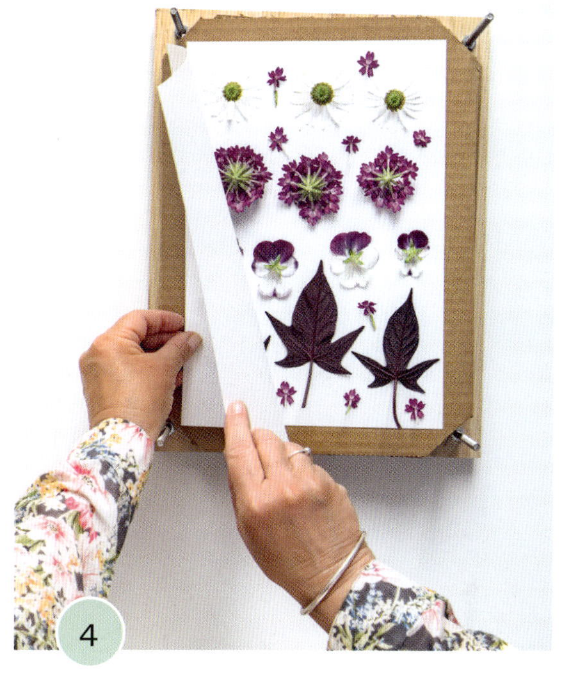

Arrange the Botanicals

Placing the botanicals is by far the most complicated and creative step. It is often a trial-and-error process to figure out which way to place each piece to get the best outcome. Try including stems and leaves, or cut the stem off as close to the flower as possible and just dry a blossom. Place blossoms facedown or on their side to see which works better. Sometimes it's useful to have both. Keep botanicals separate and well spaced, as they tend to stick together if they overlap.

Layer Up

Make layers of cardboard, paper, and botanicals, then repeat. You can assemble as many layers as your press will hold. You can also add layers over time, although try to keep track of the dates of your additions so you know when to start checking to see if they are dry. And on the topic of record-keeping, if you are truly organized (as I am only in my dreams), it is wise to try to also keep track of what you dry. A flower can look completely different once it is dry, and without notes you may not remember what it was originally.

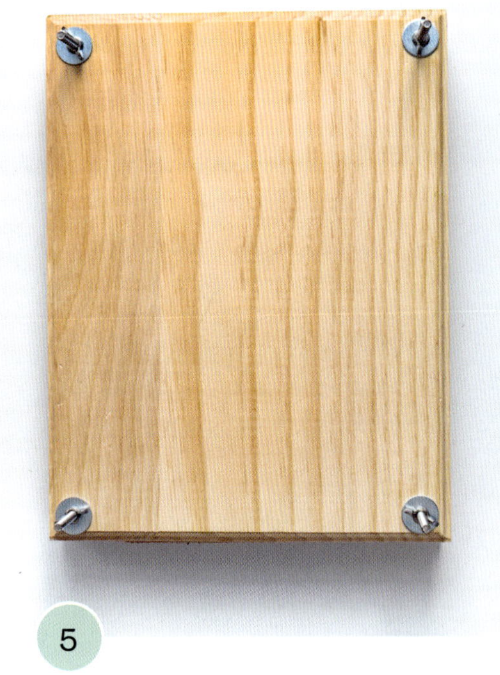

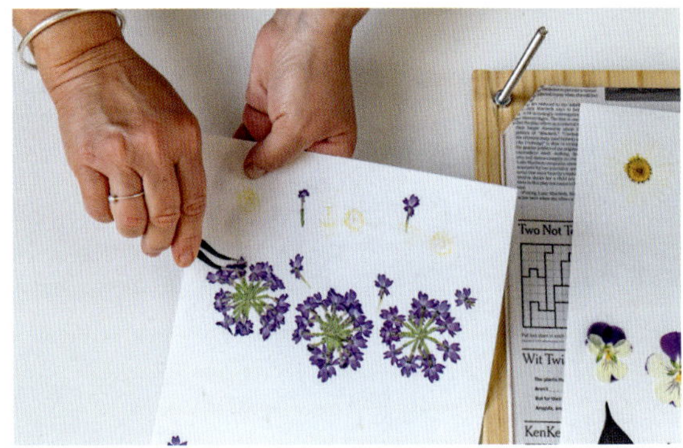

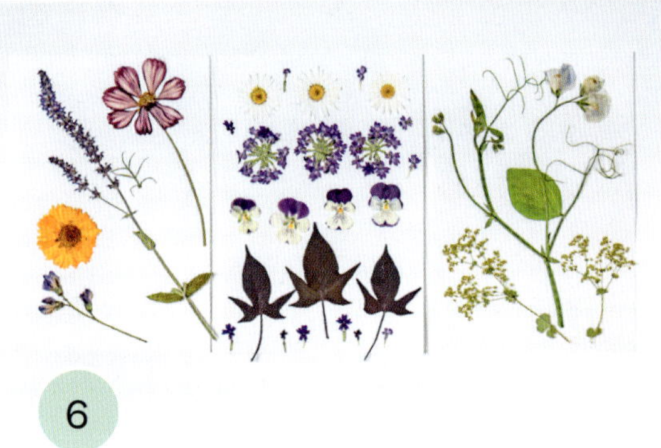

5

Close the Press

Once you have filled the press, slide the top board over the bolts until it sits on the top layer. Place the washers then the wing nuts on the bolts. Tighten the nuts until they are firmly in place. It helps to first tighten the nuts kitty-corner to keep the pressure even. Every few days, check the wing nuts and tighten them further to maintain pressure as the botanicals shrink and dry.

6

Open the Press

Depending on how thick and moist your botanicals were going in and if you had pre-dried them in the microwave, drying can take anywhere from a few days to many weeks. Be patient. Opening the press is always a surprise—sometimes delightful and sometimes … not so much. The colors may have changed, some for better and some for worse, or perhaps you find that a handful of flowers have gone brown or moldy. But you may also find that they have transformed into elegant, graceful shapes that you didn't anticipate. Carefully peel back the paper, because the botanicals can stick and then tear. If everything is dry (stiff and papery), peel off the keepers, using tweezers if necessary. If some botanicals are still moist, but not moldy, replace the surrounding layers with dry paper. Reclose the press and give the botanicals more time to fully dry. Anything moldy should be pitched.

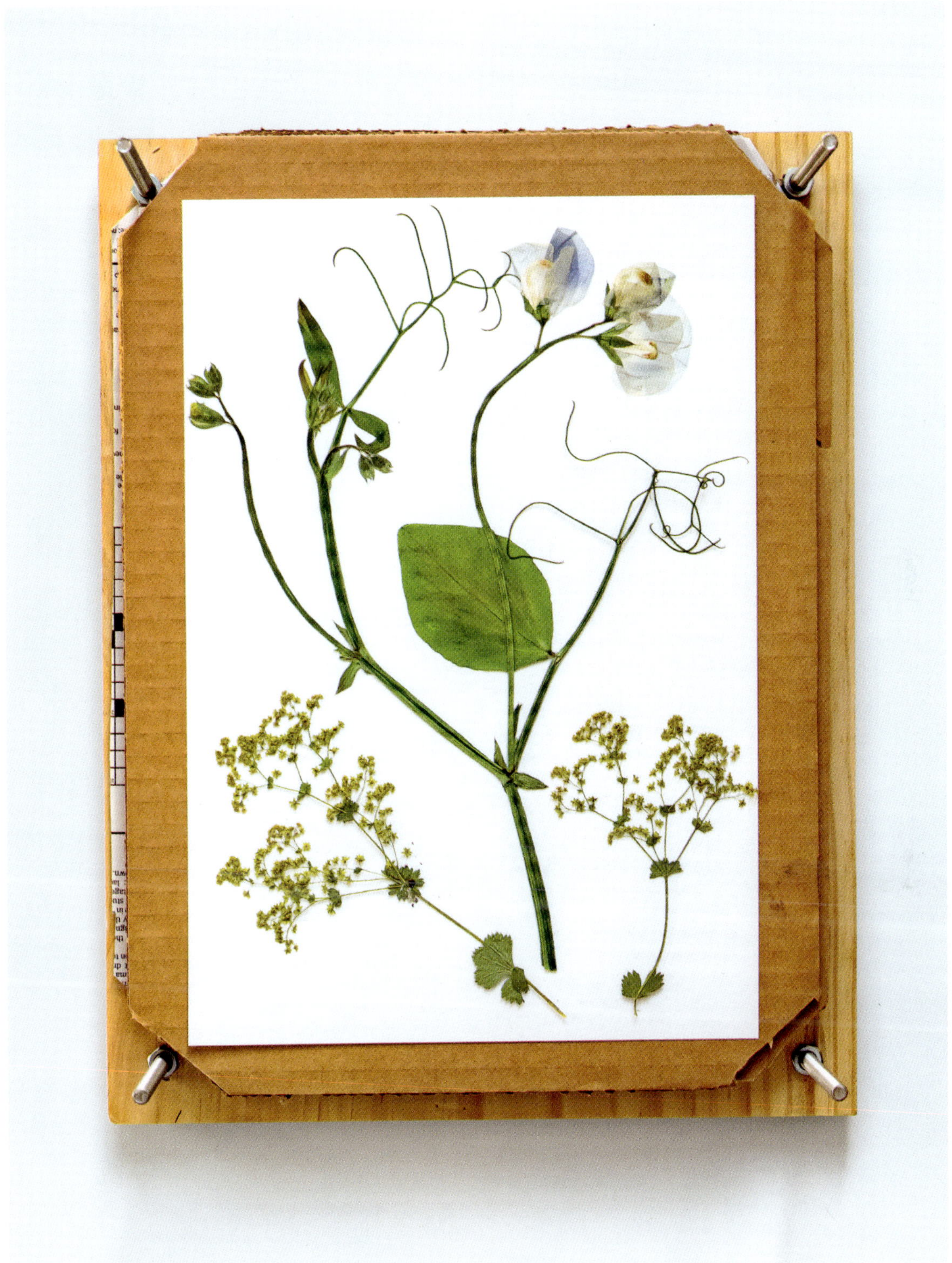

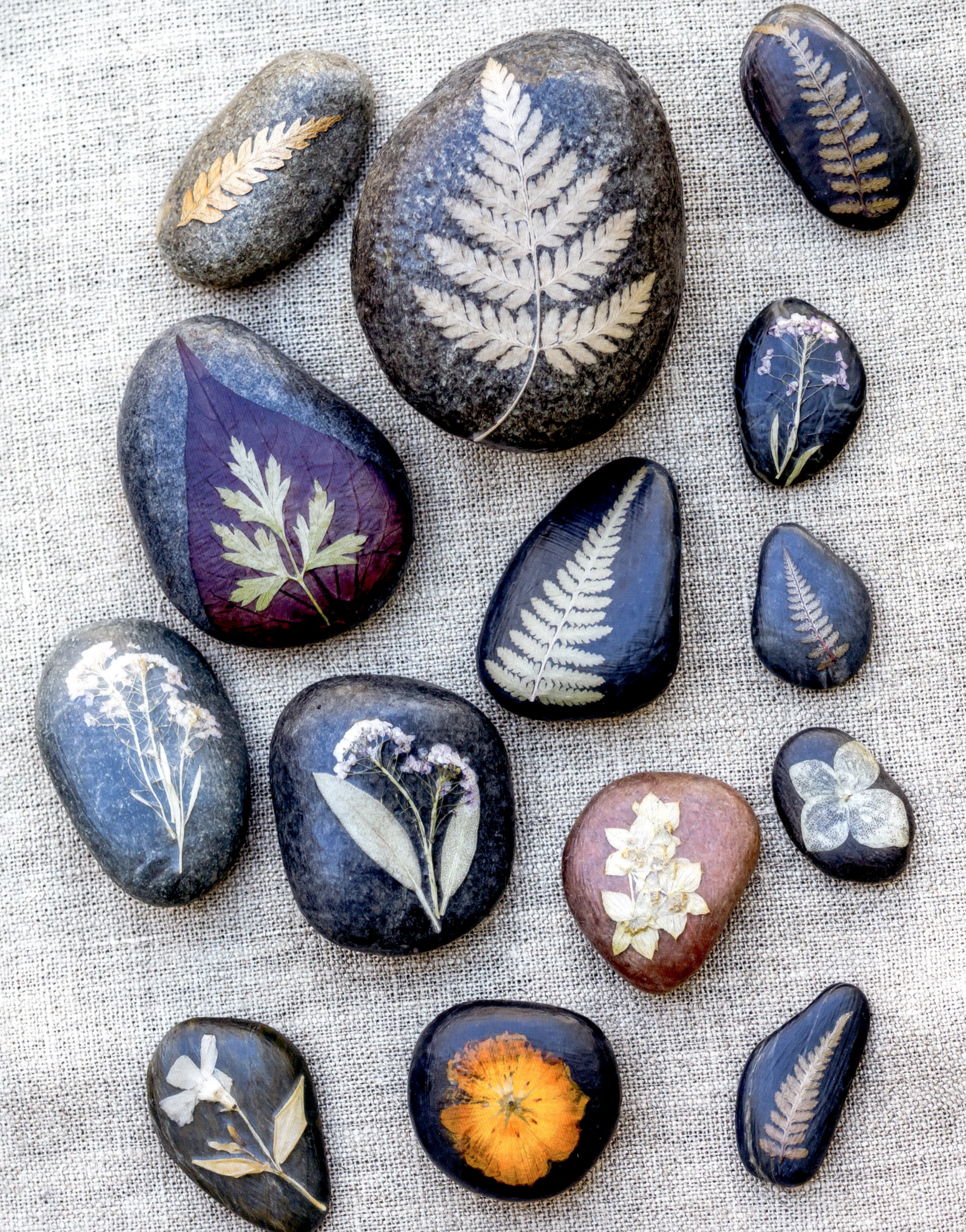

WHAT YOU NEED

- Rocks
- Dried botanicals
- Small brush (foam or bristle)
- Mod Podge decoupage glue in matte or super matte
- Tweezers (optional)
- Toothpick (optional)

4

Botanical Rocks

This has become one of my favorite projects. It is easy to do, and the finished product is both tactile and beautiful. The pieces are lovely on their own or grouped in a bowl or on a shelf. You can use any rock, but I prefer smooth, rounded rocks that feel good in my hand. A small stone may look delicate; a large stone can become sculptural. As for botanicals, my favorites are dried ferns because they are flat and, depending on their color, can look like fossils once they are glued down. I love experimenting with different plants and flowers, though I have found the flatter the better.

While very easy to create, these rocks take some time. You need to build up many layers of Mod Podge to make the botanical feel fused to the stone. Of course, the smaller the stone, the quicker each layer is to apply, but even on large stones applying a layer is relatively fast. It is also a forgiving process, because you are applying thin layers of glue, which makes it relatively easy to achieve a smooth surface.

A note about rocks: Who knew that finding rocks worthy of turning into art would be such a challenge? While I have found some gorgeous and useful rocks in the wilds of my backyard, I have two confessions to make: I have foraged (okay, swiped) a few fabulous, large round rocks from the parking lot of a local strip mall. My second confession: I have resorted to buying rocks—yes, buying rocks.

I look for several characteristics in a rock, and the rock that fits them all is rare. First, the smoother the rock, the better for most of my purposes. For this project, I have even used stones meant for terrariums. The second criteria is shape. Generally, I look for round(ish) rocks, but I also check to see that the rock face I want to use has a pleasing shape and that

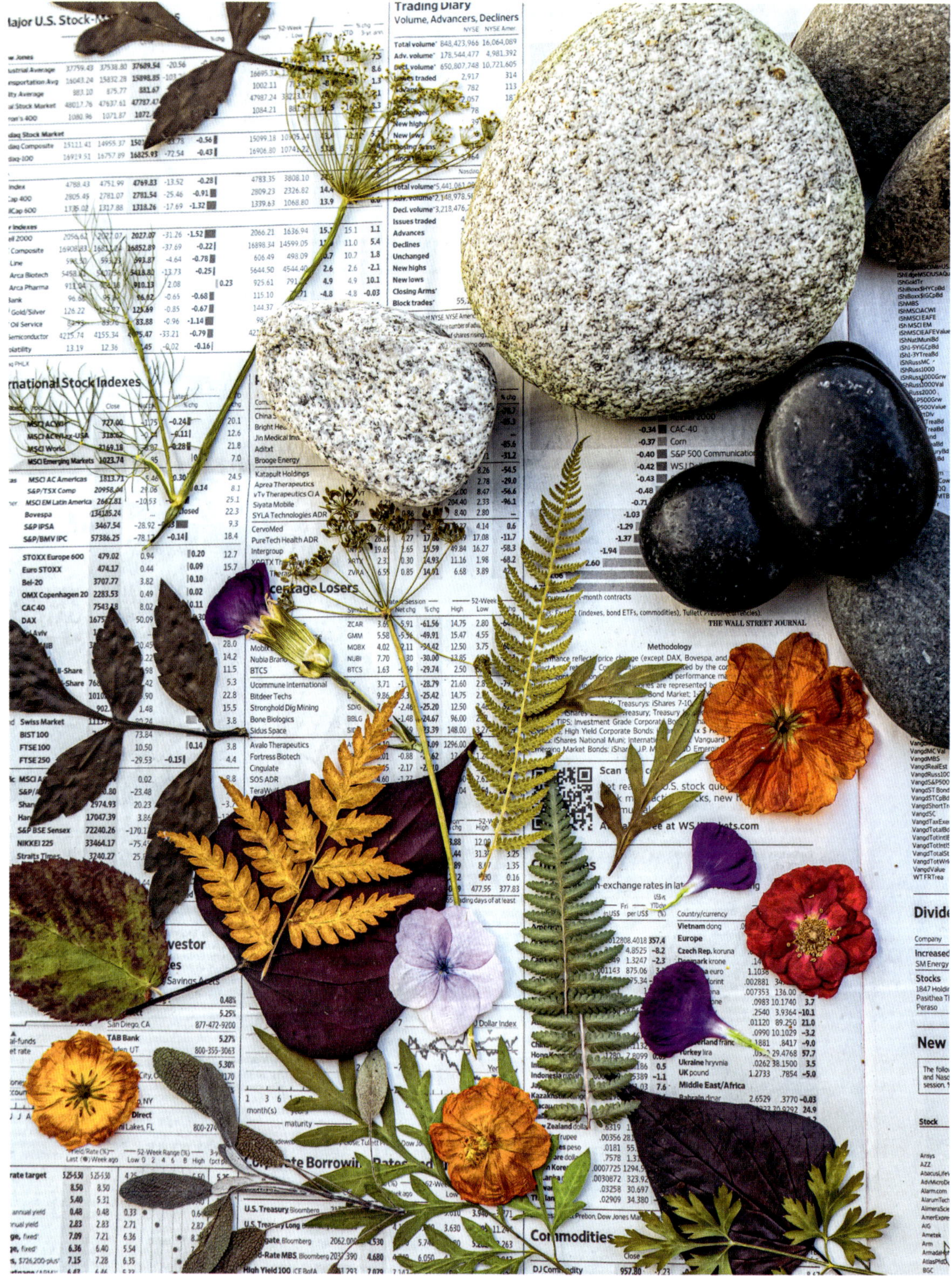
Trading Diary
Volume, Advancers, Decliners
THE WALL STREET JOURNAL
Methodology

my chosen face sits upright and visible when placed on a surface. You can always glue a pebble to the back of a rock to have it sit more favorably, but I prefer rocks that present their best face naturally.

Keep in mind that the color of your botanical may fade or change over time. This isn't necessarily a bad thing, but the more colorful the botanical, the greater the chances for substantial color shift.

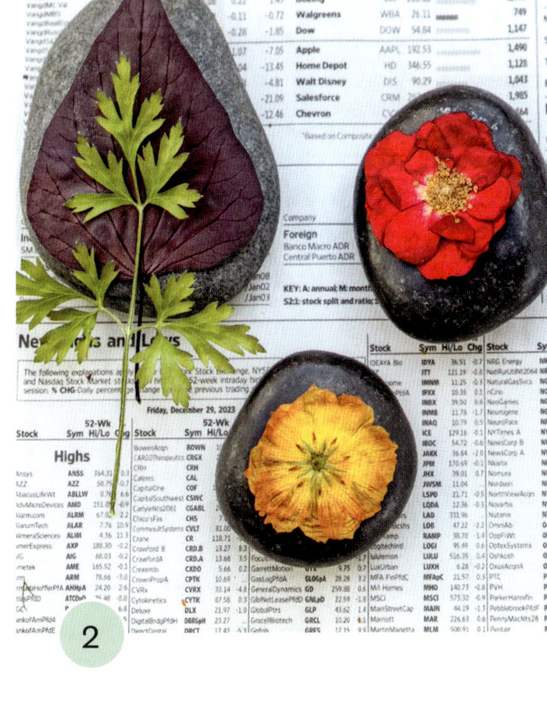

1

Choose Your Rock and Botanical

In choosing a rock and the botanical that goes with it, you will want to make sure there is enough contrast so that the botanical doesn't just disappear after it has been glued. If your rock isn't flat, you will need to choose a botanical that has some flexibility even when dried. Ferns are perfect to start with, as they are naturally flat and usually somewhat flexible. It can add a level of grace to the design if the lines of the botanical follow the curve of the stone. You can cut off and use just the tip of a fern, or I often pull the branches (called the pinnae) off the spine (also known as the midrib) and use those.

2

Design

Experiment with different compositions to see which botanicals look best on which stones. You can also try layering botanicals on top of each other, keeping in mind that over time the colors of the botanicals will change and fade.

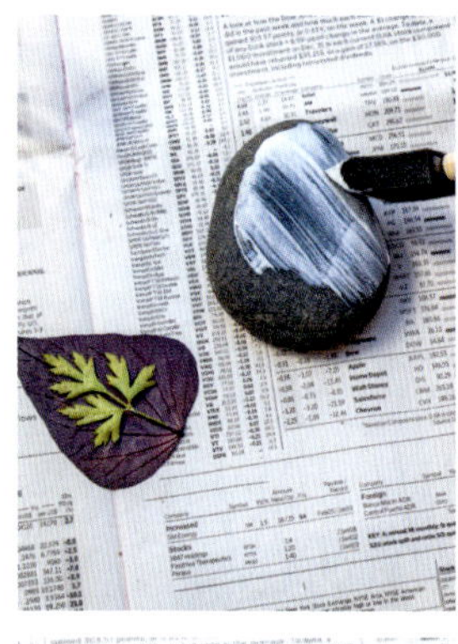

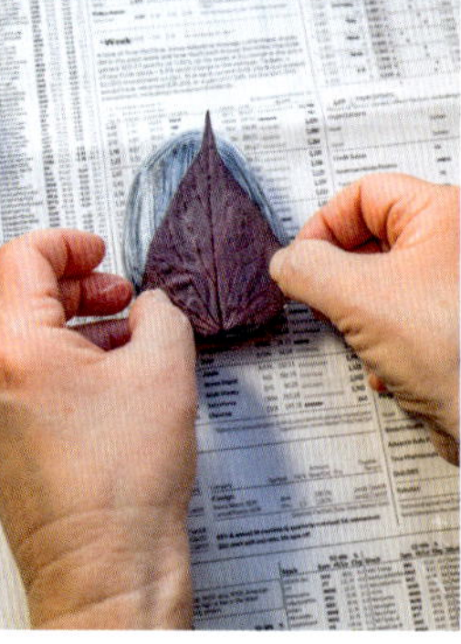

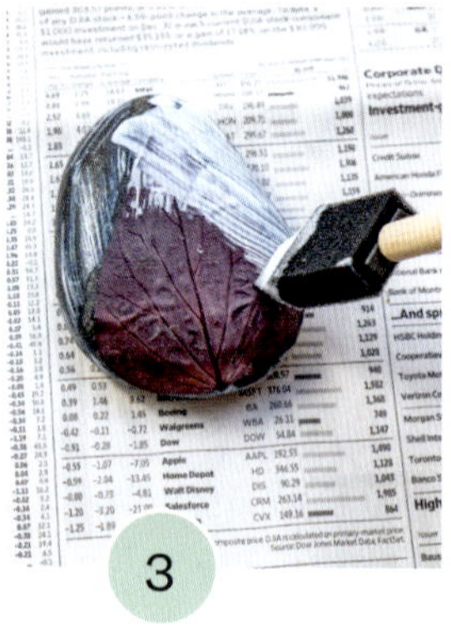

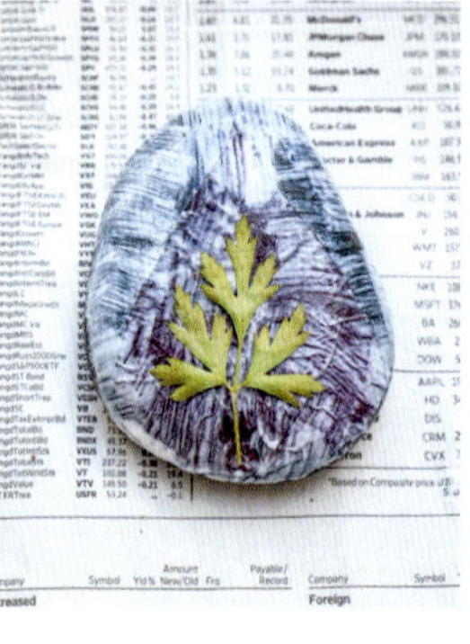

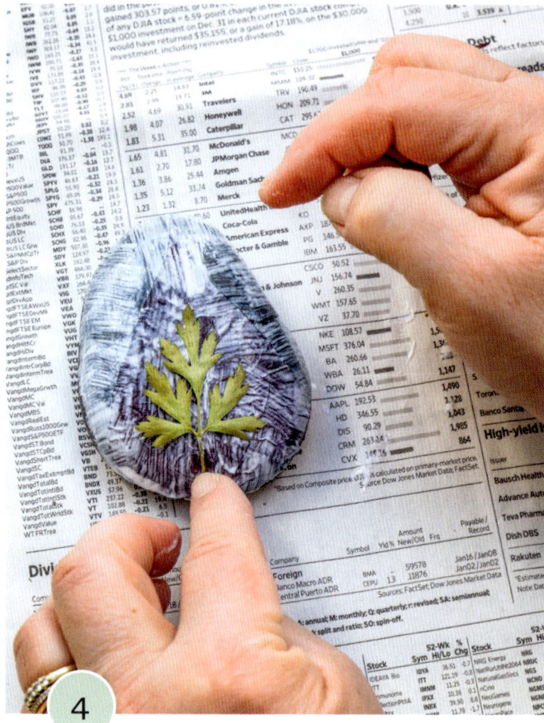

3

Glue

Using a small brush, put a thin layer of decoupage glue (I use Mod Podge) on the face of the stone. Place the botanical on top of the wet glue and press the botanical smooth, so it adheres to the stone. Make sure there are no unsightly folds or edges sticking up. Then put a layer of Mod Podge on top of the botanical.

4

Adhere the Botanical

Sometimes you have to hold the botanical so that it bends and sticks to the curve of the rock. You can use your fingers, though sometimes they will stick to the surface and you will need to carefully unstick yourself, or you can hold down the botanical with a toothpick. Let the Mod Podge dry to the touch—usually about 30 minutes.

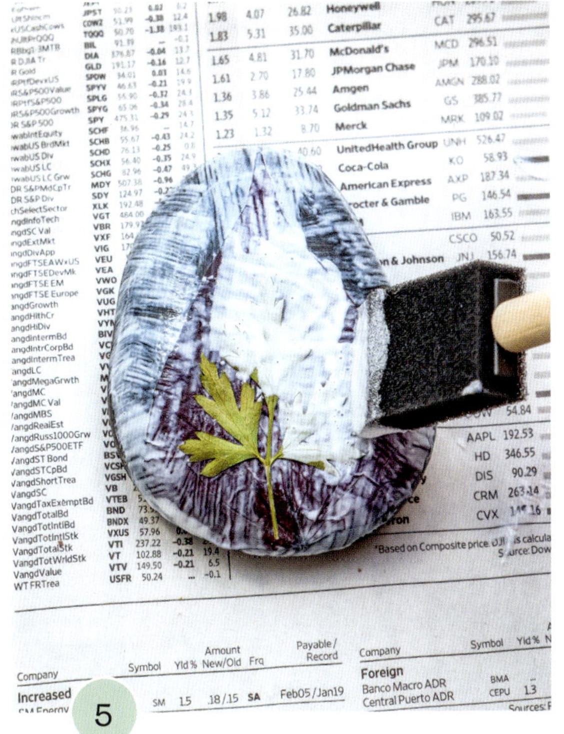

Layer with Mod Podge

Repeat the gluing process a ridiculous number of times. Sometimes it can take ten coats to get the botanical to look fused to the stone. The number of coats will depend on how flat your botanical is to start with and how smooth you want your finished stone.

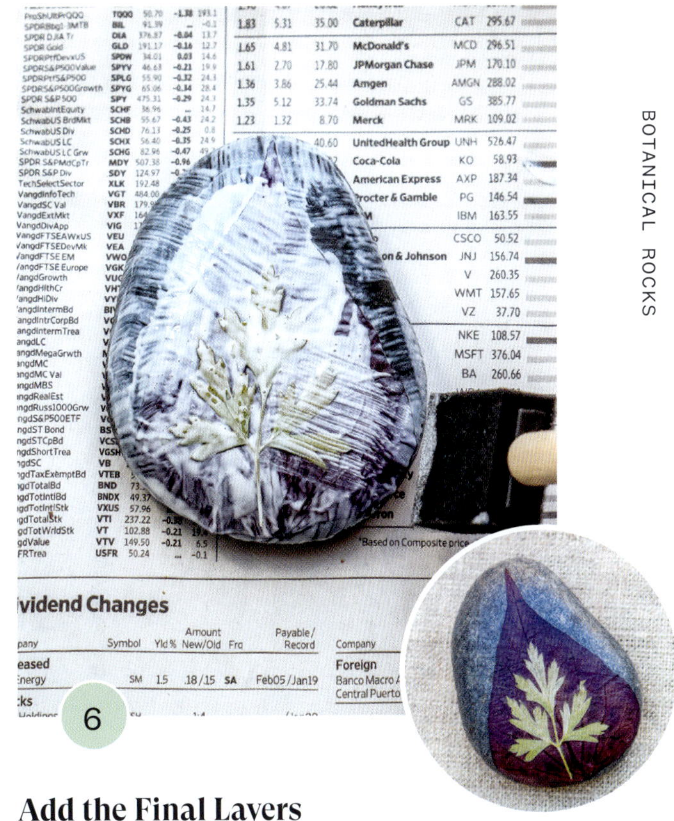

Add the Final Layers

Keep layering until the stone and its botanical have the look and feel that make you happy. It helps to keep the project in a place where you can access it easily, as it is super quick to do each layer but you need to do it so many times.

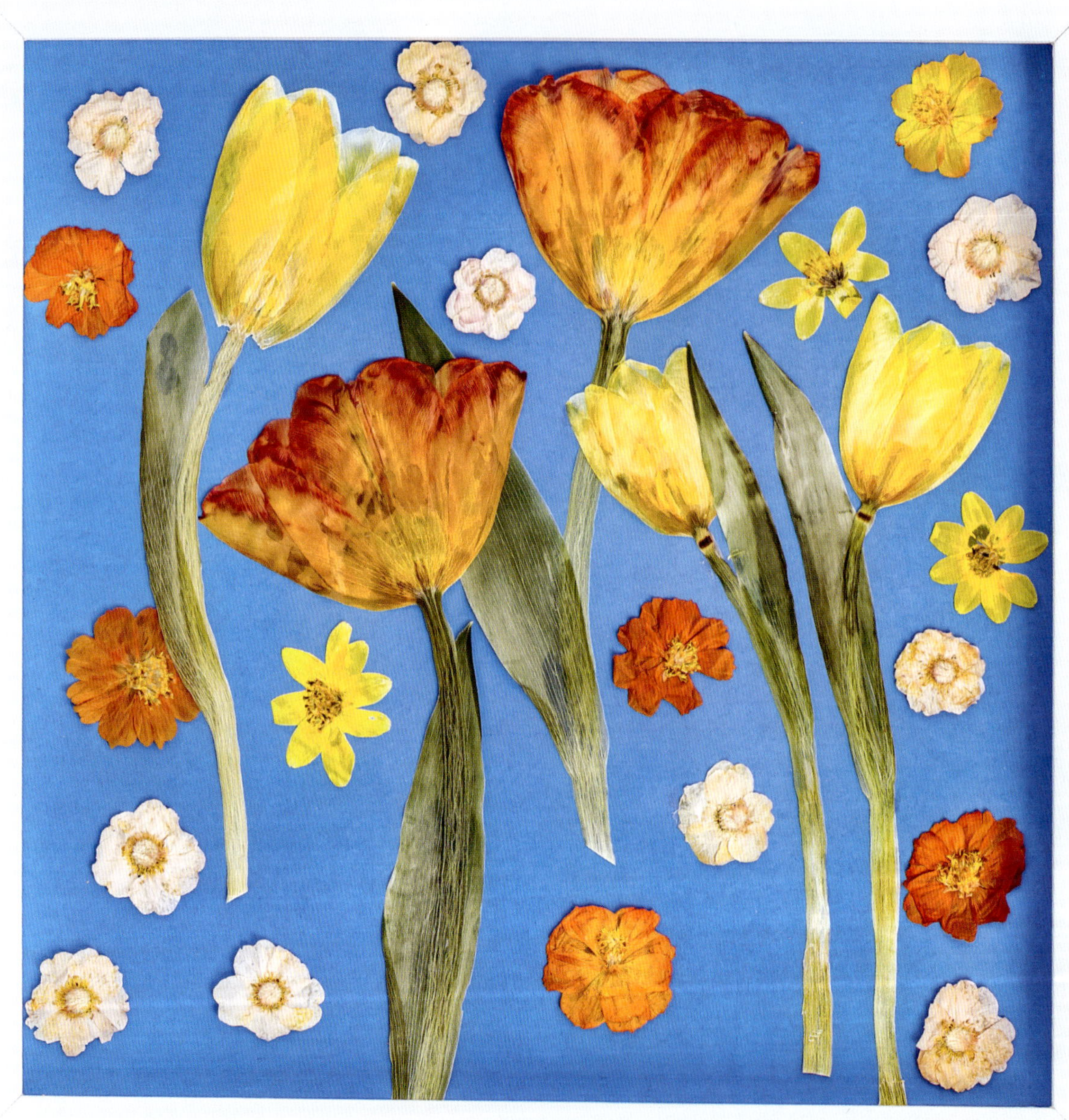

WHAT YOU NEED

- Dried botanicals
- Background material (paper or glass)
- Tweezers
- Picture frame (with or without mat)
- Liquid PVA glue
- Small brush
- Spray adhesive (optional)
- Toothpicks
- Cotton swabs
- Scissors

5

Dried Flower Collage

You don't have to search far on social media to find masses of videos of people creating dried flower collages. There is a thriving business in transforming wedding bouquets into elaborate art pieces. Of course the videos make those collages seem incredibly fast and ridiculously easy to create. Well, not necessarily. In reality, creating a stunning collage of dried flowers is a challenge. A delightful challenge, but a challenge nonetheless.

First, you need to dry the flowers . . . lots of them. On top of that, you need dried flowers in a harmonious color palette. Add to that the necessity of a steady and gentle touch for placing and gluing flowers that can be as delicate as dragonfly wings, and you have your challenge.

After that description, you might wonder why you would want to attempt this project. There are many reasons: the challenge is part of the fun, the final product can be fabulous, and the intense focus you need to create it is fulfilling.

There are some ways to increase your odds for success: First, start small. A project on the smaller side needs fewer flowers, which means less to dry and fewer to glue. Second, try picking just a few varieties of flowers to work with, and keep your color palette either warm (yellows, oranges, reds) or cool (blues, greens, purples). Place larger flowers first and then fill in with smaller flowers, leaves, and petals. Another option is to choose one, two, or three spectacular blossoms and use only those. Alternatively, just have fun and be spontaneous, which sometimes leads to the best results.

You can use anything for the collage's background, including pages from illustrated books, sheet music, maps, old calendars, photographs, even fancy rice paper. Or simply glue the flowers directly onto the glass of a floating, double-glass frame. That said, if you want your piece to last long enough to become an heirloom, choose archival paper and glue. (Note: By choosing materials that are archival, you give your projects the best chance for longevity because they are less likely to deteriorate, yellow, or become brittle over time.)

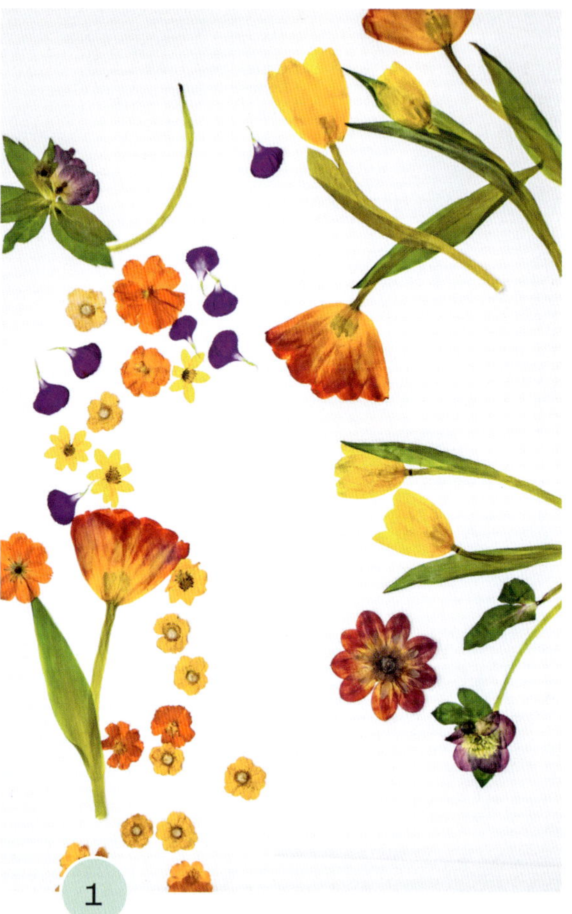

1

Select the Botanicals

Assemble an assortment of dried botanicals on a neutral background. Consider their size, color, and texture and whether you want to include stems.

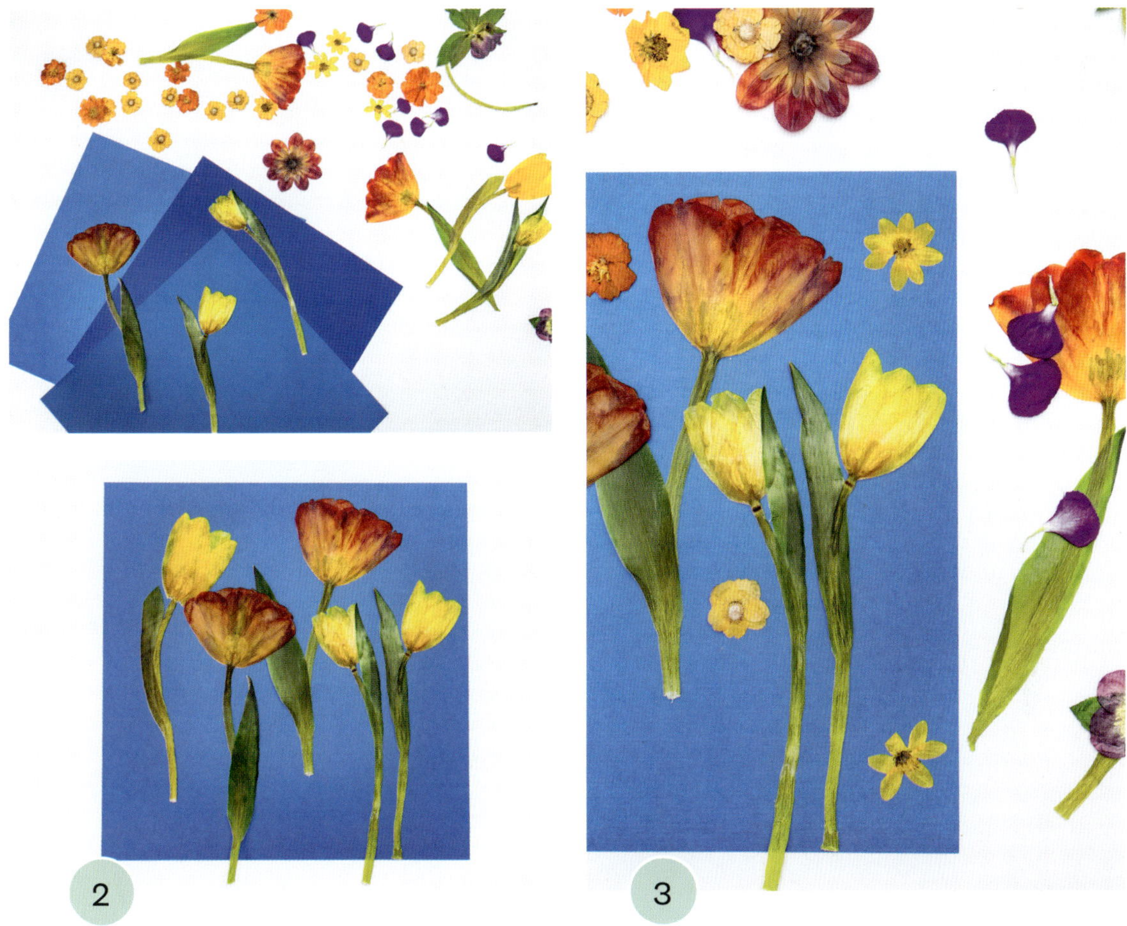

Design the Layout

Choose a background for the collage, then lay out your design. Tweezers are helpful with this, as the botanicals can be fragile and very difficult to pick up and can stick to your fingers.

Play

Try different flowers—adding and subtracting and moving things around until the design coheres. You can either keep the botanicals separated or overlap them, though the latter will make the gluing step a little more challenging.

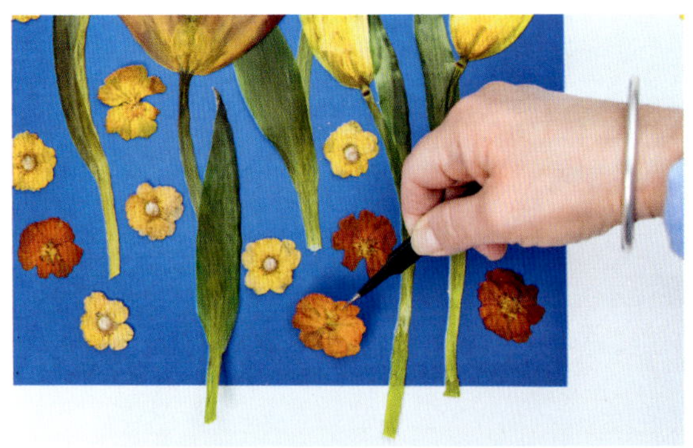

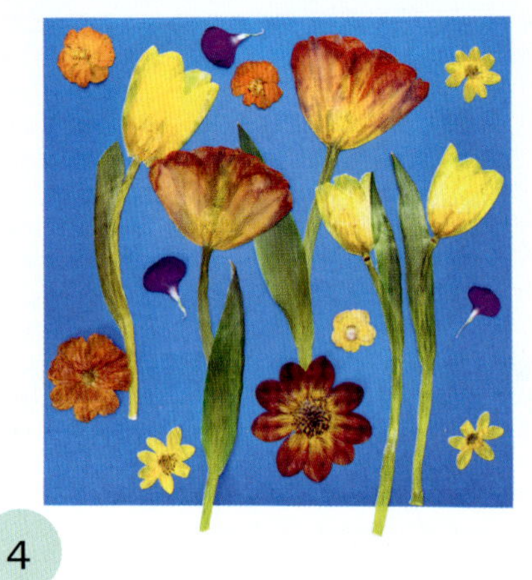

4

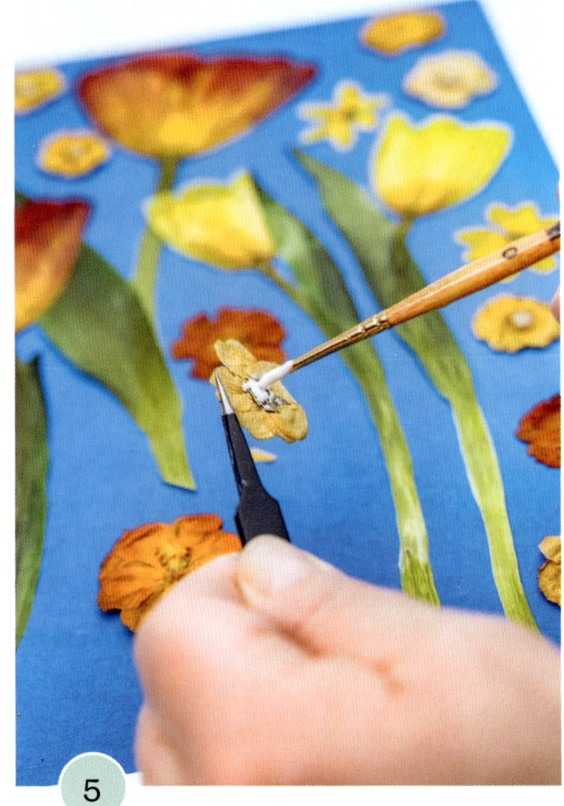

5

Step Back

Step back and check your design before you start gluing to see if specific elements aren't working or could be improved. It can also help to take a picture of the collage with your phone, as you may see holes or unwanted patterns in the photo that you would otherwise miss. If you plan to frame the finished piece, try placing the frame, without the glass, around your design to see how the edges look.

Start Gluing

Once you are happy with your design, pick up a botanical with the tweezers, flip it over, and apply dabs of glue to the back side with a small brush. You want enough glue that the botanical will hold, but not so much that glue will squish out the sides when you press it down. Alternatively, use a toothpick or cotton swab to apply the glue. You can also use a spray adhesive, though it is less environmentally friendly and requires good ventilation and the use of a quality face mask or respirator.

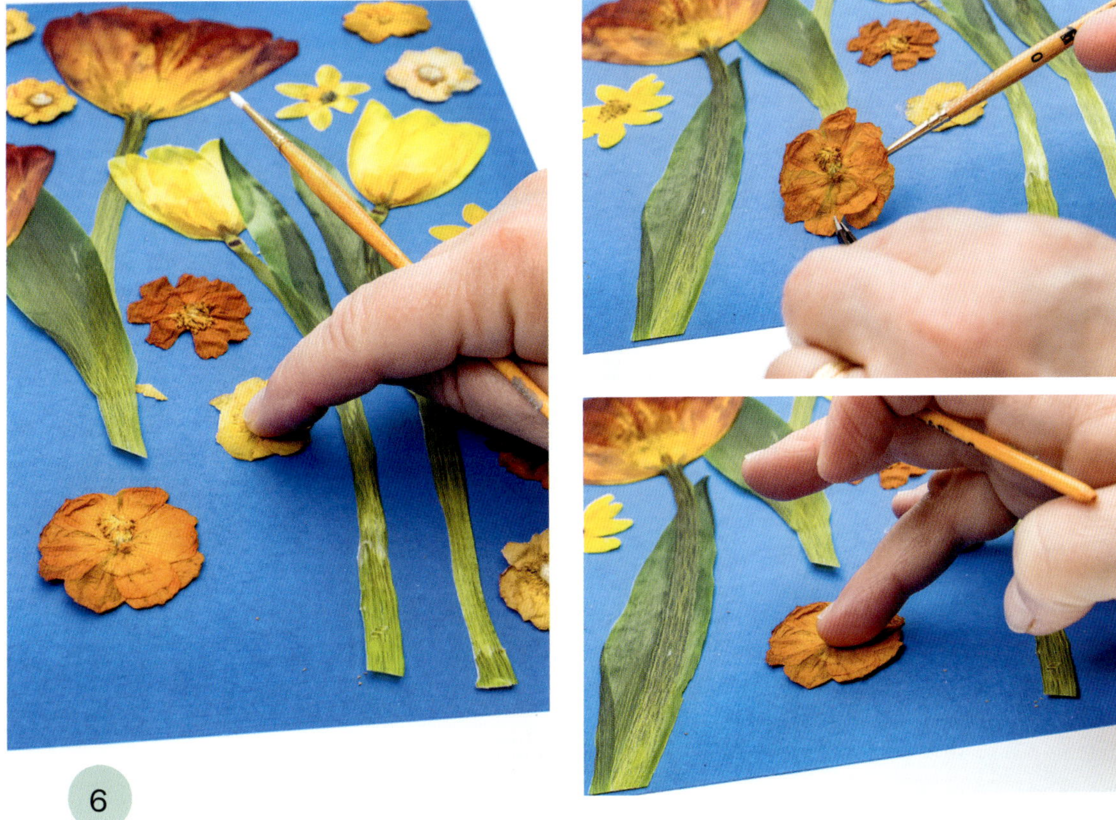

6

Adhere the Botanicals

Carefully place your flower as close to its original spot as possible, and gently press it down. If something breaks off, you may be able to repair it by gluing it back together or by gluing pieces from other flowers to fill in holes. An alternative method for gluing is to lift up the side of your botanical and slide some glue underneath it. This tends to work better with smaller and less complex flowers and leaves, or when things overlap.

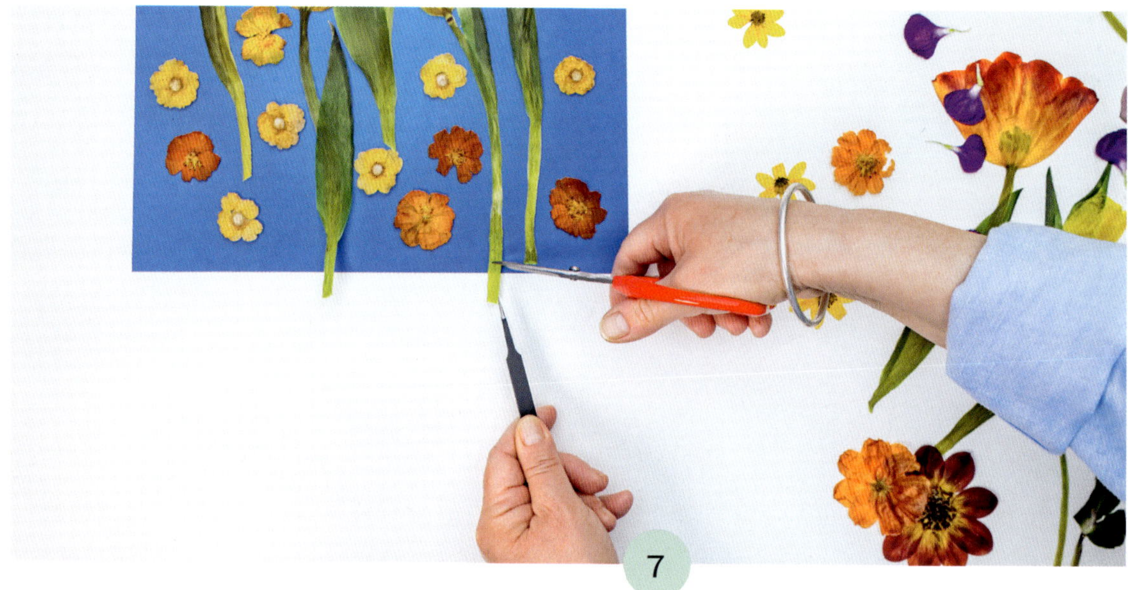

7

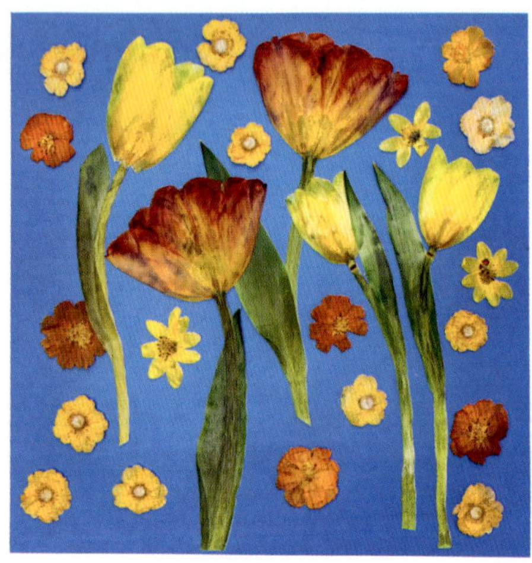

Trim

Once all your pieces are glued and have dried in place, trim any bits that overhang the edges. Then, using the tweezers, clean up any stray fluff, debris, or pet hair that have inevitably landed in the middle of your design.

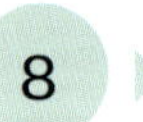

Display

There are any number of ways to frame and display collages depending on how flat the botanicals are. You can use a mat (the paperboard border sometimes used around artwork) to keep the glass from squashing your dried botanicals. Or if your botanicals stick out from the surface, you can use a box frame with or without a mat, so the glass sits significantly above the surface of the collage. Just make sure that if you want your design to last as long as possible, use archival materials when framing as well.

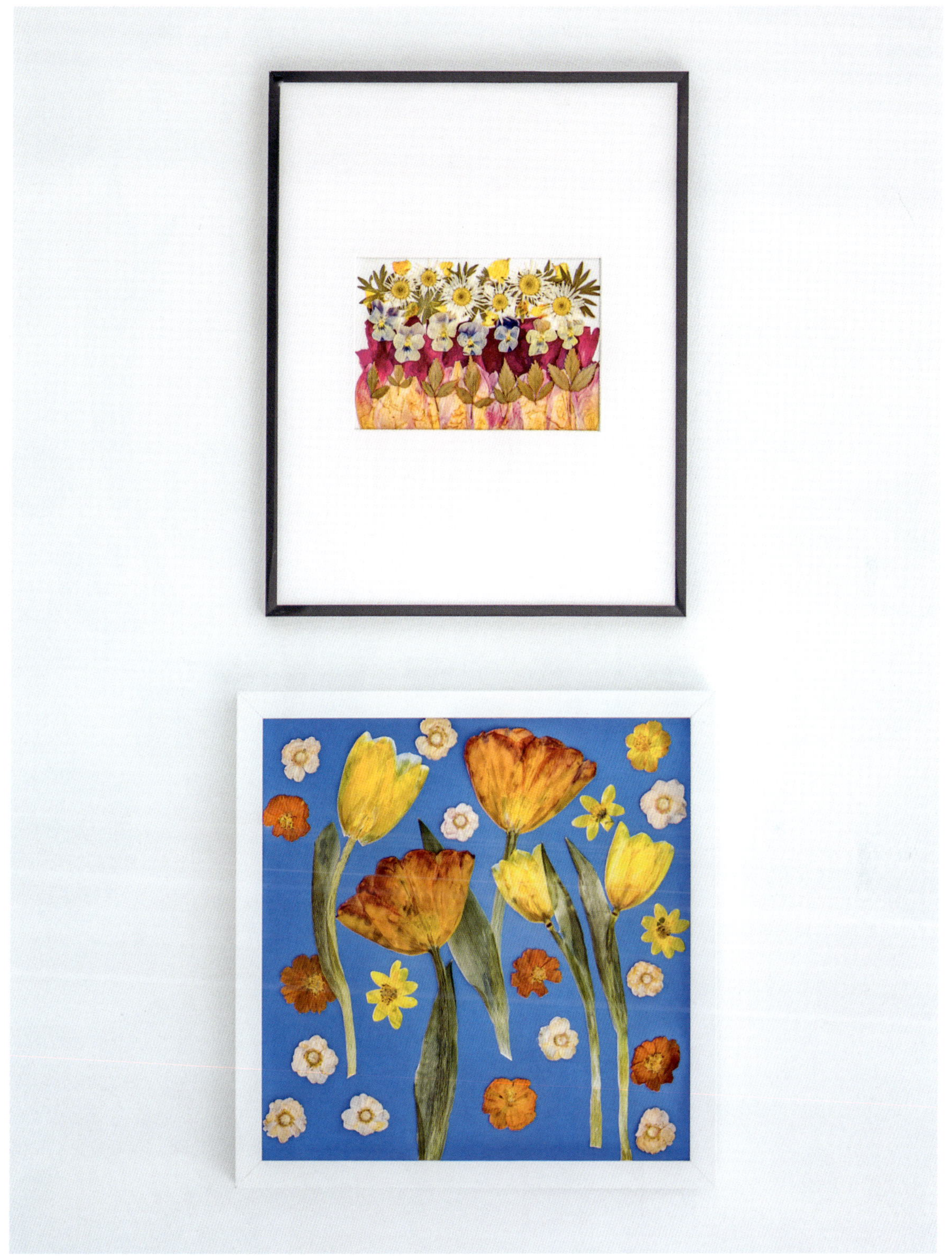

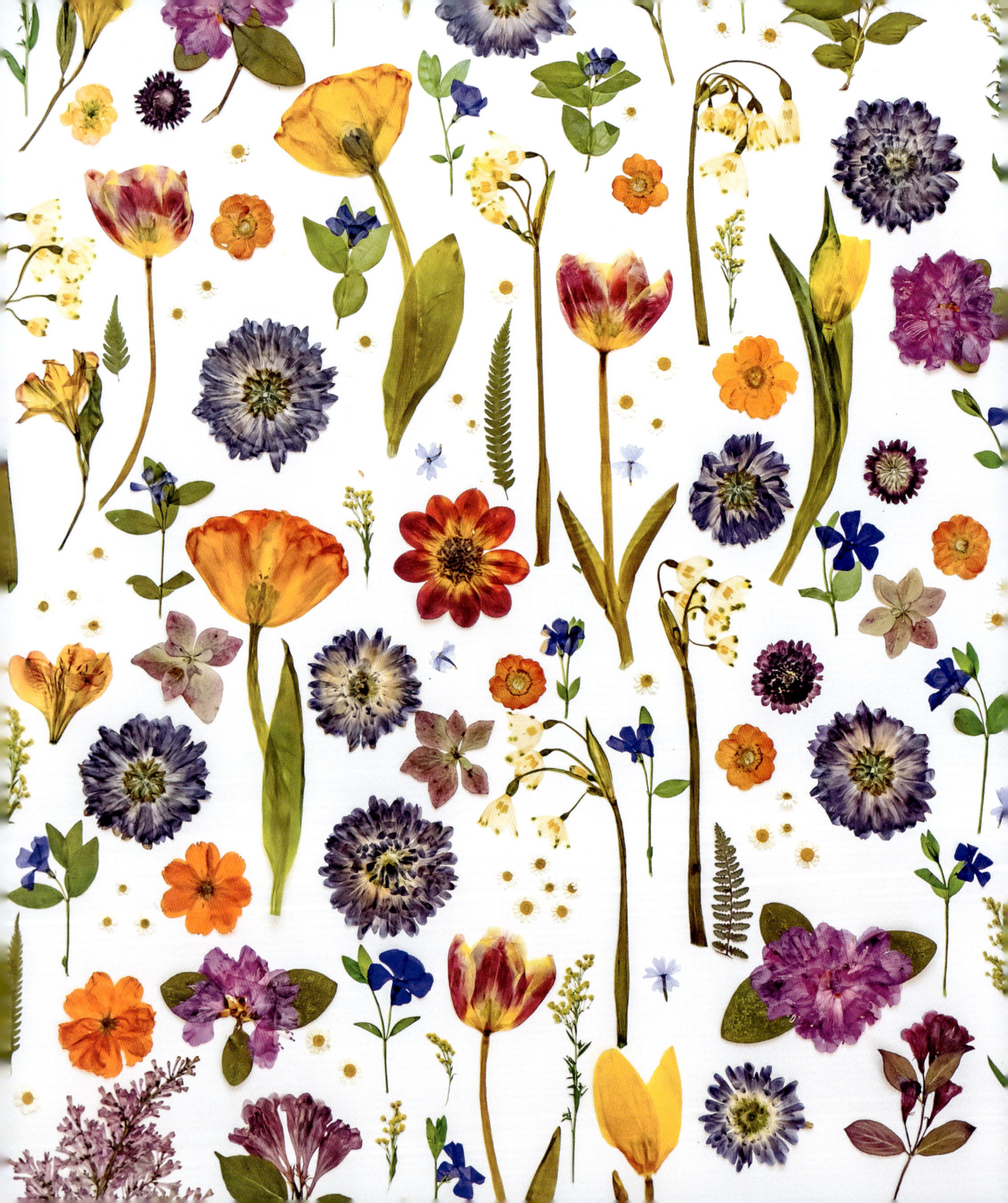

WHAT YOU NEED

- Flat background
- Dried botanicals
- Tweezers
- Digital camera or phone camera

6

Free-Spirit Collage

While it is conceivable that these could be considered cheaters' collages because the botanicals aren't adhered to the surfaces, I prefer to think of them as free-spirited creations. And while these glue-less collages are ephemeral and delicate, paradoxically they become more durable and permanent than a traditional collage by photographing them.

There are lots of reasons to photograph your dried flower projects, but perhaps the most compelling is that it captures and preserves the original color of the leaves and flowers before they inevitably fade. Whether you shoot with a phone or a digital camera, the resulting electronic files allow you to create a vast array of products. The range of print-on-demand services is astonishing. From wallpaper to dinner plates, guitar cases to phone cases, shower curtains to bikinis: there is an online business that can create it for you from a digital image.

Newer camera phones are amazing and can take stunning images, but no matter how good your phone is, a dedicated camera generally will have better lenses, yield higher-quality images, and produce larger digital files. A large file offers several advantages; perhaps the most important is that it allows you to crop an image and still have a usable and robust digital file. This gives you more options for printing. If your resulting file isn't big enough for the project you choose, you can sometimes upscale the image with photo editing software.

The flexibility a free-spirit collage gives you is limitless. While the dimensionality of some flowers can make them hard to glue, for these collages you just need the botanicals to be able to sit flat.

Of course, the primary downside of these glueless collages is that they are super fragile. Even a slight breeze or a sudden sneeze can obliterate your intricate design in a nanosecond (trust me . . . it happens). The good news is this impermanence allows you to move things around easily and shoot as many iterations of the collage as you have time, patience, and botanicals.

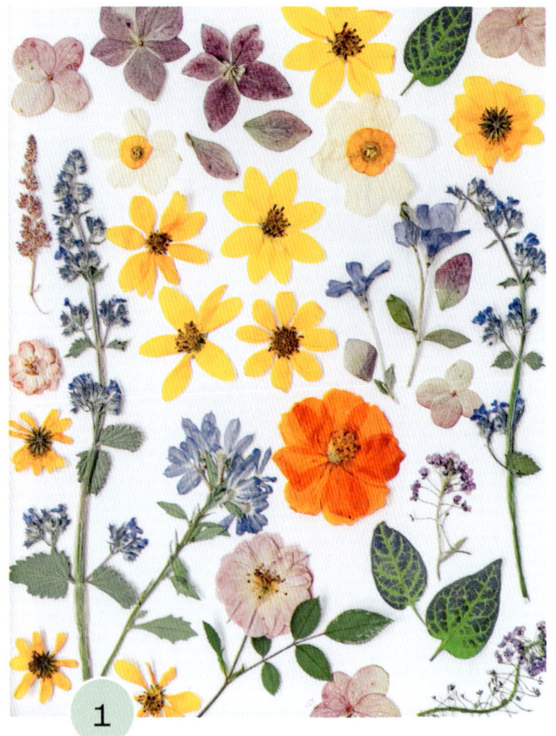

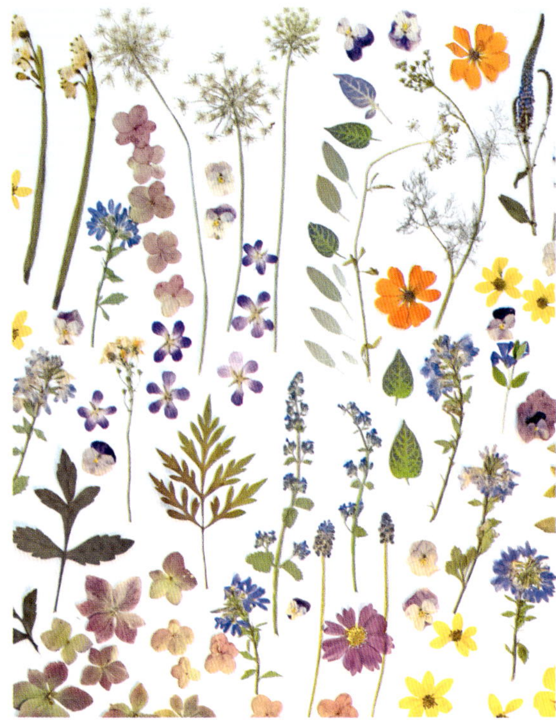

Choose Your Background and Assemble the Botanicals

Lay out an assortment of dried botanicals. Your choice of background for your collage will partially depend on how many botanicals you have and how densely packed you want your collage to be. You might want to start with a small collage and experiment with creating a design that satisfies you. It helps if your background is flat and stiff so you can oh-so-carefully move it. Beware, though, that the breeze created by even walking slowly can blow the botanicals away. You can use a piece of foam core; a heavy, stiff piece of paper; or a tabletop. White is probably the easiest background color to shoot, but don't hesitate to play with different materials, colors, and textures to see what works best for you. However, avoid shiny backgrounds, as they are difficult to photograph. Lay out your botanicals somewhere accessible where you can see them—the more you have to choose from, the better. Also, when choosing a size for your collage, keep in mind that you will need to shoot down, from above, and the image will have to fit into the frame of your phone or camera, so sometimes placing your background on the floor is the easiest. If your design is large, you may need to shoot from a stepladder so that the collage fits inside your camera frame.

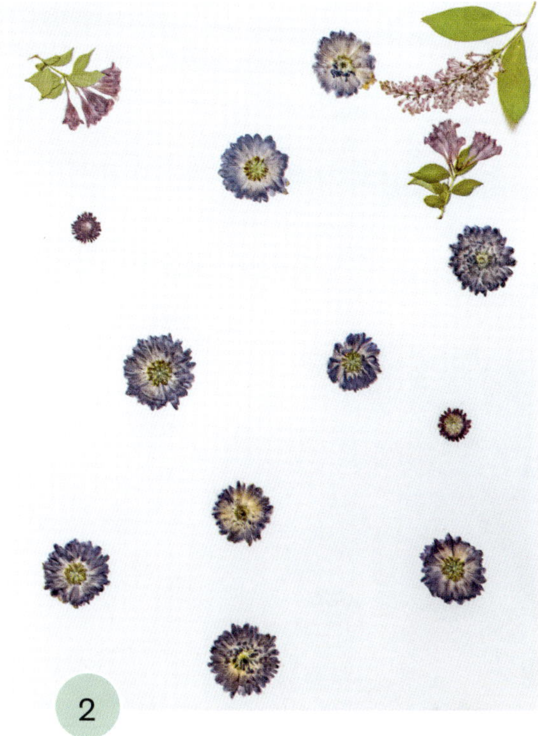

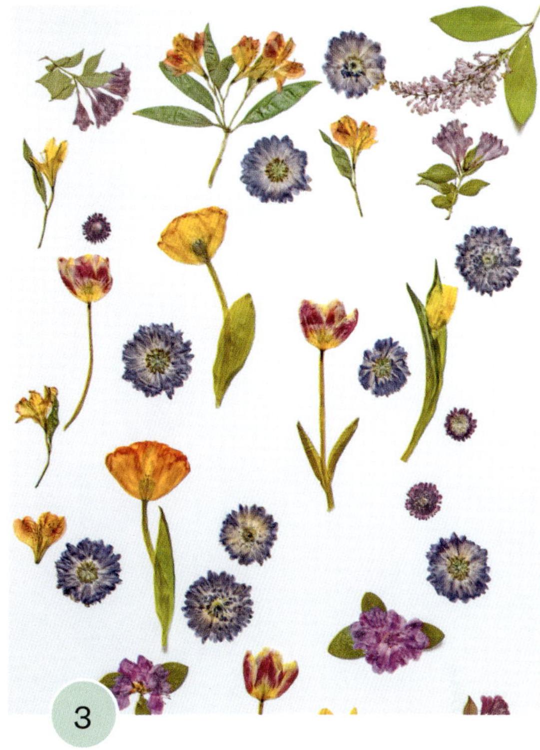

Start Designing

It's often helpful to lay out larger flowers first. They provide the most visual impact, and they take up the most space in the collage. If you have several of the same type of botanicals, try putting them out in a random pattern at the beginning. This is harder than it sounds. Large flowers in particular often seem to want to line up diagonally or start to form the eyes, nose, and mouth of a face. You can always move things around later, but it's good to look for these inadvertent patterns from the beginning.

Fill Out the Space

Your design will evolve at this point. Keep experimenting by moving pieces around and adding botanicals, while looking for ways in which the shapes relate to each other. Be aware of negative space: the space between objects. In these collages, considering the negative space can be as important as the placement of the botanicals in achieving a cohesive design. There is a kind of magical moment where it almost feels like the shapes start talking to each other or dancing together.

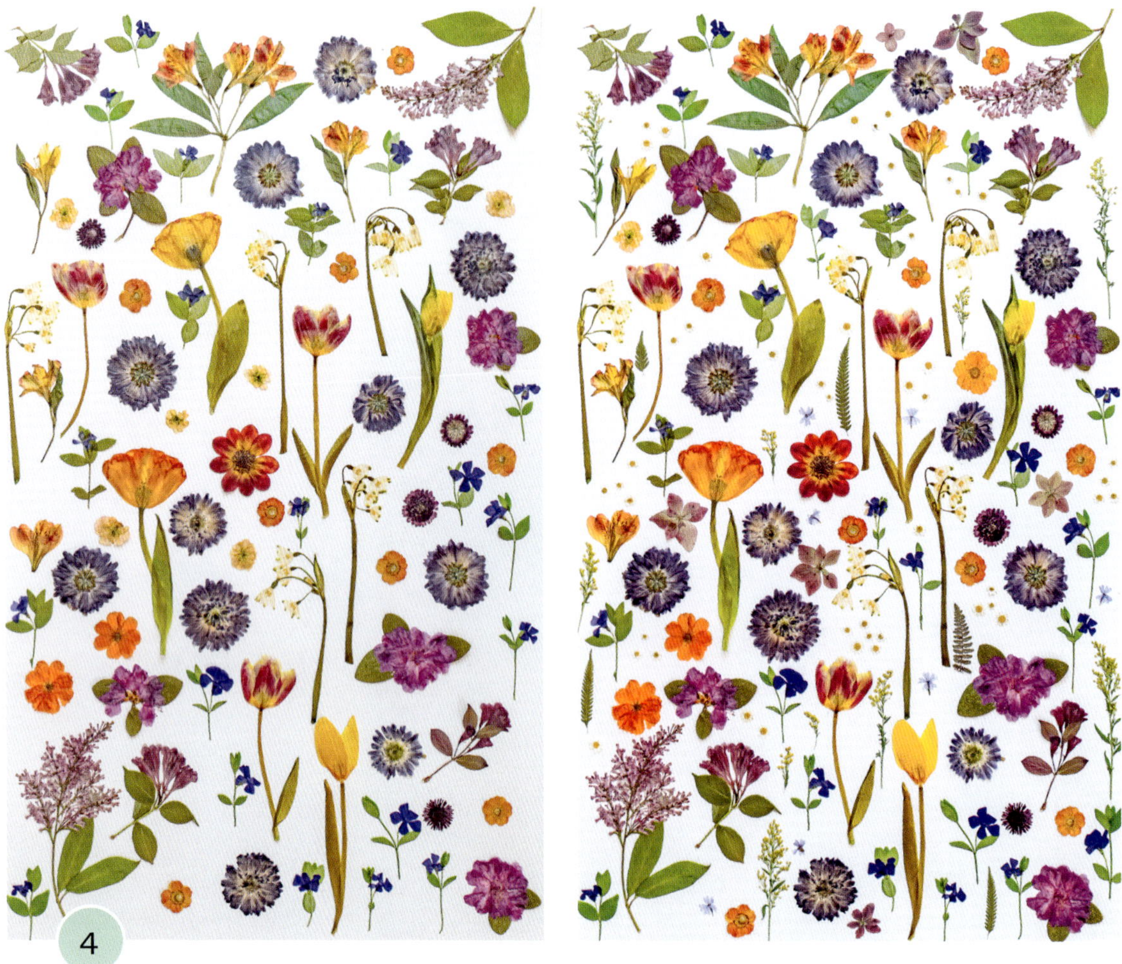

4

Add the Little Guys

Throughout the design process, it is helpful to take pictures of your collage. Sometimes you will see things in a photo that you miss when looking at the actual piece. If you see holes or places where your design isn't working, you can try adding small botanicals to tie it together. Placing small leaves, petals, or flowers throughout the collage so that they flow through the design can help move the viewer's eye through the piece, making it more cohesive.

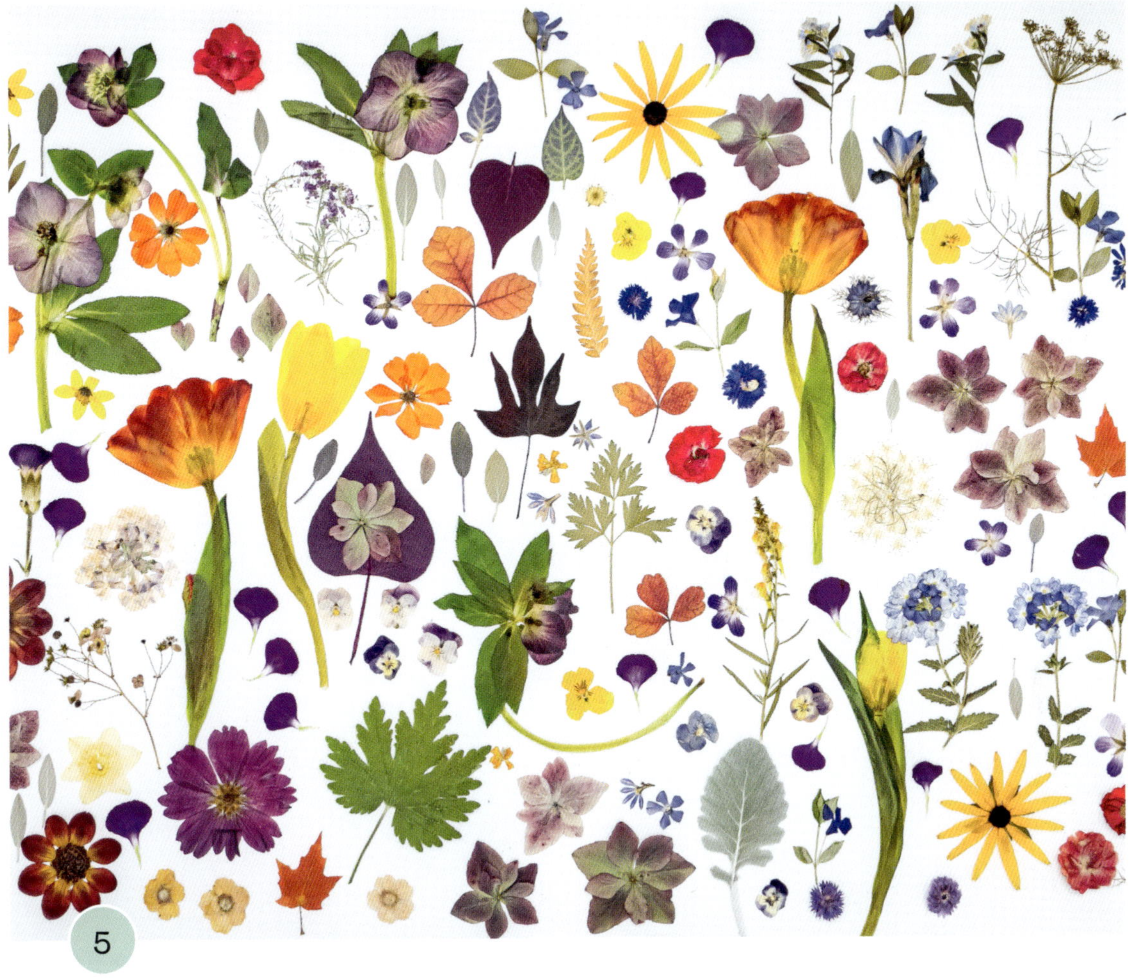

5

Photograph Your Collage

The hardest part of photographing collages is getting the plane of the camera lens level with the plane of the collage. If your camera or phone is tilted in any direction, the perspective of the collage will be skewed. Your phone or camera probably has a built-in level, so use it whenever you can. If you have made a large collage, you may have to get on a stepladder to fit the entire project into your photo. Your second challenge is ensuring the light is uniform over the entire collage. Find a window or someplace (without wind!) that has diffused natural light, or use a piece of white cloth or a purpose-built diffuser to soften direct light. And be careful not to cast shadows with your arms or camera as you shoot.

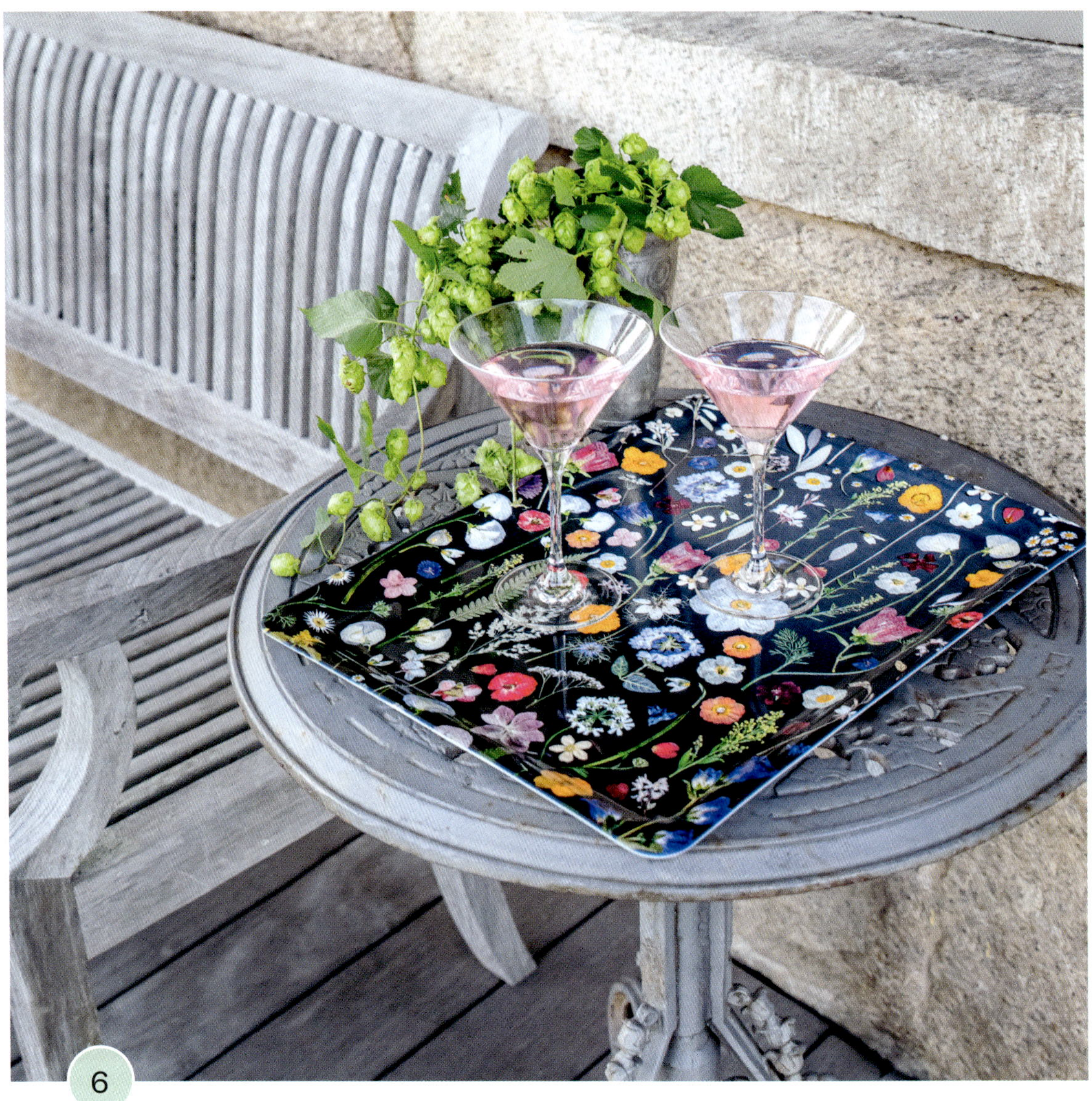

6

Create Products

There are a vast number of businesses that can turn your digital files into products that differ enormously in quality and cost. When ordering products, keep in mind that the backlit image on your computer screen may look brighter and more colorful than the printed object. You may want to print your image on paper at home or order prints online to check for accurate color, brightness, and contrast, especially if you will be ordering an expensive product. Also, be sure to read the company's image specifications before you send in your file.

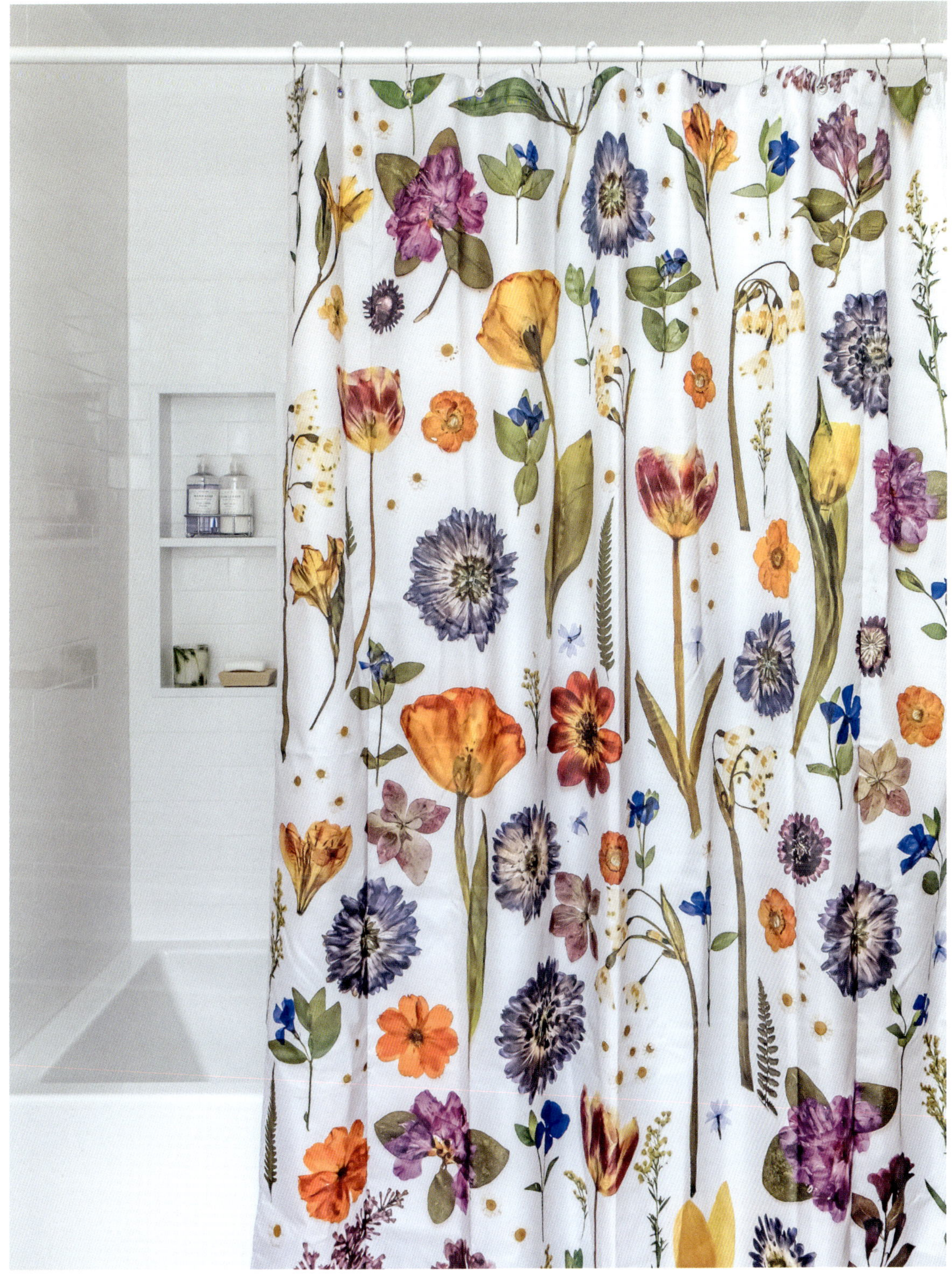

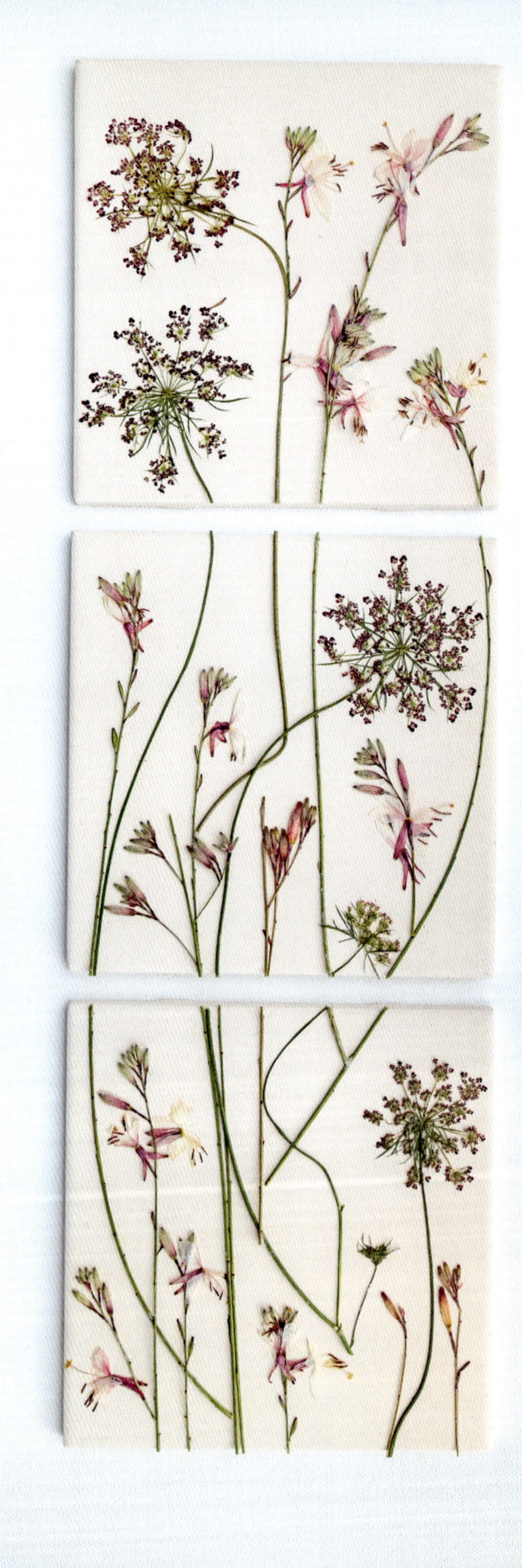

WHAT YOU NEED

- Dried botanicals
- Paper
- Pencil
- Newspaper
- Bisque-fired tiles
- Spray adhesive
- Tweezers
- Sharp scissors
- Precision utility knife
- Liquid PVA glue
- Toothpick or small brush
- Clear matte acrylic spray

7

Dried Flower Tile Tryptic

If you already have dried flowers, this project can be completed in an afternoon. A spray adhesive works remarkably well and quickly, and it's particularly good for lacy flowers. A word of caution: Make sure you have good ventilation when using an aerosol, and consider wearing a quality face mask (like an N95) or a respirator when spraying.

For this project, you can use a series of three tiles, or you can make a single tile or include as many tiles as you want in a series. The tiles can be connected visually by using long-stemmed plants like Queen Anne's lace and gaura, as done here. Alternatively, you can arrange the flowers and leaves so they appear to flow from tile to tile, creating a unified piece.

There are several ways to display the tiles, from hanging them with tile or plate hangers to mounting them in a glass-covered box frame. You can also mount them directly on the wall by gluing hangers to the backs of the tiles. Depending on where you want to hang your finished piece, the orientation can be horizontal or vertical.

Keep in mind that this project is crafted with dried flowers, which by nature are ephemeral and delicate. The colors will fade over time and, even if they are treated with an acrylic spray, they will remain incredibly fragile and will still fade. To increase their longevity and vibrancy, keep the tiles out of direct sunlight and in a location where they won't be bumped or jostled.

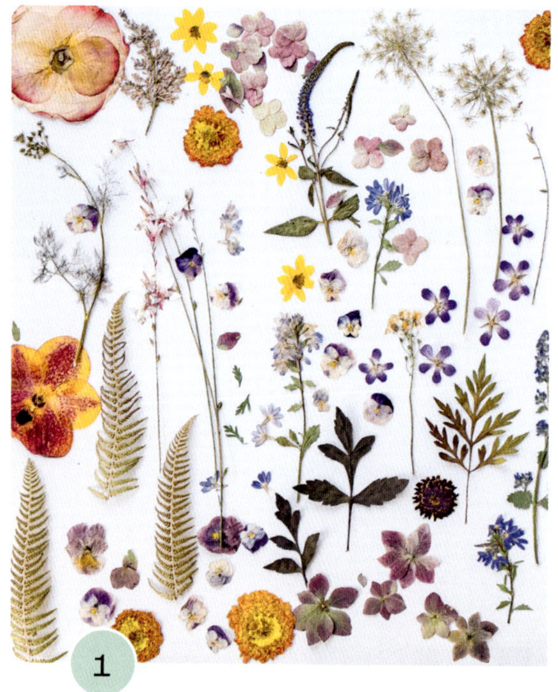

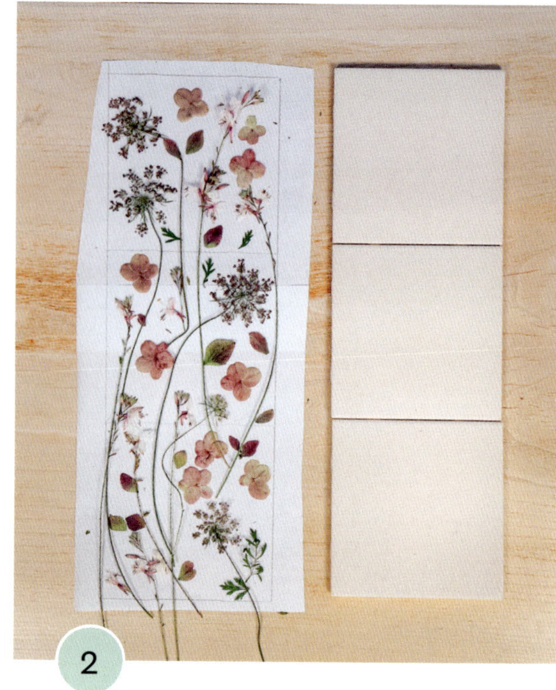

Choose the Botanicals

It is always a delight to spread out dried flowers. The good news is that you almost can't go wrong in what you choose. Some things to think about are color and form. Do you want to include stems? Do you want bright colors or a more muted palette? See if you can find botanicals that seem to talk to each other and don't all face the same way. And check both sides, as the back of a botanical is sometimes more interesting than the front.

Make a Template and Lay Out the Design

Making sure your paper is big enough (you can tape two pieces together, if needed), draw an outline the size of your tiles, and mark the lines between the tiles as well. Lay out your botanicals on the paper template. This is just a draft, and your design will inevitably change as you transfer the design from the template to the tiles, but it's a good place to start. Of course, if you prefer, you can design right on the tiles, but I find it is sometimes easier to begin on paper.

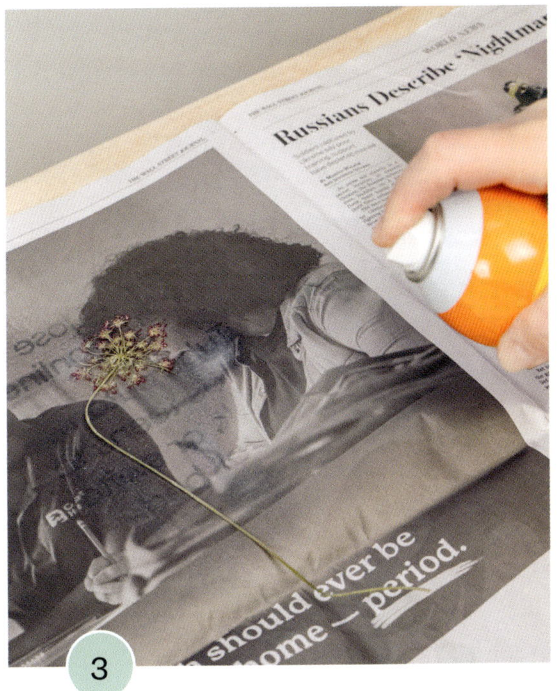

3

Apply Glue and Adhere the First Botanical

Once you are happy with your layout, it's time to glue the elements. Spread newspaper on your work surface. Try working from the top down to establish the flow and spacing of your design. Pick up the first flower and spray it with adhesive on the back side, making sure it's completely covered. Following the directions on the adhesive, wait the designated time before placing your flower on the tile.

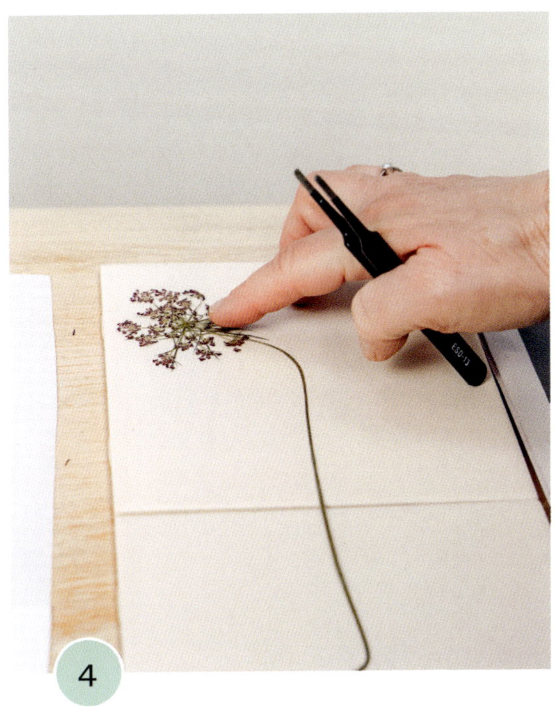

4

Place Your Design

Place the flower on the tile in approximately the same place as it was on the paper template. The sprayed botanical will be a bit damp, which can increase the stem's flexibility and let you slightly bend or adjust it for a more pleasing placement. Gently press the glued botanical onto the tile, making sure it adheres completely.

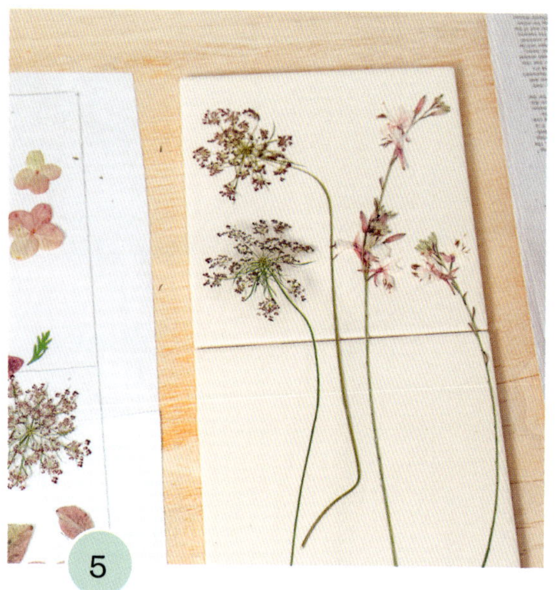
5

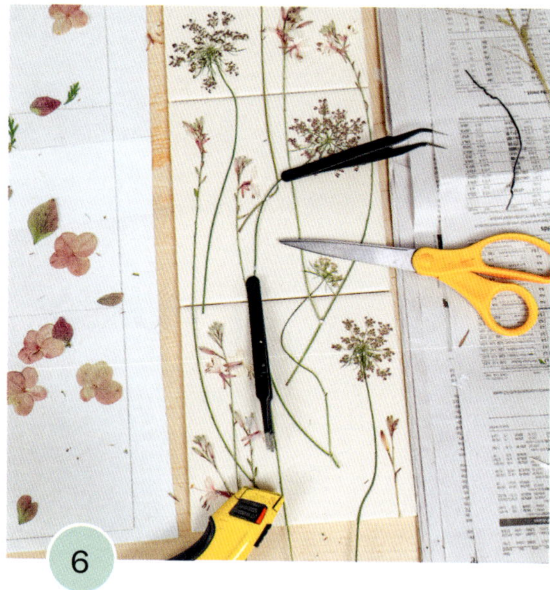
6

Add More Botanicals

Continue spraying and adding botanicals, making sure that anything crossing the tile divisions can be cut cleanly—stems are easier to slice than blossoms.

Weight Uncooperative Botanicals

As you glue, you may find that some parts of a botanical may not be in complete contact with the tile. To solve this issue, use whatever you have on hand to weigh down the wayward botanicals. Choose something heavy enough to press down pieces that are sticking up, but not so heavy that it will squash them. Weigh down any areas you think may not be adhering properly and let them dry with the weight on top.

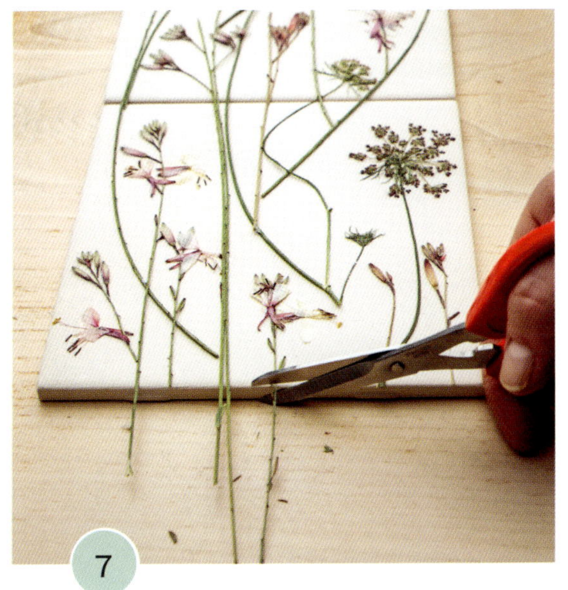

7

Trim

Using sharp scissors or a utility knife, trim any stems that extend past the tile edges.

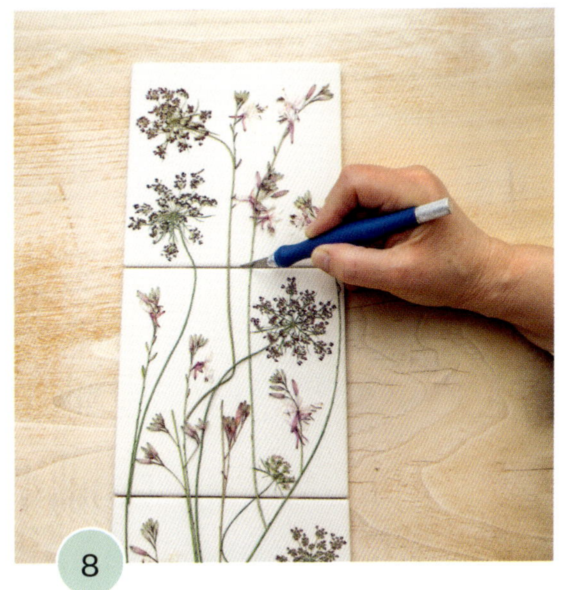

8

Separate the Tiles

Use a thin, sharp utility knife to cut anything connecting the tiles, holding down stems that might come loose as you cut.

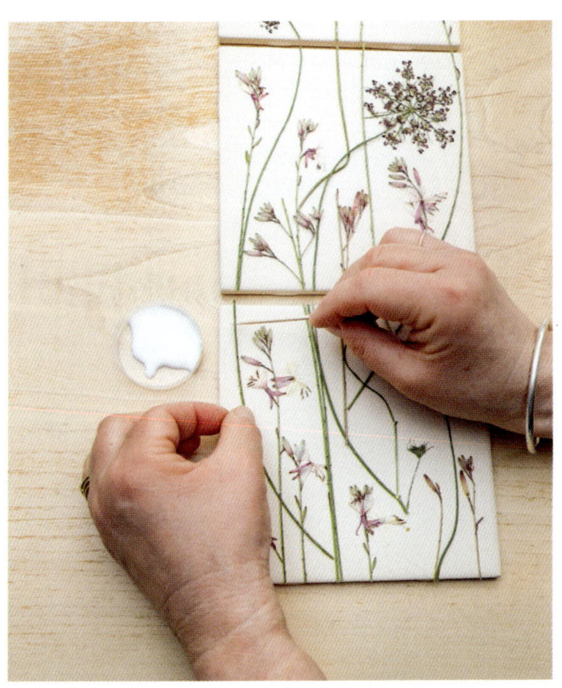

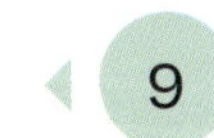

9

Do a Final Check

Inspect your tiles to see if anything is loose, sticking up, or not fully adhered. Using liquid PVA glue and a toothpick or small brush, carefully dab small amounts of glue onto any loose parts. Then using your finger, tweezers, or a toothpick, press and hold until the piece has stuck. To preserve your tiles, you can use a clear matte acrylic spray, covering the entire surface of the botanicals and the tiles in an even layer.

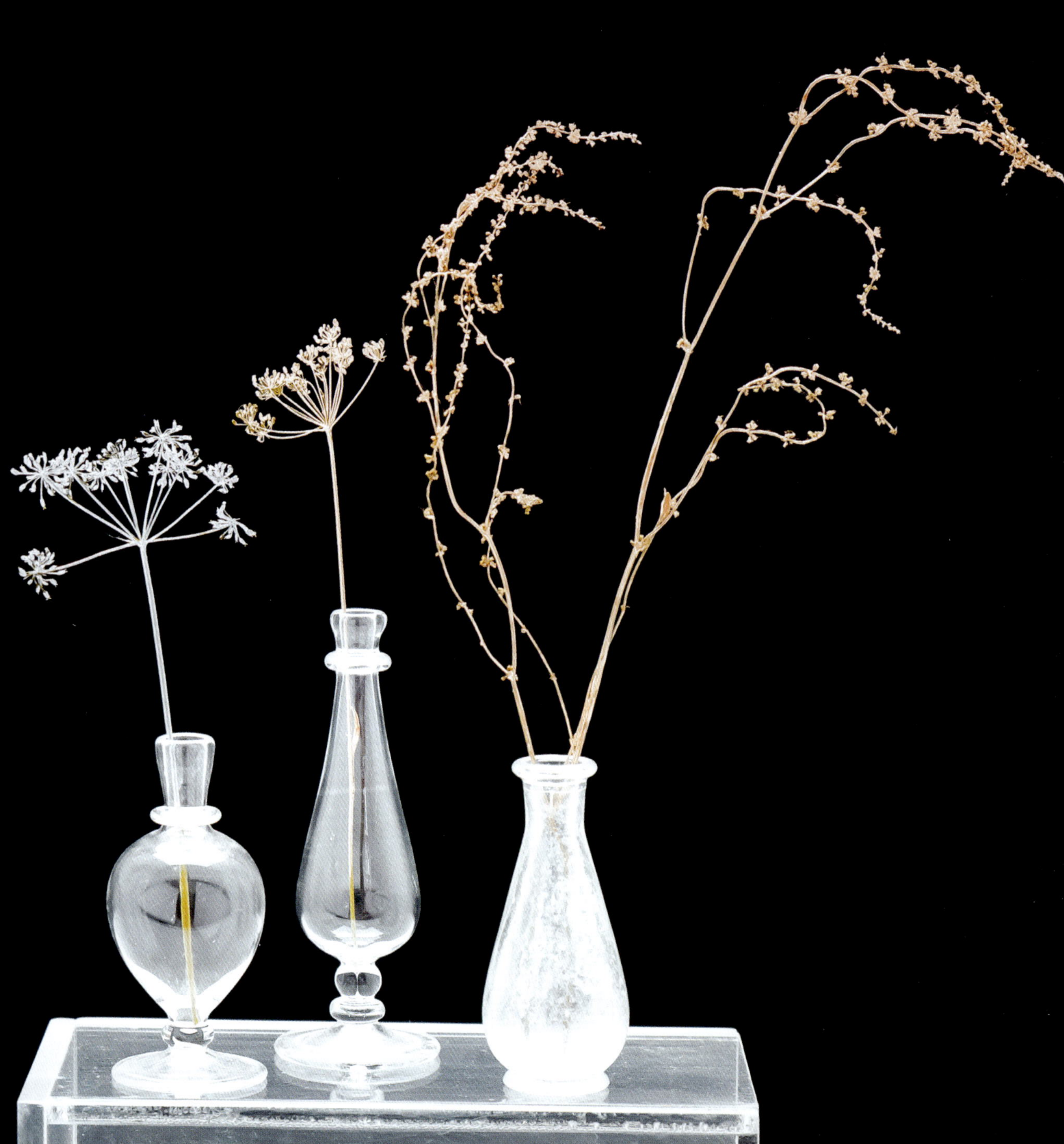

WHAT YOU NEED

- Dried weeds or sturdy plants
- Metallic gold and/or silver paint
- Small bristle brush
- Jar, holder, or clothespins
- Clear matte acrylic spray (optional)

8

Gilded Weeds

What would the world be, once bereft
Of wet and of wildness? Let them be left,
O let them be left, wildness and wet;
Long live the weeds and the wilderness yet.

—Gerard Manley Hopkins

Well, I'm with the poem on the wilderness part. And the weeds. Yes. Just not in my garden. That said, some weeds are so elegant, graceful, and abundant that we may as well make use of them. And you have to admire weeds' vigor and tenacity—their ability to thrive in the most inhospitable places, even bursting through pavement and gaining toeholds on sheer rock faces.

Foraging for weeds and drying them (see Drying Botanicals, page 20) can be joyful and help you view weeds in a new way. And what is a weed, really? The definition of a weed can fall into a gray area. Take, for example, lily of the valley. To some, it's a precious and fragrant garden staple; to others, it's a pestilent weed.

One way to celebrate and elevate weeds is to dry them and paint them with metallics. Of course you can gild any dried plant, but you want to choose those that are not too terribly delicate, as fragile blossoms and tendrils can easily shred when you're trying to paint them.

Though I try to avoid noxious materials as much as possible, I love this gold paint, which though smelly and probably toxic and not great to inhale, is easy to apply and great looking. To minimize the hazard, wear a quality face mask or respirator and work in a well-ventilated space. If possible, apply this paint outdoors, though there is always a risk of an insect flying in and getting stuck in the paint (trust me, it happens).

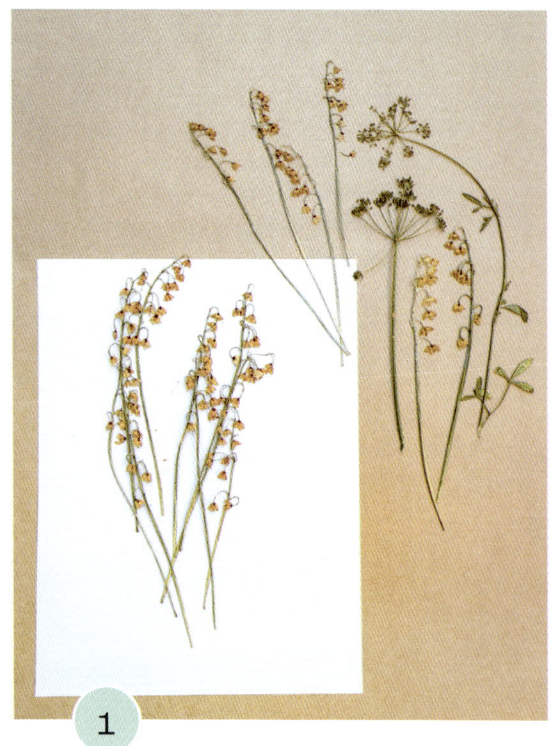

1

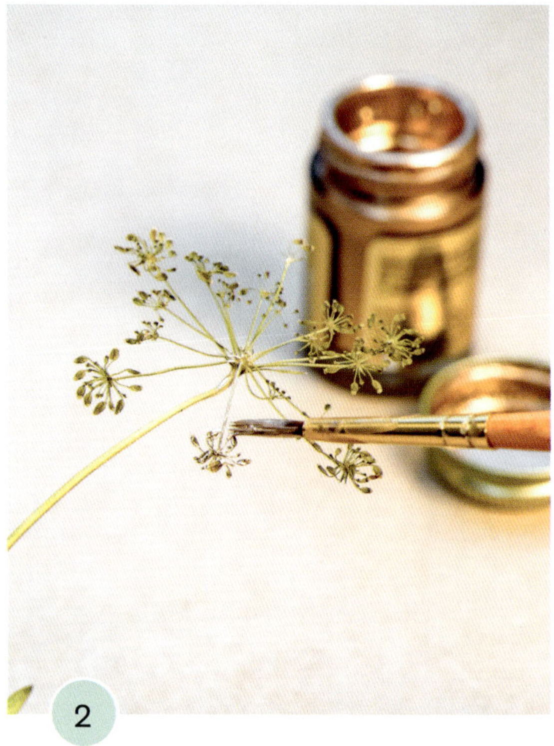

2

Select the Dried Botanicals

For this project, look for plants or weeds that are somewhat structured and textured—delicate yet robust. Lily of the valley, when dried, can turn a not-too-attractive shade of brown. But its structure is still pretty, so it's a perfect candidate for gilding. Make sure to have plenty of spare botanicals on hand, as it is possible (okay, likely) that some (or many) will break in the painting process.

Paint

With a small amount of paint on your brush, start carefully painting a dried botanical, applying a thin, even coat. Laying the weed or plant on a flat surface can make it easier to do the fussy, intricate bits. You may need to gently dab the paint into hard-to-reach spots. Then pick up the painted botanical so it doesn't stick to the surface, and gently wave it or blow on the painted areas to help them dry. When dry to the touch, turn the botanical over and paint the reverse side. Look at the piece from all angles to be sure you've covered the entire plant. Repeat for any other botanicals.

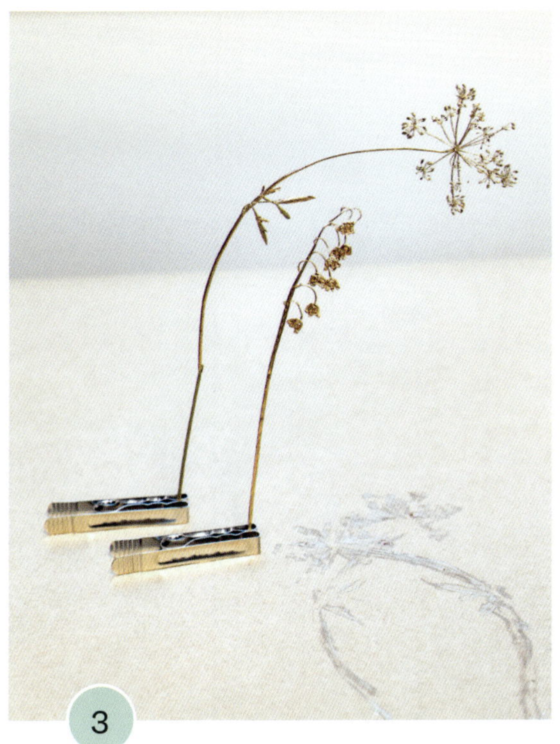

Dry

Place the painted plants to dry in a jar or clip them into a holder or clothespin and leave there until all sides dry.

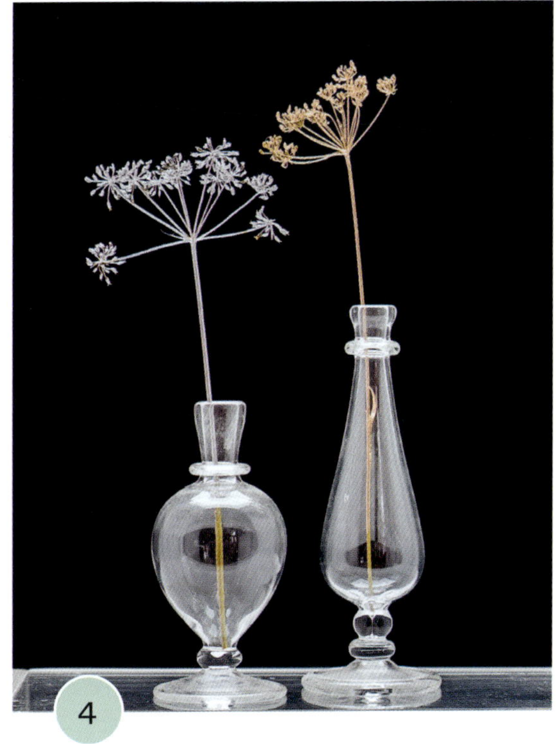

Display

Display your gilded weeds in small vases or create a floral collage with them (see page 57). You may also want to spray your gilded botanicals with clear matte acrylic to prevent them from possibly tarnishing.

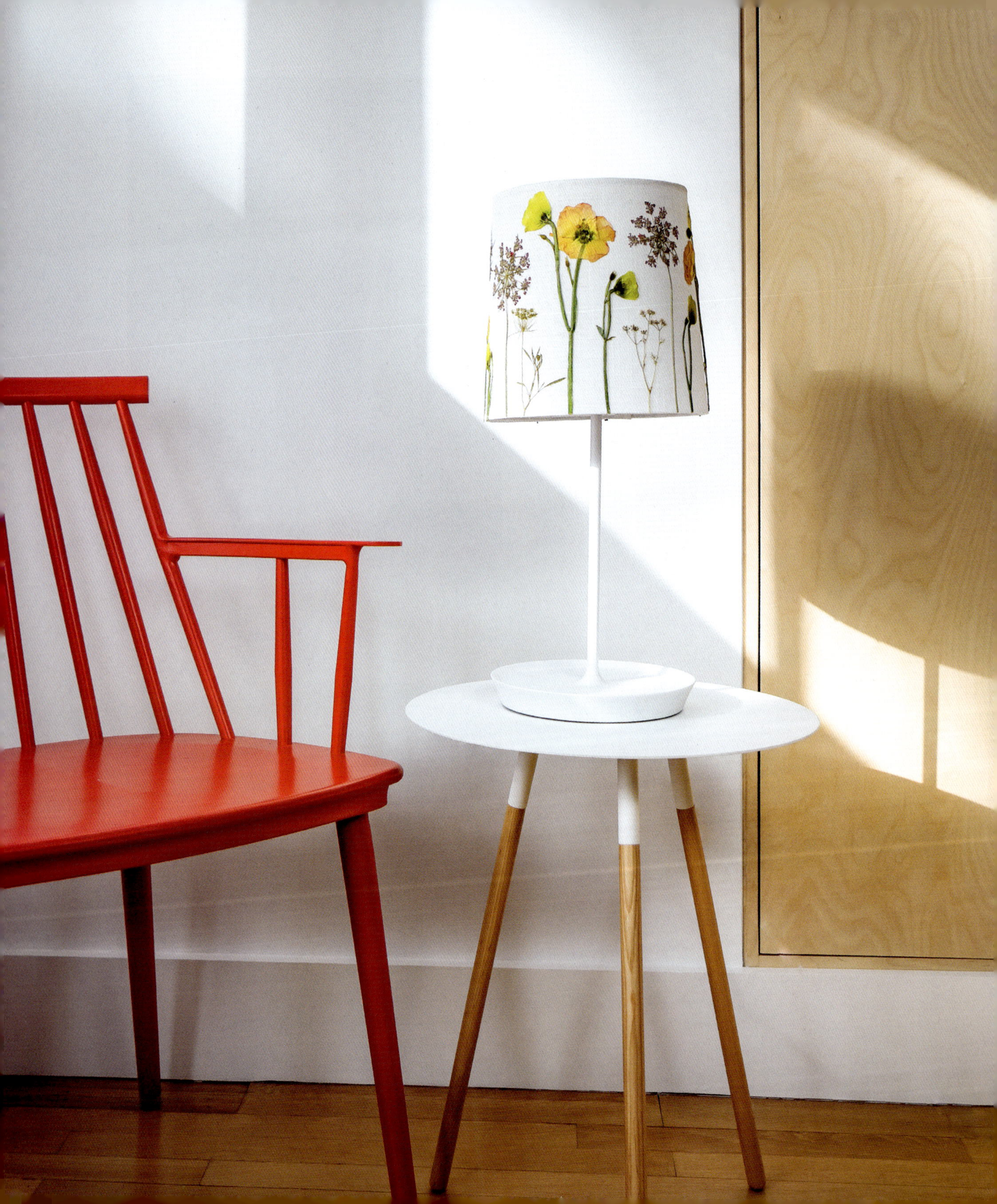

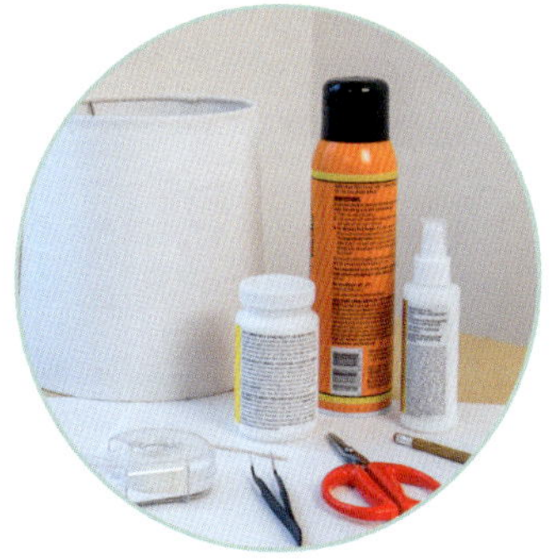

WHAT YOU NEED

- Dried botanicals
- Lampshade with a smooth paper or fabric surface
- Pencil
- Paper or wrapping paper
- Clear tape
- Sharp scissors
- Newspaper or scrap paper
- Spray adhesive
- Liquid PVA glue
- Tweezers
- Small brush or toothpick
- Matte acrylic spray (optional)

9

Flowered Lampshade

When contemplating projects to make with dried flowers, I wasn't initially that excited about decorating a lampshade. Now, however, every lampshade looks like a blank canvas that I want to "flower." There is something lovely about seeing flowers on a shade, suspended in midair atop a lamp. Also, when the light shines through the shade, the flowers become translucent and luminescent—as if the sun were rising behind them.

Depending on the shape of your shade (it never ceases to amaze me how many different sizes, shapes, materials, and colors they come in), you will probably want to create a paper template to help in the design process. The template will also be useful to determine approximately how many flowers are needed to fill the circumference.

To attach the flowers, a spray adhesive works well, especially if the lampshade is paper or a reasonably smooth fabric. The spray is also a particularly good choice for adhering lacy flowers. In addition, it's useful to have some liquid PVA glue handy to tack down hard-to-reach or tiny bits. To be honest, it is impossible to know how long the adhesive will last, but even if a botanical falls off, chances are good you'll be able to glue it back on or replace it.

Most dried botanicals are extremely brittle, so make sure to choose ones that will conform to the curve of your shade. The spray adhesive can make the botanicals a little more flexible and a bit less brittle while they are damp, but you won't know until you have tried spraying a particular flower how much it will bend. Whenever working with a spray adhesive, make sure to have good ventilation and wear a quality face mask or respirator.

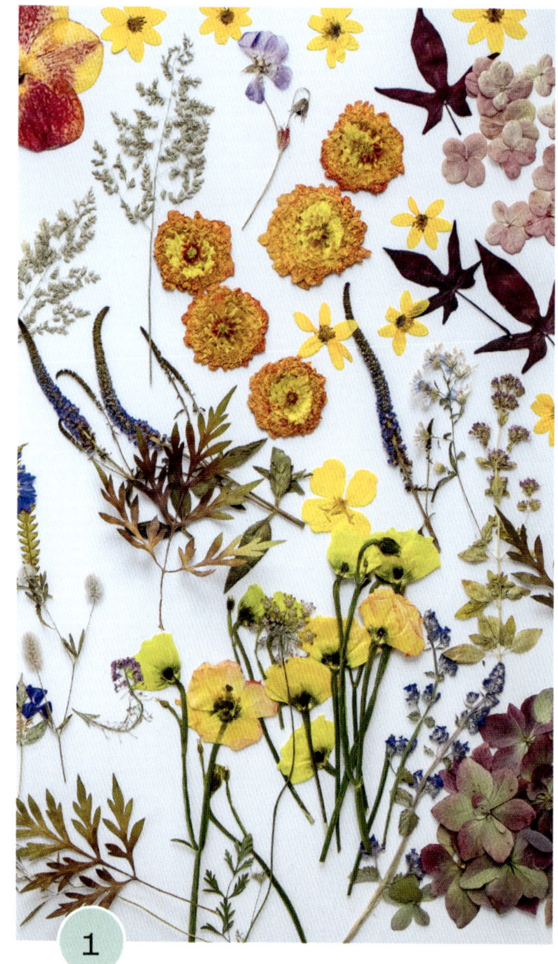

1

Select the Botanicals

Hopefully you have a lot of dried flowers to choose from. Think about color palette as well as size and durability. Also, depending on the curve of your shade, the botanicals may need to curve as well, so keep that in mind when making your selection.

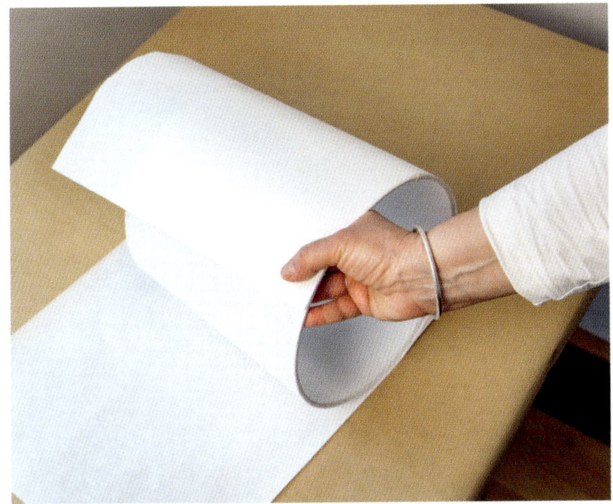

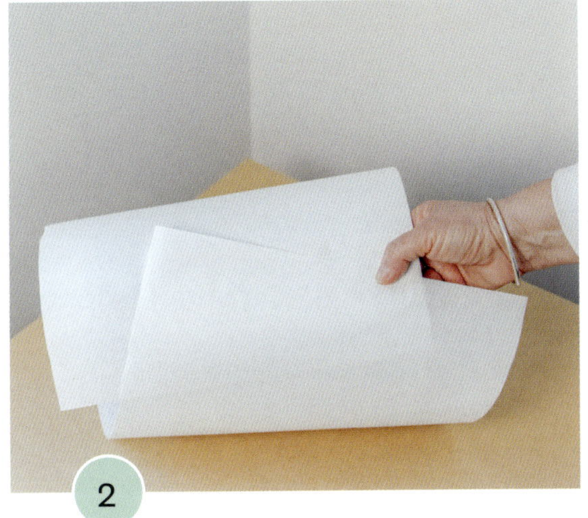

2

Make the Template

Create a template the size and shape of your lampshade using pencil and paper. If your shade is new and came with a plastic wrapper, carefully cut off the wrapper and trace its outline onto paper. Otherwise, tape pieces of paper together or use wrapping paper to form a sheet large enough to encircle the shade.

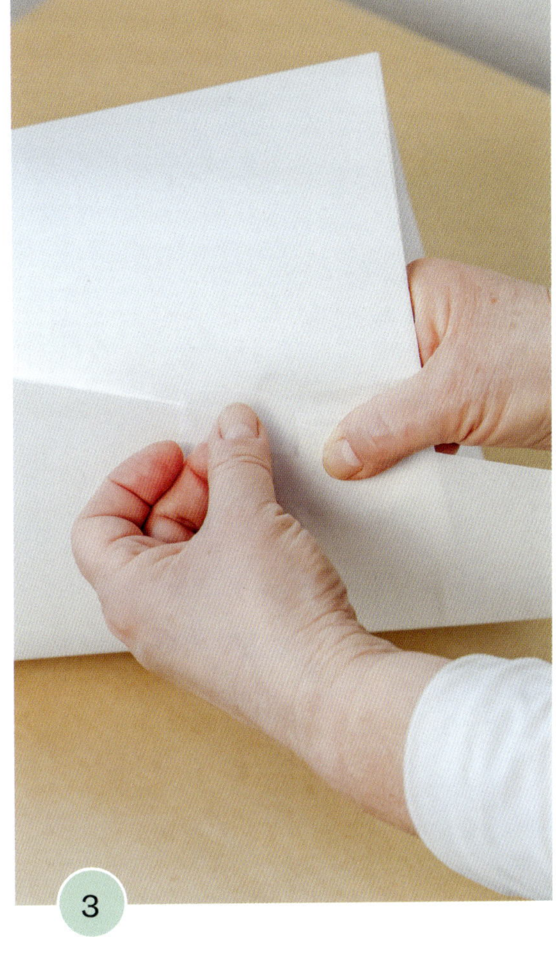

3

Refine the Template

Wrap the paper template tightly around the shade and tape it together. If your shade is smaller at the top than at the bottom, the paper will look askew, but that is fine if your paper is long enough to go around the shade fully.

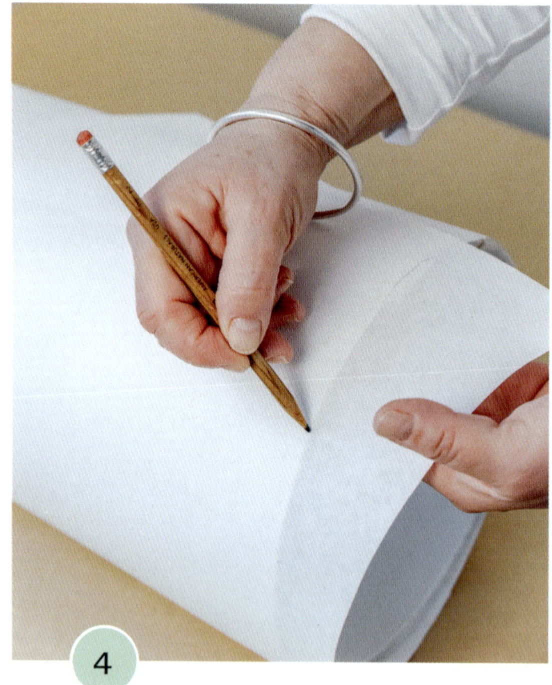

Draw the Edges

Using the pencil, trace the bottom and top edges of the shade onto the template. Draw a line down from the top edge of the shade to the bottom edge. This line determines where you will cut to get the length of the paper template.

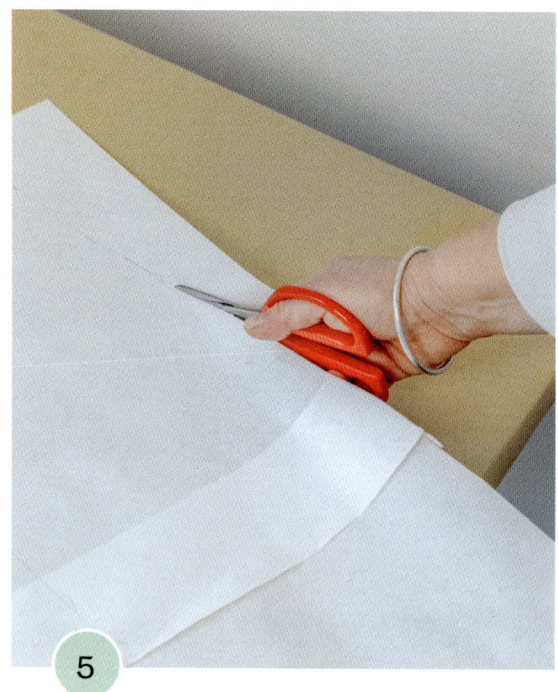

Cut Out the Template (Optional)

Remove the tape to unwrap the paper and lay the template flat. Using the lines you have drawn, you can either cut out your template or use the drawn lines to define the design. Once you have finished cutting, it's a good idea to wrap the template back around the shade to double-check that it is the right size.

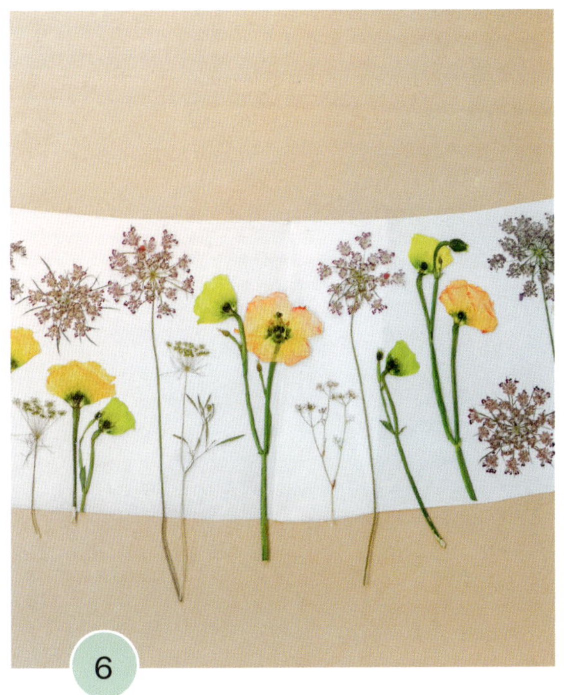

6

Lay Out the Botanicals

Lay out your design on the template. It's fine if stems extend over the edges: you will be able to cut them off later.

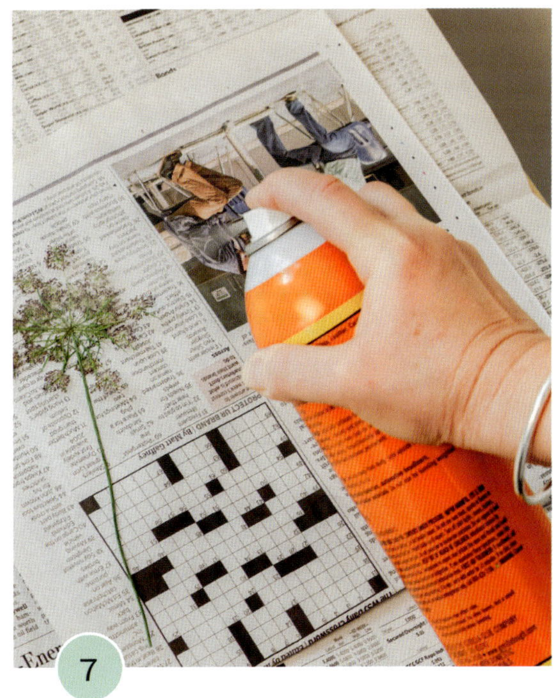

7

Start Gluing

Begin transferring your design from the template to the shade by picking up a botanical with tweezers and flipping it over onto a piece of newspaper or scrap paper. Spray the adhesive on the backside (the side currently facing up) of the botanical, making sure to coat it evenly and completely. Let the adhesive cure for the manufacturer's recommended time before adding the botanical to your shade.

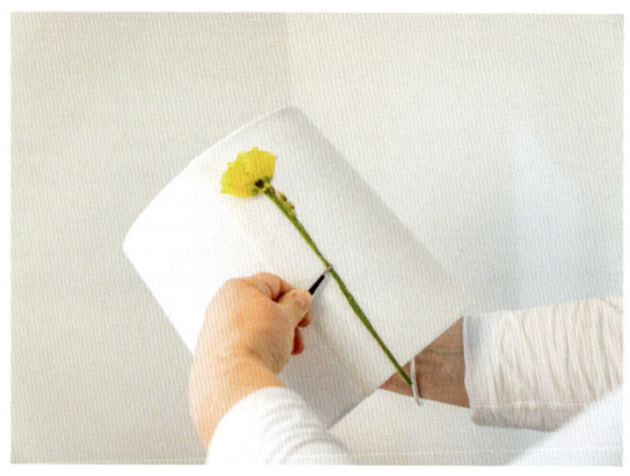

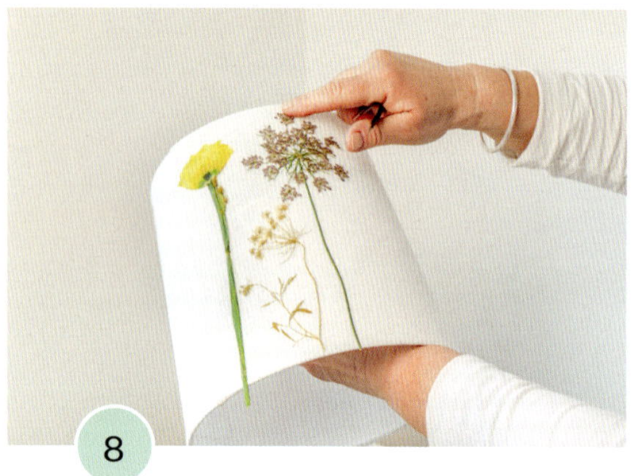

8

Adhere

Place the botanical, sticky-side down, on the shade in the spot indicated on your template. Gently but firmly press the botanical to the shade, making sure it completely adheres. Continue transferring botanicals from your template to the shade, following the template design and spacing as closely as you can. Chances are good that the shade won't be perfectly identical to your template, so as you get to the end, before you glue the last botanicals in place, hold the remaining flowers up to the shade to see if they will actually fit. You may have to add or subtract, depending on how accurate your transfer from template to shade was.

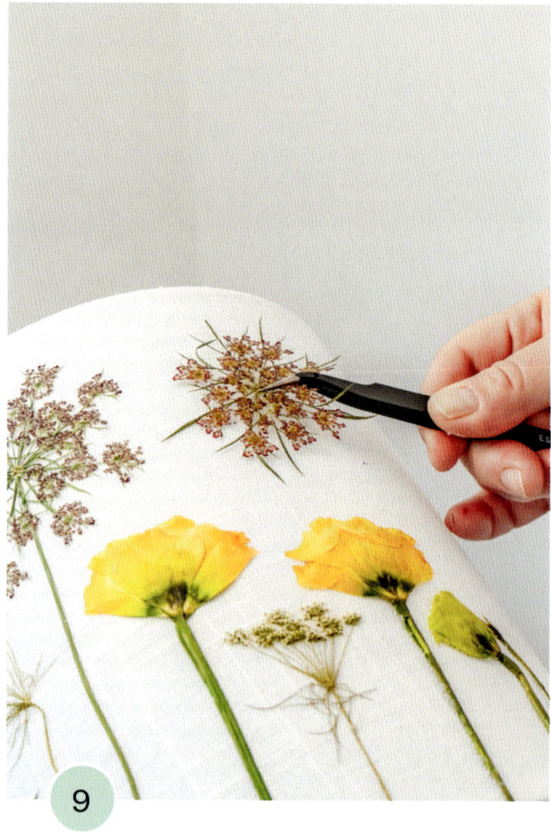

9

Finish the Shade

Cut off any stems that extend beyond the edge of the shade. Check to see if anything has come loose or isn't completely adhered. Secure any loose bits by carefully applying a dab of liquid PVA glue with a small brush or toothpick and hold until it sticks. However, be careful with how much glue you apply, as a blob of glue can show through a translucent flower when the lamp is turned on. If you choose to, apply the matte acrylic spray to the entire shade.

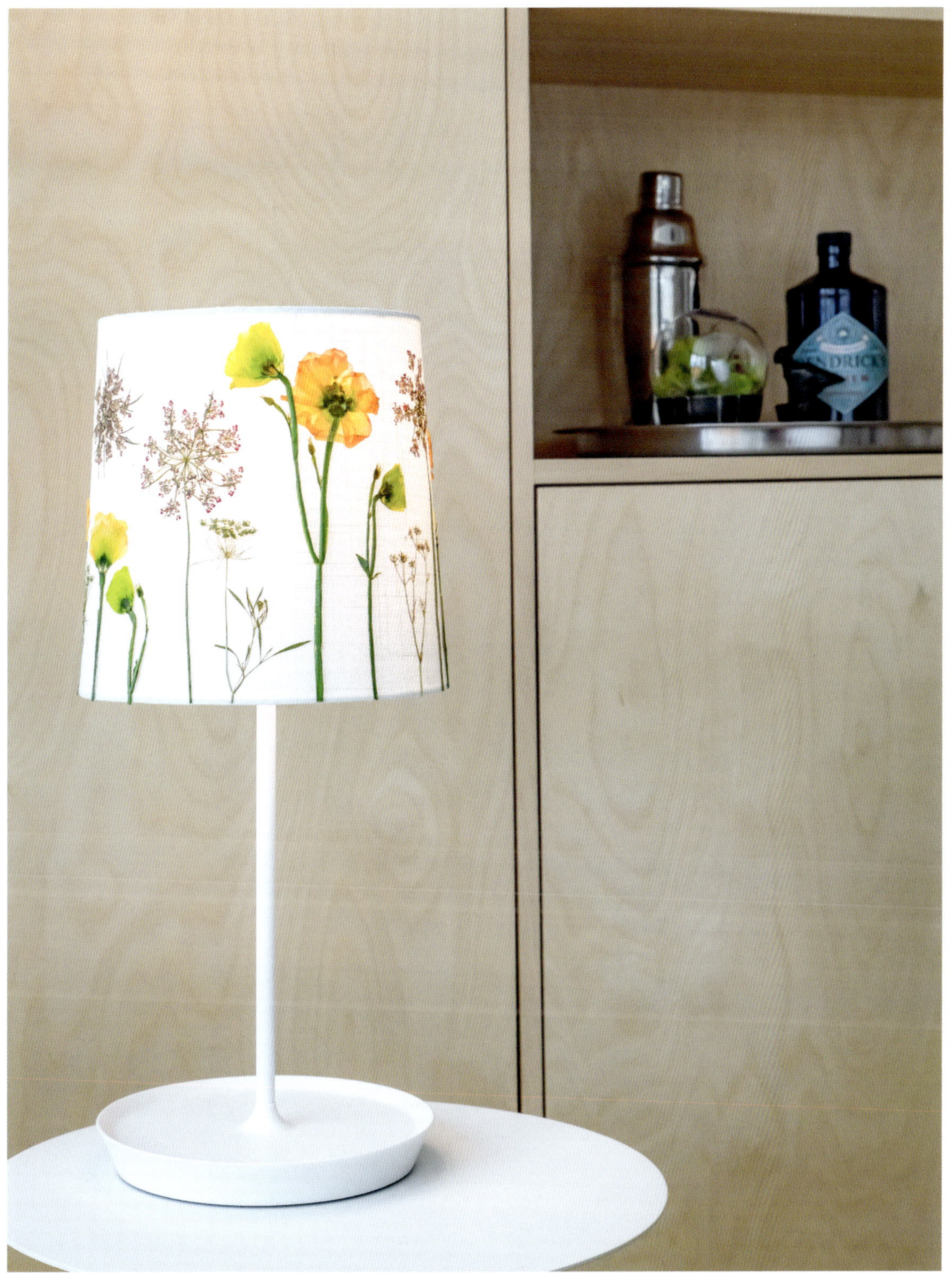

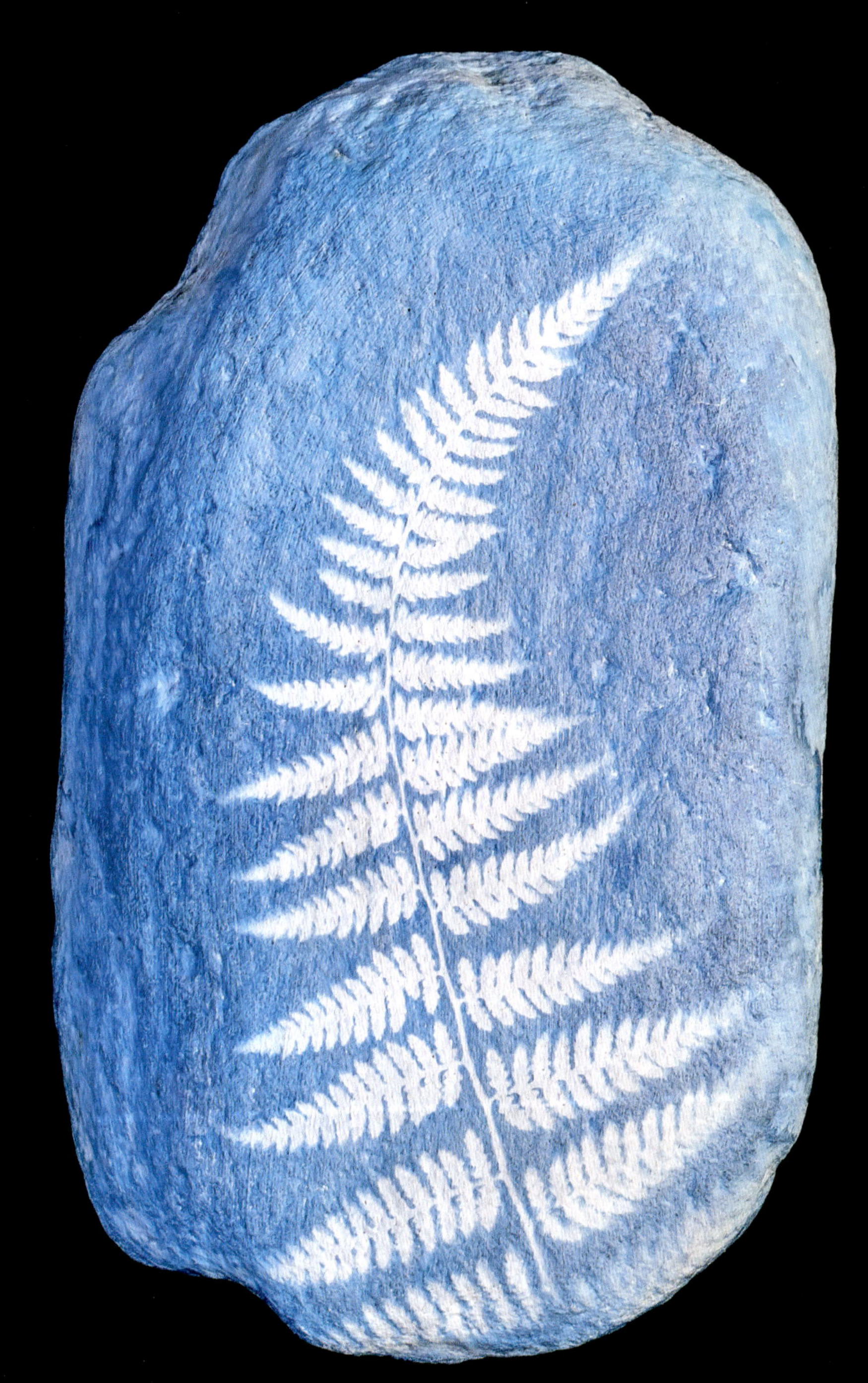

CYANOTYPES

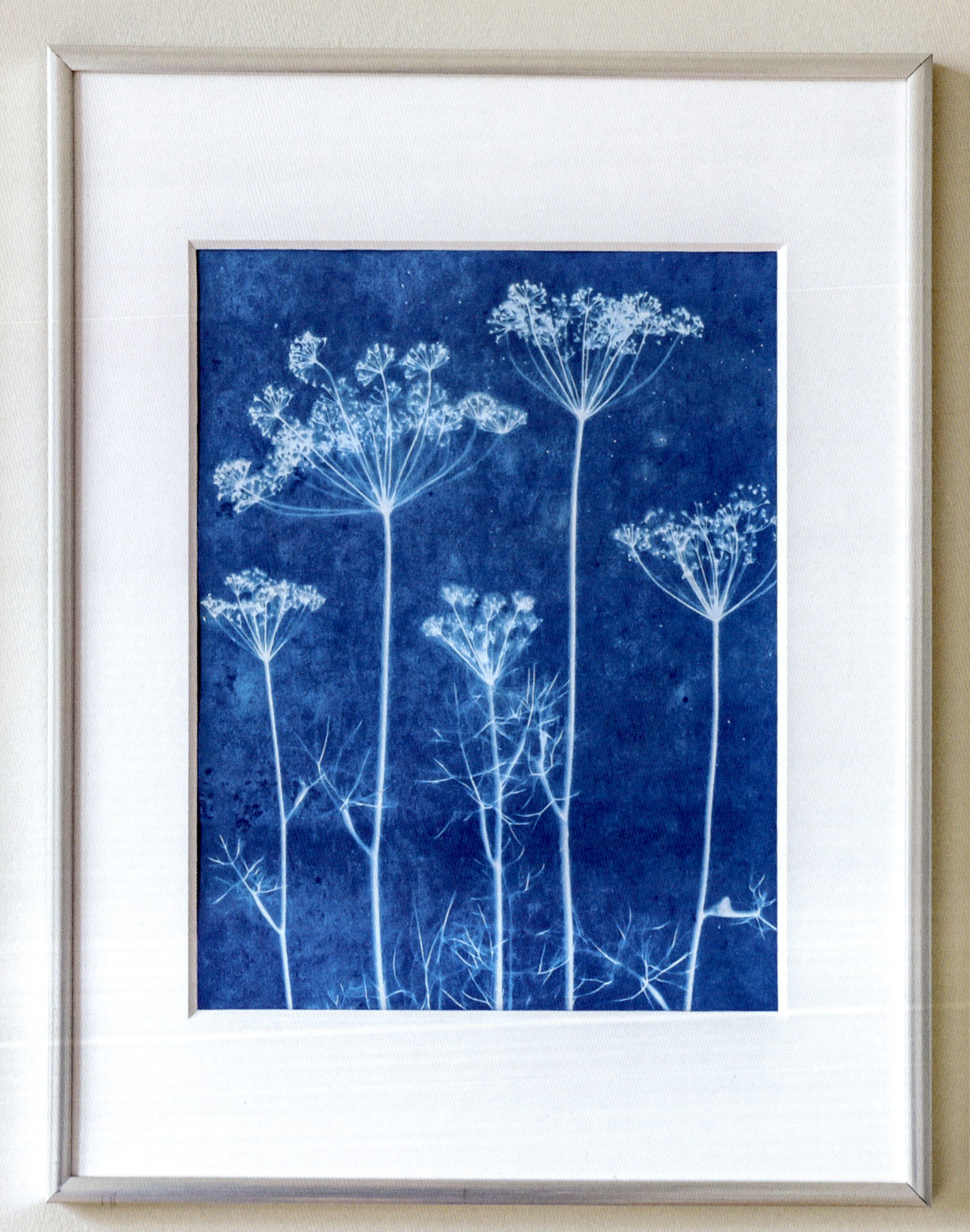

WHAT YOU NEED

- Foraged flowers, leaves, and/or grasses, fresh or dried
- Pretreated cyanotype paper
- Stiff piece of cardboard or foam core larger than the cyanotype paper
- Tweezers (optional)
- 1 sheet of non-UV glass larger than the paper (make sure the glass has smooth edges, or cover the edges with a thin piece of masking tape to prevent cuts)
- 2 bulldog clips or other large clips (more if your piece is very large) or tape
- Sink, plastic box, or hose with access to water
- Spray bottle with peroxide, or a bath with about a 9 to 1 ratio of water to peroxide (optional)
- Wire baking rack and sheet pan or clothespins and clothesline

10

Cyanotype on Paper

Cyanotype, known for its striking Prussian blue color, is a venerable photographic process invented in 1842. While today's (relatively) simple chemical process is surprisingly similar to the original, contemporary artists are pushing the boundaries of cyanotype and making amazing, sometimes otherworldly pieces. For example, Meghann Riepenhoff uses not only the sun but tides, wind, rain, and sediment to create room-sized cyanotypes, some of which are not even blue at all. Max Kellenberger makes stunning prints with everything from spaghetti to aspirin to cotton swabs; some of his creations are a luminous brown-gold color created by toning the finished prints with wine tannins.

The cyanotype process may be limitless in its possibilities, but it's also a great project to start with because it can be as simple or as complicated as you choose. Although you can create your own photosensitive cyanotype paper relatively easily, you also can buy papers that are heavy, high quality, and pretreated with photosensitive chemicals. The items placed on top of the paper block the emulsion underneath from being exposed to the sun, so those parts remain white (if you use white paper), resulting in a photogram—a photographic image made without a camera. The part of the paper exposed to sunlight, once washed, turns a gorgeous blue. The saturation level of the blue is largely determined by how long you expose the paper to the sun.

Making a cyanotype print using pretreated paper is minimally messy and quick, with a great chance for success. As is true with most new art adventures, however, there is a bit of trial and error involved to get consistent results. It takes a while to figure out how much time it takes to get a good exposure and which botanicals work best.

You can use almost any botanical, but keep in mind that a large, simple leaf, such as a maple or oak leaf, or a flower, like a black-eyed Susan, will create a large white area which can be great if you want a graphic look. Items that are feathery or intricate, like ferns or grasses, will give a textured look to your design, and the finished piece will show more blue.

The flatter the botanical, the easier it is to picture what shape it will make and what your print will look like once exposed. Thin and delicate botanicals can sometimes let a bit of light through, so the resulting image is more nuanced. Dried flowers and leaves can also work well because they are already flat, won't curl in the sun, and can often be reused.

While you can just go for it, without planning, and place your foraged botanicals on the treated cyanotype paper and see what happens, you may also want to be more intentional in planning your design. I'm a fan of both ways. Sometimes spontaneous designs are energetic and fun. Sometimes a planned design makes more of a statement. Cyanotypes can be bold or simple, graphic or complex. You might experiment with a design by laying out your botanicals on a plain white piece of paper before removing the photosensitive paper from its plastic wrapper. It is also helpful to squint your eyes when you lay out the design so you see patterns—how the positive as well as the negative spaces will look once the paper is exposed and the botanicals removed.

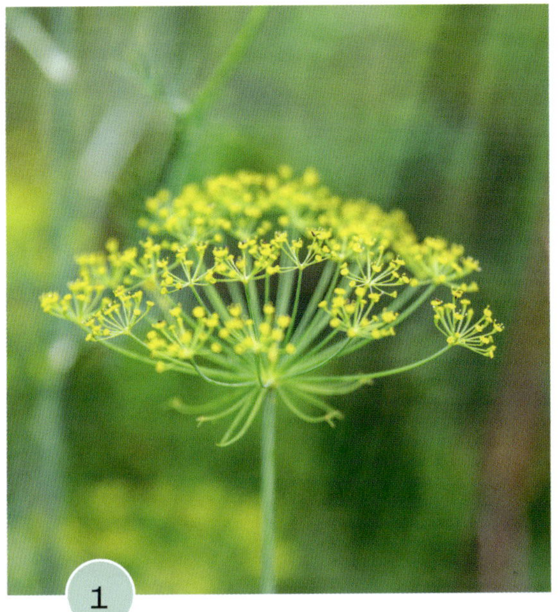

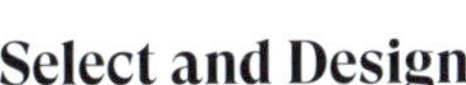

Select and Design

Select plant materials that suit your mood. Flowers, leaves, grasses, even whole branches can make great prints. Dried botanicals will give a more predictable outline. Be aware that you can get some surprises (blobs) if you are using a three-dimensional item, such as a berry, or a thick flower like a rose or peony.

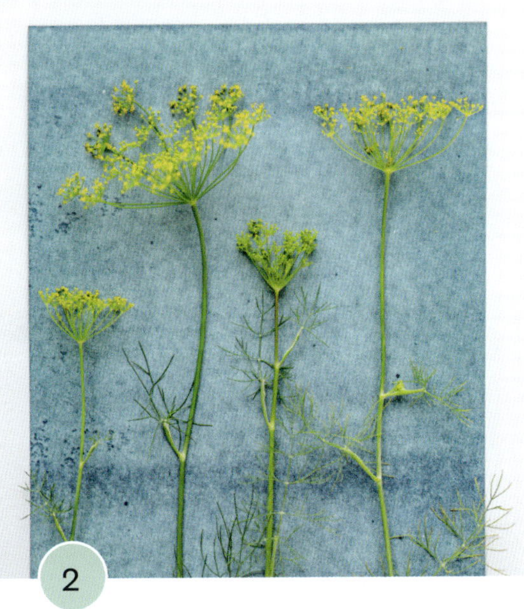

Place the Design on the Cyanotype Paper

Once you have decided on a design, you will need to dim the lights. The room doesn't need to be pitch dark, but you don't want to expose the cyanotype paper to bright light before you are ready. Once the room is dim, take one piece of cyanotype paper out of the black plastic bag, then carefully reseal the package. At this point the paper will be a greenish color.

Place the cyanotype paper on the cardboard or foam core. Then arrange your foraged pieces on top of the treated paper to create a design, remembering that where the sun is blocked, the paper will ultimately turn white, and where the sun hits, the paper will turn blue.

As long as you're not in direct sunlight, you can play with your design until you have a composition you like. That said, don't take too long: even ambient light will eventually affect the paper. Tweezers can really come in handy here to unfold fragile petals or move fussy leaves that might otherwise stick to your fingers.

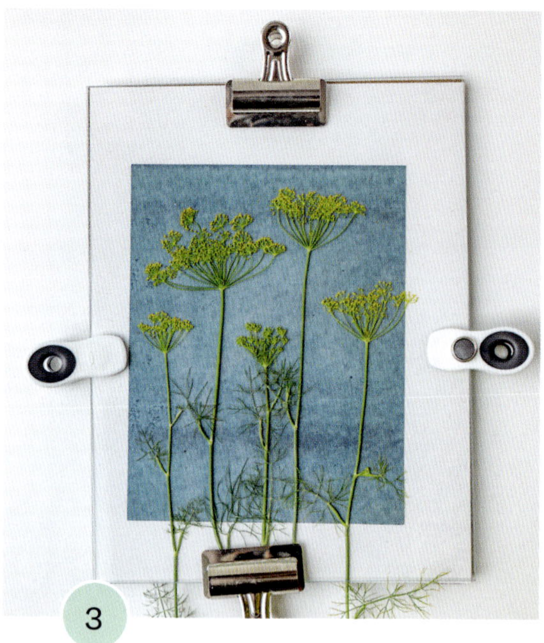

3

4

Secure the Design

Once you are happy with your design, carefully lay your piece of glass on top of the botanicals. The glass will help smoosh the botanicals flat, keeping the pieces in good contact with the paper for a crisper, more well-defined image, and prevent your painstaking design from being blown to smithereens by even the merest movement or breeze. The weight of the glass also stops fresh botanicals from curling in the sun. Secure this arrangement with bulldog clips, making sure the clips are far enough from the edge of the cyanotype paper that they won't cast a shadow on your print.

Expose the Cyanotype

Put your cyanotype sandwich (board, cyanotype paper, plant materials, and glass) outside, in direct sun, in a location where no branch shadows or shady areas will fall onto the paper as the sun moves. If the sun is at an angle, you might want to prop up your sandwich at a slight angle as well, but only if you have fastened it together with clips so the design doesn't slide. If you are not using the glass, you may want to place your botanicals on the paper (albeit quickly) in your sunny location, as even the slightest air movement can disturb or ruin the design.

Depending on the strength of the sun—determined by your location, the time of day and year, and how clear the sky is—leave your print in the direct sun for 5 to 20 minutes to get a good, deep blue. If you want a lighter blue, use less time. Your paper will turn a grayish color when it is exposed and if you carefully lift a corner of a botanical, being careful not to shift it, you should be able to see its imprint.

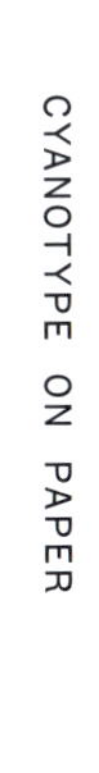

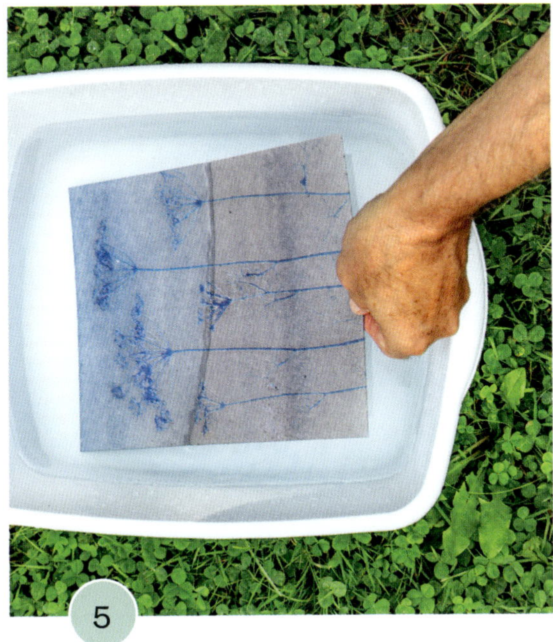

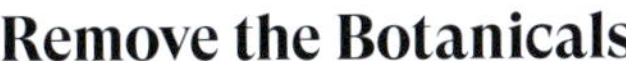

Remove the Botanicals

Working out of bright light in shade or indoors, take apart the sandwich and remove the plant material. You should be able to see your imprint (which will become white after washing), but it will still have color.

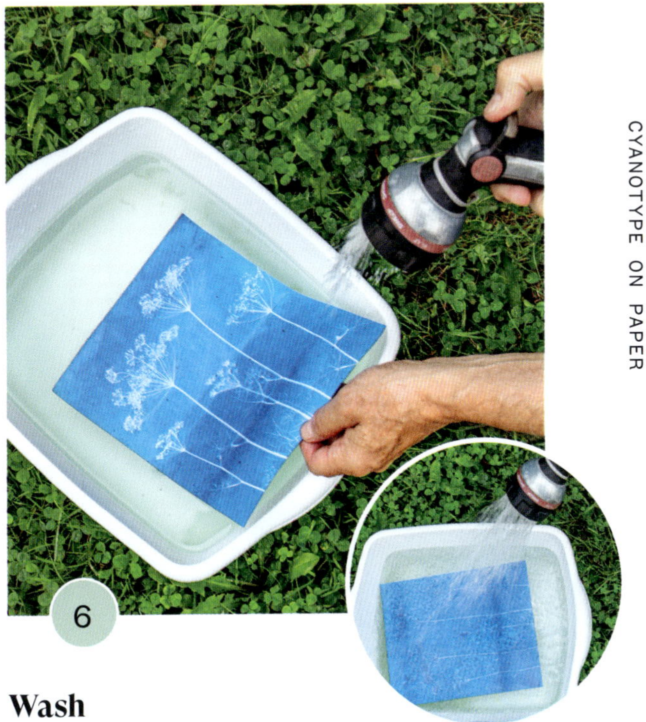

Wash

Take the exposed cyanotype paper and place it in a sink or plastic tub filled with a few inches of cool water, then gently wash the chemicals out of the paper with running water. If you are outside, you can gently wash the paper with a hose. The paper is surprisingly robust, and if you take some care in washing, you don't have to worry about it tearing.

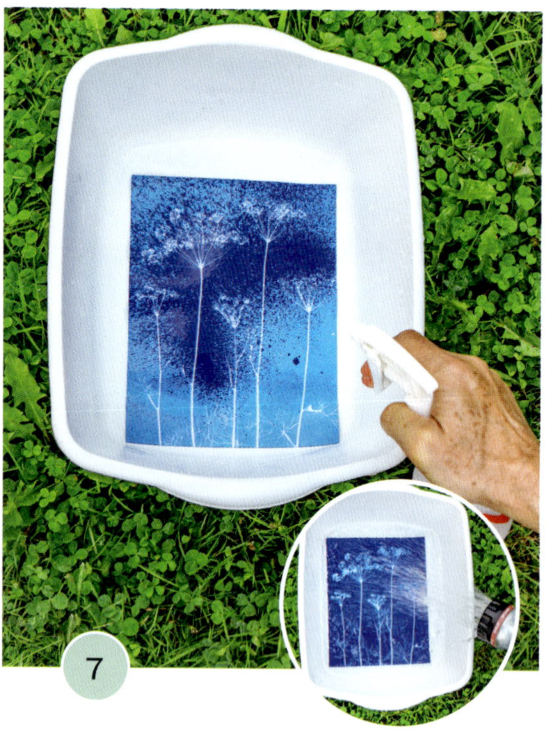

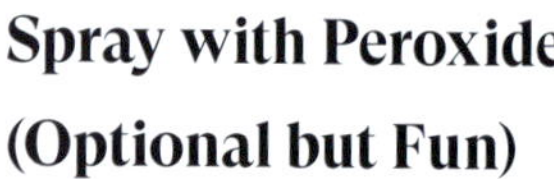

7

Spray with Peroxide (Optional but Fun)

After a few minutes of washing, once the whites turn white and the rest of the paper turns blue, you can either take your print out of the water to dry or use your bottle with peroxide and spray the wet print all over. Alternatively, you can add a few tablespoons of peroxide to the water bath (shoot for approximately a 9 to 1 water to peroxide ratio), but I think spraying is more fun. This is a magical moment, as the intensity of the blue suddenly deepens. After the peroxide spray or bath, do another quick rinse with water and your print is complete.

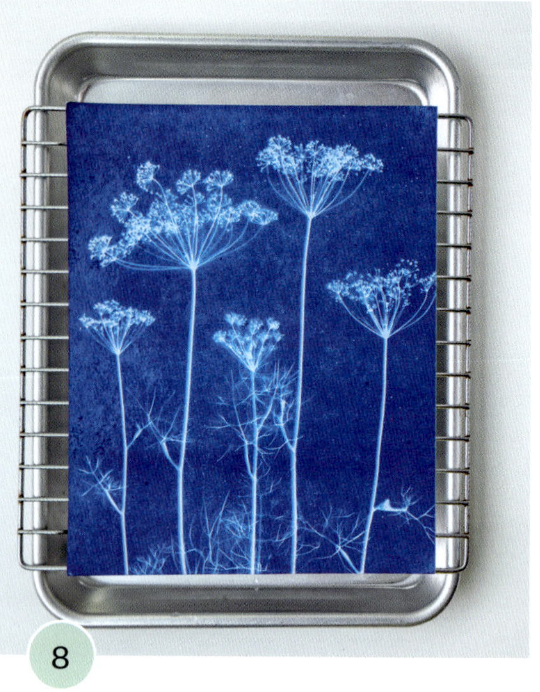

8

Dry

To dry your paper so that the final print is flat enough for framing, put it on a wire baking rack set over a sheet pan or hang it by clothespins from a line in the shade or inside. Be careful, as the wet paper is flexible and somewhat fragile at this point, and you don't want to put any dents or marks in it. The amount of time it takes your print to dry will vary according to humidity and temperature. Once the paper feels totally dry to the touch, if it is not completely flat, you can put it under a pile of heavy books and leave it for a few days to flatten.

Cyanotype Tips

- Before laying fresh botanicals on the cyanotype paper, make sure they don't have any moisture on them, as it will make splotches.
- If you want your cyanotype to have a layered look, experiment by adding botanicals to your design every few minutes during the exposure. That way some areas will be whiter (those that were covered at the beginning of the exposure), and some will be semi-exposed, showing different intensities of blue.
- To establish optimal timing for the perfect blue, cut a piece of cyanotype paper into strips and do a timing test: Put all the strips into the sun at the same time. After 3 to 5 minutes, start taking them out of the sun one at a time with a minute or two spacing in between. Wash them and make sure to label each strip with the number of minutes it was in the sun. The results of the timing test will be applicable only around the time of day you do the experiment, but it will give you a better ballpark for your prints than just winging it.
- To make note cards or place cards, cut the cyanotype paper into smaller pieces or change the shape in step 2, while you are indoors and before exposing it.
- To make multiple copies of your cyanotype, photograph or scan it and then make prints.
- Although some prepared cyanotype paper is two-sided and can be exposed twice, exposing the second side can create issues with your first print because sunlight may leak under the paper. If you like your first design, it's safer not to expose the other side.
- If you do want to use both sides of the paper, don't wash the paper after the first exposure. Simply turn the paper over, repeat steps 2 through 5, and wash and dry the print.
- As much as possible, hold the unexposed paper by the edges.
- Some translucent flowers, like buttercups, will let some light through, which can create a nice effect.

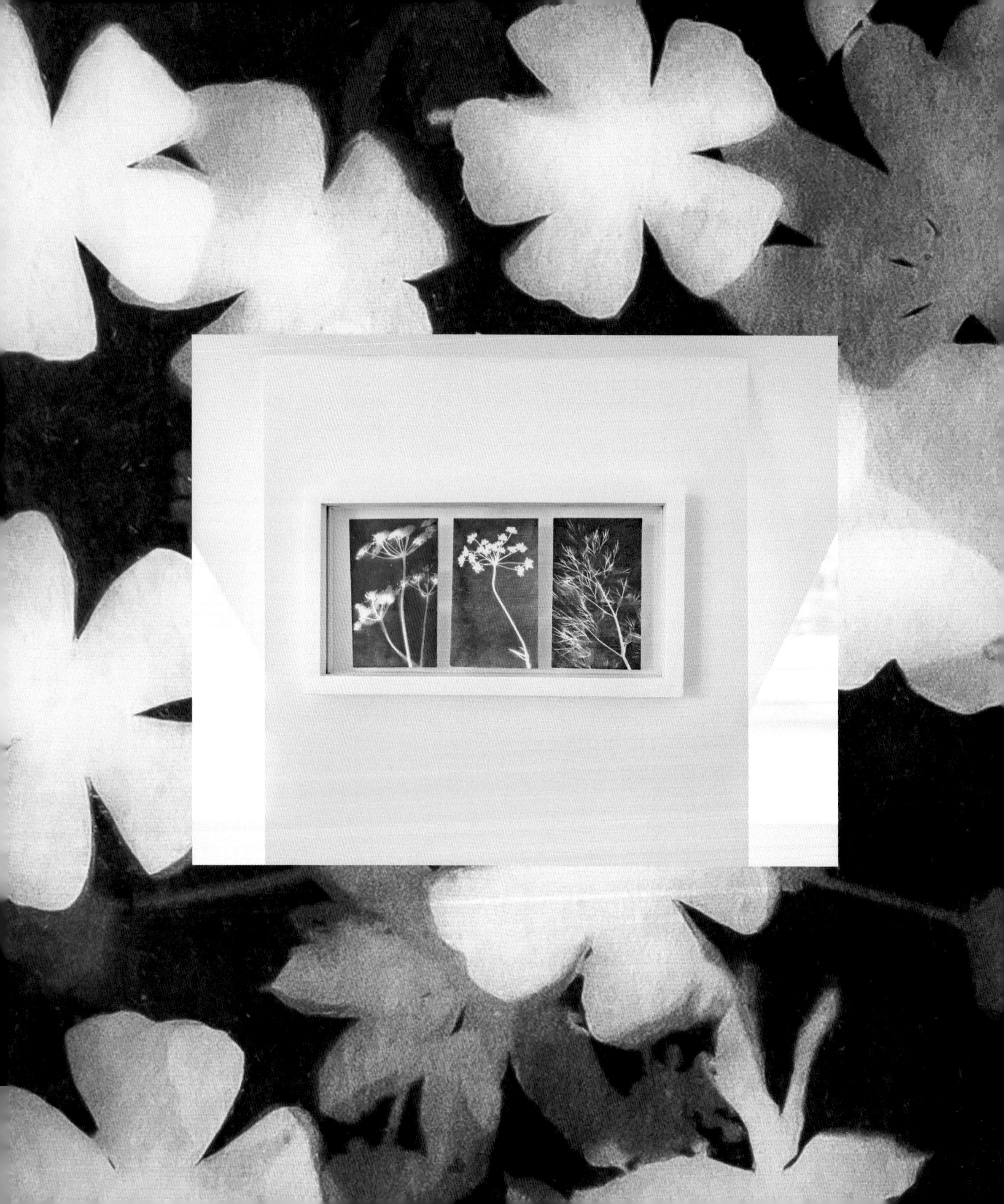

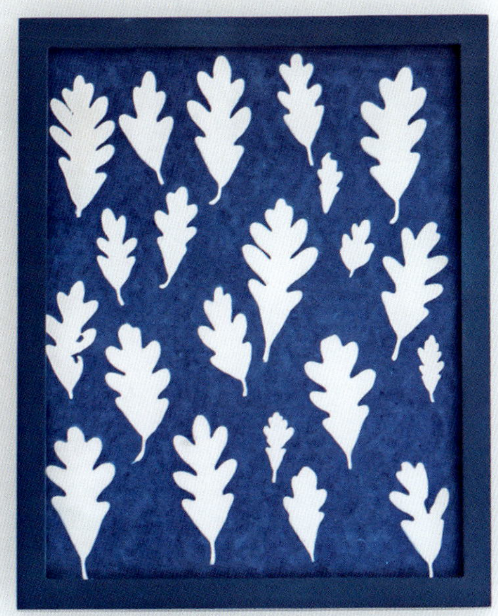

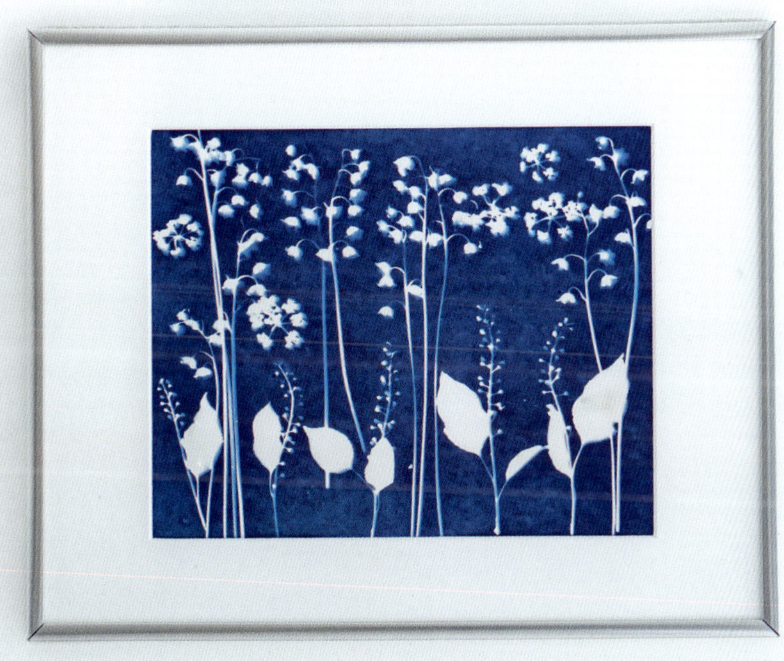

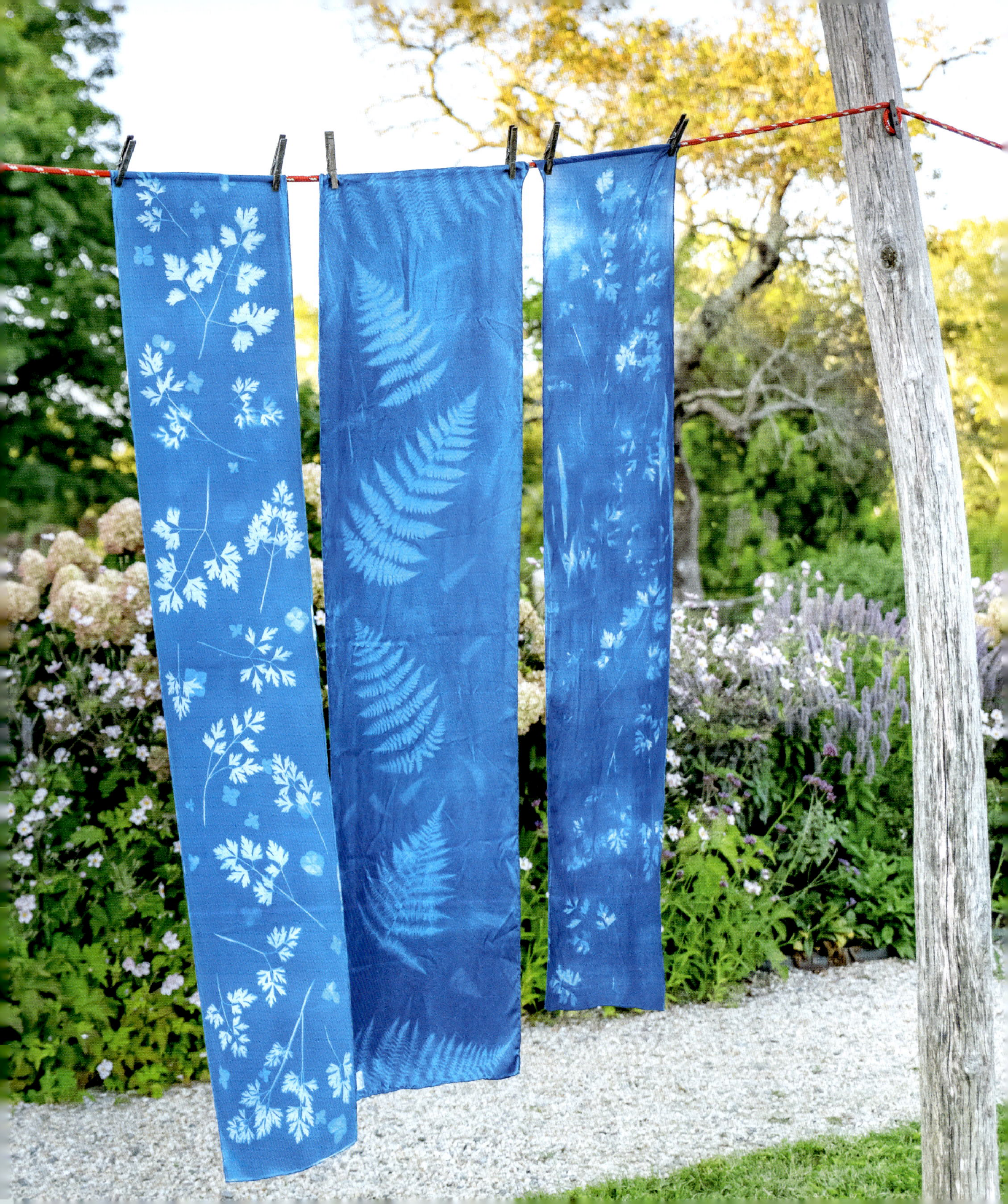

WHAT YOU NEED

- Botanicals
- Paper
- Pretreated cyanotype-ready silk scarf
- 1 or more sheets of non-UV glass (optional)
- Paper the size of the scarf (optional)
- Sink, bucket, or hose with access to water
- Spray bottle with peroxide, or a bath with about a 9 to 1 ratio of water to peroxide (optional)

11

Cyanotype Silk Scarves

I am a scarf person. At all times of year you will find me wearing a scarf—cotton, linen, silk, wool, or a combination of fibers. Scarves make me happy. Colors, neutrals, patterns, or textures: I love how scarves feel, and I love the pop of color they can provide.

Silk scarves are perhaps the most delicious. The feeling of silk on skin is one of the most luxurious things we can sartorially experience. To think that a single filament of silk, created by worms, is stronger than a comparable filament of steel is so cognitively dissonant that it makes the fabric even more remarkable. The silk filament comes, most commonly, from the cocoon of a mulberry-leaf-eating silkworm (*Bombyx mori*). Each cocoon is made from a single thread that can be 1000 to 3000 feet long. It takes about 2500 silkworms to create a pound of raw silk.

You can buy bulk silk fabric and make your own scarves or find finished, plain white silk scarves. You can treat them with cyanotype solution yourself, though it is somewhat challenging to get an even distribution of the chemicals. The easiest path, used here, is to get pretreated scarves, which makes the whole process super easy, though a bit pricey.

I have tried three pretreated silk scarves: chiffon, which is lighter weight and somewhat sheer; crepe de chine, which is heavier and smoother;

and charmeuse, which is the heaviest and most luxurious.

The most difficult part of the process is finding a way to put botanicals down on the long scarves and keep them from blowing off or curling up into an unappealing shape as they sit in the sun. I have dealt with this issue in two ways: The first is by taking a long piece of rigid foam insulation, placing the scarf on top, and pinning the botanicals and the scarf in place. This is time-consuming but effective. The second solution is taking panes of glass and laying them down on top of the botanicals. I was concerned this would leave lines because I had to lay the glass down in a patchwork because I didn't have a piece long enough to cover the whole scarf. However, the glass edges leave no discernable lines—and the images come out crisply because the glass presses the entire botanical flat onto the fabric.

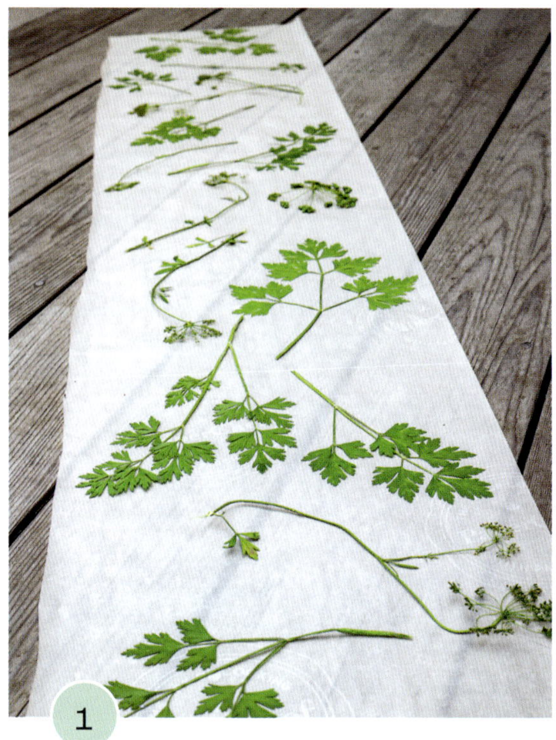

1

Select the Botanicals and Prepare the Template (if Using)

You can use either fresh or dried botanicals, keeping in mind that dried plants will be pre-flattened and curl less in the sun than fresh. Be aware that the areas that block the sun will turn white, so if your botanicals are large and solid (peonies, for example), they will create large white shapes—which can look like blobs if the petal edges don't form an interesting pattern. It's helpful to make a paper template the dimensions of your scarf and lay out the botanicals. This ensures that you will have enough botanicals to cover your scarf and that the design is satisfactory before you expose the fabric to the sun.

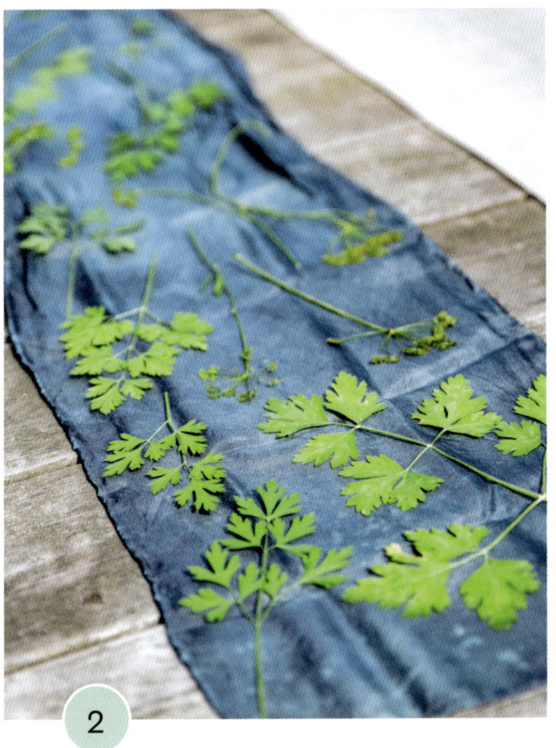

2

Lay Out the Scarf and Botanicals

Take the scarf out of the light-protective packaging. If it is very wrinkled you can iron it, but be sure not to use steam. Lay the pretreated scarf on a flat surface in direct sun. Place your botanicals on the scarf as quickly as you can, because the exposure starts as soon as bright light hits the fabric.

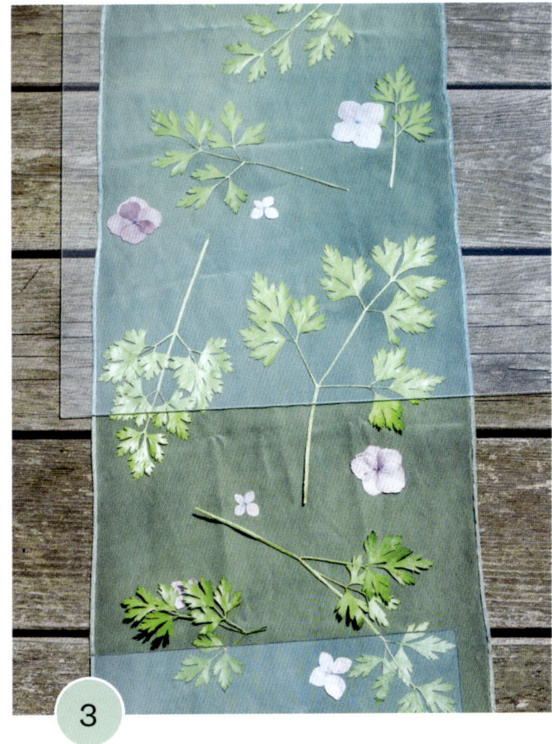

3

Expose

If you are using glass, carefully place the sheet(s) on top of your botanicals. The glass will ensure the botanicals don't blow away, which can easily happen with even the faintest breath of wind. The amount of time you need to expose the scarf will vary widely, depending on cloud cover, time of day, location, and how deep you would like the shade of blue to be. It can take from 5 to 20 minutes in full, bright sun. One way to know when the fabric is properly exposed is that it turns from a greenish color to a gray. To further check exposure, carefully lift a corner of a botanical, without shifting it, to see if it has made an image on the silk. Knowing when your cyanotype has had enough sun exposure takes some practice. The good news is that the process is very forgiving and there is a lot of room for error.

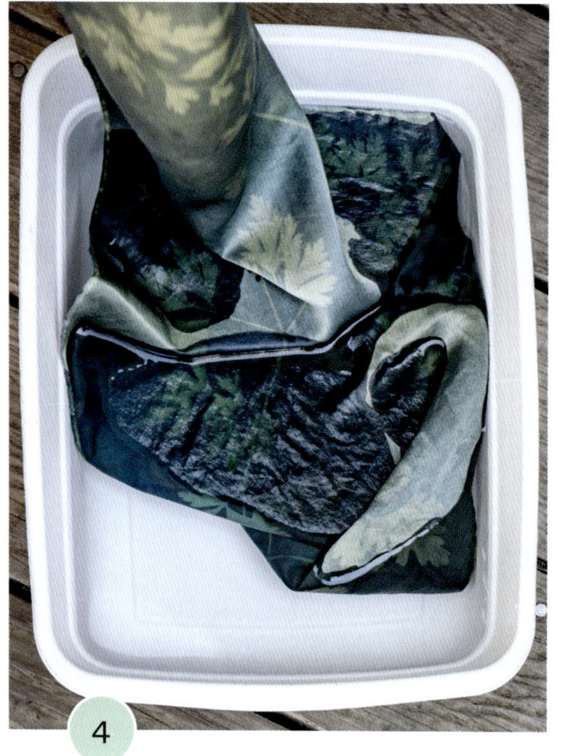

4

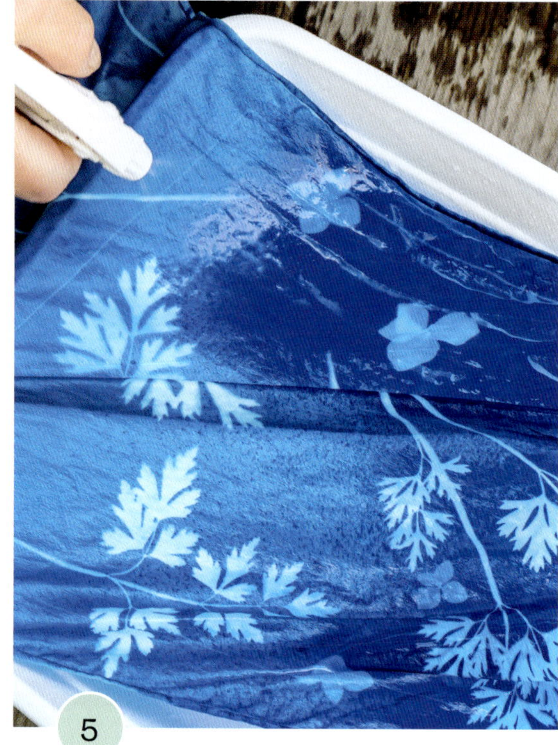

5

Rinse

When your scarf is sufficiently exposed, remove the botanicals, then gently rinse it in cool water until the water runs clear and color washes out of the white areas. You can do this under a faucet, in a bucket, or outside with a hose.

Treat with Peroxide (Optional) and Dry

If you choose, you can spray the rinsed scarf with peroxide or add the peroxide to a water bath (approximately a 9 to 1 water to peroxide ratio) and dip the scarf in. The peroxide hastens the oxidizing of the cyanotype chemicals, instantly turning the fabric a vibrant blue. Give the scarf a quick final rinse to remove the peroxide. Dry your scarf out of direct sunlight.

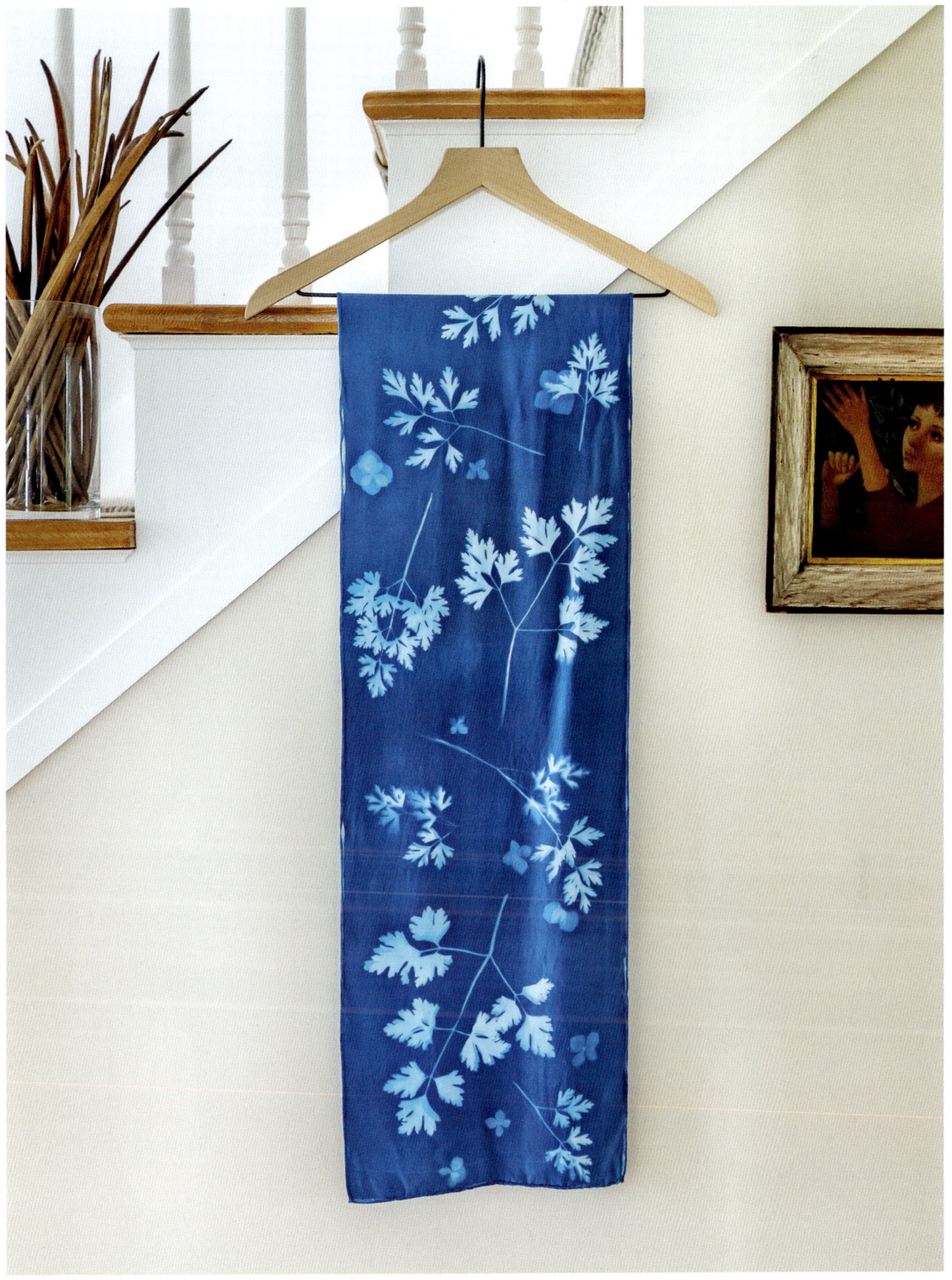

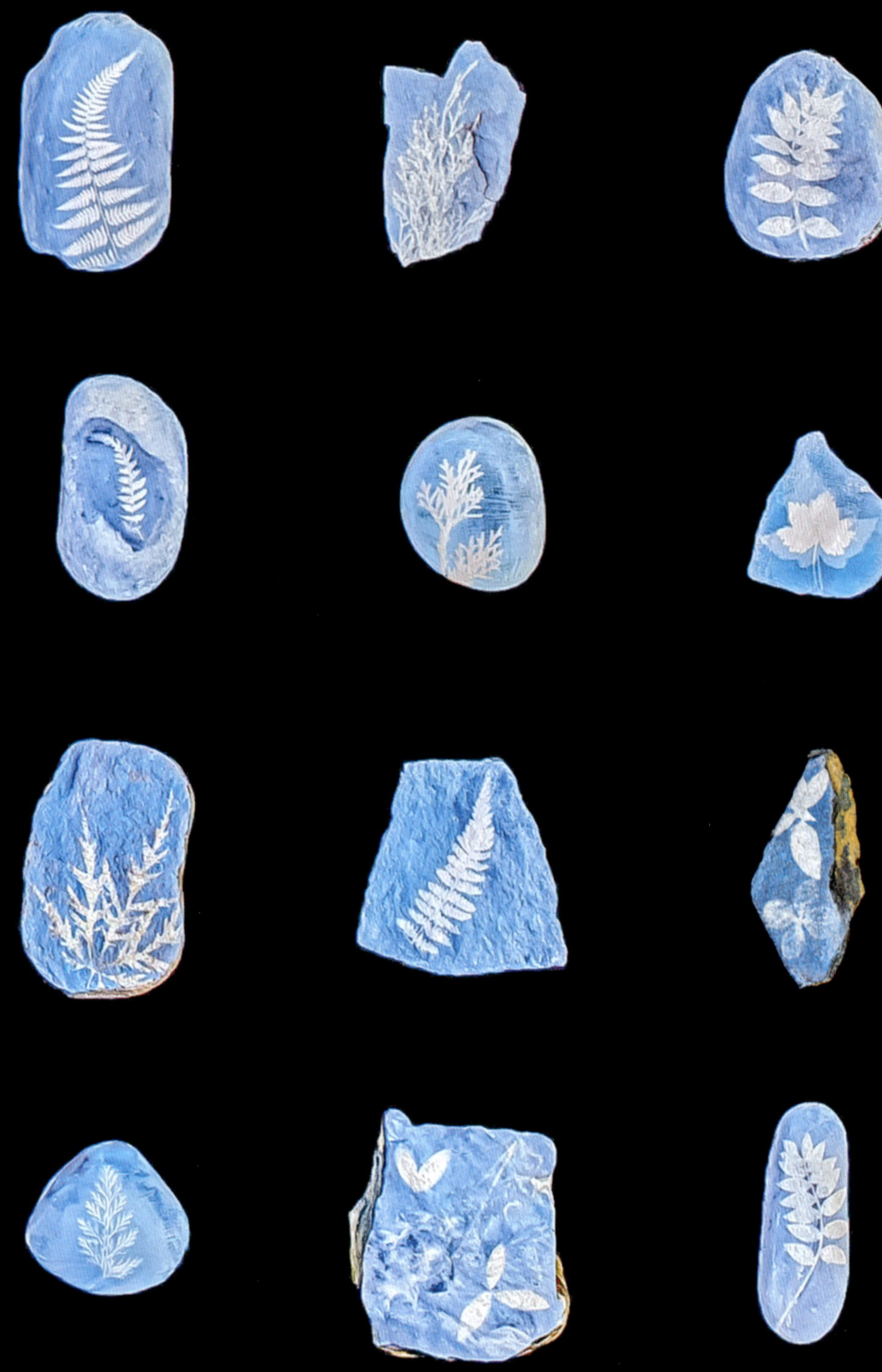

WHAT YOU NEED

- Stones
- Botanicals
- Brush
- Gesso
- Cyanotype chemicals (potassium ferricyanide and ferric ammonium citrate)
- Small jar with a lid
- Shot glass or small measuring cup
- Plastic wrap or sheet of non-UV glass (optional)
- Sink, hose, tray, or bucket with access to water
- Spray bottle of peroxide, or a bath with about a 9 to 1 ratio water to peroxide (optional)
- Masking or painters tape (optional)

12

Cyanotype Stones

There is something intriguing about seeing a photogram of a delicate leaf or flower imprinted on stone. I'm not sure if it is the implausibility of it or the transformational quality, but something about it fascinates me. I also love turning rocks blue.

I have found that applying a coat of gesso (a white paintlike mixture) to the stone helps the cyanotype chemicals adhere and gives the images more contrast. When I skipped the gesso step, the rocks were a flop—they didn't have enough contrast to show the botanicals, even when using light-colored stones.

The rocks I like the best are painted with a coat of watered-down gesso, which allows some of the stone's colors and texture to show through. If you want more contrast and a classic white-and-blue cyanotype, use the gesso without diluting it or paint on a few coats.

Any size stone can work, but try to choose one with a smooth but not shiny surface. The entire gesso-and-cyanotype surface tends to peel off shiny stones. To get a crisp photogram, if your rock is flat, you may be able to place a piece of non-UV glass on top of the botanical. If your stone is round or irregularly shaped, you can tightly bind the botanical to the stone with plastic wrap, fastening the wrap in the back.

Several different chemical combinations can be used to create cyanotypes, which you can buy from many art or photo supply stores. However, the easiest way to create the cyanotype solution is to buy a set of two chemicals, either ready to use, or dry and premeasured chemicals to which you just add water.

This is a great project for experimentation. Rocks are free, and the cyanotype chemicals and gesso are relatively inexpensive.

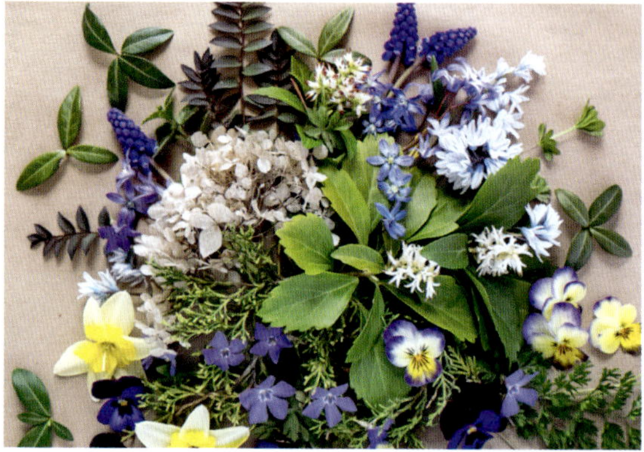

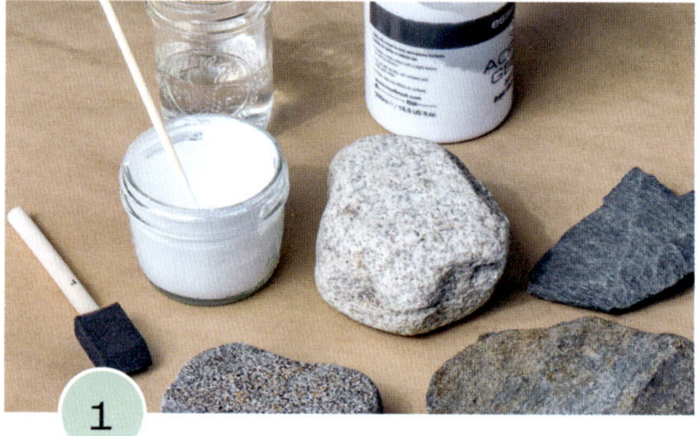

1

Gather the Stones and Botanicals

Any stone and any botanical will work, but it pays to experiment. If you want a stark contrast, a solid flower or a leaf like an oak or maple with interesting edges might be a good choice. If you prefer something subtle and feathery, an intricate leaf like a Japanese maple or a fern frond might work well. If your stone is round, keep in mind when fitting your botanical that the sun will hit only the face that is exposed.

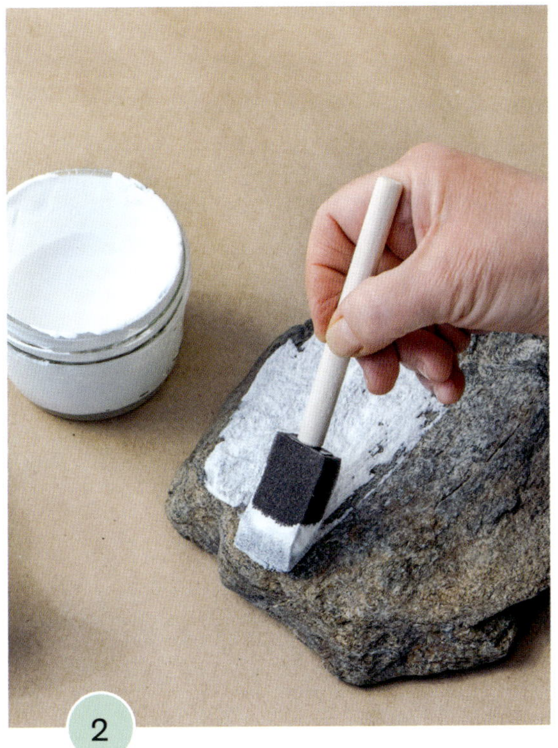

2

Prep the Stones

Wash and dry your stones, then brush on a coat of either diluted (to let some of the stone show through) or full-strength gesso. You can coat the entire stone or just the parts you want to cyanotype. If your goal is an opaque white, you may have to apply a second or even a third coat. Let dry completely.

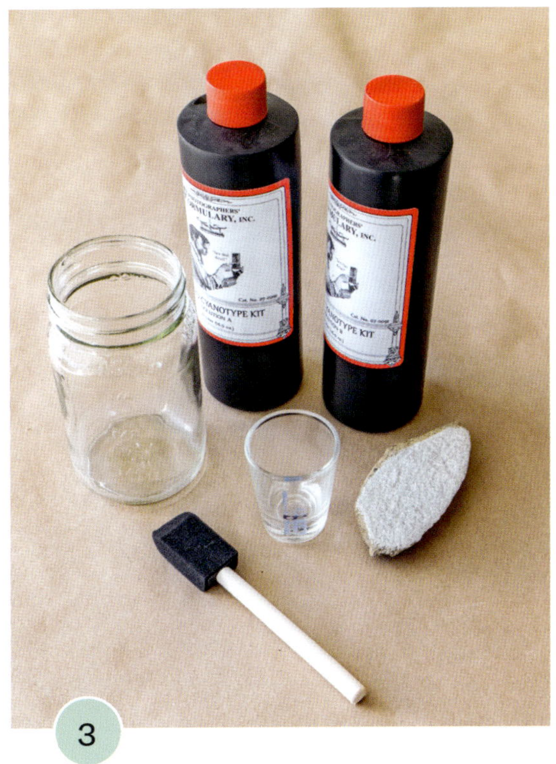

3

Mix the Chemicals

You must do this step in dim light. Read the directions on your chemicals and either mix them with water if called for, or, if using a premixed liquid, measure and mix the two chemicals together in a small jar or container, usually in a one-to-one ratio (if you are using dry chemicals, follow the manufacturer's instructions). The chemicals, once mixed, will last just a few hours, so combine only as much as you need for a first coat. Half of a shot glass of each solution should be enough for coating roughly ten medium-sized rocks, depending on how heavy a coat you apply.

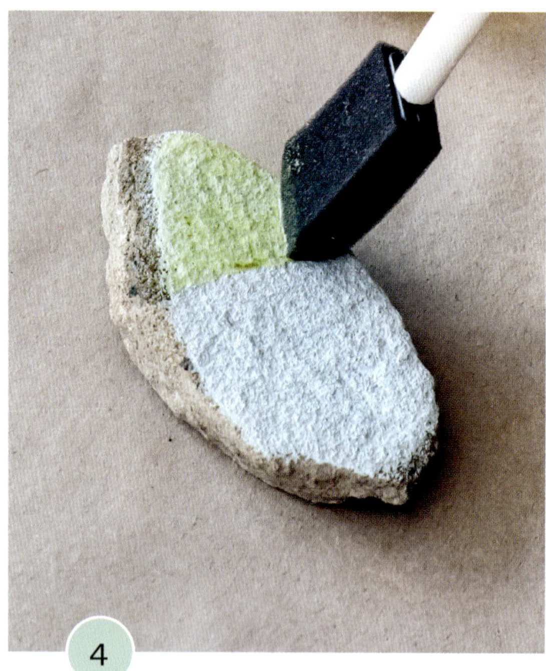

4

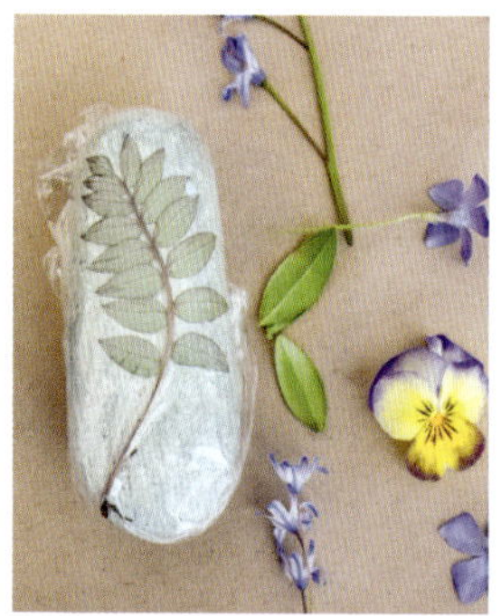

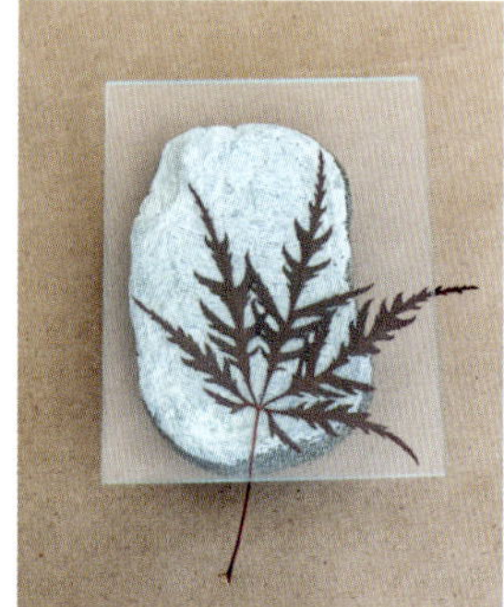

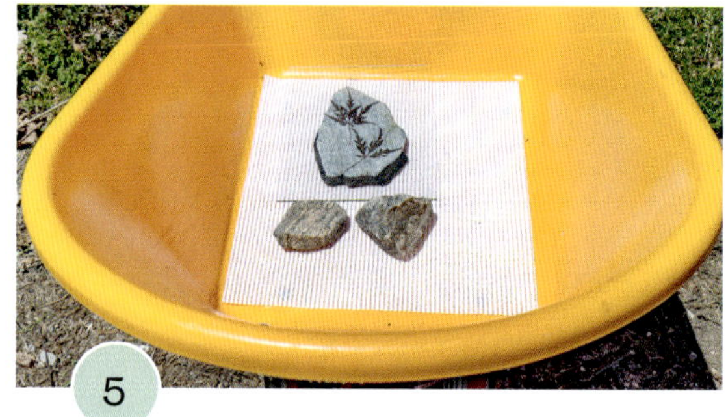

5

Paint the Stones

Make sure your cyanotype solution is well mixed, and then paint a thin layer on your gessoed stones wherever you want them to be blue. Let dry completely, then apply a second thin coat. If more than a few hours have passed, create a new batch of solution before reapplying. For complete coverage, try to paint in a different orientation than the first coat. Let dry completely in the dark.

Design and Expose

In dim light, place the botanicals on top of your stones. Make sure the botanicals are dry, as water will create splotches. To create crisp images, either tightly adhere the botanical to each stone with a layer plastic wrap, securing the wrap on the back with tape, or if a stone is flat, place a piece of glass over the botanical. Keeping the glass on top of a stone can be tricky, and you may need to prop up the glass so it doesn't slide or get blown off. The wrapped stone may also need propping up so the face with the botanical stays exposed to the sun. Place your stone in direct sunlight. Exposure is an experimental guessing game. It can take anywhere from 5 minutes to several hours depending on the strength of the sun. Enough time has passed for a good exposure when the photosensitive solution has turned gray. You can also check your impression, by carefully lifting a piece of a botanical, without shifting it, making sure it has created a shadow.

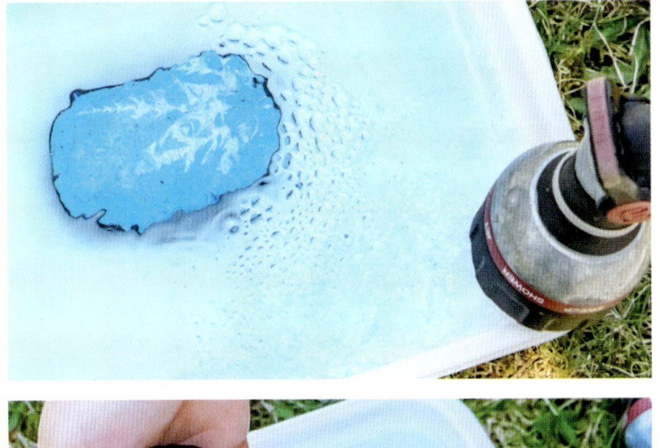

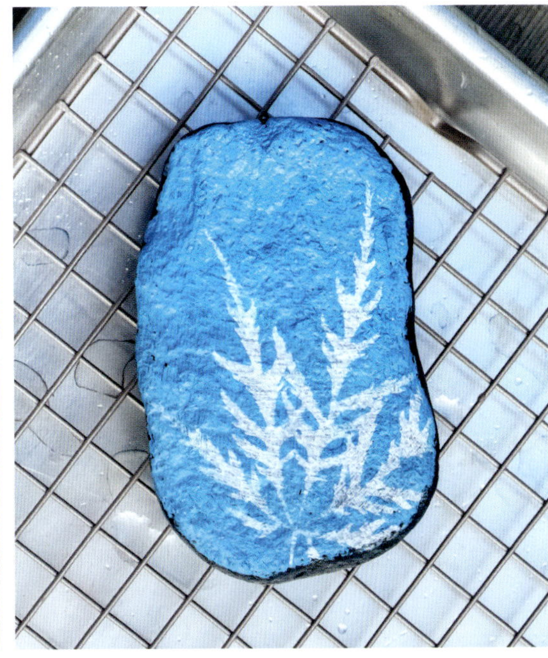

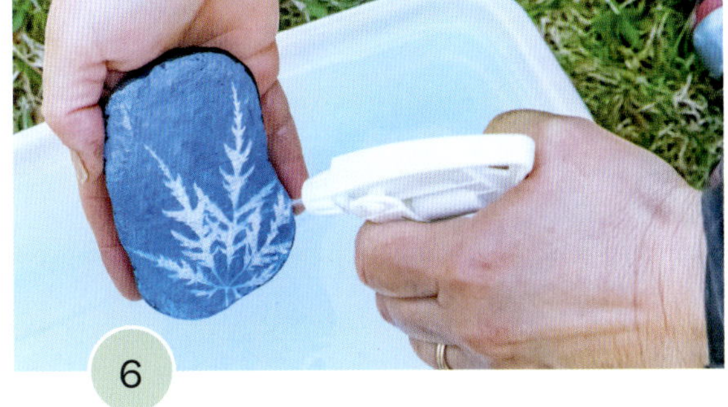

6

Rinse and Dry

Now comes the alchemy. Remove the wrapping or glass and the botanicals and rinse the stones with fresh water for several minutes until the water runs clear and your protected areas have turned white. For some instant gratification, spray your stone with peroxide or add a few tablespoons of the peroxide to a water bath and dip in the stone (shoot for approximately a 9 to 1 ratio of water to peroxide). The peroxide will instantly intensify the blue areas. Rinse off the peroxide and let the stone dry. When displaying any cyanotype, it's best to keep it out of direct sunlight.

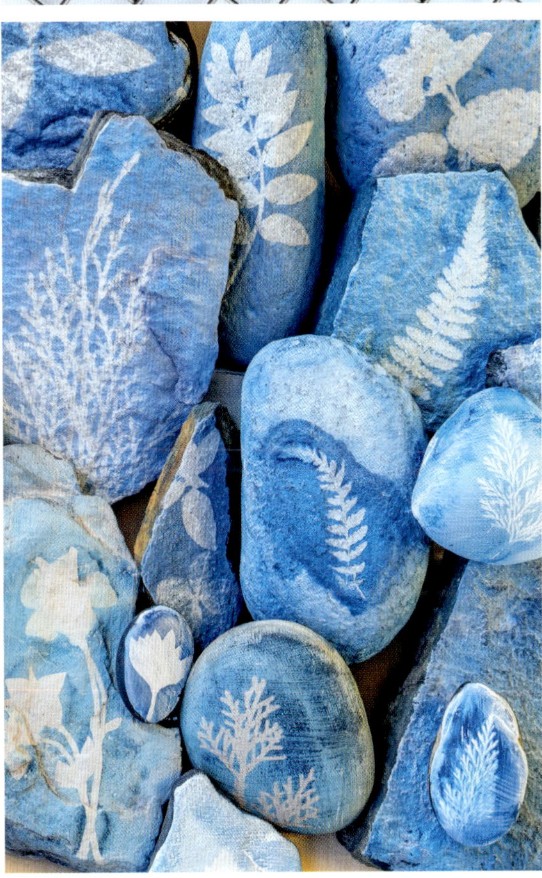

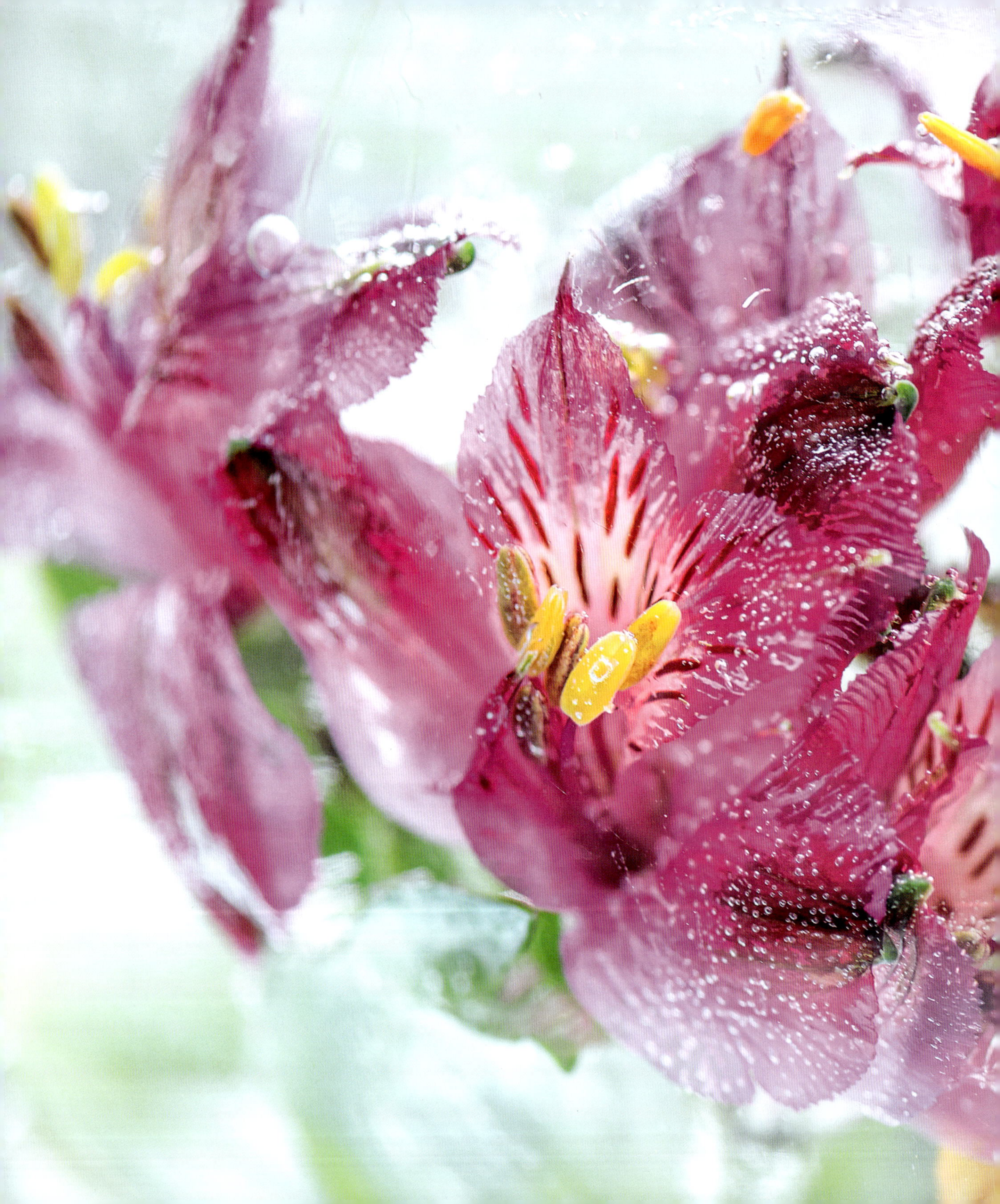

FROZEN FLOWERS

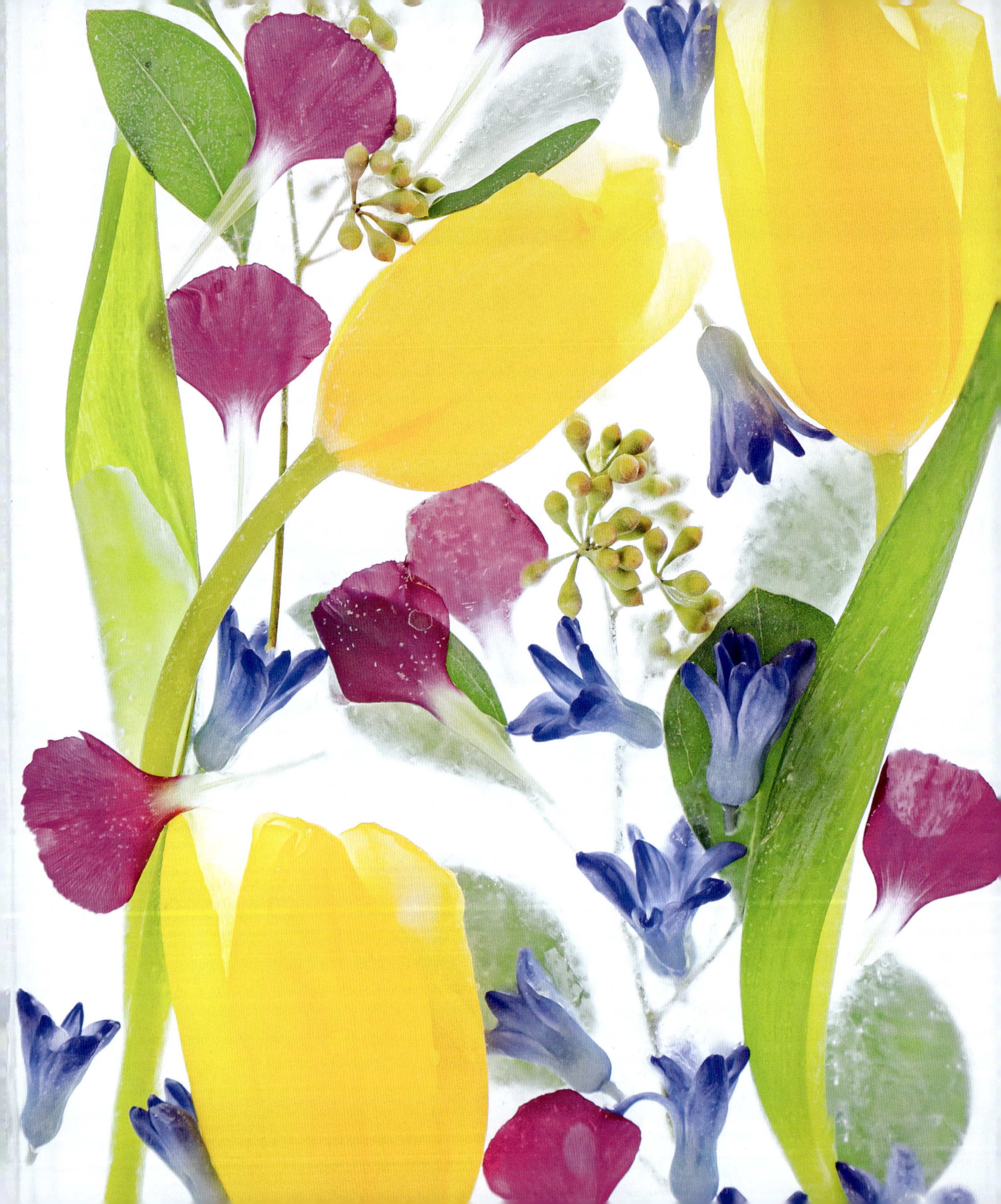

WHAT YOU NEED

- Fresh botanicals
- Smooth-sided container (plastic, silicone, or glass rated for freezing)
- Freezer or outdoor temperatures below freezing
- Phone with camera (or a digital camera)
- Cooler (optional)
- Foam wrap or bubble pack (optional)
- Funnel (optional)
- Aluminum foil, white paper, or cardstock (optional)

13

Flower Still Life

During the winter of the pandemic, I became completely enamored (okay, obsessed) with freezing flowers. It became my antidote to the cold, monochromatic days endemic to winter in Maine. Instead of dreading the frigid temperatures, I began to look forward to them. From reading everything I could about getting clear ice (most of the articles are geared toward clear cubes for cocktails), I discovered that the key is to cool the water slowly and in one direction so the bubbles sink to the bottom, leaving clear ice at the top. I found the best way to do that was outside on cold nights. I started experimenting, by setting flowers out in glass and plastic containers. I would add water, wrap the containers in bubble pack, and place them in coolers with the tops open so that they would freeze slowly from the top down. The results were an incredible alchemy. Even if the ice wasn't clear every time, the resulting floral ice pieces were almost always fascinating, and sometimes staggeringly beautiful. Taking photos of the pieces became a meditation. I would shoot some pieces as sculptures in the landscape surrounded by snow. With others, I would zoom in as close as possible to an area that had color and movement, and I found myself transported into the ice, shooting multiple and varied close-ups.

Once summer arrived, I became infatuated with making frozen still lifes with botanicals from my gardens and surrounding woods. My freezer became crammed with them—no room for food! I also found that shooting these pieces in hot weather, as they melted, added a new and delightful dynamic.

I have had great results taking photos with phone cameras as well as with my professional cameras and lenses. There are times when I even prefer to use my phone, as I can move around the ice more easily. You can make prints using your home printer or by sending digital files to an online or local printer. Digital files can be made into cards, framed prints, posters, or almost anything imaginable. You can have your images printed on wood, fabric, metal, glass, even surfboards or furniture.

Here's the thing to be aware of before you start: almost all flowers float. You have several options to deal with this. First, embrace the look of flowers half submerged in ice—it can be interesting to see half a blossom or even just the edge of a petal breaking through the ice's surface. Second, freeze in two stages, which is what has been done here—freeze the flowers in place and later add water to submerge them. Third, keep your flowers submerged by using small glass jars, discs, or even rocks to weight the stems (these objects will be visible through the ice but can become part of the design). Sometimes the weights work, and sometimes, despite all efforts, things float anyhow. Finally, try wedging your flowers into your container, so the walls of the container and other flowers keep the botanicals submerged. Again, sometimes it works and sometimes it doesn't; either way, chances are great that you'll get something worthwhile.

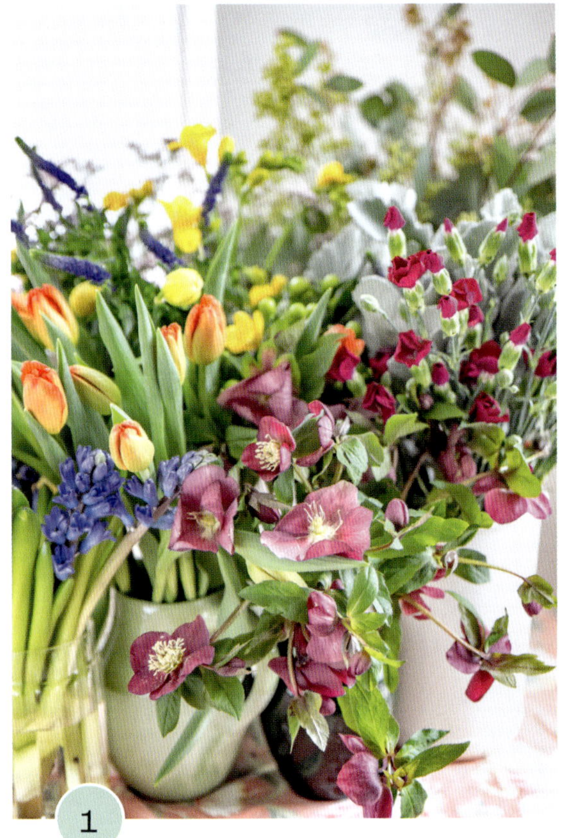

1

Gather Fresh Botanicals

Select the botanicals to freeze. In winter, depending on where you live, that might mean a trip to the store. You can use almost any flower, petal, leaf, or berry to create your still life. You can use one type of flower or even a single blossom to great effect, or you can compose a multicolored collage using a combination of flowers, petals, leaves, even fruit. As you consider what to include, think about the color palette and size and texture.

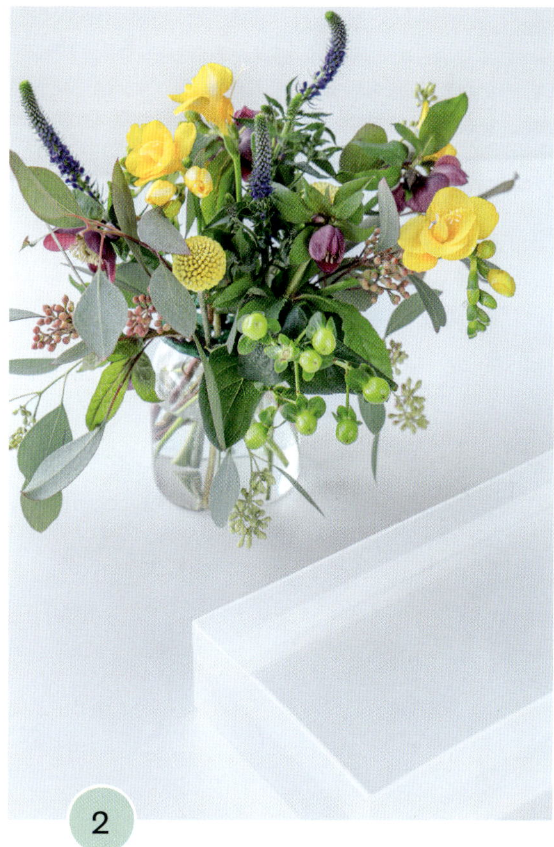

2

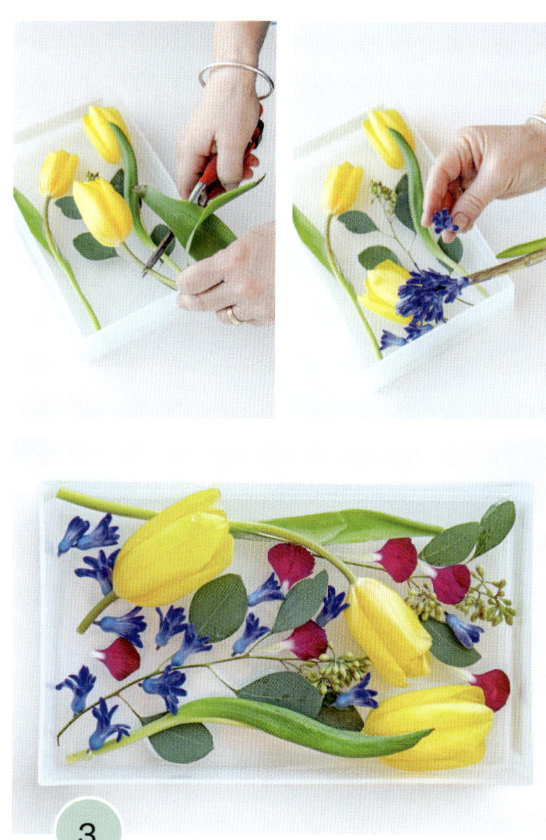

3

Begin Filling the Container

You can use any container that will safely freeze. Glass, plastic, and silicone all work well. Make sure the container has smooth, straight sides so that the ice will slip out (which won't happen if there are ridges or textures) and that the top of the container is as wide as or wider than the bottom. Pour in an inch or two of water—more if you're using a very large container. You need just enough water so that the flowers will freeze in place. Lots of websites will tell you to boil your water to get crystal-clear ice, some will tell you to boil it twice, and others will say to use distilled water. I have found (and some research agrees) that if you have clean tap water, no other treatment is necessary.

Arrange the Botanicals

Try to construct your still life close to where you will freeze it so the water and flowers don't slosh around too much as you carry the filled container. Place and arrange your botanicals. Have fun and play with the composition, making sure to pick out any unsightly bits of detritus. At this point, the botanicals will only be partially submerged and easily disturbed, so be careful when you pick up your container. Set the container in a freezer (or outside in a cooler if temperatures will stay below freezing long enough). Once placed, you may have to rearrange some flowers if they shifted. If you choose to, you can wrap the outside of the container in thin foam or bubble pack to slow the freezing process, as this may result in clearer ice.

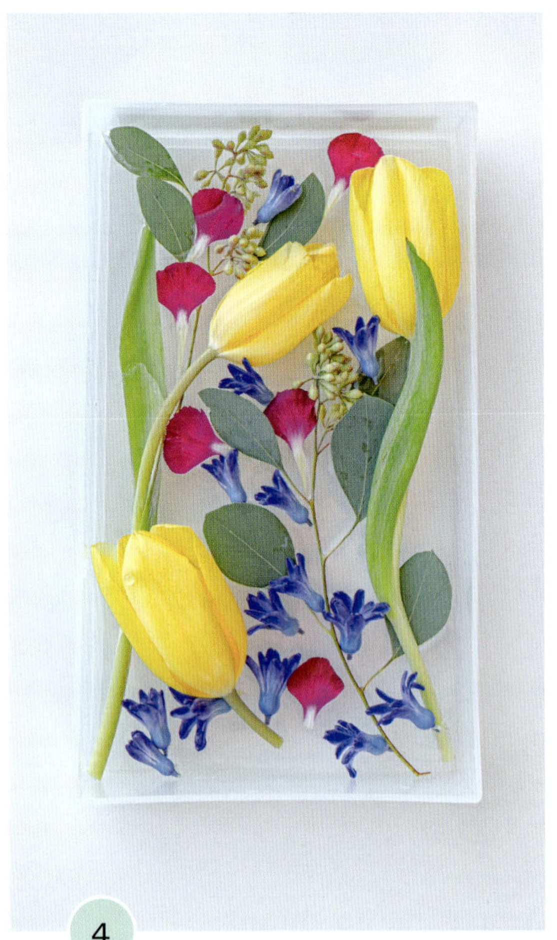

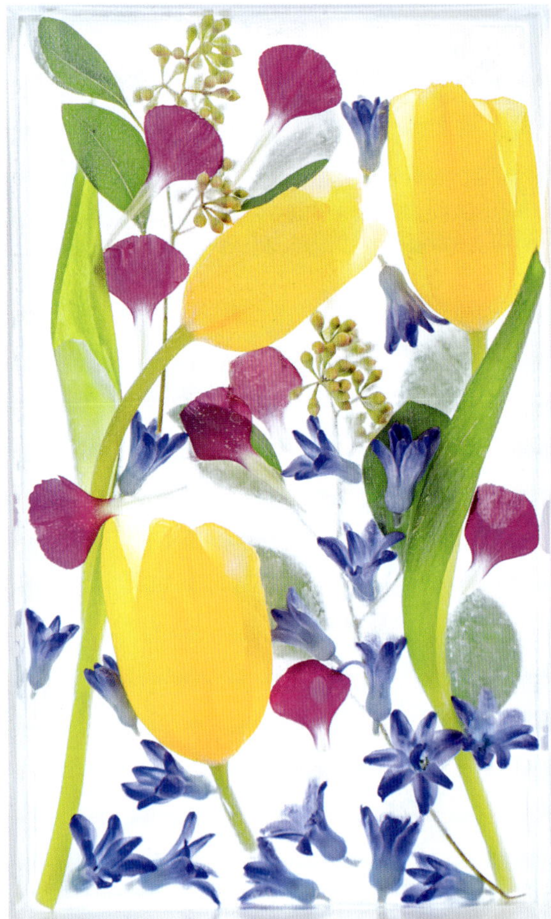

4

First Freeze

Many variables will determine how long your piece will take to freeze: air temperature, water temperature, volume of water, and density of flowers, to name a few. To check if your piece is fully frozen, pick up the container once the surface is hard and tilt it. If there are bubbles moving under the surface of the ice, you will need to continue freezing. At this point, though, you might want to take a few photos, even if the piece is not completely frozen. Sometimes the most beautiful stage is when flowers are frozen but not yet completely encased in ice.

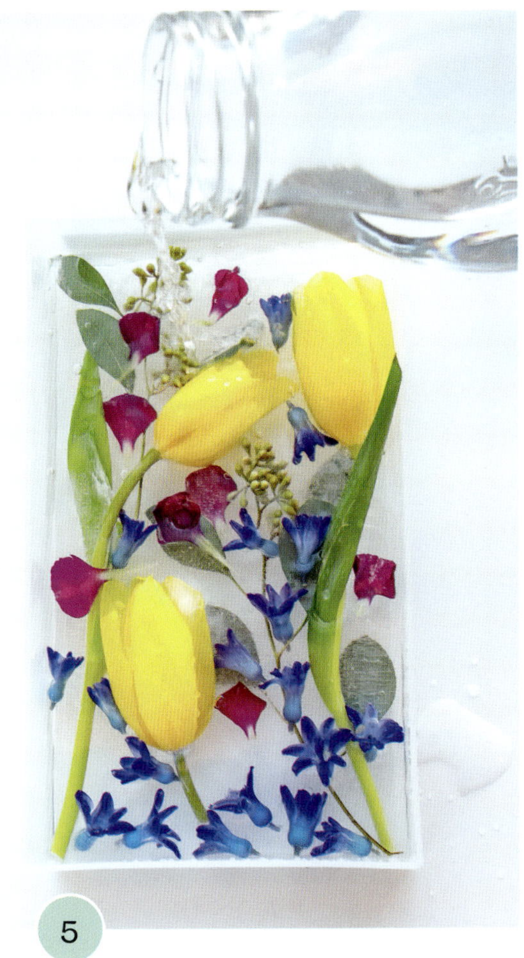

5

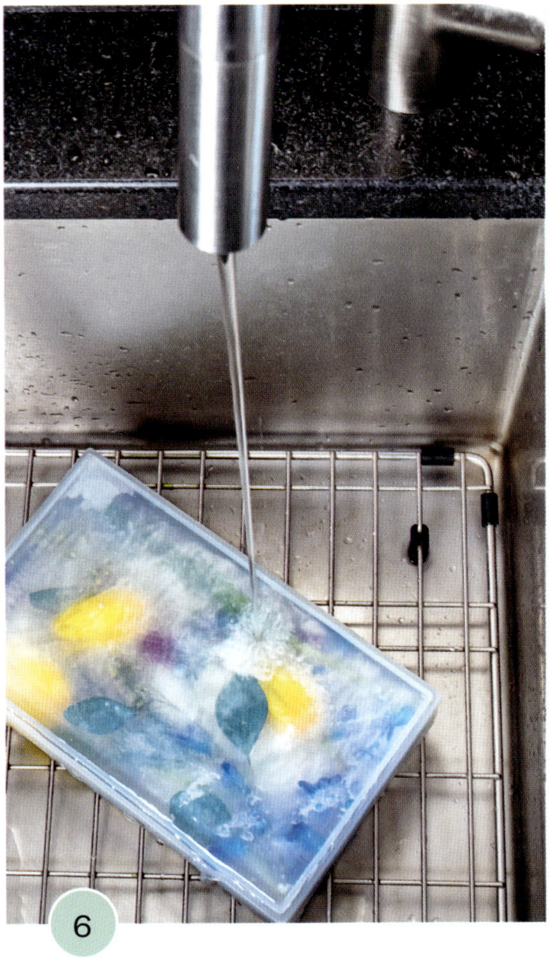

6

Add More Water

When the first freeze is complete, slowly add more water, taking care not to pour directly on top of fragile botanicals, until it almost reaches the top of the container or has completely submerged the flowers. Unless you have incredibly steady hands, you may want to add the last bit of water while the container is in the freezer (or outside) to avoid spilling in transit. If it's a bad angle for pouring, sometimes a funnel is useful. Let the still life fully freeze.

Release the Ice

Before releasing your ice piece, you may want to photograph it while it's still in the container. There is a chance that the ice will crack when you take it out. The cracks often have their own beauty, but it's also great to have some uncracked images. To release the ice piece, you can either leave it out at room temperature until it just starts to melt, or you can run the back side of the container under cool water until the piece slides out.

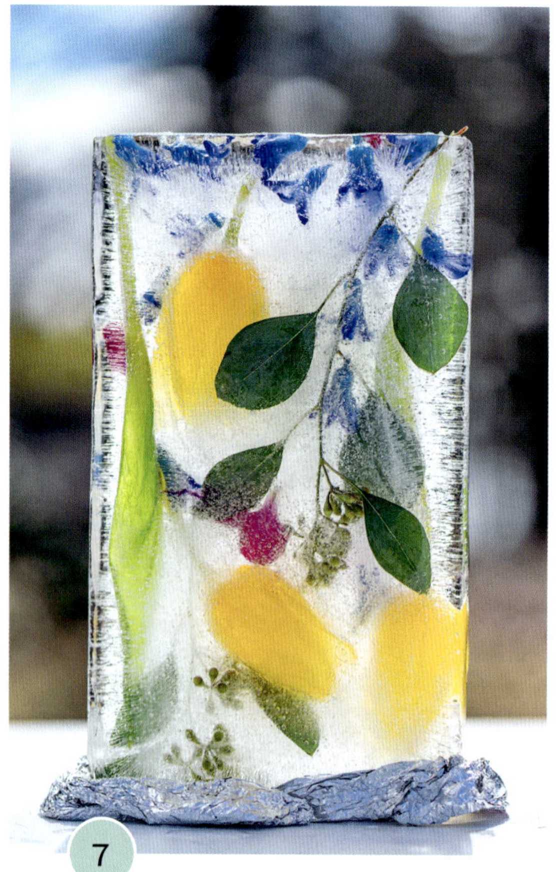

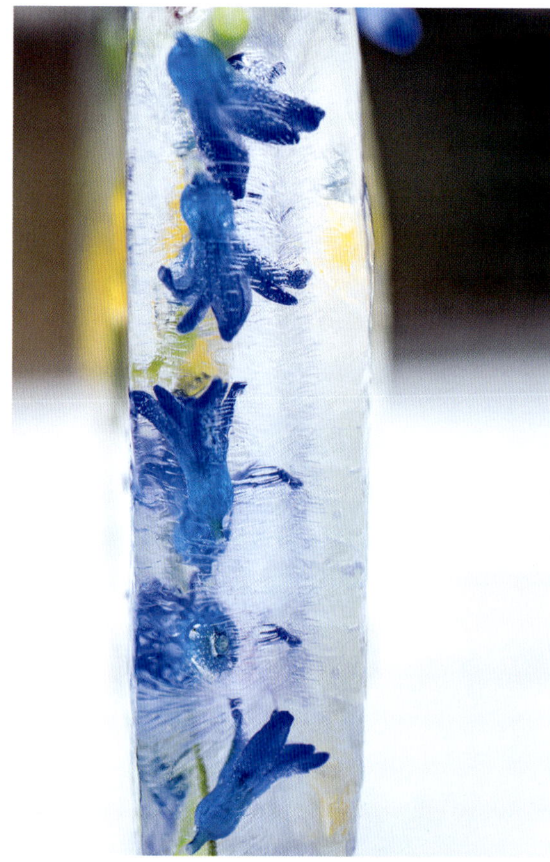

Shoot

Keep in mind that ice is very slippery; as the still life melts, it can easily skitter off any surface and smash to bits. As you're photographing the piece, it often looks best to have the light coming from behind it. You can use crumpled foil, ice cubes, or snow to prop up the ice piece vertically if you want the light to come through it. You can also use a piece of foil, a white piece of paper, or cardstock to bounce light through the ice. Take time to look at your piece from every angle and experiment with different techniques. Try close-ups and longer shots. Shoot from above and below. Try different backgrounds—black, white, colors. You can use a wall, the side of your house, or a piece of paper or wood as a background. Shoot outdoors or indoors. Shine a flashlight or other bright light through the ice. Try as many things as you can think of. As the ice melts, all sorts of interesting things can happen, so keep shooting until your piece is just a puddle.

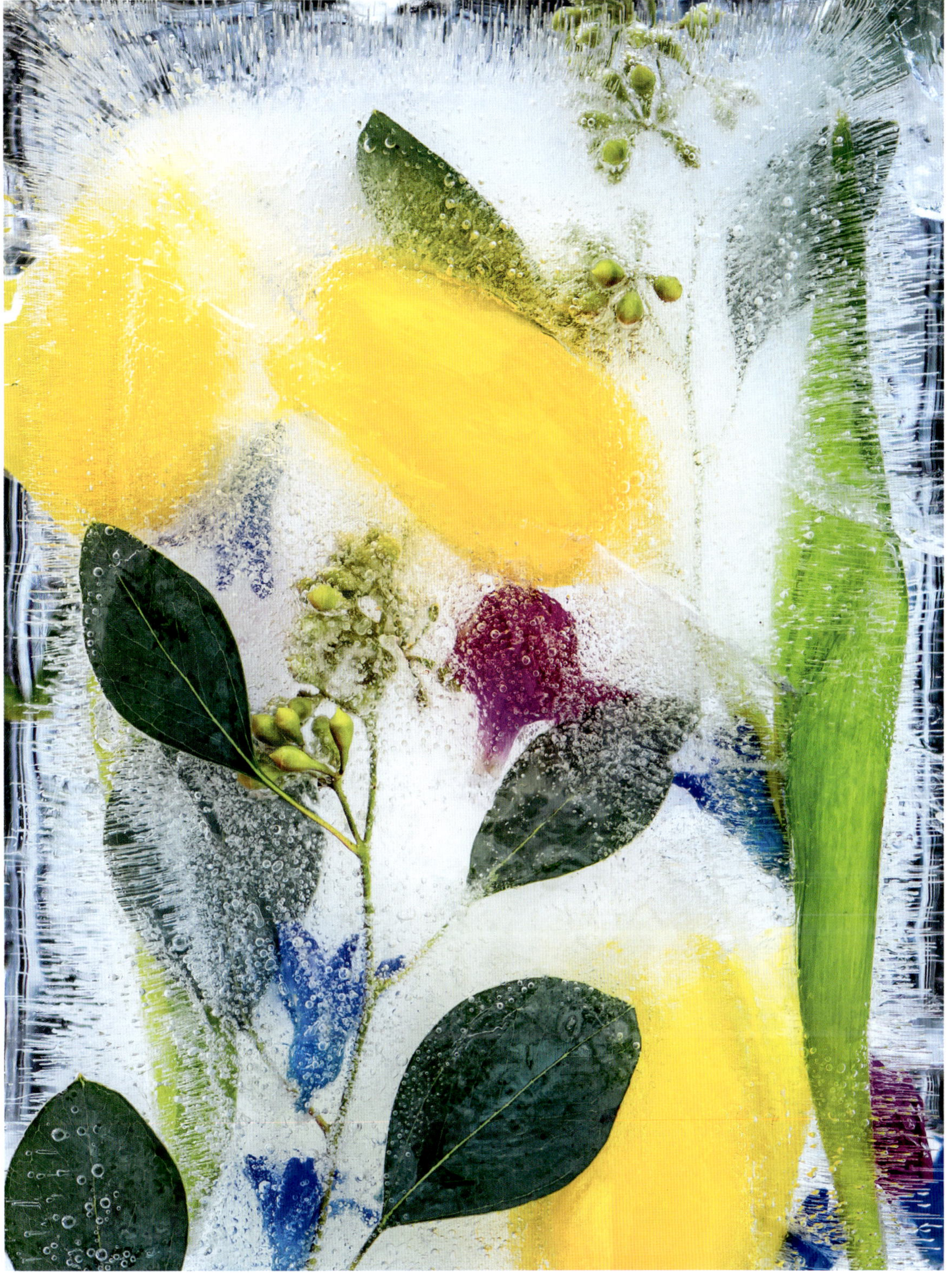

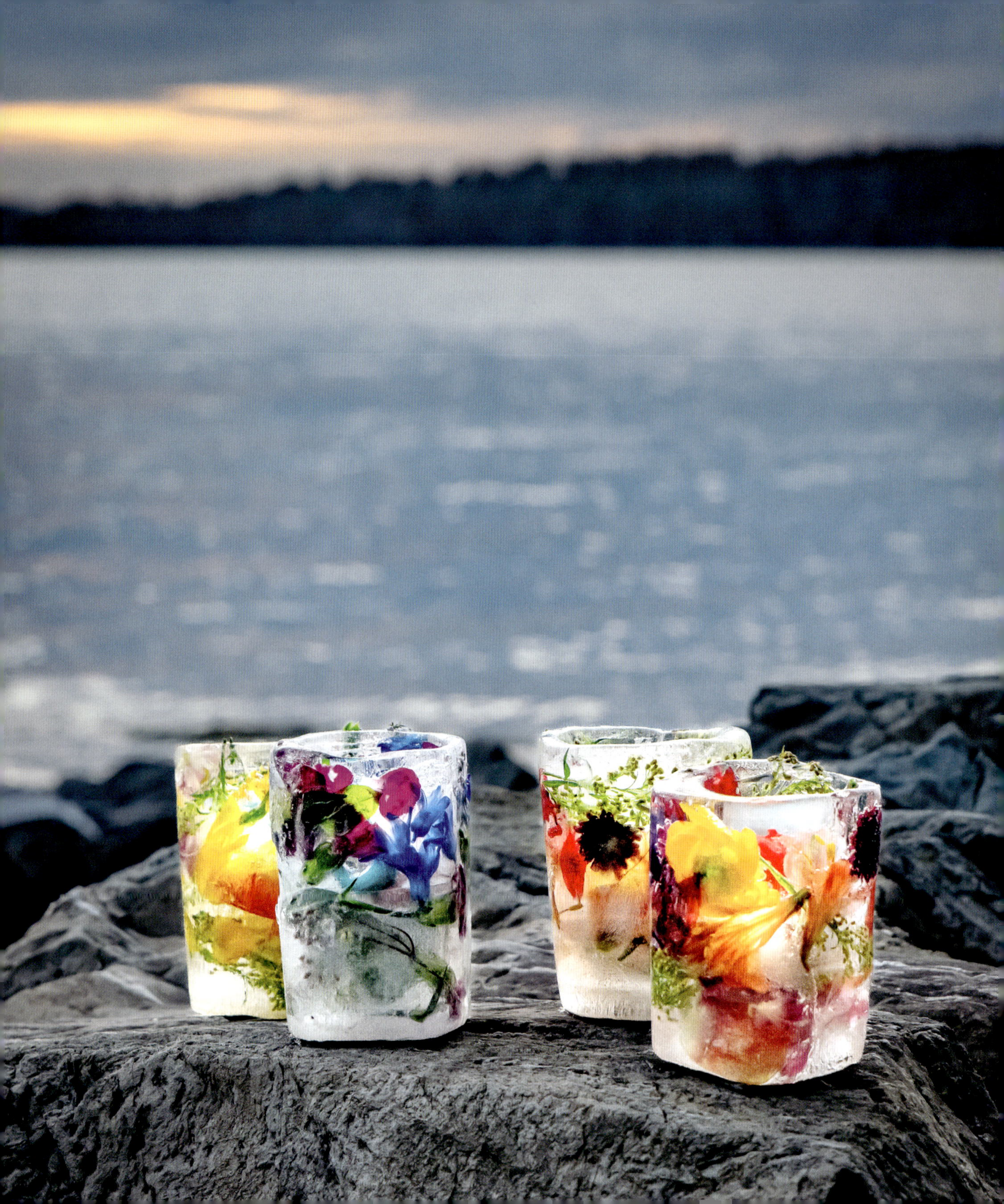

WHAT YOU NEED

- Botanicals
- Large, deep, smooth, and straight-sided container (plastic, silicone, or glass rated for freezing)
- Smaller smooth-sided container to fit inside the large container (plastic, silicone, or glass rated for freezing)
- Battery-operated light or candle
- Masking tape or painter's tape
- Sharp scissors
- Chopsticks or skewer (optional)
- Freezer space or outdoor temperatures below freezing
- Stones or weights (optional)
- Funnel (optional)

14

Floral Luminaria or Ice Bucket

The only difference between making floral luminaria and ice buckets is scale. And be warned, an ice bucket needs serious freezer real estate. Both are surprisingly easy to create but take some time to freeze. The ice bucket will require many more botanicals and longer to freeze, but on the other hand, it will also last longer before it melts.

If you have enough space in your freezer—or outdoor temperatures will be below freezing long enough—you may want to make several luminaria at once, as they look lovely in a grouping. To illuminate your luminaria, you can use battery-operated tea lights, fairy lights, or even a candle, though a real flame will melt the ice more quickly. You can even turn an ice bucket into a giant luminaria by just adding light.

If using the ice bucket or luminaria indoors, place it on a tray or something that will catch or absorb the water as it melts. The good news is that both the luminaria and the ice bucket usually look cool even as they melt and fall apart.

These ice pieces can be so striking that you may want to photograph them close-up for prints or cards, as described in the Flower Still Life project.

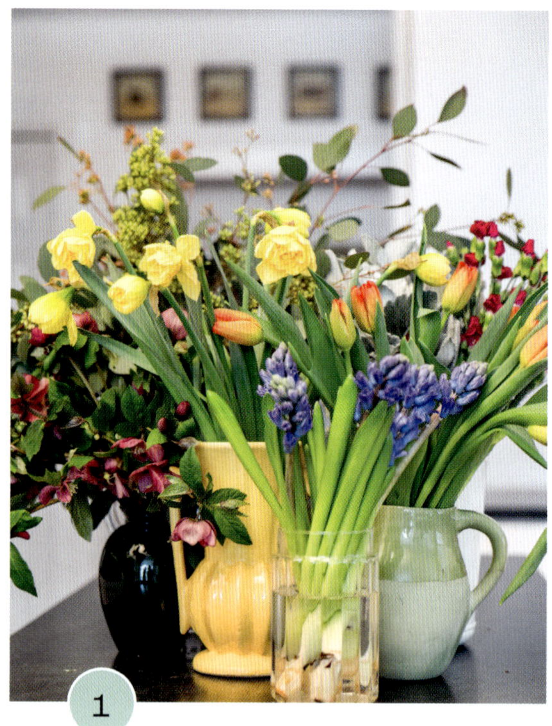

1

Select Fresh Botanicals

One of the beauties of this project is that so many different types of flowers and foliage will work. Think about color combinations and texture as well as size. The flowers have to fit in the container, so keep that in mind.

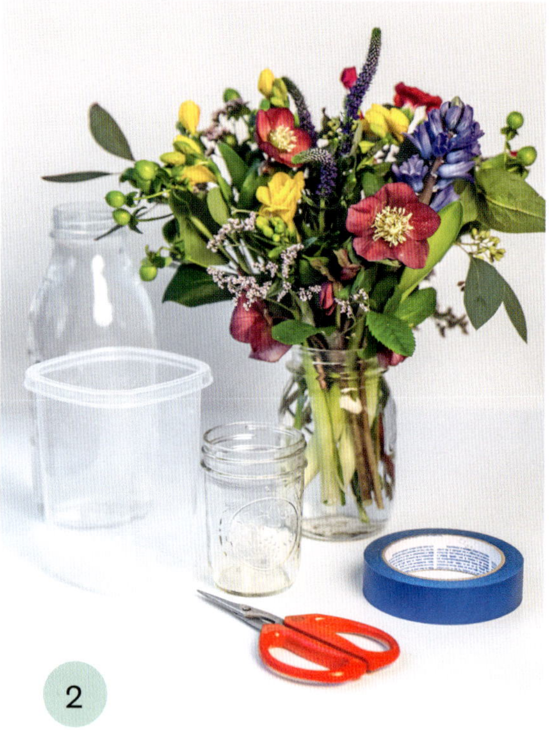

2

Select the Containers

Double-check that you have two smooth, straight-sided containers—one that will fit inside the other—made of plastic, silicone, or glass rated for freezing. The containers should be free of ridges, texture, or shoulders so the ice will slide out when the time comes. If you are making an ice bucket, check to see that your bottle will fit in the smaller container that will form the well to hold the bottle. If you are making a luminaria, make sure the light you choose will fit into the smaller container. Also be sure to allow enough space between the nested containers so that the ice wall is thick enough to be durable and won't melt too quickly. For the luminaria, shoot for a ¾-inch minimum thickness; for the ice bucket, aim for walls at least 1 inch.

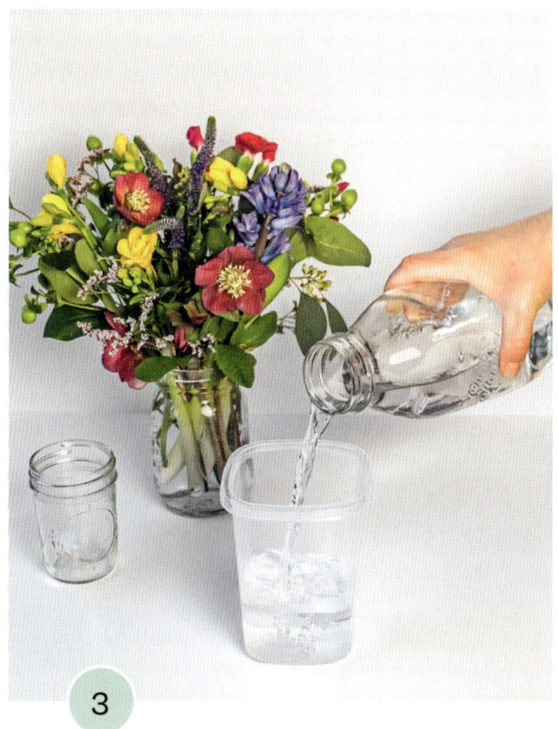

3

Add Water to Form the Vessel Bottom

Pour a few inches of water into the larger container; when frozen, this water will form the bottom of the luminaria or ice bucket, and the smaller container will eventually sit on top of this ice. The exact amount of water will depend on the size of the smaller container: you want the rim of the smaller container to sit at the same height or above the rim of the larger container when it is sitting on top of this first frozen layer.

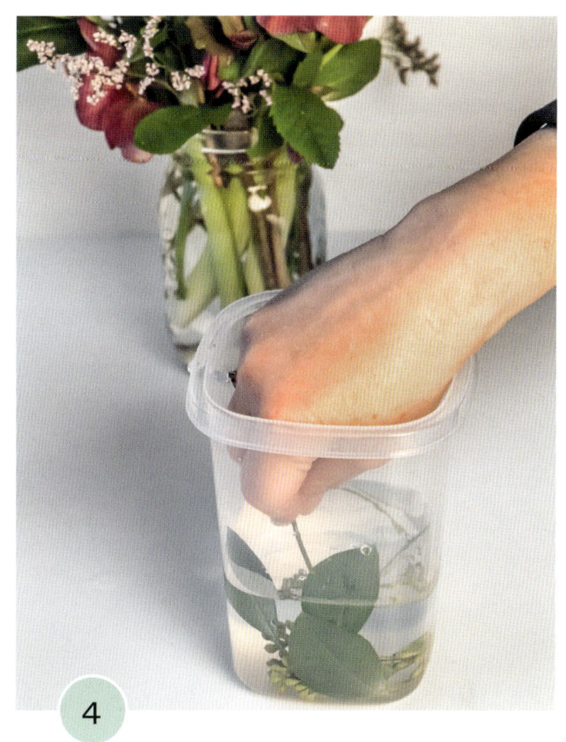

4

First Freeze

Add botanicals to the bottom layer. Most flowers float, so try to wedge your botanicals into the container in a way that keeps them submerged. You may want to cut stems to fit and/or pluck blossoms off their stems for color. Once you have placed your botanicals, chill the container, on an even surface, until the water is completely frozen. Check this by holding the container up to the light and tilting it; if bubbles move under the ice, give it more time to freeze.

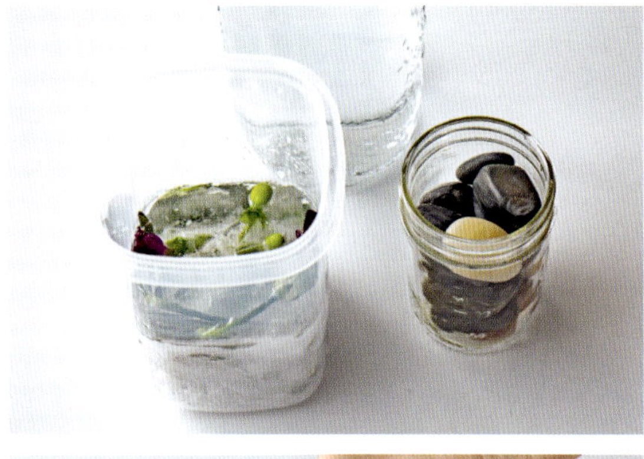

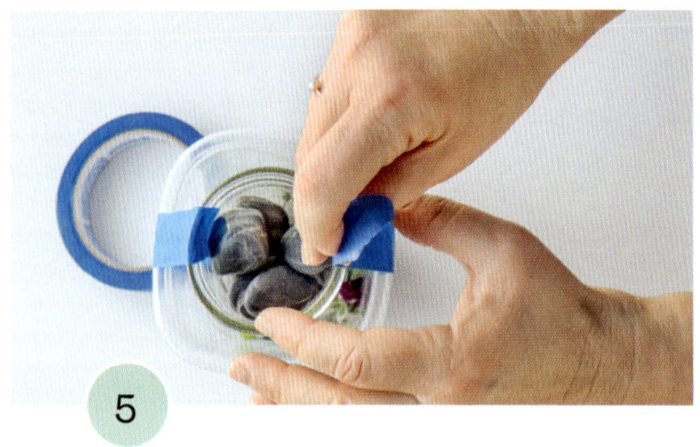

5

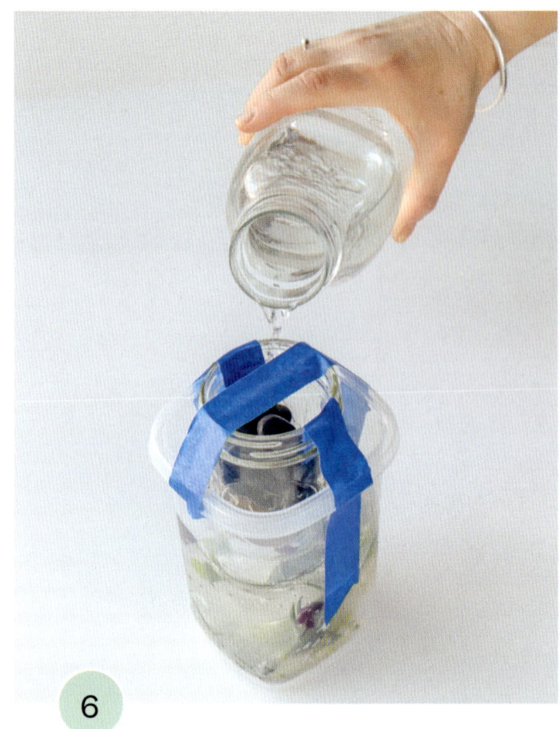

6

Place the Inner Container

Once the first layer is completely frozen, you may choose to add weights to the smaller container. They aren't essential, but they will make it easier to tape the container and add stability. Slip the smaller container inside the larger container so that the bottom rests on top of the ice "floor." Place it as close to the center and as level as possible. The ice floor may not be flat, so just do your best. The rims of both containers should be even, or the inner container rim can stick out above the outer. Tape the two vessels securely in place, leaving room to add the botanicals.

Add Water

Fill the space in between the containers with water. Keep in mind that adding your botanicals will raise the water level, so leave some room at the top.

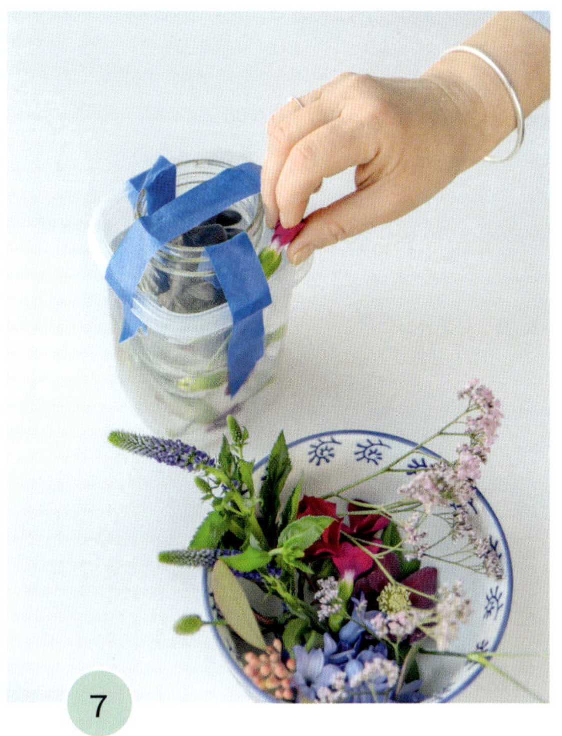

7

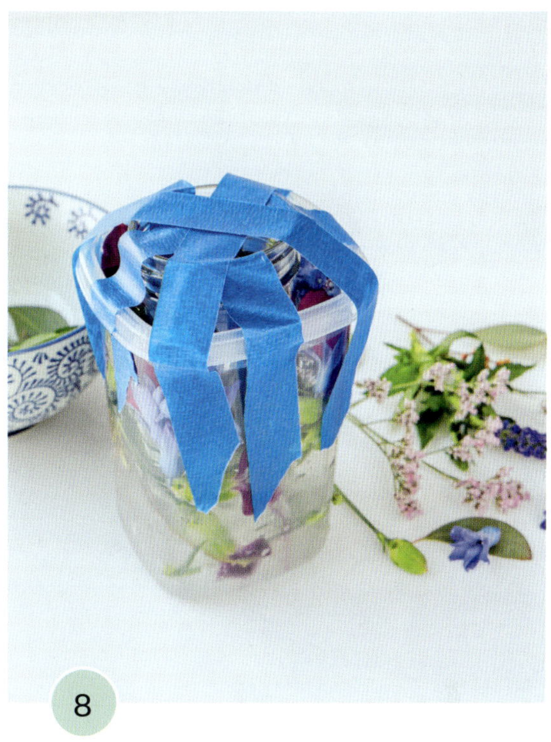

8

Add the Botanicals

Carefully stuff your botanicals into the water in the space between the containers. They will want to float, so if you can wedge them in without squishing them, that is a good thing. Use your fingers or chopsticks to move them around to get a good distribution of color and texture. Once you are happy with your design, top up the water until it almost reaches the rim—keeping in mind that the volume will expand as it turns into ice.

Secure with More Tape

The inner container will want to float and may be a bit wobbly, so once you've added the flowers and are happy with their distribution, apply more tape to the top so the inner container won't shift as the ice freezes around it. Put the whole construction into the freezer or into freezing temperatures outside and leave until completely frozen.

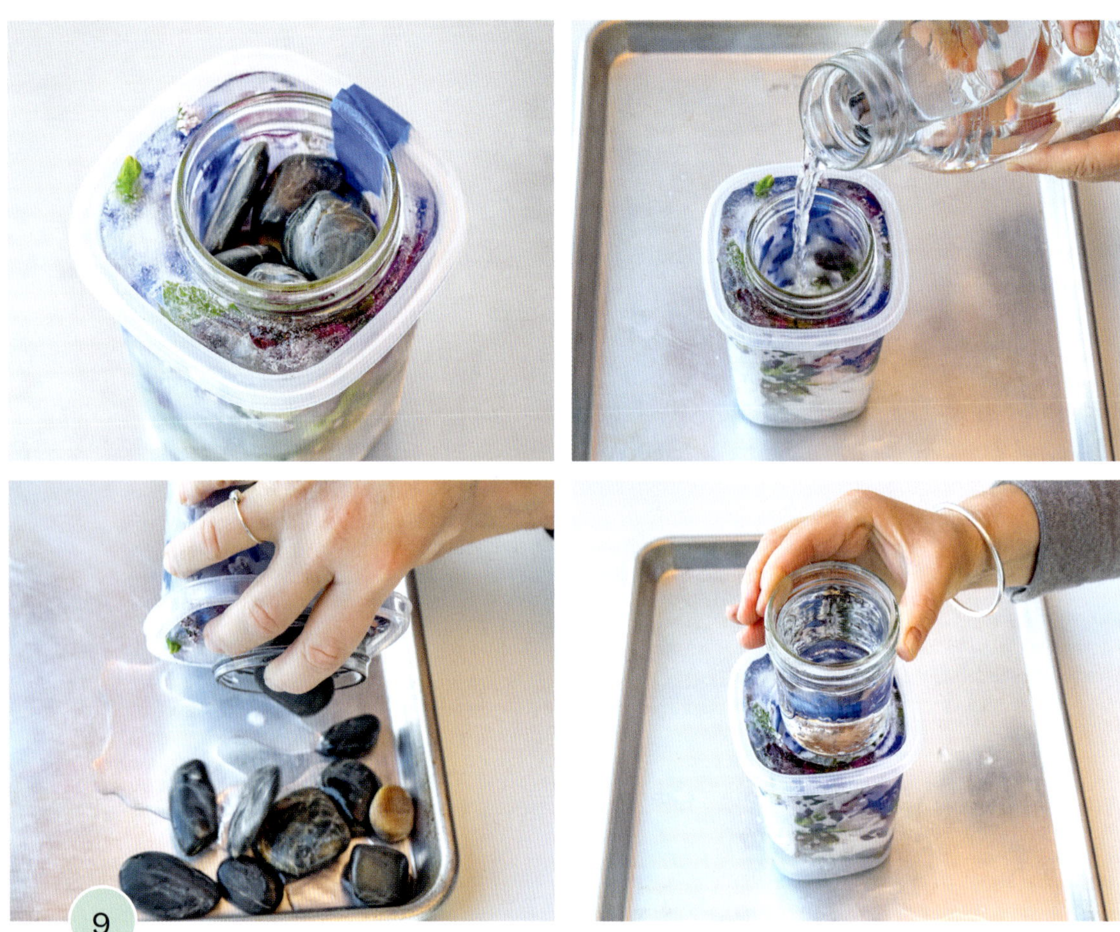

9

Release the Inner Container

Once the ice is solid (again, check for this by holding it up to the light and tilting it to see if bubbles are moving inside the ice), remove the luminaria or ice bucket from the freezer. To release the ice from the containers, you can let the whole thing melt just a little—enough to slide out the inner container. Or you can remove the rocks and add cool water to the inner container, which will melt the ice enough that you can free it.

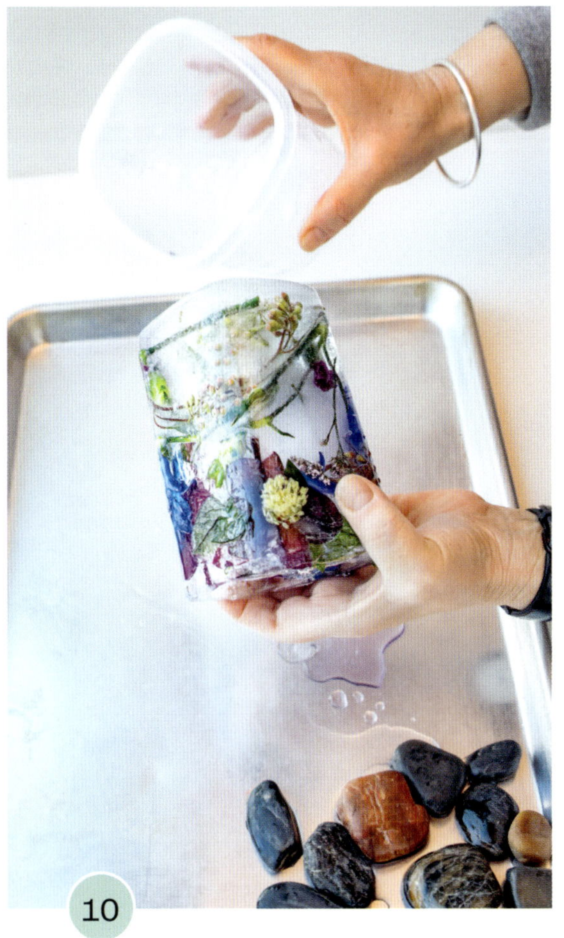

10

Release the Outer Container

Once the inner container has been removed, run the outside of the outer container under cool water. Note that if you use warm water, it will cause more cracking in the ice. This is okay, as it usually occurs on the surface and doesn't hurt the integrity of the ice, but at this point you probably want to minimize cracking. Slide out the luminaria or ice bucket carefully, as it will be very slippery.

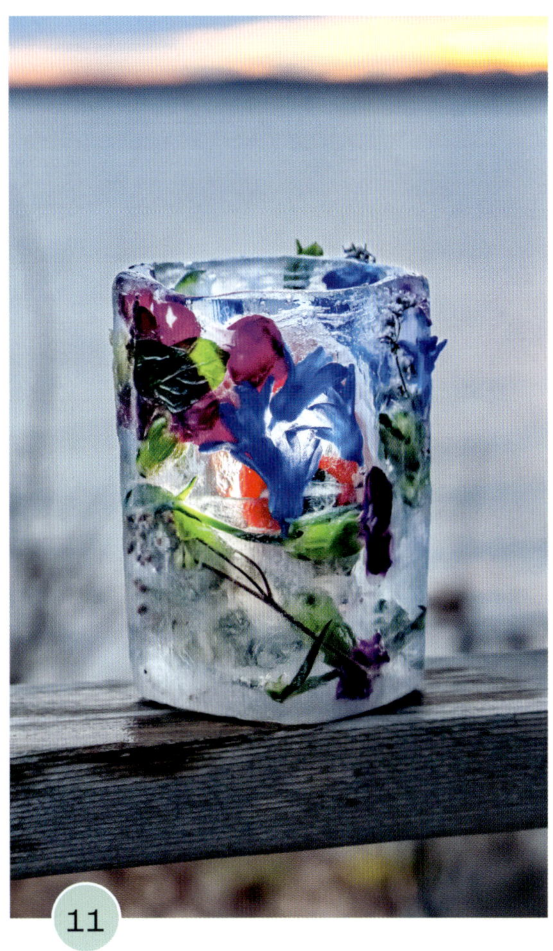

11

Display

To display your luminaria or ice bucket, try placing it on a tray or plate and surrounding the base with greens. You also may want to shoot a few close-up photographs before it melts.

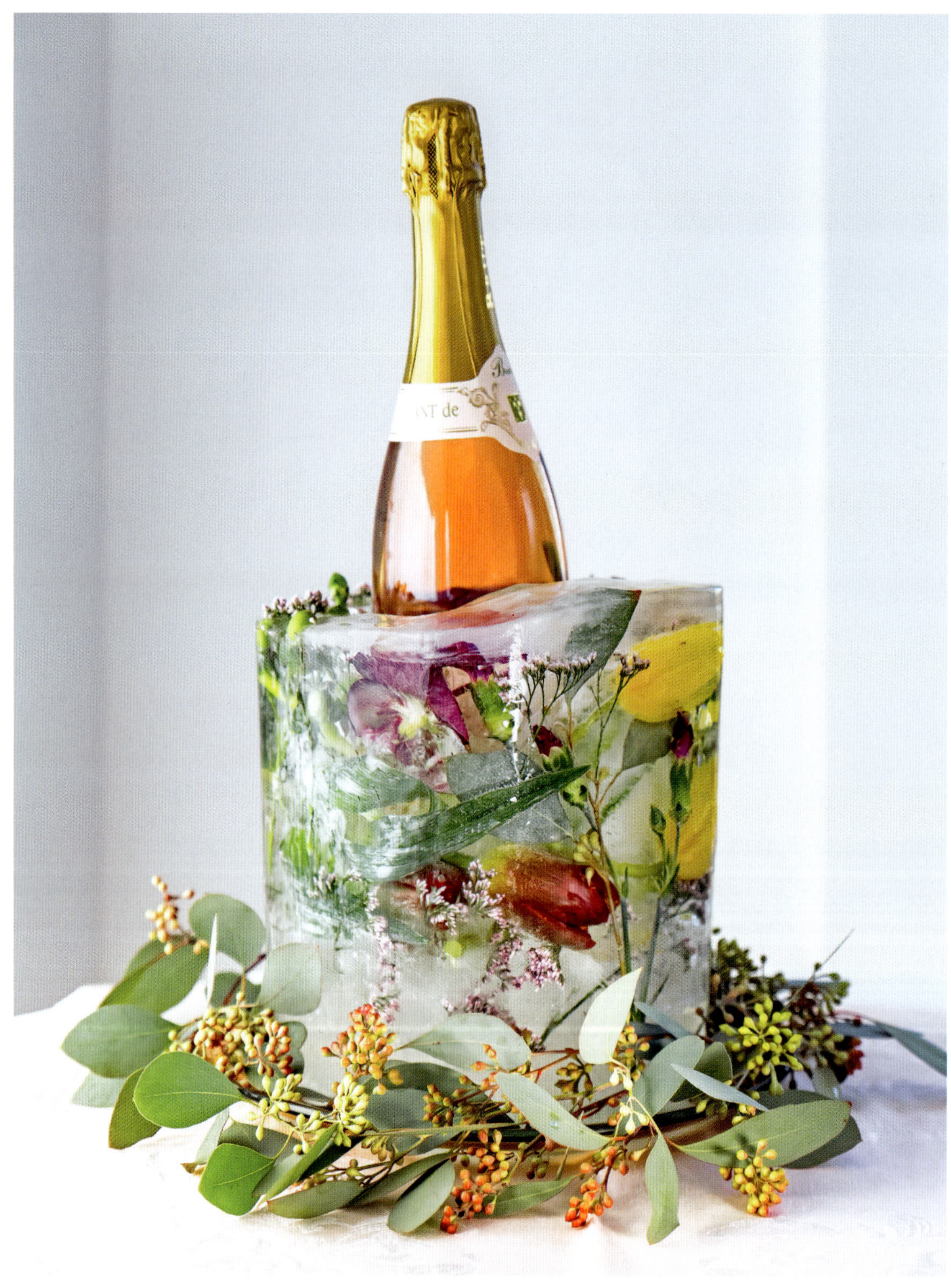

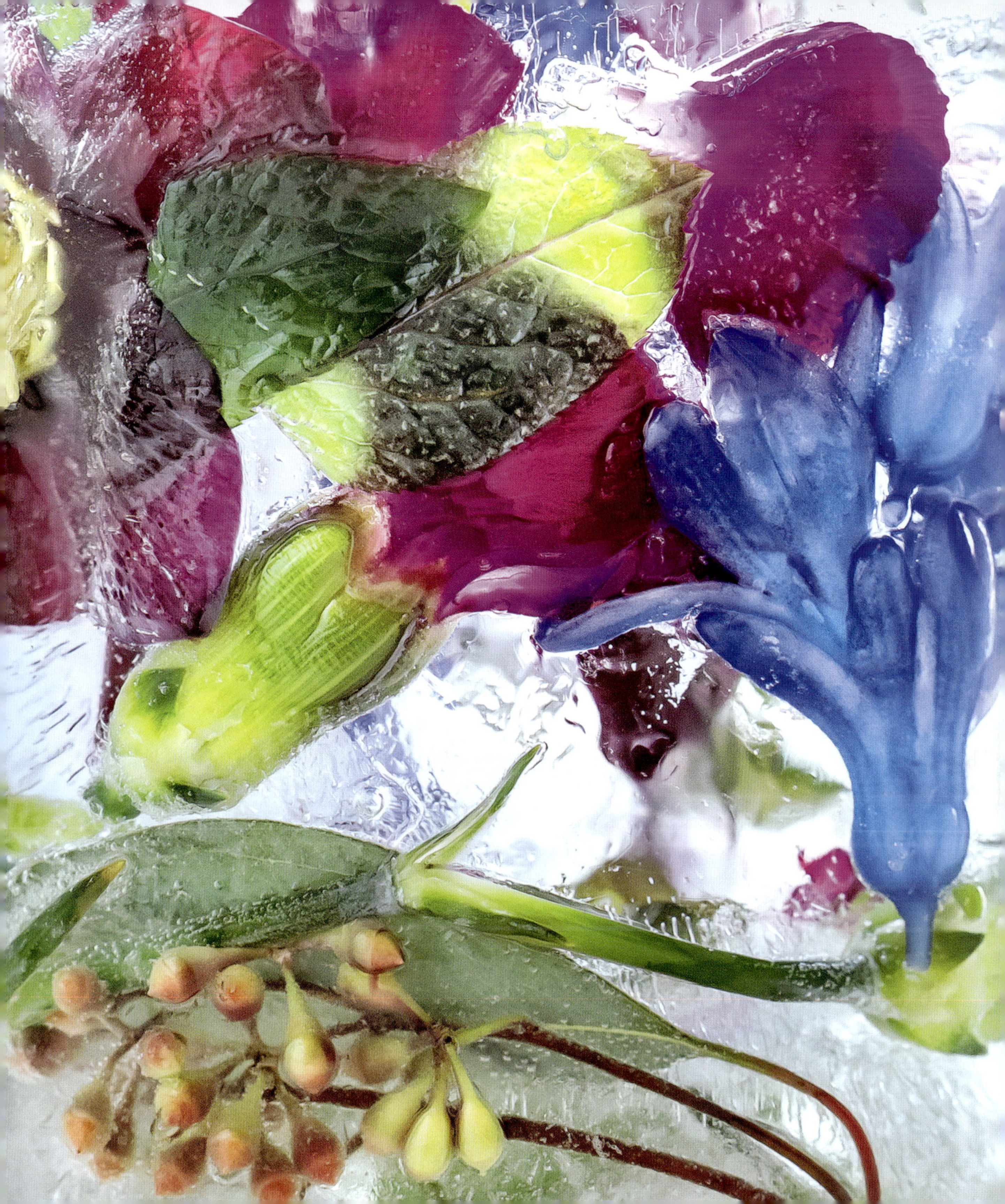

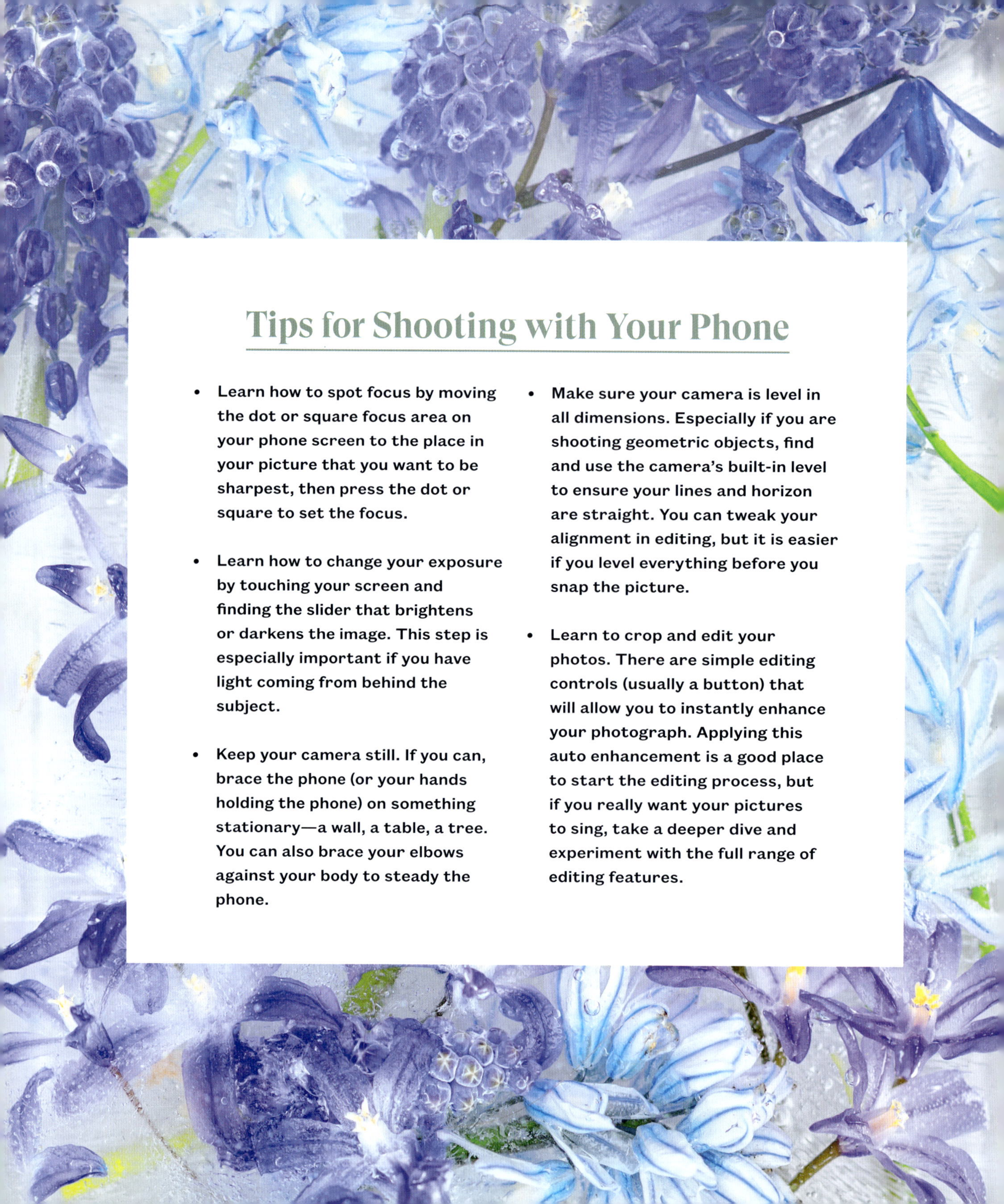

Tips for Shooting with Your Phone

- Learn how to spot focus by moving the dot or square focus area on your phone screen to the place in your picture that you want to be sharpest, then press the dot or square to set the focus.

- Learn how to change your exposure by touching your screen and finding the slider that brightens or darkens the image. This step is especially important if you have light coming from behind the subject.

- Keep your camera still. If you can, brace the phone (or your hands holding the phone) on something stationary—a wall, a table, a tree. You can also brace your elbows against your body to steady the phone.

- Make sure your camera is level in all dimensions. Especially if you are shooting geometric objects, find and use the camera's built-in level to ensure your lines and horizon are straight. You can tweak your alignment in editing, but it is easier if you level everything before you snap the picture.

- Learn to crop and edit your photos. There are simple editing controls (usually a button) that will allow you to instantly enhance your photograph. Applying this auto enhancement is a good place to start the editing process, but if you really want your pictures to sing, take a deeper dive and experiment with the full range of editing features.

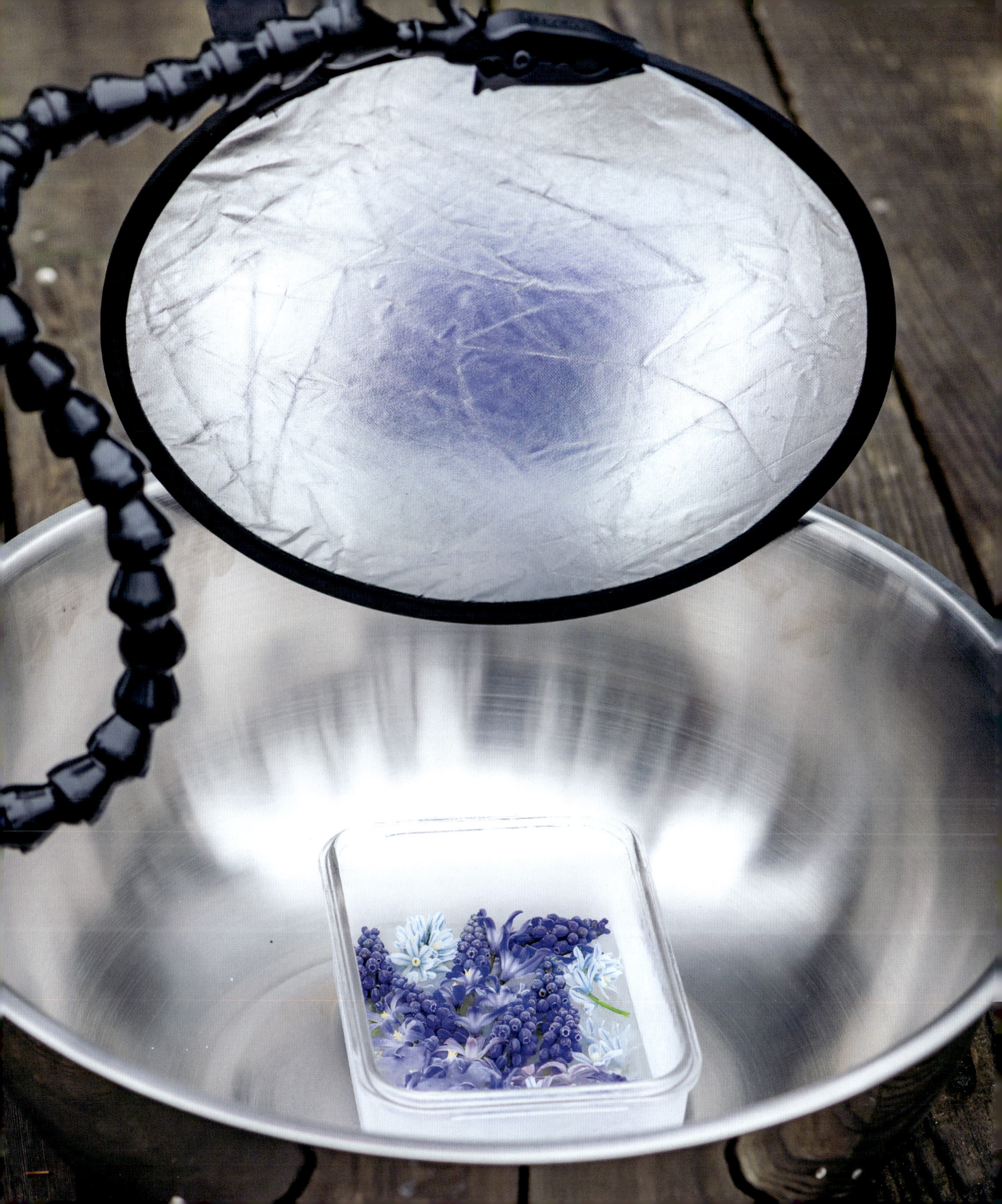

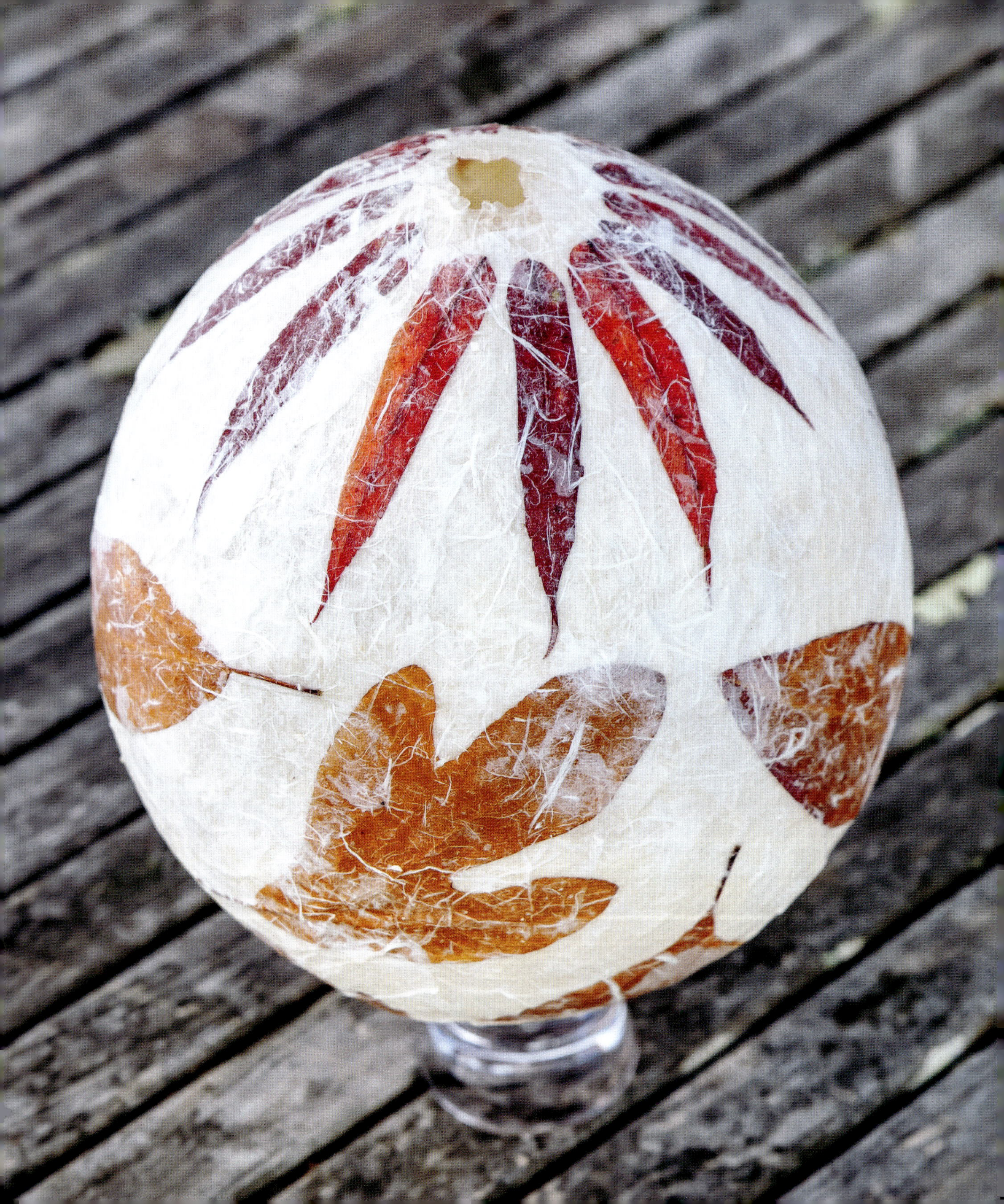

PAPIER-MÂCHÉ

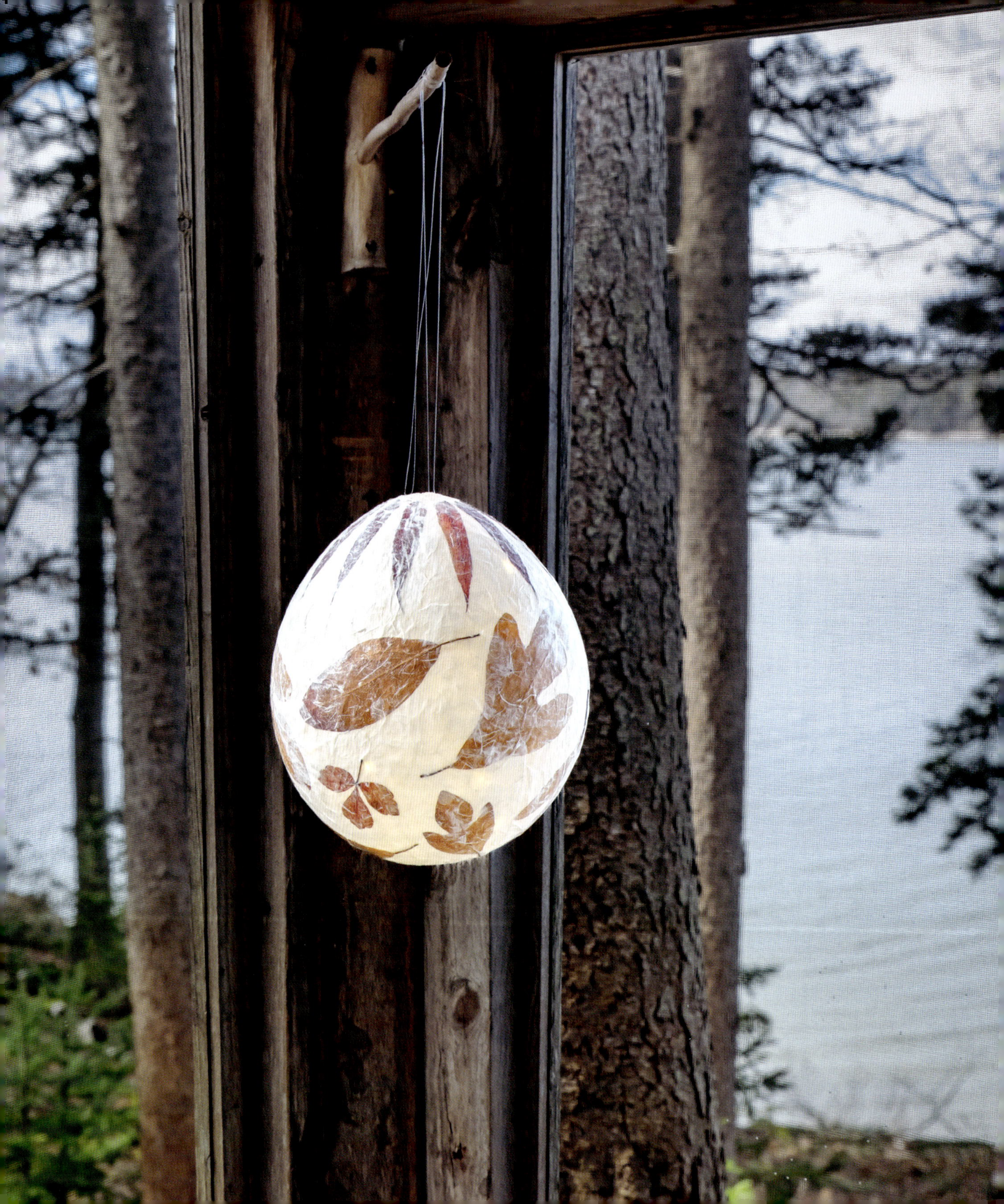

WHAT YOU NEED

- Fresh leaves
- Paper and books or a flower press
- Thin rice paper or a tissue-type paper
- Balloon
- Plastic cup or container
- Mod Podge decoupage glue or watered-down liquid PVA glue
- Small brush
- Scissors
- Dull knife or long spoon (optional)
- Utility knife
- Battery-powered fairy lights
- Large needle or awl (if hanging the lantern)
- String, fishing line, or wire for hanging (optional)

15

Leaf Lantern

While making this papier-mâché lantern, I became completely enamored with collecting fall leaves. I searched everywhere for perfect or perfectly interesting leaves. Oddly enough, though I live in the country and take my dog for daily walks in woods, the best leaves I found were in a drugstore parking lot. I did wonder if they were in such pristine condition precisely because they were in a parking lot and hadn't been ravaged by bugs.

The lantern can take a few days to make: you will need to flatten fresh leaves overnight, and each layer of papier-mâché must be dry before you add the next. That said, the process is straightforward and hugely satisfying. I used an inexpensive Japanese mulberry paper, but you can use tissue paper or even toilet paper or facial tissues.

The lantern can be any size. A balloon makes a good mold—although when I was experimenting with the papier-mâché process, one balloon completely collapsed before the project was done, so I had to start over. Maybe the problem was caused by a faulty knot, or perhaps I took too long and the balloon deflated over a few days, as some balloons are wont to do.

If you don't live in a part of the world where leaves turn color in autumn, or you don't want to wait for fall, you can make this project at any time of year using dried flowers or flattened leaves.

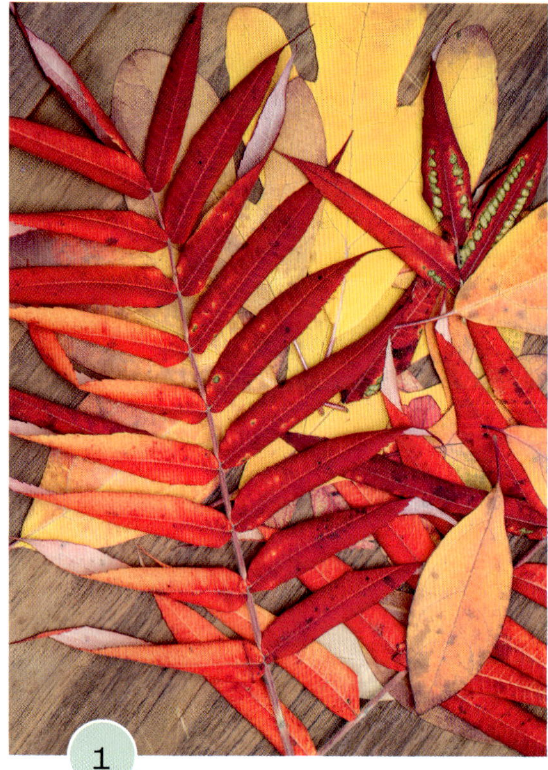

1

Select the Leaves

Collect fresh, flat leaves, many more than you think you will need. You have a design choice here: to use leaves of different sizes and shapes or to stick with just one type of leaf.

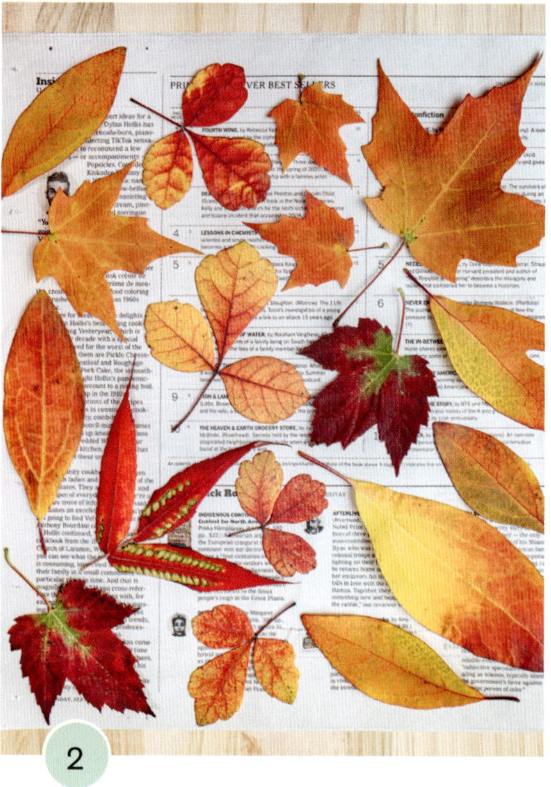

2

Flatten the Leaves

Sandwich your leaves between sheets of paper in a book or place them in a flower press. Flatten them overnight. Don't wait too long or they will become too dry and brittle to work with.

3

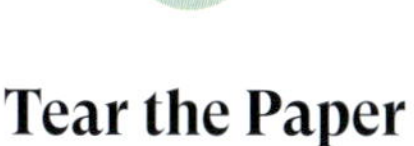

Tear the Paper

Tear your paper into strips. Any width and length will work, but about 1 inch wide and 6 inches long is a good place to start.

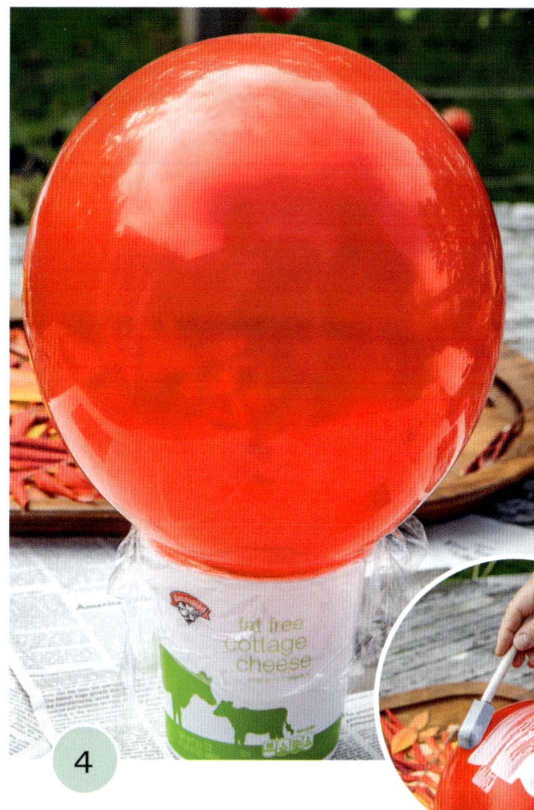

4

Coat Part of the Balloon

Blow up a balloon and set it on the open end of the plastic cup. Paint an area the size of about the size of your paper strip with a thin layer of glue. Warning! The balloon can get staticky and literally jump out of the cup or your hand, so carefully hold on to it tightly as you do the project. The advantage of resting the balloon on the plastic cup is that it's easy to unstick. As you move the balloon around on the cup to paste paper on different areas, the strips can dry without sticking to your work surface.

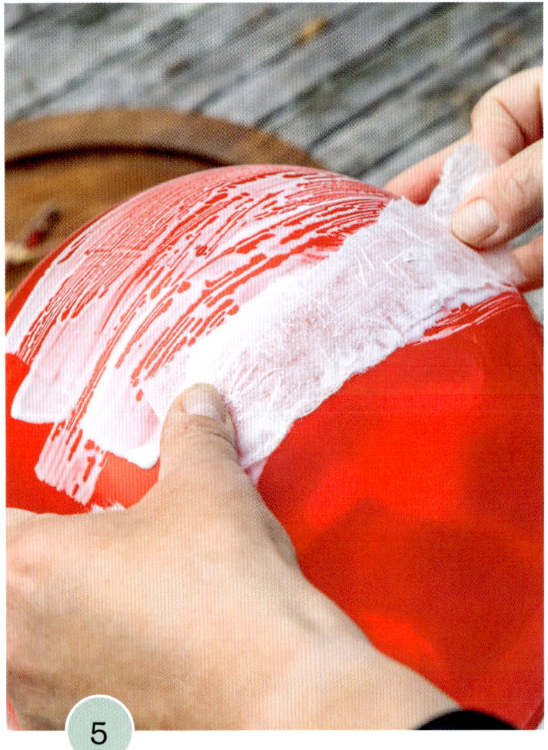

Apply a Strip of Paper

Place a paper strip on top of the glue, smoothing it as you go.

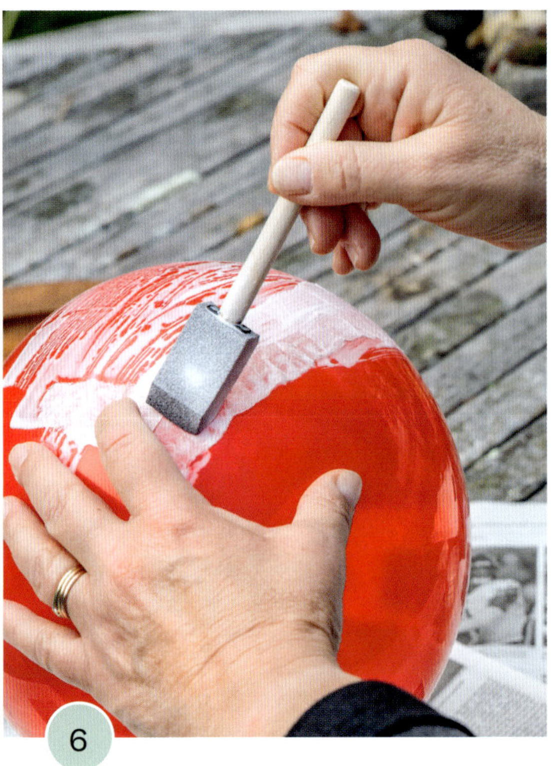

Coat the Strip

Paint a thin layer of glue on top of the paper strip.

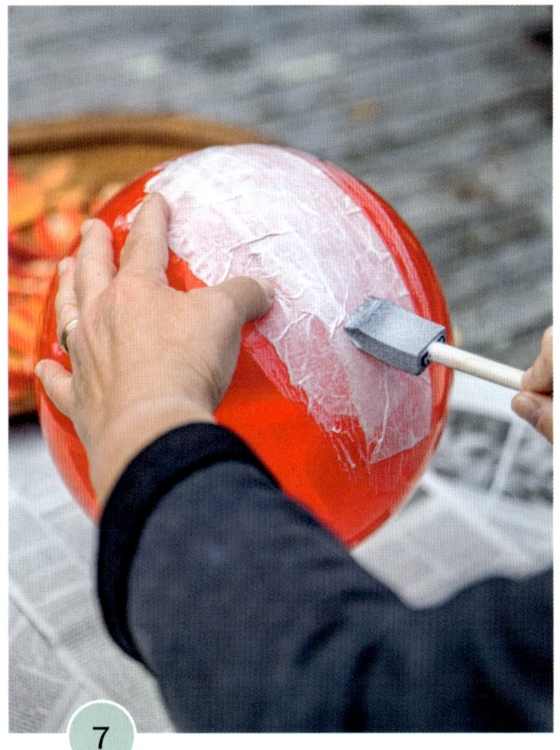
7

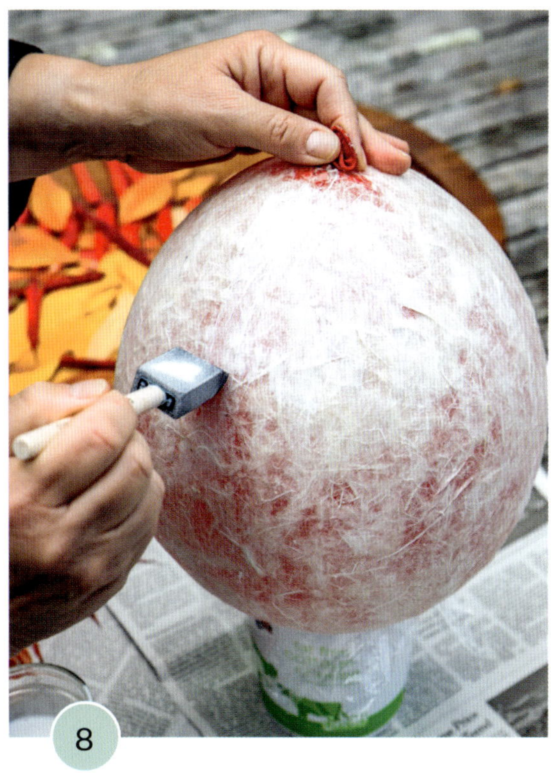
8

Cover the Balloon

Continue painting glue on the balloon, then laying on overlapping paper strips, then painting over the strips with glue until the balloon is covered. As you layer, leave an area free of papier-mâché around the knot. The size of this area will depend on what kind of light you want to insert in the lantern, and whether you want to hang it or use it on a table. Leave the coated balloon undisturbed on its cup until it feels dry to the touch. This could take anywhere from 30 minutes to several hours depending on the paper, the humidity, and how much glue you have used.

Apply More Paper Layers

Repeat step 7 until you have at least four layers of glue and paper, making sure to let each layer dry before applying the next.

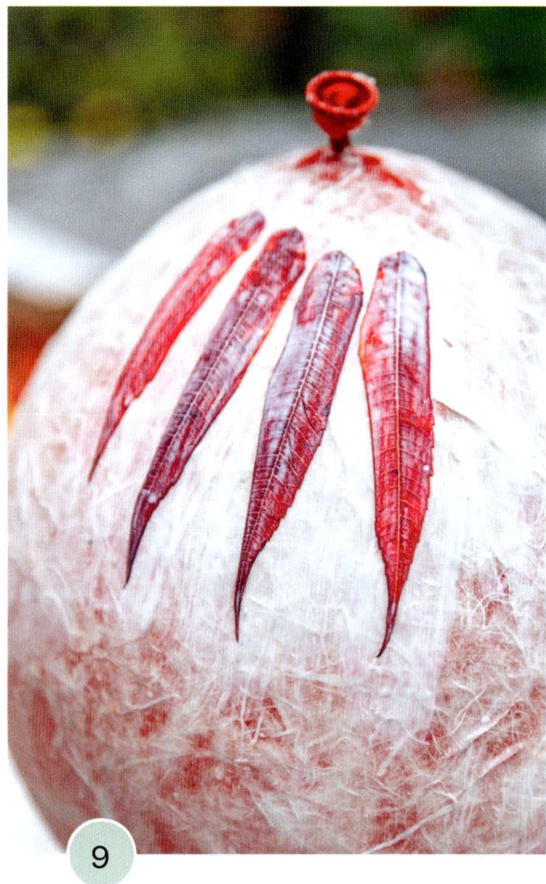

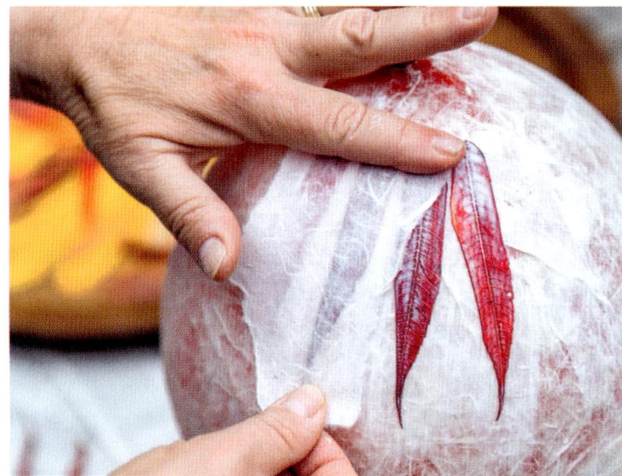

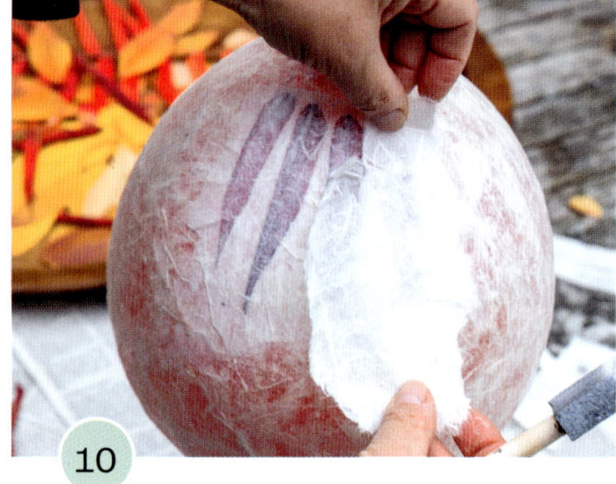

Apply a Leaf

Paint a thin layer of glue on the balloon and place one leaf—or several, depending on their size—on top of the glue.

Coat the Leaf

Paint a thin layer of glue on top of the leaf. Place a piece of torn paper on top of the coated leaf.

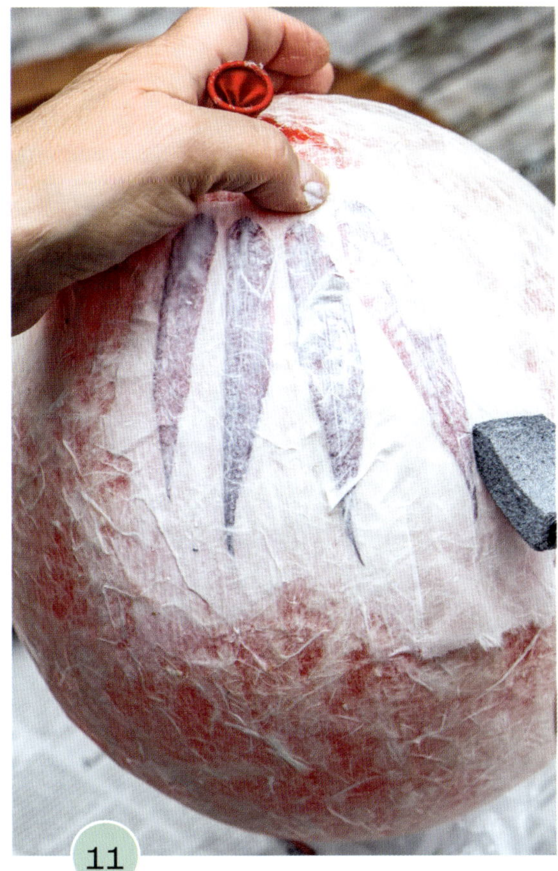

Coat the Paper

Apply a thin layer of glue on top of the paper that is over the leaf or leaves.

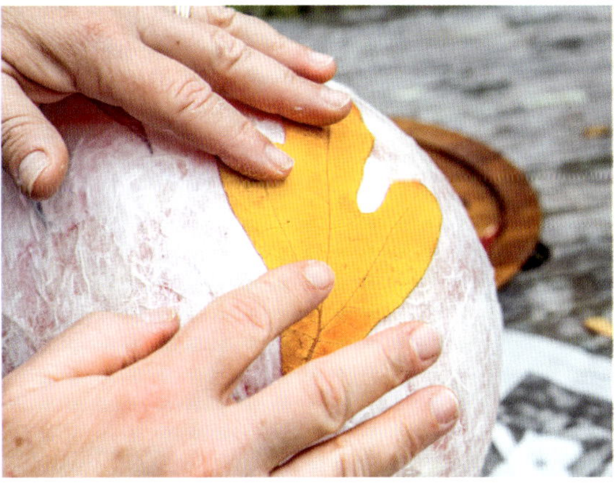

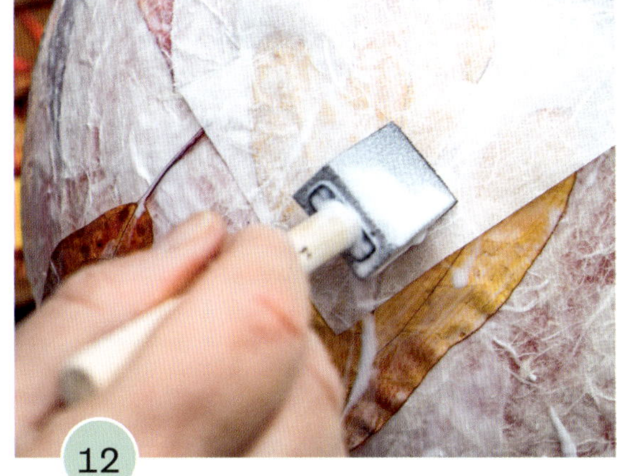

Continue Adding Leaves

Continue adding leaves, paper, and layers of glue until you are happy with your design. Let dry completely. Note: After the glue dries, it becomes more translucent, and the leaves' colors become more vivid.

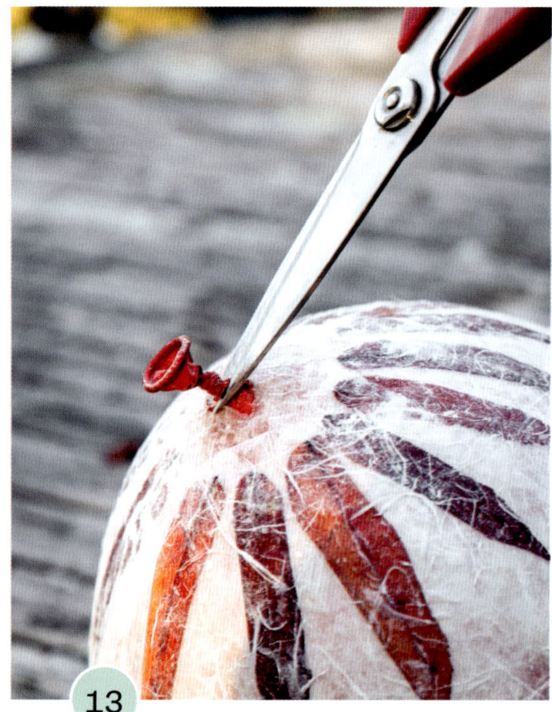

13

Pop the Balloon

Once you're happy with the lantern, cut the balloon below the knot. If the balloon doesn't pop and deflate by itself, you may have to take a dull knife or long spoon to help gently peel the balloon off the inside of your now-hardened shell. Discard the deflated balloon once you have freed it from the lantern.

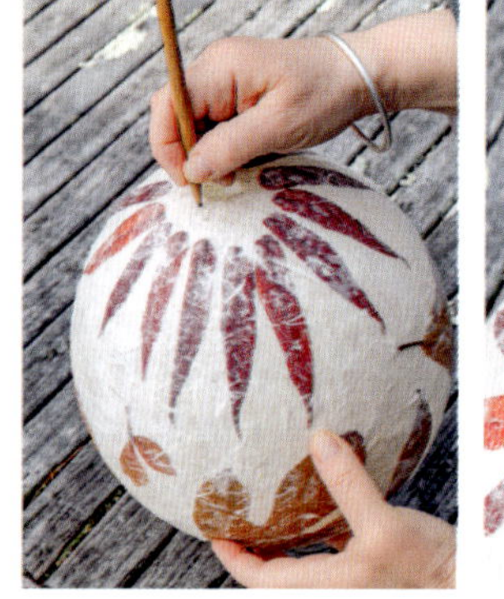

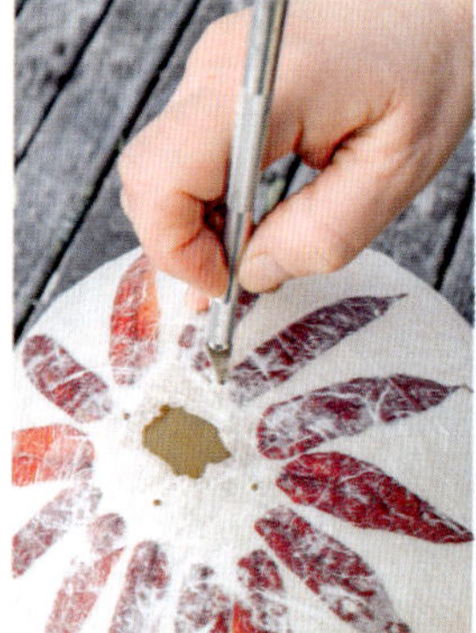

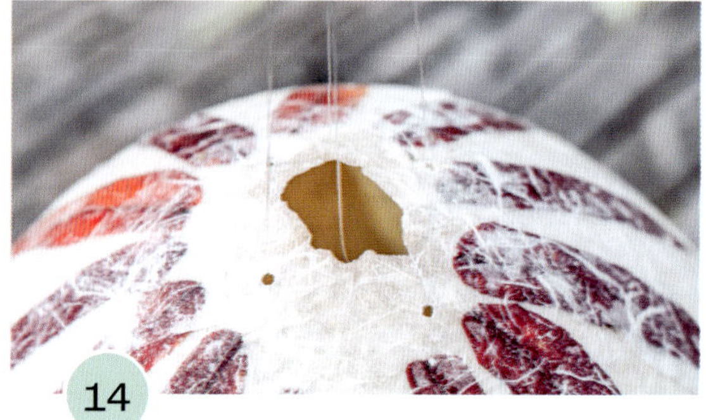

14

Enlarge the Hole

If you need more space to insert lights, mark a hole with a pencil, then use a utility knife to carefully cut the papier-mâché to your desired shape. If you want to hang your lantern, poke three or four small holes in your lamp with the needle or awl and attach the string, fishing line, or wire.

15 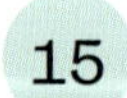

Add the Lights

Insert the fairy lights and hang, or simply place on top of a bowl.

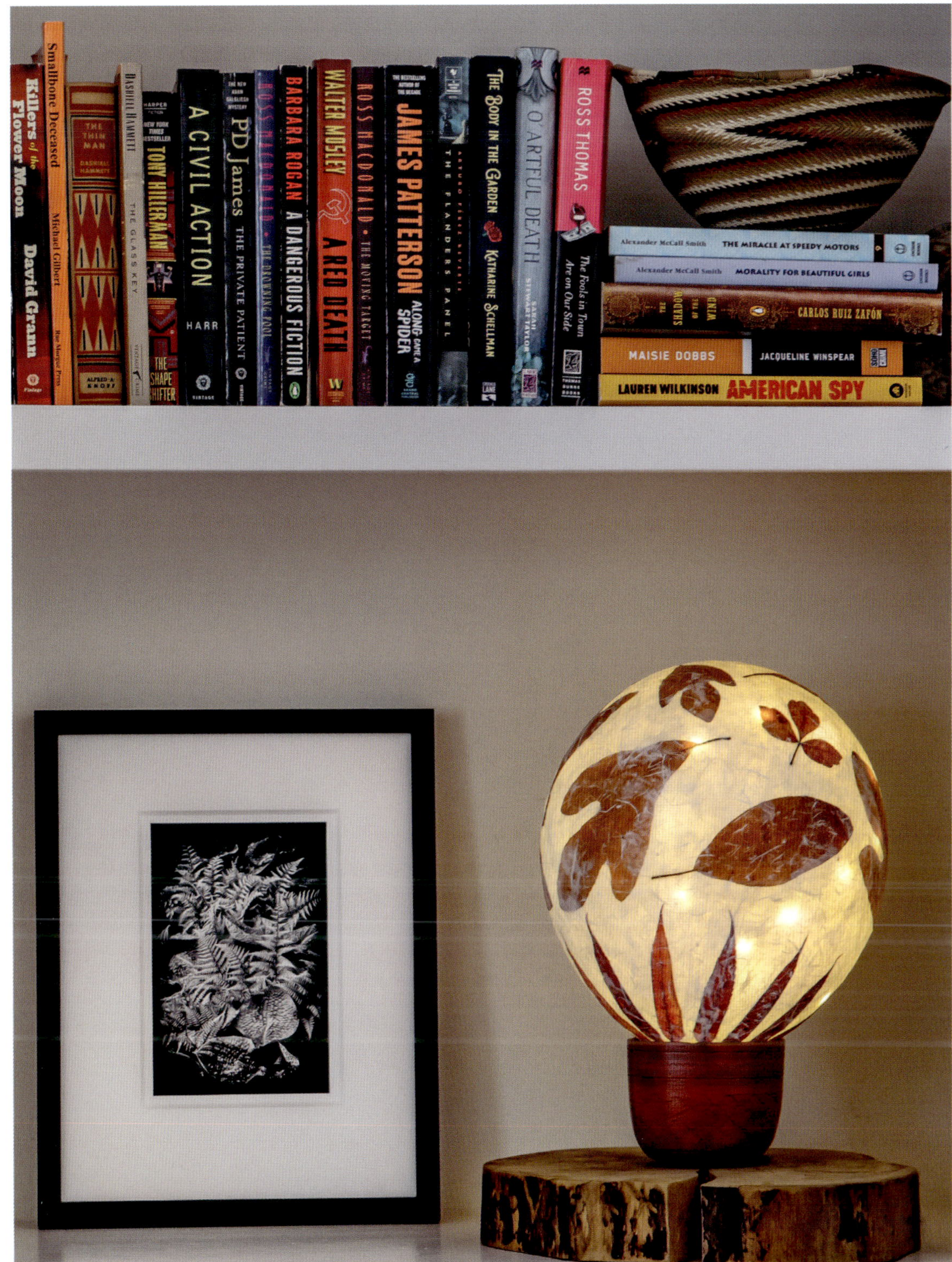
Killers of the Flower Moon
David Grann
Smallbone Deceased
Michael Gilbert
THE THIN MAN
DASHIELL HAMMETT
ALFRED A. KNOPF
DASHIELL HAMMETT
THE GLASS KEY
TONY HILLERMAN
THE SHAPE SHIFTER
A CIVIL ACTION
HARR
PD James
THE PRIVATE PATIENT
ROSS MACDONALD
THE DROWNING POOL
BARBARA ROGAN
A DANGEROUS FICTION
WALTER MOSLEY
A RED DEATH
ROSS MACDONALD
THE MOVING TARGET
JAMES PATTERSON
ALONG CAME A SPIDER
THE FLANDERS PANEL
THE BODY IN THE GARDEN
KATHARINE SCHELLMAN
O'ARTFUL DEATH
SARAH STEWART TAYLOR
ROSS THOMAS
The Fools in Town Are on Our Side
Alexander McCall Smith
THE MIRACLE AT SPEEDY MOTORS
Alexander McCall Smith
MORALITY FOR BEAUTIFUL GIRLS
CARLOS RUIZ ZAFÓN
MAISIE DOBBS
JACQUELINE WINSPEAR
LAUREN WILKINSON
AMERICAN SPY

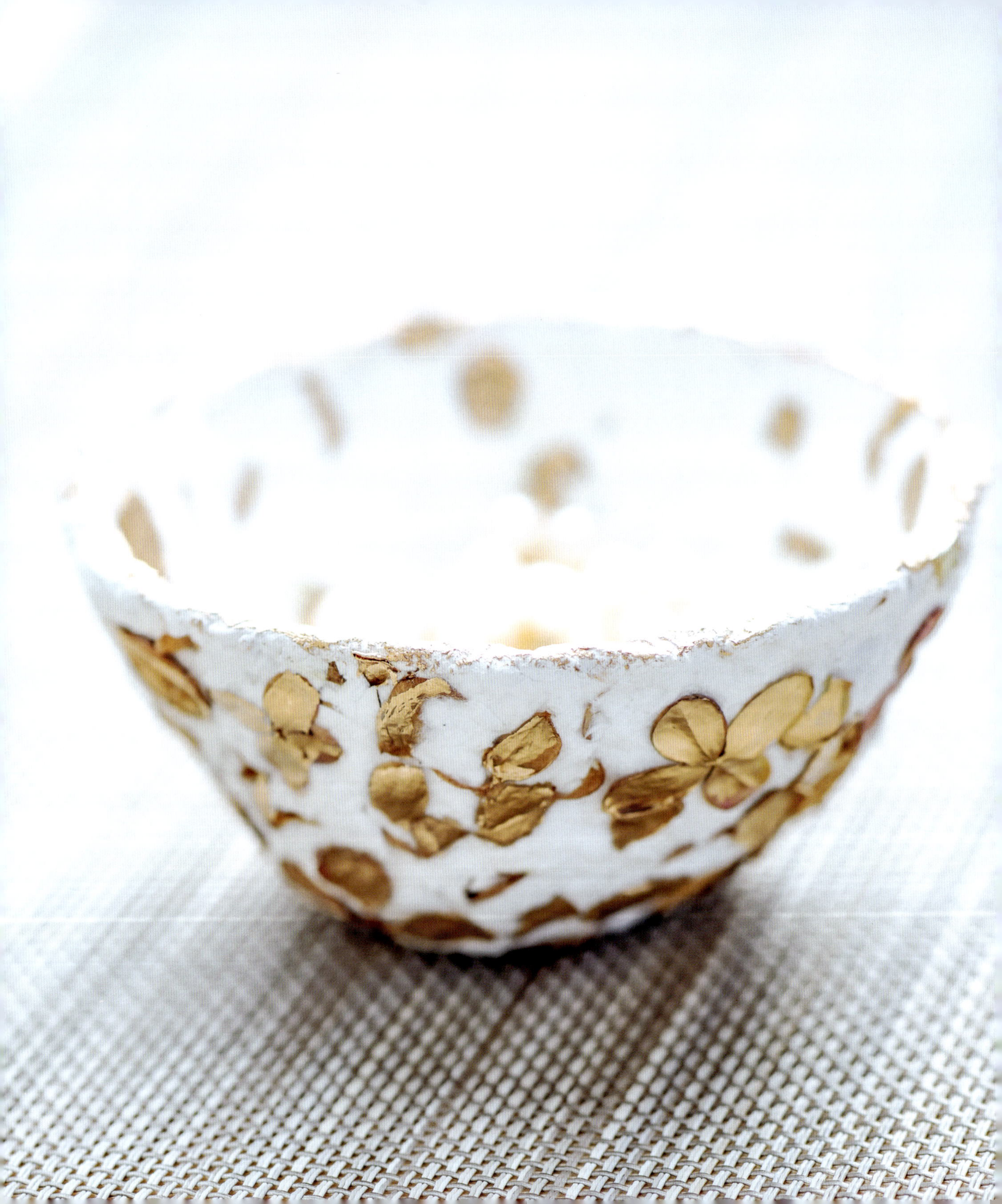

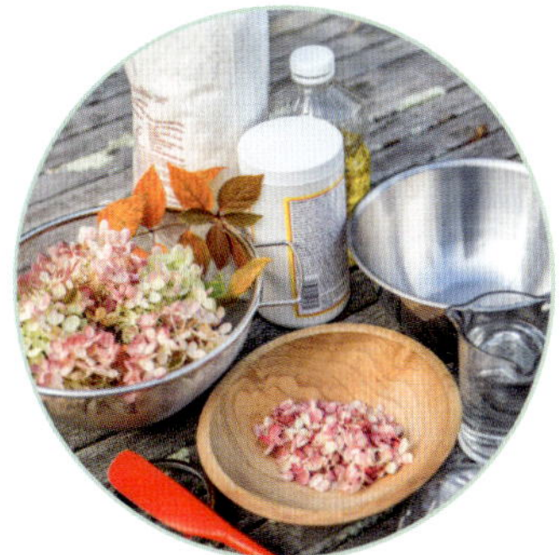

WHAT YOU NEED

- Dried hydrangeas
- Bowl for mold (plastic, glass, or ceramic is fine, or use the top of an inflated balloon)
- Plastic wrap (optional)
- Vegetable oil (optional)
- Water
- Large mixing bowl
- Bag of instant papier-mâché pulp
- Spoon
- Liquid PVA glue (optional)
- Butter knife or silicone spatula
- Jar or bottle
- Metallic paint or gilding (optional)

16

Hydrangea Bowl

I love that you can create lightweight and relatively durable vessels quickly and without much difficulty with papier-mâché. Using this incredibly flexible medium is reminiscent of the childhood pleasure of making mud pies. While you can create papier-mâché using the technique in the previous project, you can also combine paper and cardboard in a blender and make your own pulp. Or just buy a bag of instant papier-mâché, which is paper that has been pulverized into a lovely fluffy fuzz to which you simply add water and voilà, you have a substance that is relatively easy to form into bowls. The size and shape of your papier-mâché vessel is limited only by your ingenuity and patience. The finished product can be painted, gilded, decoupaged, or left as is.

I found making flower bowls to be somewhat of a delightful crapshoot. As the bowls dried, the colors from some flowers, even if dried, would bleed. The results were often beautiful, but sometimes red flowers turned the papier-mâché brown, and purple flowers turned black.

When I tried hydrangeas, I discovered that they didn't bleed as much as softer flowers, and often they remained pretty true to color. Sometimes, however, even the hydrangeas turned brown. Happily, if you aren't pleased with the final colors, you can use gold or silver paint to cover them.

You can use almost anything for a mold. I like using a cheap, lightweight, clear plastic bowl that I can always break if I have trouble releasing the dried papier-mâché. Using a clear mold—plastic or glass—also allows you to see the inside of your bowl to check for thin areas, holes, or cracks in the papier-mâché.

If you can, keep the bowl inverted for the whole process until the outside is dry to the touch. If you flip it over while the papier-mâché is still wet, chances are great that the whole thing will completely fall apart.

A cautionary note: Papier-mâché pulp produces a fair amount of dust, no matter how careful you are. The package claims that this dust is safe and nontoxic, but I still don't want to breathe it in. If possible, do the dusty bits (steps 2 and 3) outside, wearing a face mask. Also if it's windy, keep your pulp downwind so it doesn't get blown in your face.

The following recipe is enough to cover a 6-inch-diameter bowl with ¼ inch of papier-mâché.

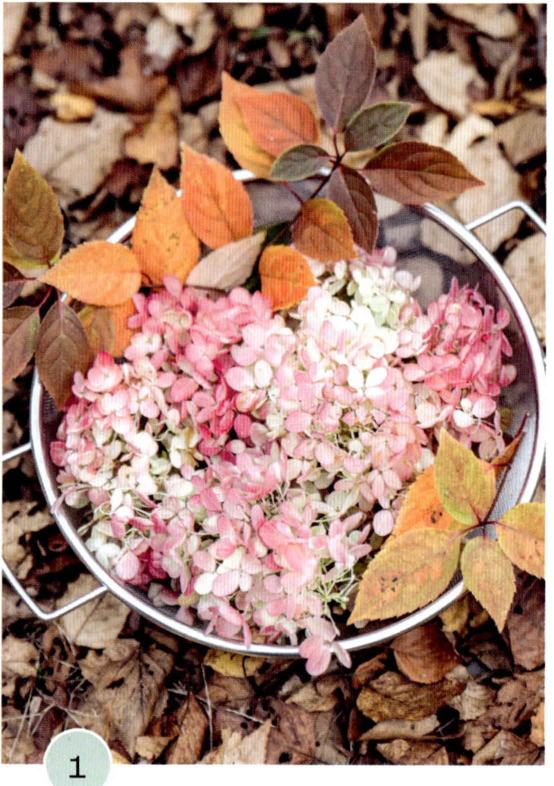

1

Separate the Hydrangeas

Separate the dry hydrangeas heads into florets. For my project, I used panicle (also called Pee-Gee) hydrangeas that had turned a soft pink in fall, when they were gathered.

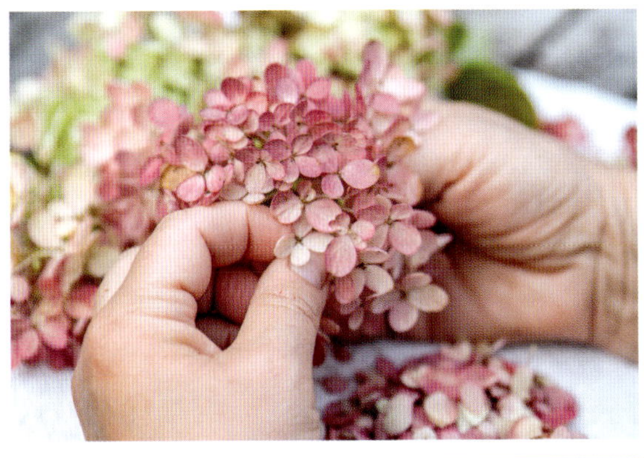

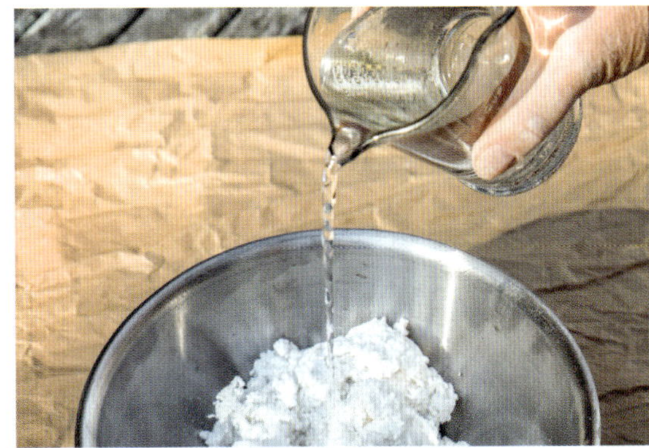

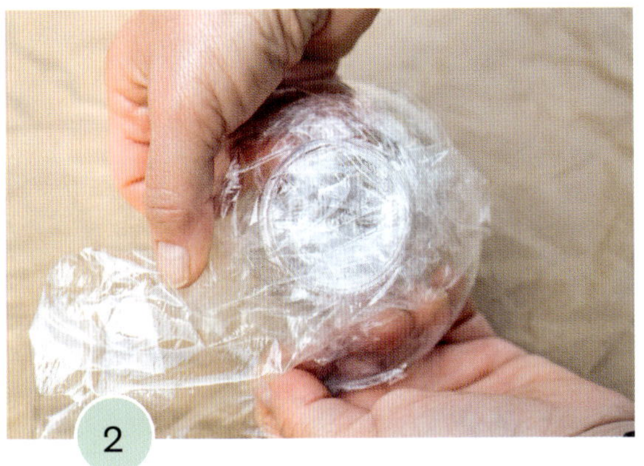

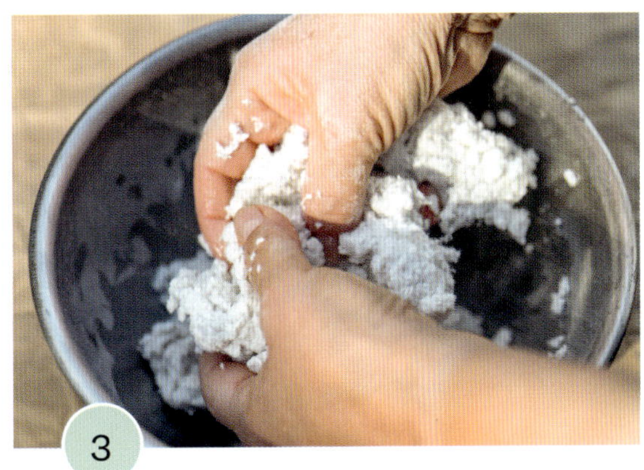

2

Cover the Mold, if Desired

You may want to cover your mold in plastic wrap to keep the papier-mâché from sticking to it. Before applying the wrap, spread a very thin layer of vegetable oil all over the outside of the mold; this will help to release your finished plastic wrap–lined bowl after it has dried. If using plastic wrap, tightly cover the outside of the bowl completely, tucking the excess inside. There will be wrinkles, but try to minimize them as much as possible.

3

Mix the Papier-Mâché

Working outside, if possible, place ½ cup of water in the large mixing bowl. Grab a handful of paper pulp and stir it into the water. Add an additional two or three handfuls of pulp, depending on the size of your mold, mixing it with the water as you go. If the mixture feels dry, add more water. It should feel like a shaggy bread dough. You want a consistency you can shape into a ball and that is easy to work with and holds together. There is huge latitude here, so whatever feels good to you will probably work. You can also stir in a few tablespoons of PVA glue at this point to help coat the flowers so they may bleed a little less. At this point, the dusty part of the project should be over, and you can move inside if you choose.

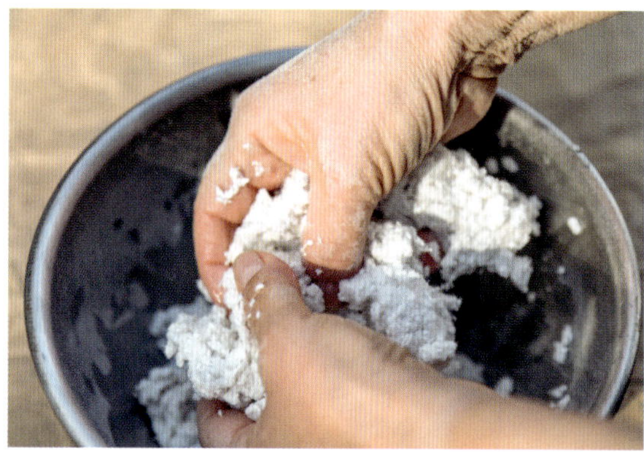

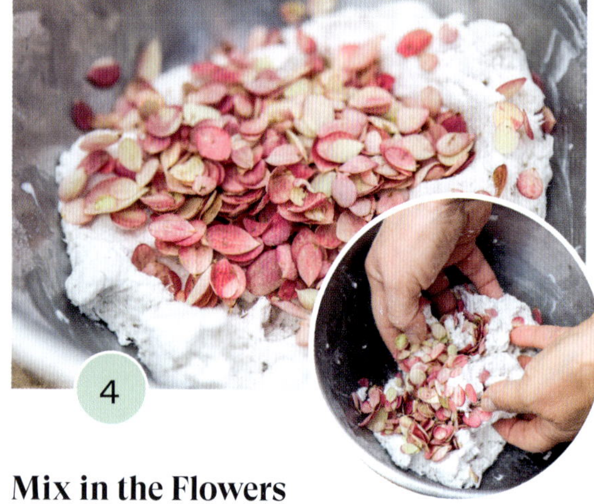

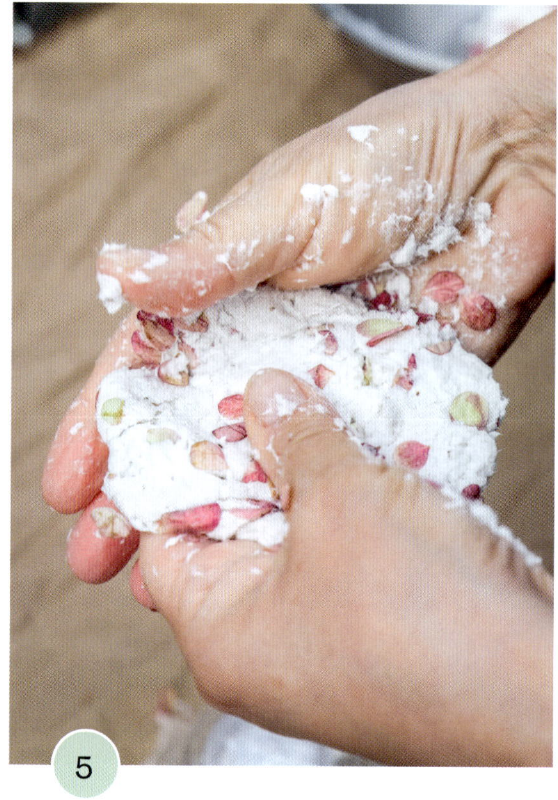

Mix in the Flowers

Gently knead the flowers into the papier-mâché. Include enough so that you can see the flowers, but don't add so many that you compromise the integrity of the papier-mâché. The amount of flowers is really guesswork, but the key thing is that the mixture should still be able to hold together when formed into a ball.

Form a Disc

Take a handful of the flower-papier-mâché mixture and form it into a flat disc about ¼ inch thick, making sure there is a fairly even distribution of flowers.

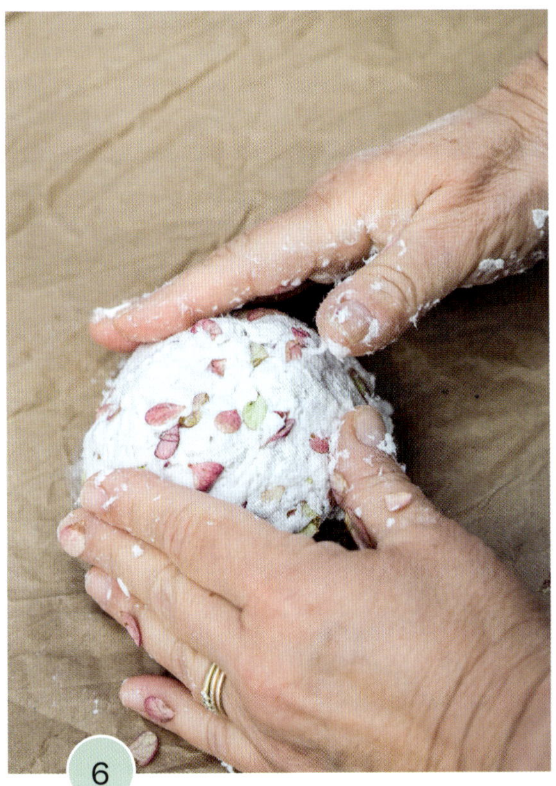
6

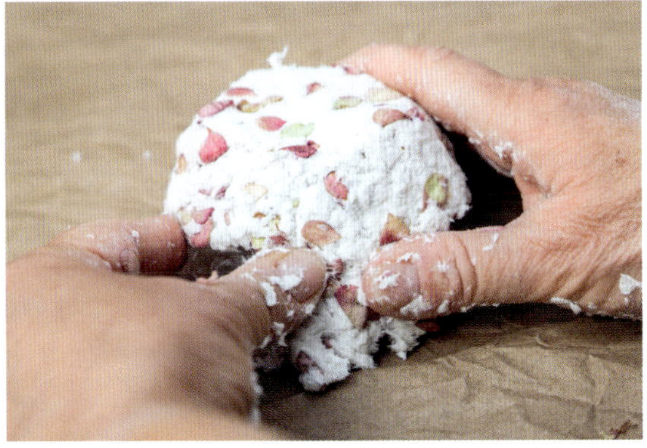

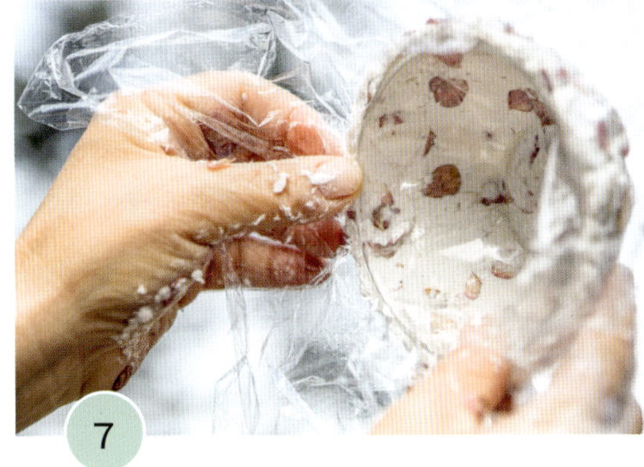
7

Form the Bowl

Press the disc over the bottom of the prepared bowl, and press it until it tightly hugs the shape of the mold.

Apply More Material

Add more of the flower-papier-mâché mixture until the entire mold is covered with about ¼ inch. Try to keep the thickness as uniform as possible, looking for and filling holes and cracks as you go. If you have used a clear bowl as the mold, you can hold it up to the light, which makes holes or thin spots easy to see.

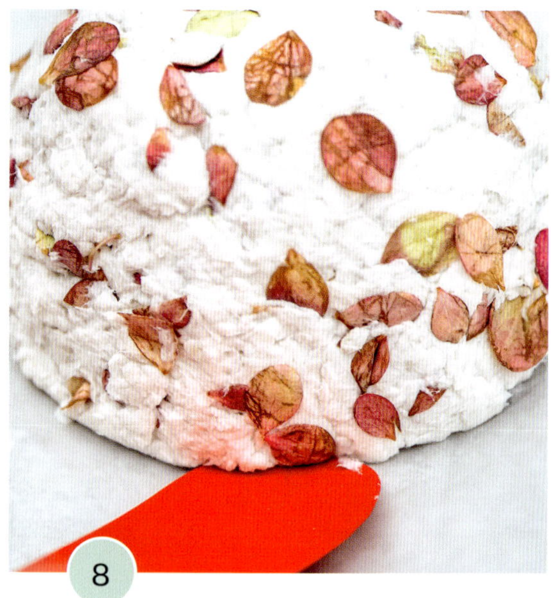

8

Smooth and Let Dry

Using the butter knife or silicone spatula, flatten any blossoms that are sticking out. Cut or press the lip of your bowl so it is flat and uniform. At this point, you may want to press additional blossoms into the outside of your bowl; be sure to press them in firmly so they stick. Then let the bowl dry inverted on a jar or bottle so the lip of the bowl doesn't stick to the work surface. When it feels dry to the touch—this can take a few days depending on temperature and humidity—gently pull the mold and plastic wrap out of the bowl.

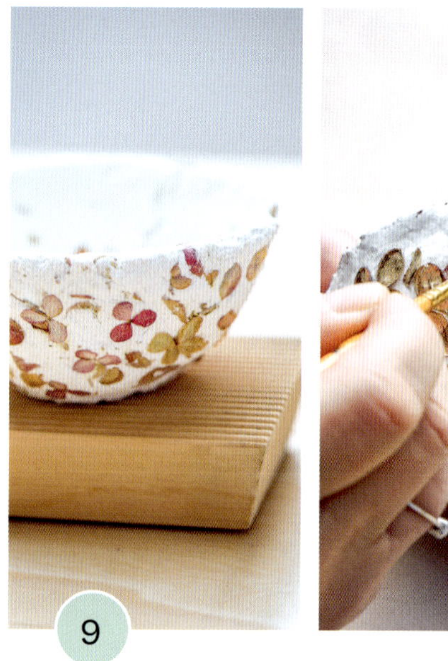

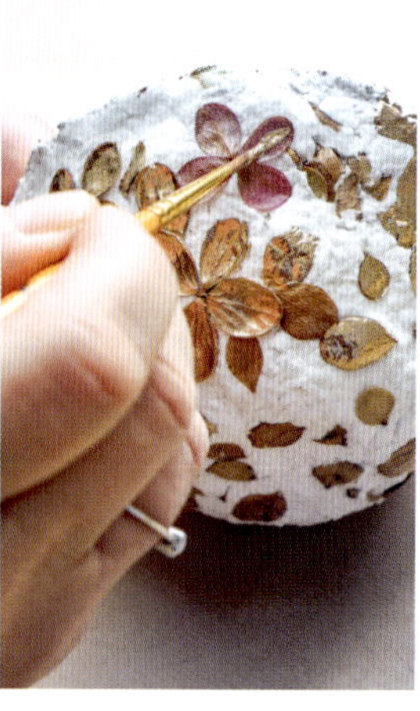

9

Paint or Gild (Optional)

If you are happy with your bowl, you can stop here. However, if your flowers have turned brown, or you just feel like adding a little bling, you can paint your blossoms with metallic paint.

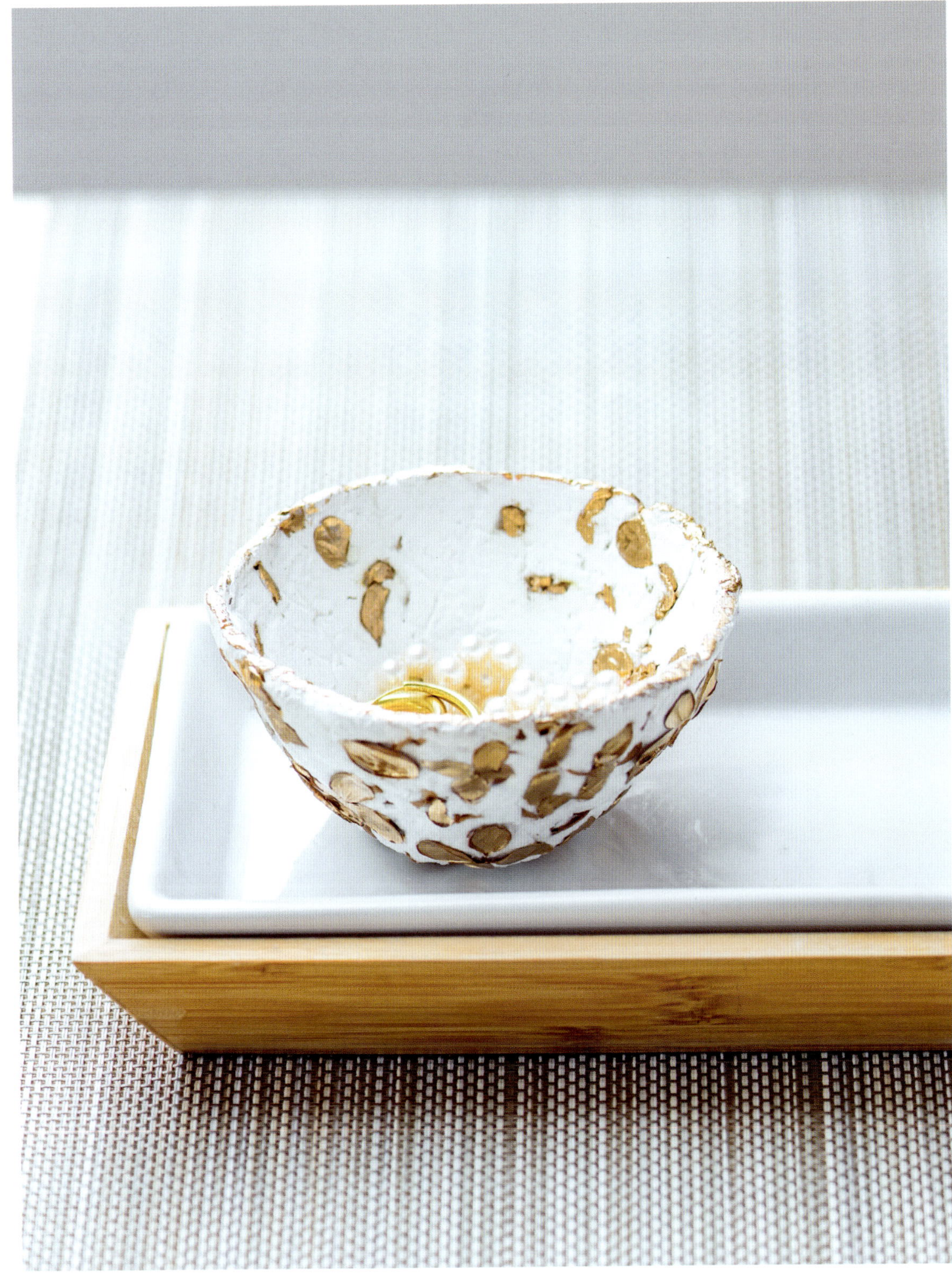

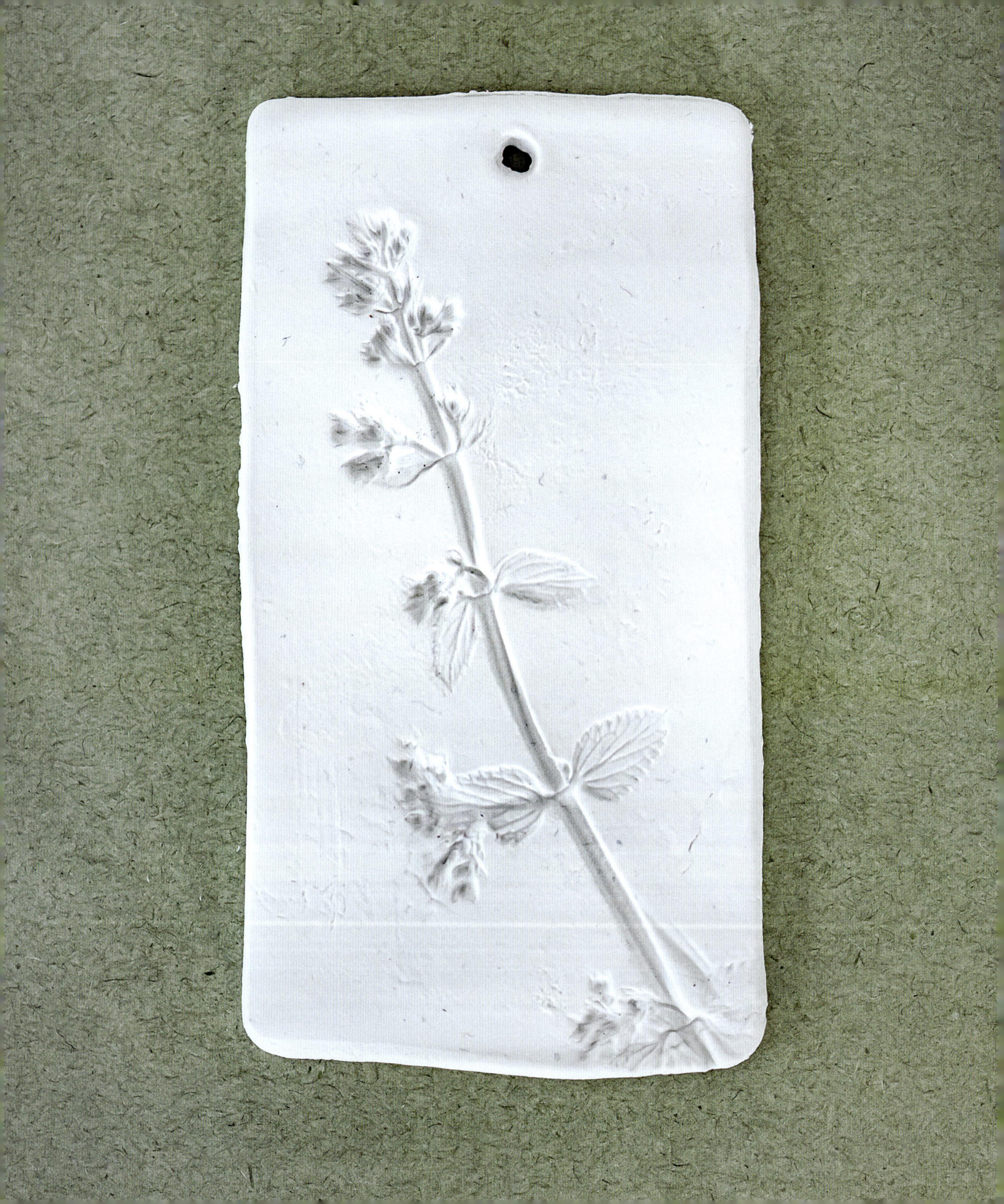

AIR-DRY CLAY

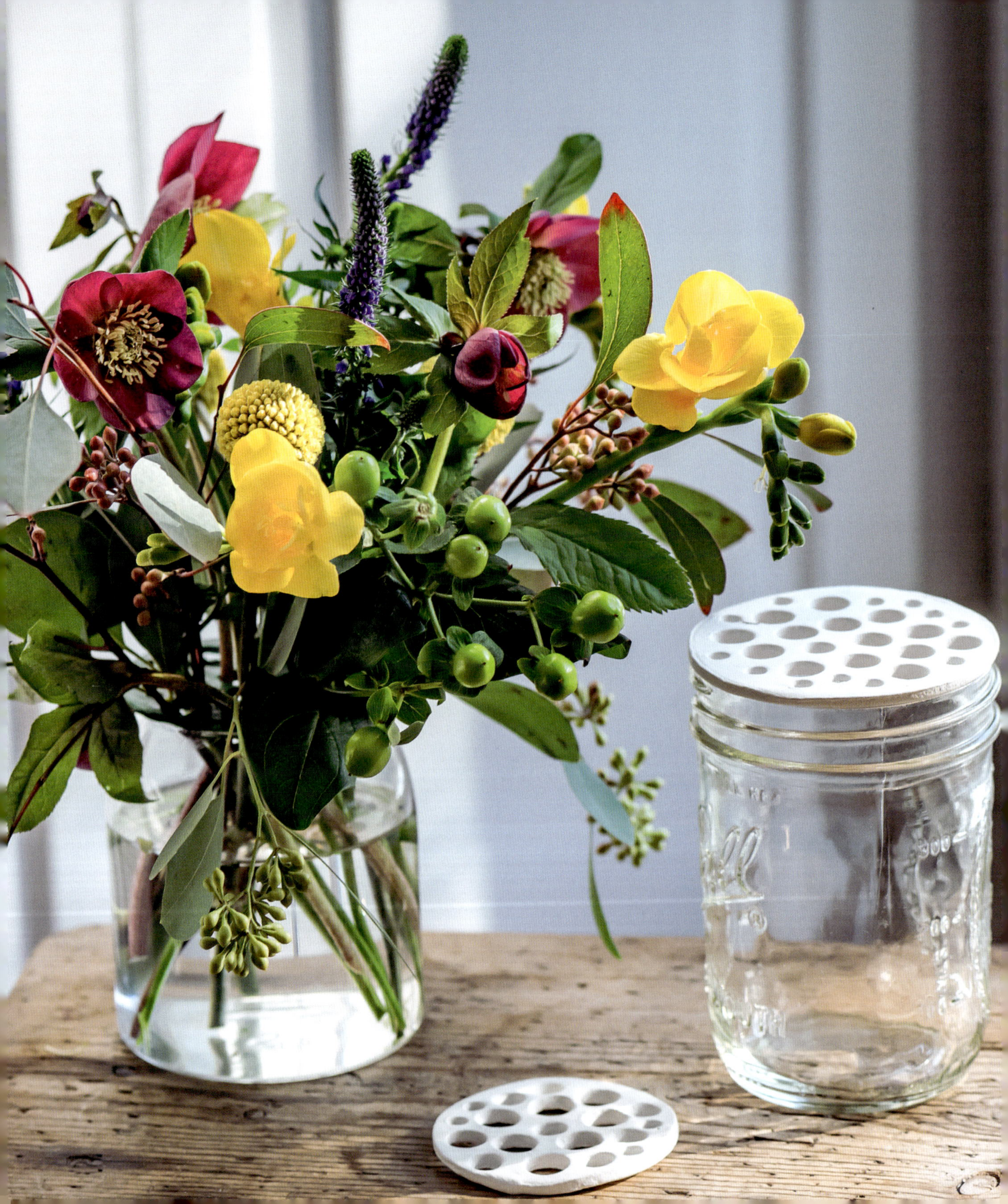

WHAT YOU NEED

- Air-dry clay
- Smooth work surface: cutting board wrapped in waxed paper or freezer paper; silicone baking mat; plastic mat; or waxed paper taped to a surface
- Mason jar or vase
- Small jar with water
- Rolling pin, straight-sided bottle, or clay roller
- Clay pin tool or knife
- Metal or stiff plastic straws (in different widths, if desired)
- Skewer or toothpick (optional)
- Acrylic paint (optional)
- Acrylic sealer (optional)

17

Flower Frog

No one seems to know definitively why flower frogs are called frogs. One plausible explanation is that they are traditionally placed underwater. Whatever the reason, this project's frogs share few similarities with amphibians or traditional flower frogs, as they sit on top of a vessel, not underwater inside it. However, they work well in doing what they are intended to do, which is to secure flowers into an arrangement and help provide structure without resorting to the use of environmentally damaging flower foam.

These frogs are created with air-dry clay, which is a lightweight material that requires few tools and is fairly easy to work with. You can leave the clay as it comes in white, gray, or terra-cotta or paint it with acrylics. When dry, it is relatively durable, though it needs to be treated with a sealant or acrylic spray to withstand moisture.

Make your frog in any shape you choose, and it can be concave, convex, or flat. The clay shrinks a bit as it dries, so take that into consideration when cutting out your shape. These frogs work particularly well with dried flowers because they separate the botanicals a bit and can help organize what otherwise may become a tangle of stems. To use your frog to arrange fresh flowers, it's a good idea to seal it first.

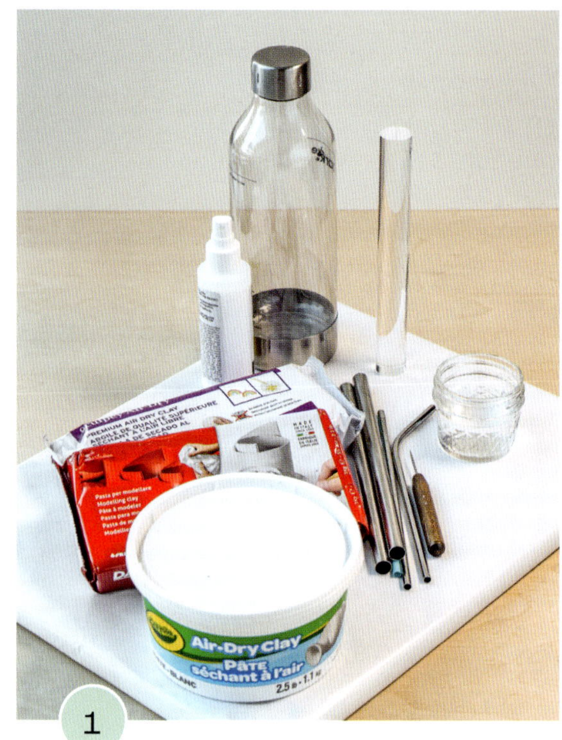

1

Prep Your Workspace

Air-dry clays vary tremendously in stickiness. The more expensive clays tend to be less sticky and therefore easier to work with. The trick when setting up your workspace is to find a surface to work on that will minimize your clay sticking. A good option is to cover a board with waxed paper or freezer paper, wrapping it tightly and securely taping the paper to the back. Other good surfaces to work on include silicone baking mats or a plastic mat.

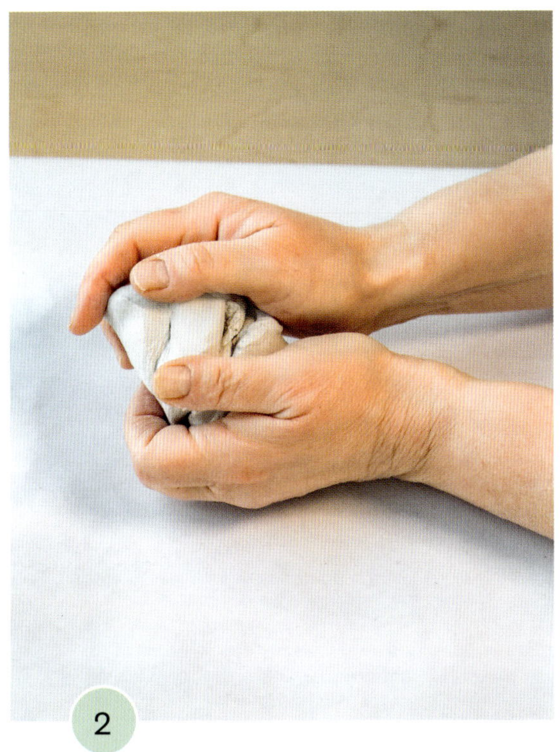

2

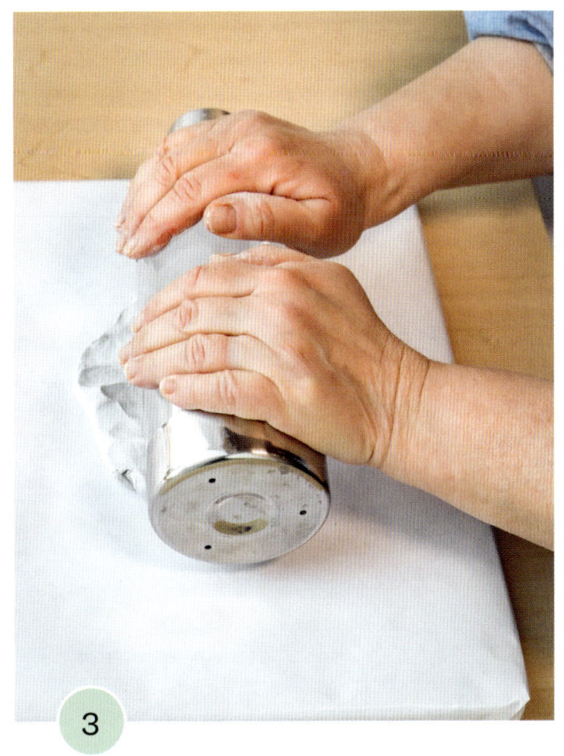

3

Knead the Clay

Start by tearing off a hunk of clay the size of your fist and resealing the unused clay so it doesn't dry out. The exact amount of clay you'll need depends on how thick you want your frog as well as the size of the opening in your jar or vase. It may take a bit of trial and error to get the right amount, but you are better off starting with too much than too little. Don't worry if you have excess; you can use it in the future. Knead the clay until it is smooth and uniform in texture and then roll it into a ball. If the clay feels dry or too stiff, wet your hands with water and knead it in.

Roll the Clay

Flatten the clay ball with your hands. Now start rolling the clay, keeping the pressure even throughout each roll. Roll in several directions until you have a disc of uniform thickness and big enough to cover the mouth of your jar or vase. A thickness between ¼ and ⅛ inch works well.

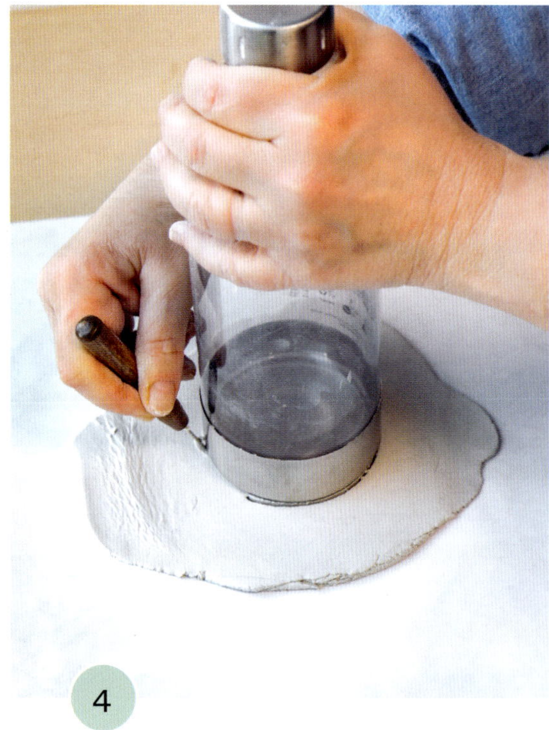

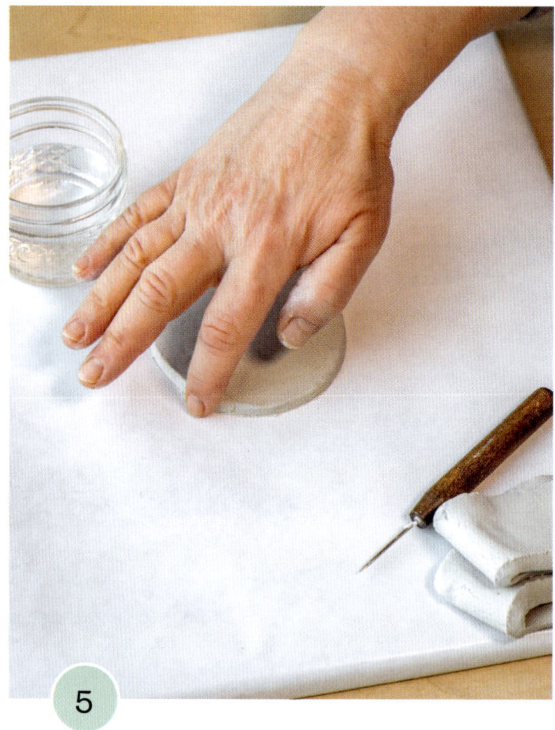

4

Cut the Shape

Using the clay pin tool or a knife, cut out a round, square, or free-form shape. Keep in mind that as the clay dries, it will shrink a bit. If you are fitting the frog to a jar or vase, you can use the top as a template, cutting around the outside and making sure to leave a little excess.

5

Smooth the Edges

Put a little water on your fingers and smooth out any rough edges.

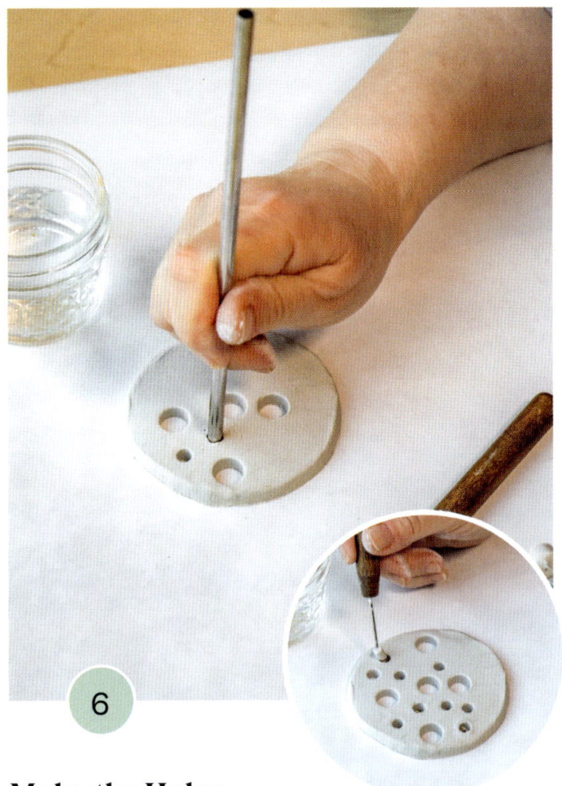

6

Make the Holes

Metal straws work best here, though if you don't have them, stiff plastic works just fine. Dip a straw in water, then press it into the clay to make holes. Rotating the straw as you press down helps make a clean cut. You can arrange the holes in a pattern or scatter them randomly and use different- or same-sized straws. Keep in mind that the larger the hole, the more options you will have for different-sized stems. Sometimes when you make a hole, the center of the hole sticks to your work surface. When it does, carefully pick or pry it out with the clay pin tool, skewer, or toothpick. You can use the same tool to pick clay out of the straw, if a piece gets stuck.

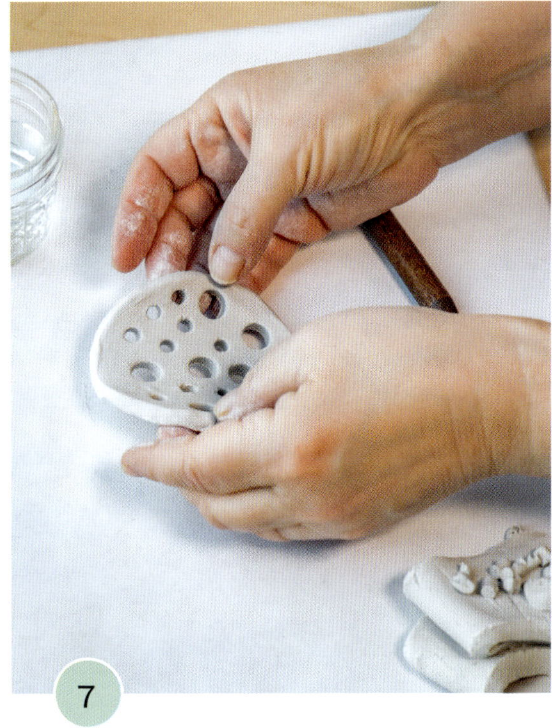

7

Dry It

Your frog will be wet and flexible at this point, so carefully lift it by the edge and peel it off the surface. You may have to smooth out anything that gets misshapen in the process. Place it on a piece of waxed or freezer paper to dry. Once it is leather hard on one side, carefully turn it over so the other side can dry. Keep flipping it over and flattening as it dries to prevent the edges from curling. Drying time will depend on temperature, type of clay, humidity, and thickness of your frog, but expect it to take one to several days to completely dry.

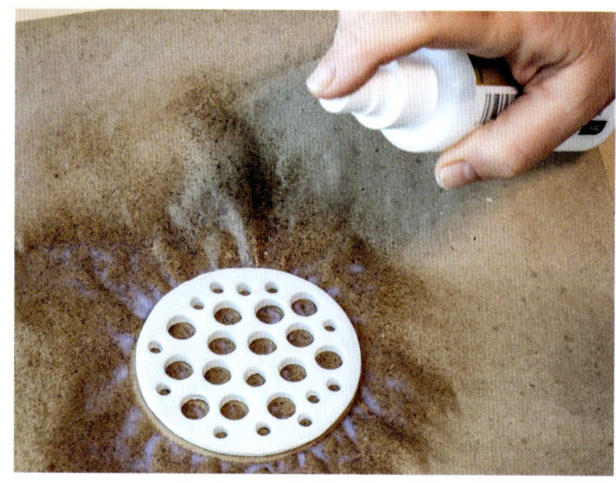

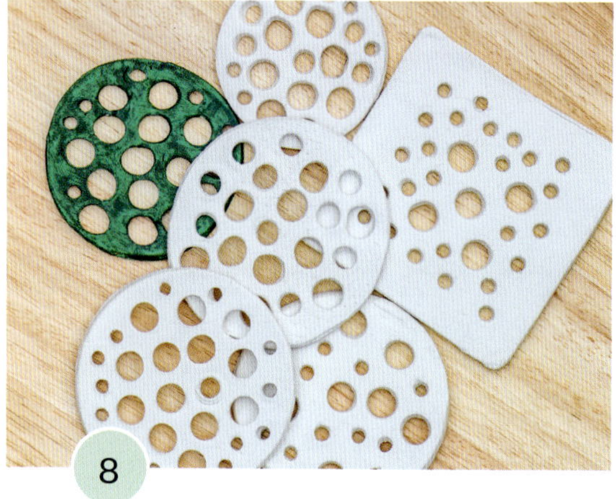

8

Seal It (Optional)

Once your frog is dry, if you choose to, you can paint it with acrylic paint and then spray it with an acrylic sealer.

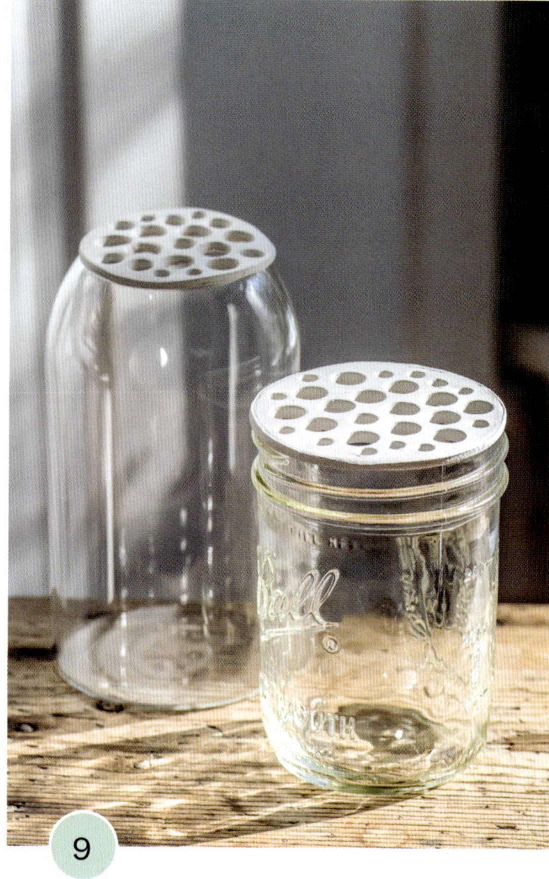

9

Arrange

Place the frog on your jar, vase, or vessel. Frogs are lightweight, and yours may slide around until you have inserted enough flowers and greens to hold it in place.

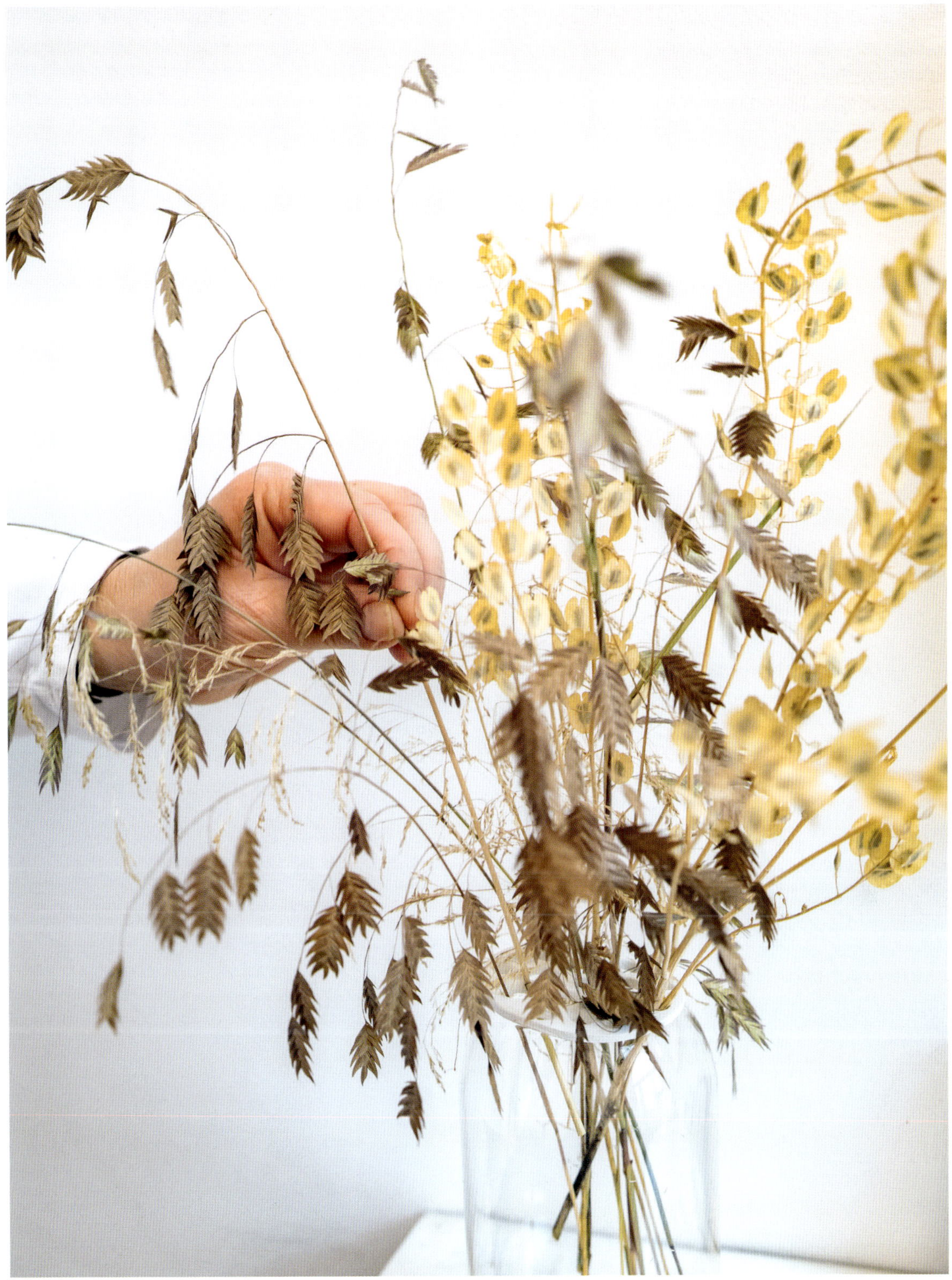

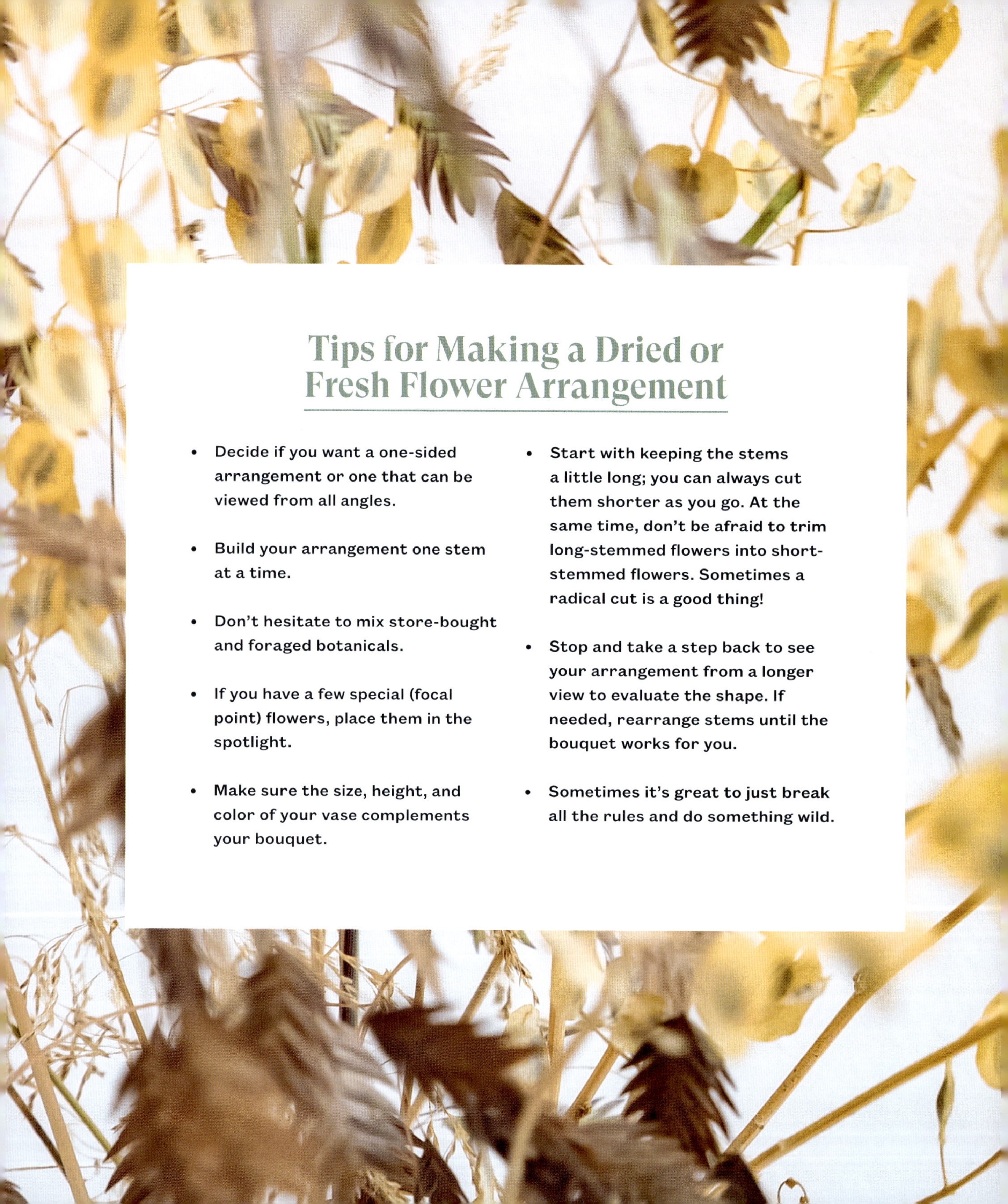

Tips for Making a Dried or Fresh Flower Arrangement

- Decide if you want a one-sided arrangement or one that can be viewed from all angles.
- Build your arrangement one stem at a time.
- Don't hesitate to mix store-bought and foraged botanicals.
- If you have a few special (focal point) flowers, place them in the spotlight.
- Make sure the size, height, and color of your vase complements your bouquet.
- Start with keeping the stems a little long; you can always cut them shorter as you go. At the same time, don't be afraid to trim long-stemmed flowers into short-stemmed flowers. Sometimes a radical cut is a good thing!
- Stop and take a step back to see your arrangement from a longer view to evaluate the shape. If needed, rearrange stems until the bouquet works for you.
- Sometimes it's great to just break all the rules and do something wild.

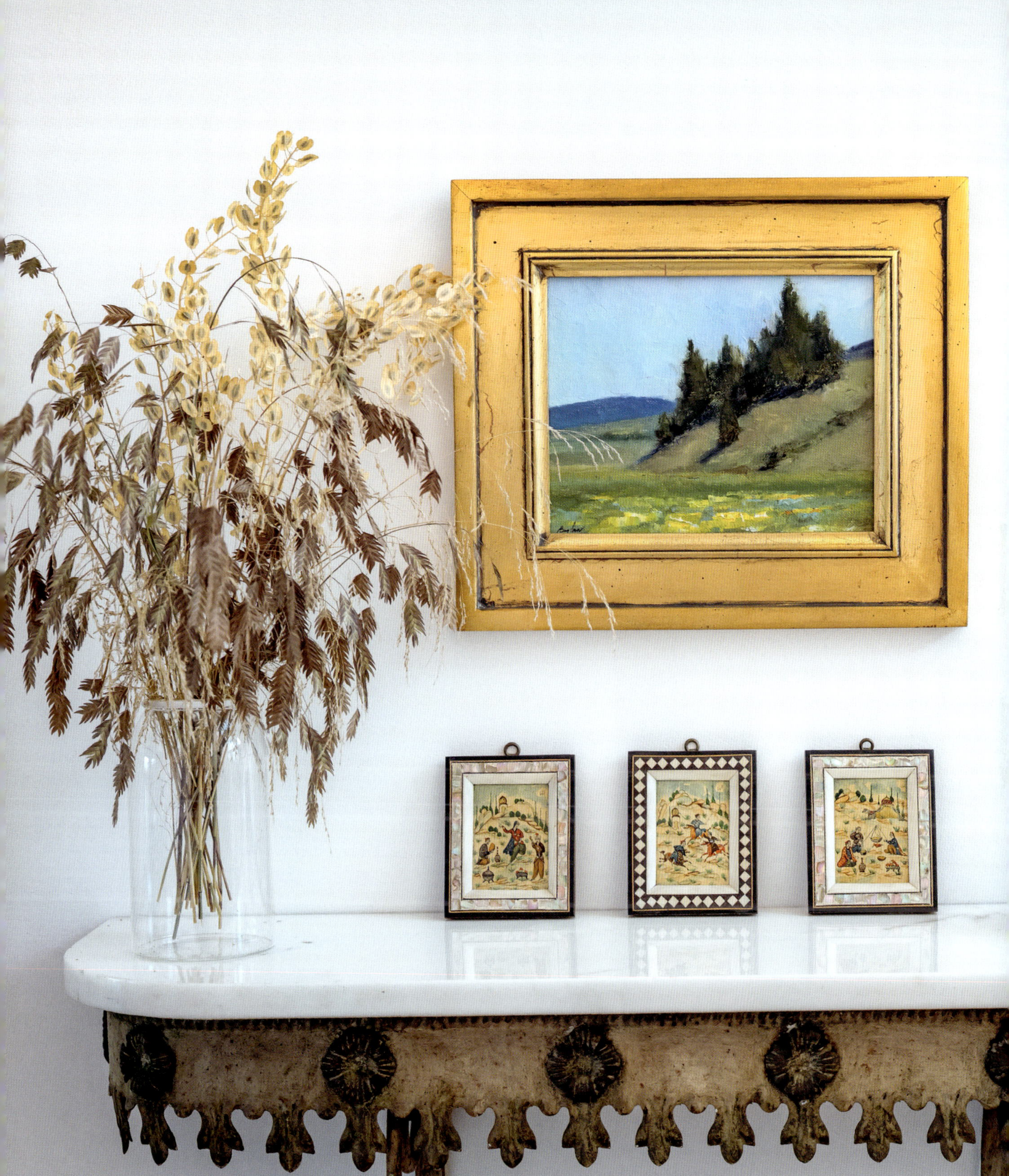

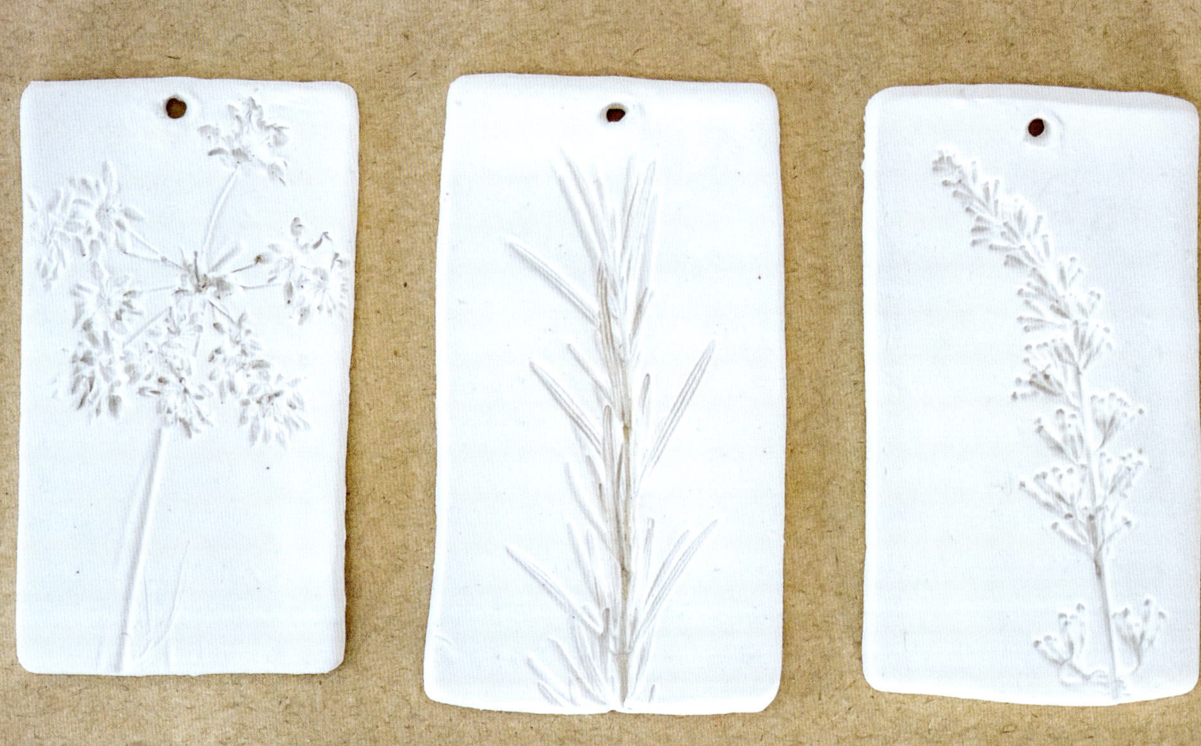

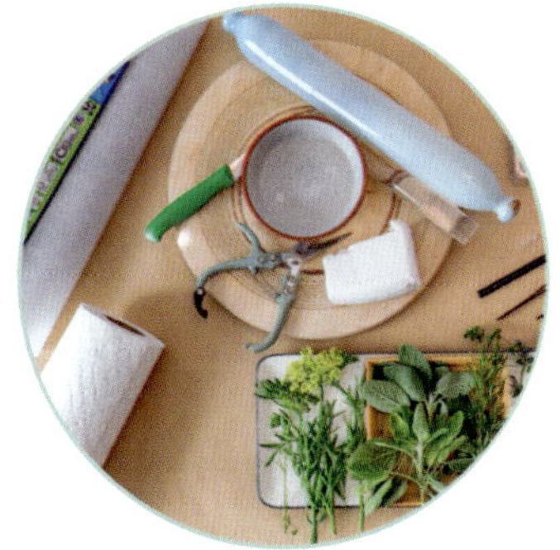

WHAT YOU NEED

- Botanicals
- Air-dry clay
- Sturdy and smooth work surface
- Rolling pin or large straight-sided, smooth bottle
- Knife
- Pointed tweezers
- Small bowl (optional)
- Colored pencils, acrylic paints, or ink (optional)

18

Botanical Wall Tile

There is something lovely about air-dry clay. Partly it is the instant gratification of not having to bake or fire the clay. And then there's how ridiculously light the clay is when it is dry—kind of like a dried marshmallow. Another plus is that you don't need a lot of tools. The clay may be a little pricey, but a little does go a long way.

These botanically imprinted tiles are easy and fast to create, although they do take about twenty-four hours to dry. When they are done, you can decorate them with acrylic paint or colored pencils, or you can leave them as is. If you poke a hole in the clay while it's wet, you can hang the tile (they can make great ornaments). Or prop the finished tile on a shelf or against a wall.

When choosing botanicals to imprint, look for interesting shapes and textures. It's all about experimentation. Some things you are certain will look amazing will turn out to be meh; other things you are skeptical of can turn out to be quite elegant.

Let me digress for a moment: When making art, it's important to use a critical eye to evaluate what to keep and what to discard. The common aphorism about writing also applies: "You must kill your darlings." Some of your pieces won't work. No matter how many hours you have toiled, if the pieces don't speak to you, then just chuck them. And while sometimes it can be hard to discern what is worth saving, try mightily to keep only your best stuff. Otherwise it is easy to quickly become overwhelmed by the volume of

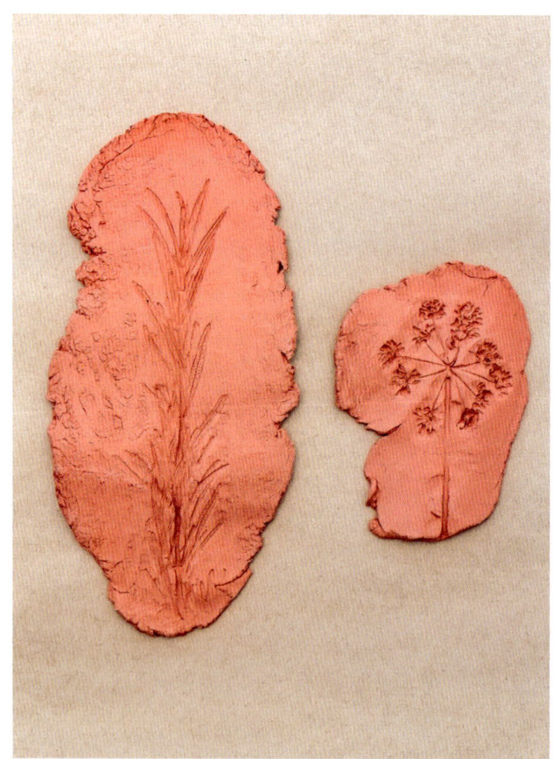

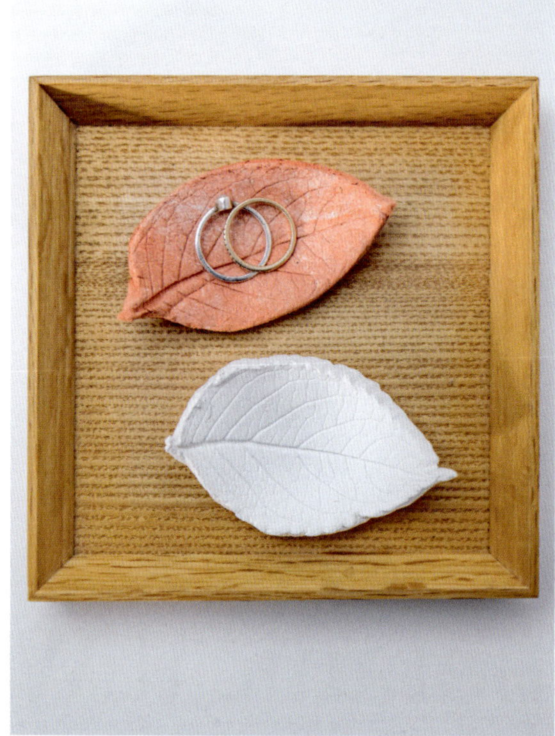

projects you may be producing, which can make you want to stop producing art altogether.

Back to clay. You can cut the clay into shapes by pressing something (like a leaf or solid object) into the clay and cutting around it. Or you can press a hollow object—think a cookie cutter—into the clay to cut out the shape.

You can also make small bowls with your cutout shapes. Hydrangea leaves work well for this, especially varieties with a pronounced vein structure and serrated edges. Simply press the leaves into the clay and then cut out the outline. Gently give the clay leaf a concave shape. Place it in a plastic-wrap-lined bowl to minimize sticking and help maintain the shape as it dries.

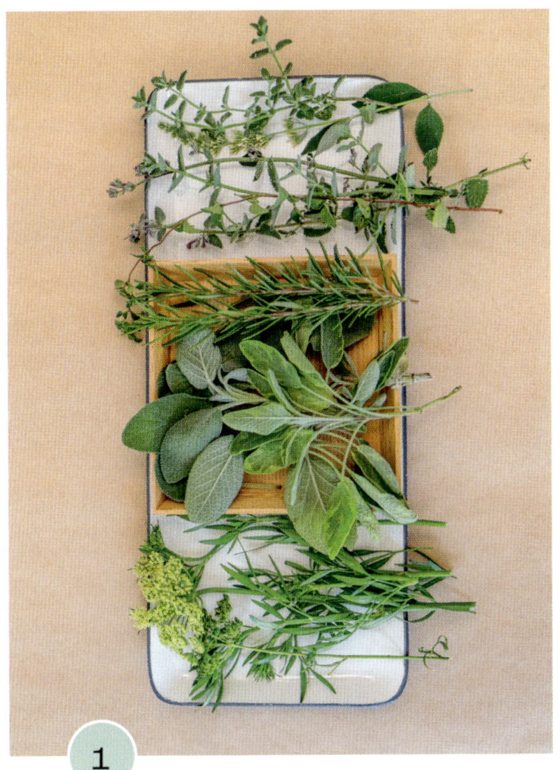

1

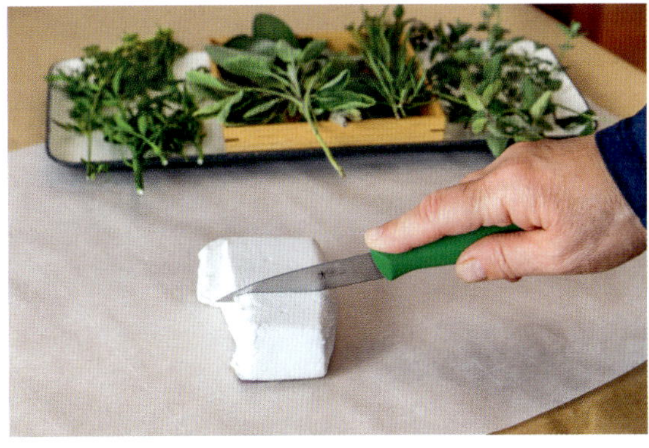

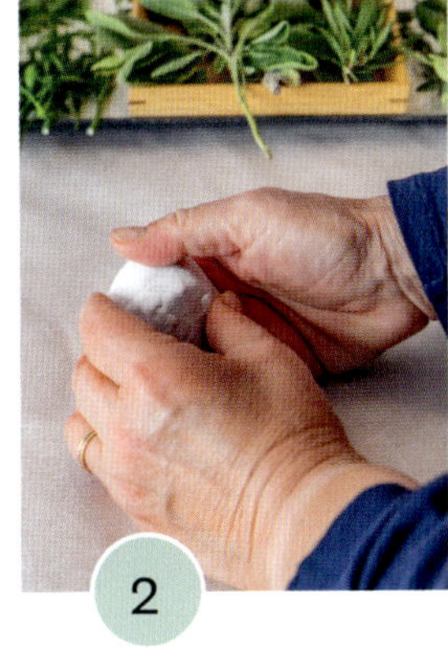

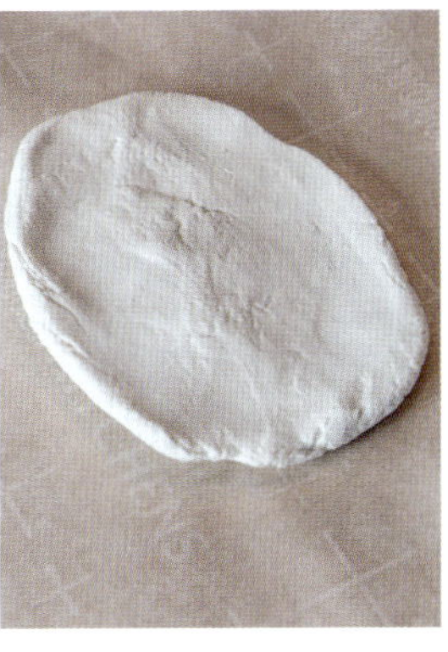

2

Select the Botanicals

Choose botanicals that have dimensionality as well as interest. They must be thick enough to make an impression in the clay and tough enough not to fall apart when they are removed. Be wary of tiny seeds: they will stick to the clay and are a pain to remove.

Knead

Air-dry clay comes in three colors—white, gray, and terra-cotta. Once you have chosen your clay, cut off a hunk and knead it on the work surface into a smooth ball. Start off with more clay than you think you need. You can always reuse any excess, but if you don't have enough you will have to start over. Consider too that making large objects is much more difficult than smaller ones, as it is hard to roll a larger piece of clay to an even thickness, and the chances of the clay cracking and warping as it dries are greater.

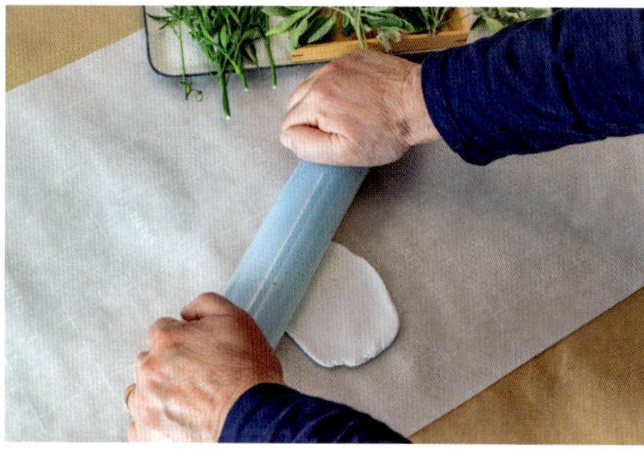

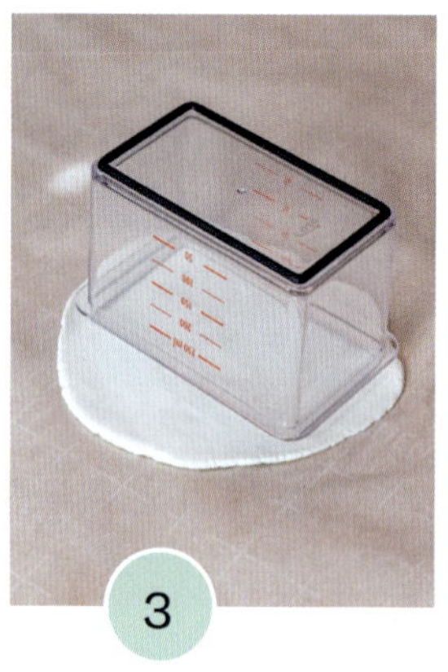

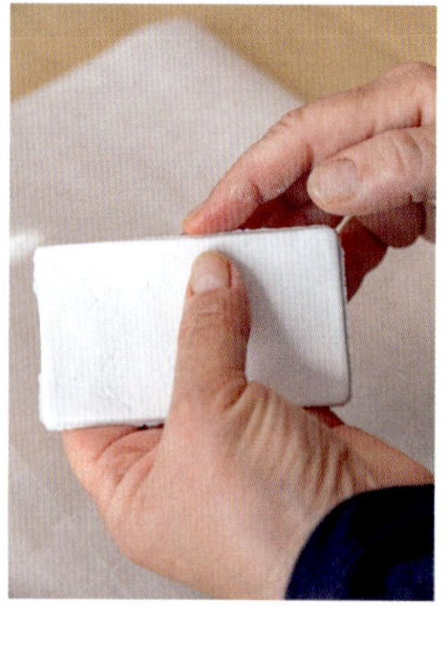

3

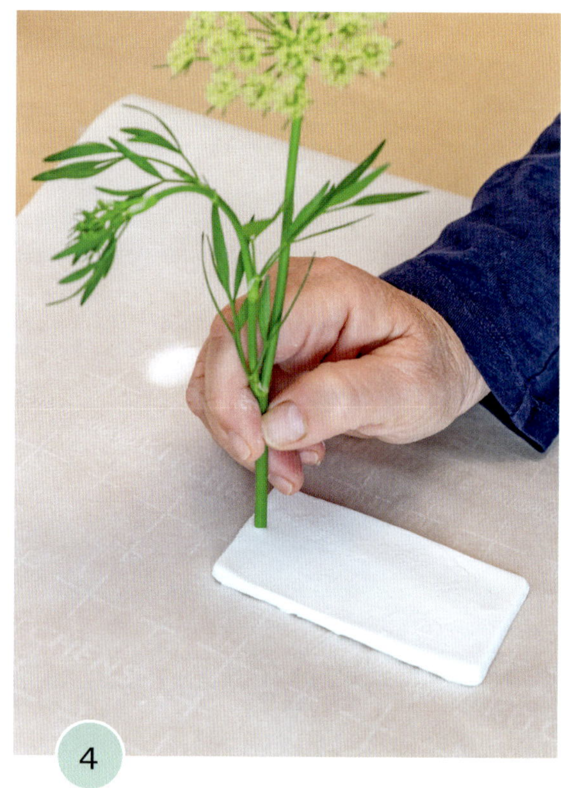

4

Roll and Cut

On your work surface, roll out the clay to an even thickness—around ¼ inch is a good thickness to shoot for. Depending on the look you're going for, you can make a free-form piece or a more regular and geometric shape, and you can choose smooth or rough edges. If your clay feels dry, or you want to smooth out the surface, rub it with a little water.

Make a Hole, if Desired

If you plan to hang your piece, pierce the clay with an object about the size of the hole you want. Then turn your clay over to smooth and flatten the edges of the hole.

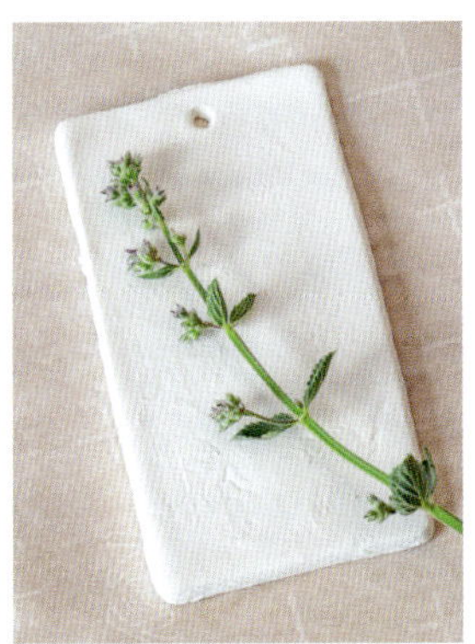

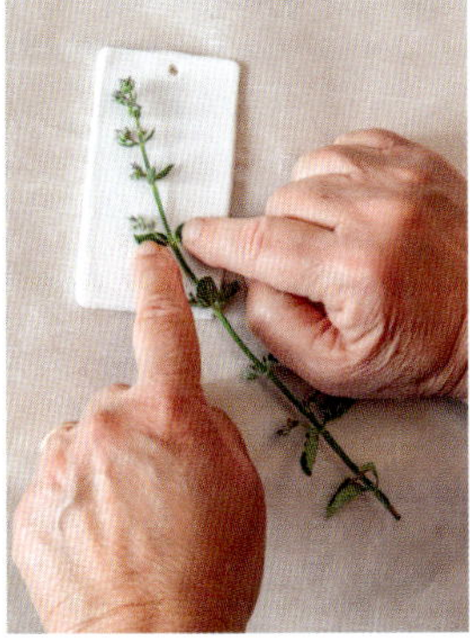

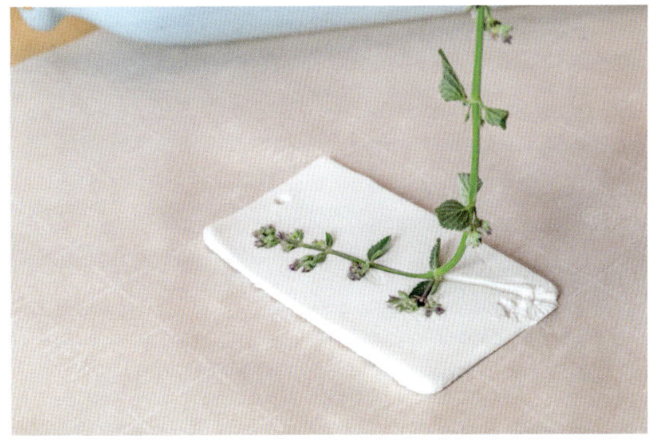

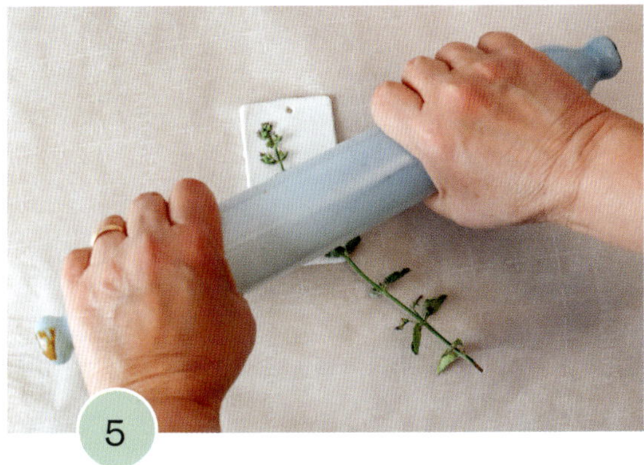

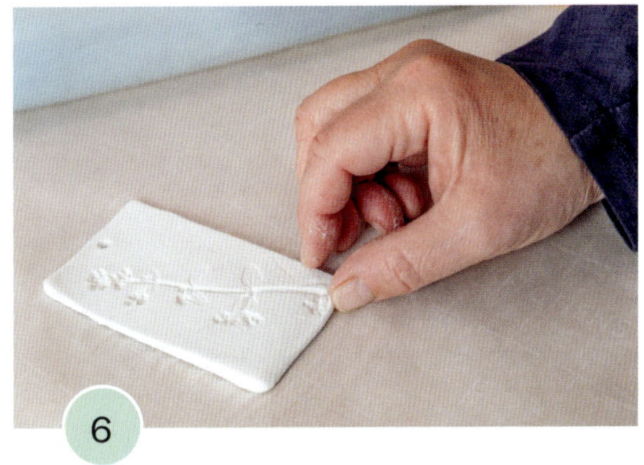

Imprint

Take your botanical and position the leaves and stems where you want them. Then press it gently into the clay with your fingers. Next, firmly, and with even pressure, roll over it with your rolling pin. You want to apply just enough pressure to get a good impression.

Remove the Botanical

Pry up an edge of the botanical and peel it away from the clay—using tweezers can be helpful. If bits of the botanical stick to the clay, remove them carefully with the tweezers. If you need to do any small repairs, fix them now before the clay begins to dry. For example, if one of the stems or some leaves didn't print, you may be able to realign them and simply press them into the clay with your fingers to get a better impression.

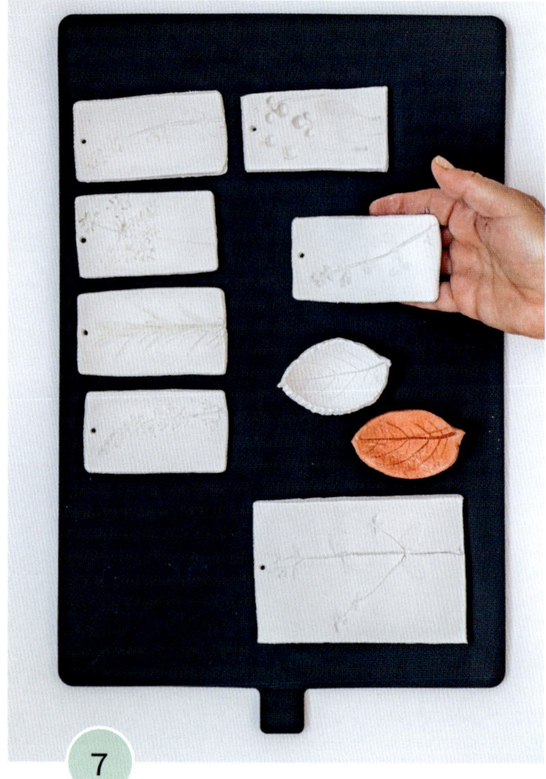

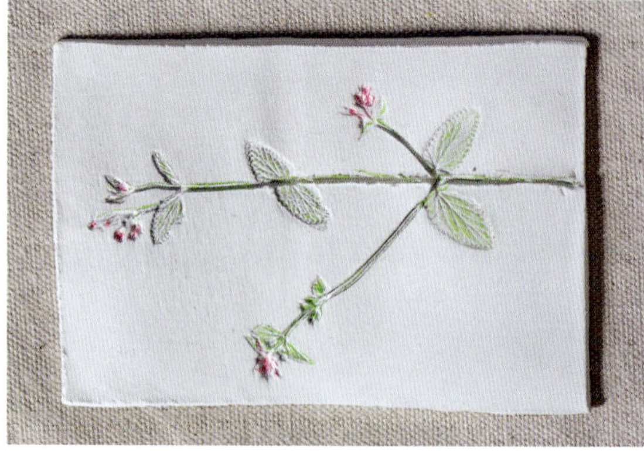

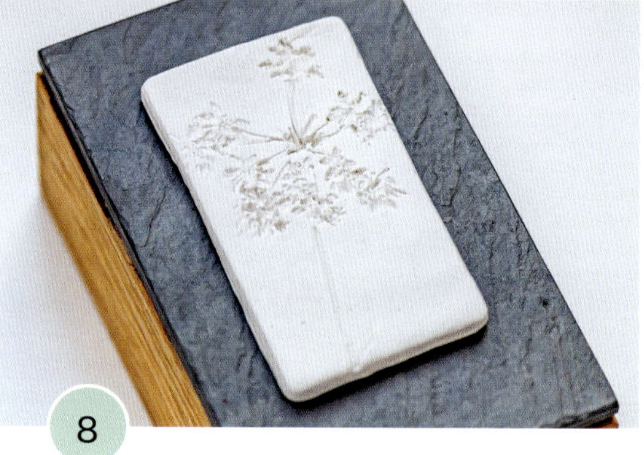

Dry

For flat tiles, gently flip over and flatten them every couple of hours as they dry, otherwise they tend to curl. For bowls, dry them inside another bowl that you have lined with plastic wrap. These bowls should also be turned over every few hours so both sides can dry, but make sure to support the center of each bowl when it's inverted so it doesn't collapse.

Decorate, if Desired, and Display

Once your clay has dried, if you choose to, you can use colored pencils, acrylic paints, or ink to enhance your designs.

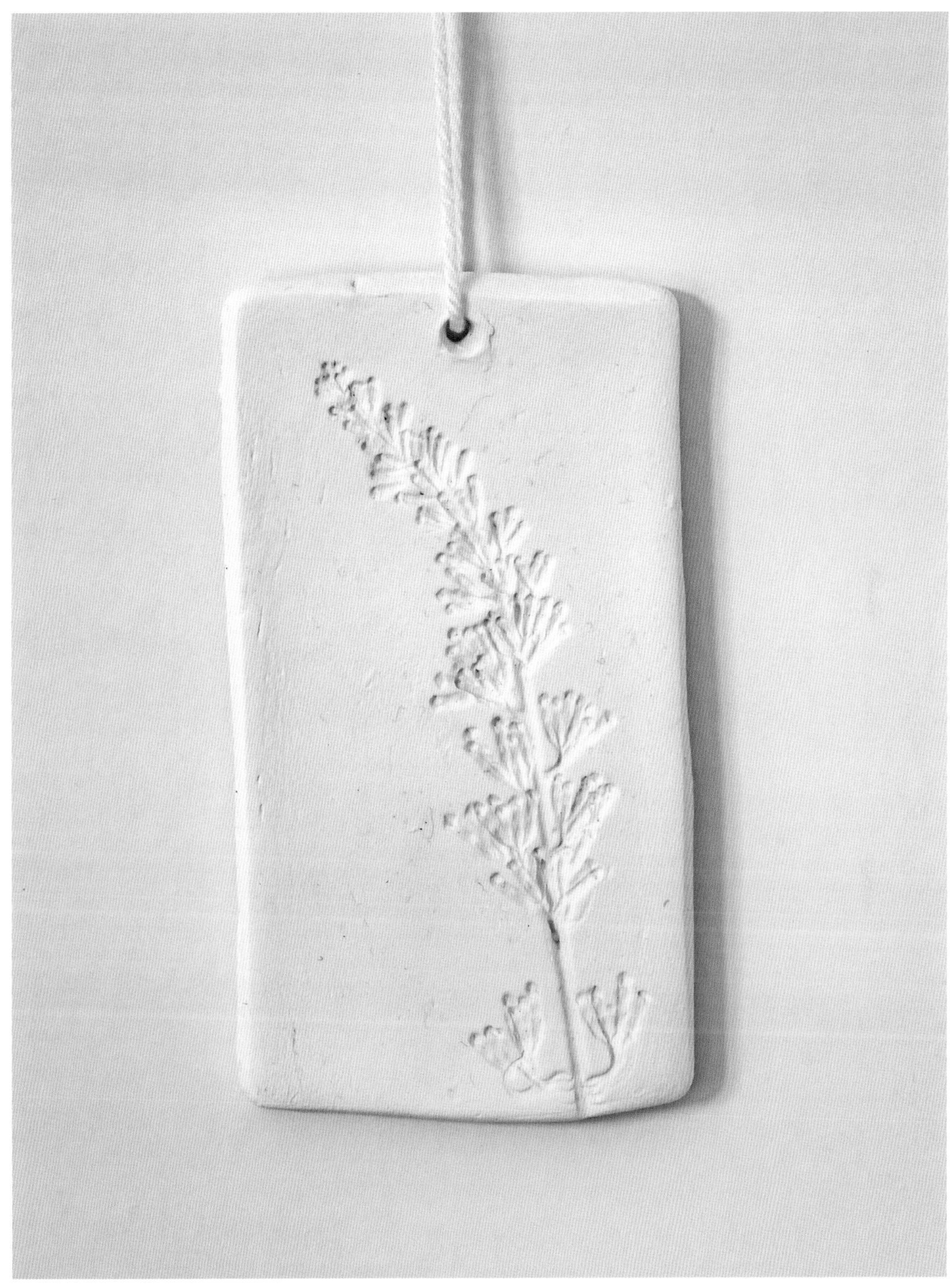

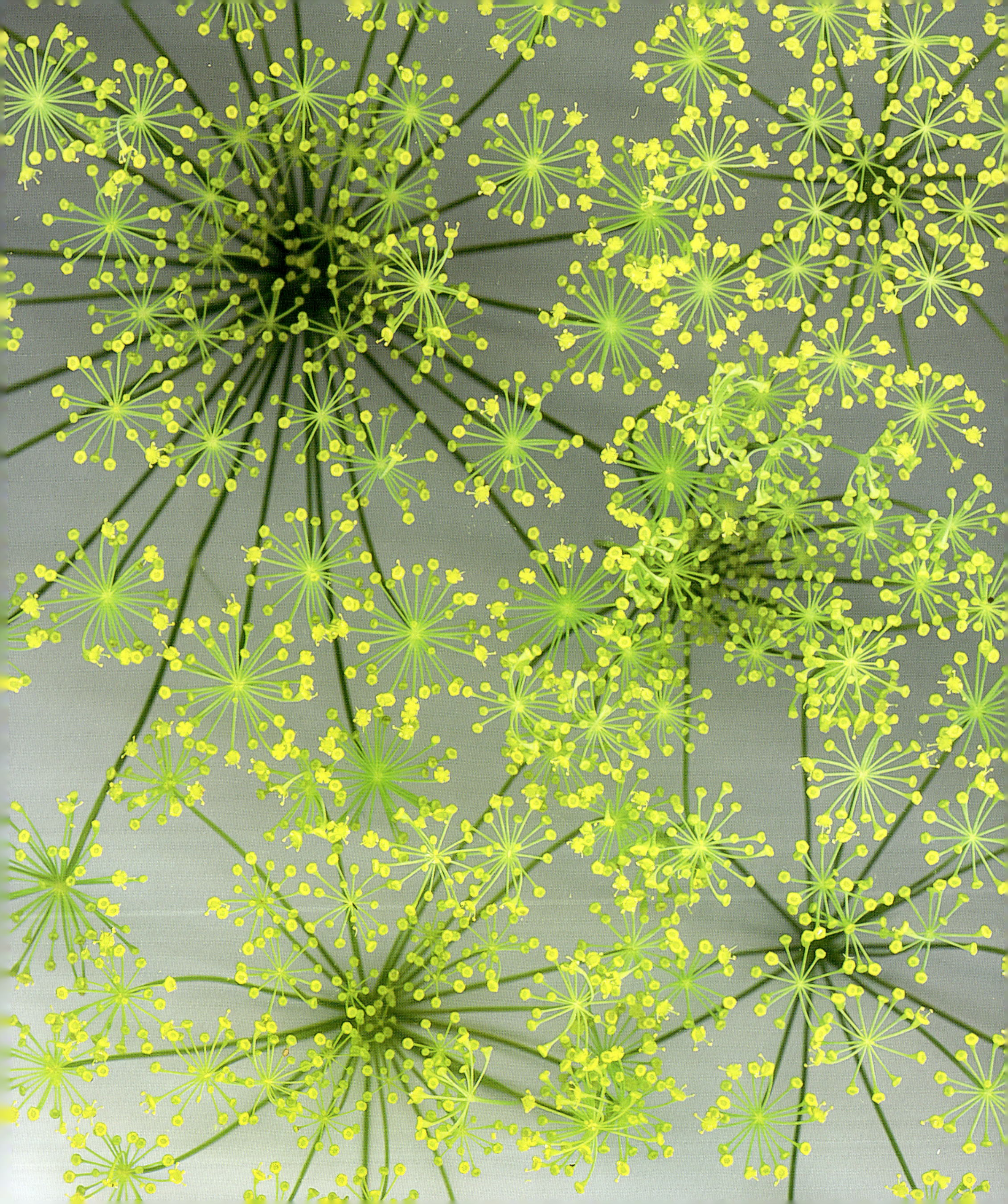

MORE PROJECTS

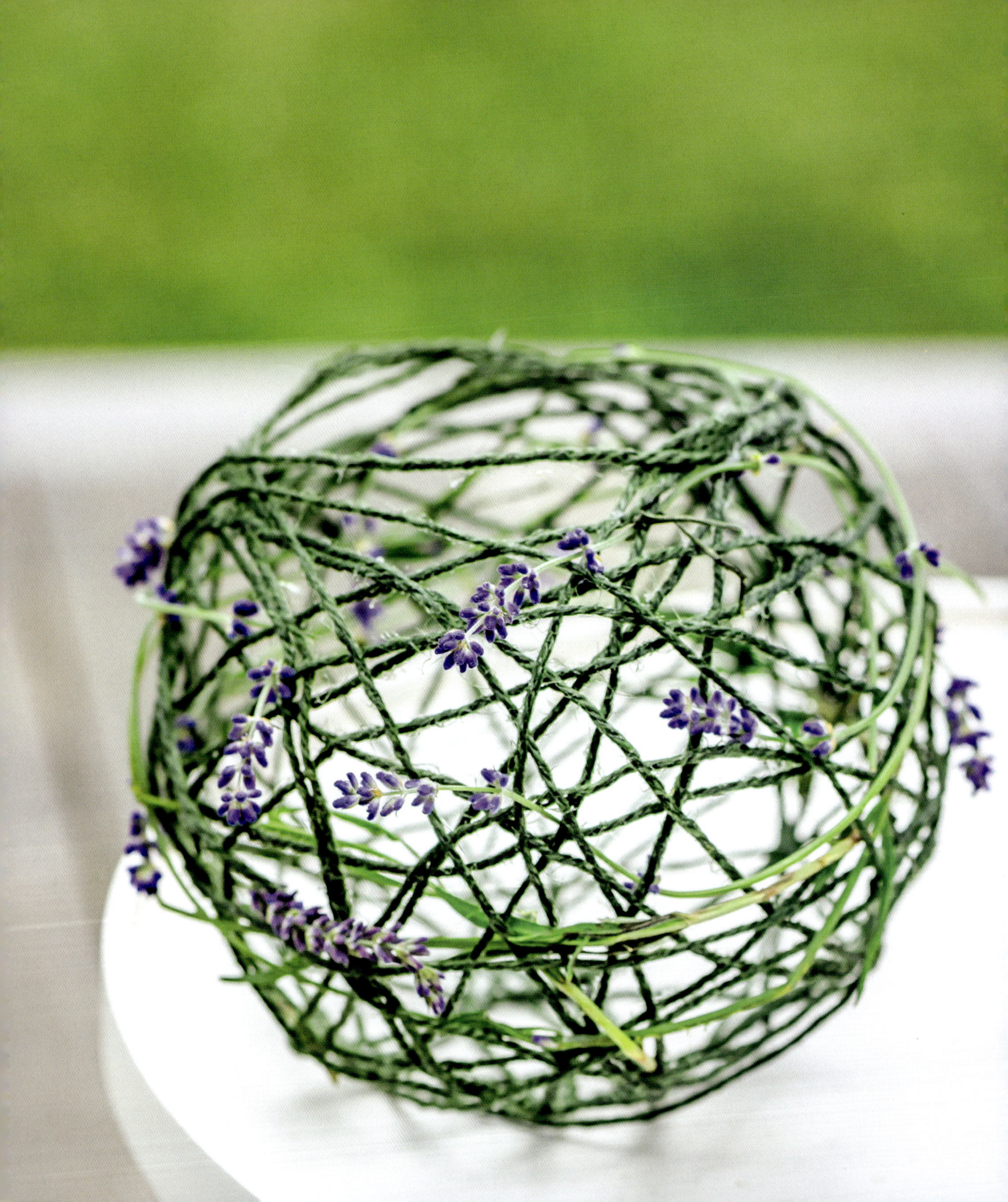

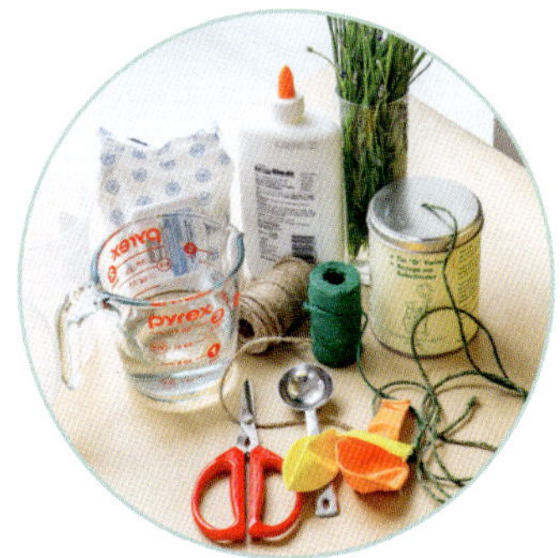

WHAT YOU NEED

- Twine or string
- Balloon or inflatable mold
- Liquid PVA glue
- Plastic container with lid
- Knife or sharp scissors
- Chopstick or stirrer
- Baby wipes or paper towels
- Soft toothbrush (optional)
- Lavender sprigs, grasses, other botanicals, or feathers (optional)
- Battery-operated fairy lights (optional)
- Fishing line or twine, for hanging (optional)

19

String Orb

I love how playful it feels to create a large string ball. The fact that this project is fast and easy adds to the fun. It's a bit messy—the glue gets everywhere—but then again, you may be tidier when creating than I am. These orbs can be sculptural objects or lanterns, either hung or stationary, to great effect. A few of them grouped together, in the same or different sizes, can look fabulous.

Balloons, beach balls, or blow-up exercise balls of any size work well as molds. Just be aware that if you choose to do a giant sphere, you will need lots of twine and glue to give the orb enough structural integrity to stand on its own.

You can use any strong string or twine, colored or neutral. For added interest, weave long, flexible botanicals through your orb. Fresh lavender works well—and as a bonus, your orb will smell heavenly. Long-stemmed grasses also look elegant. To make some grass stems more flexible, so they bend instead of snap, try pulling the stem between the end of your thumbnail and your index finger. This will also flatten them and make them easier to weave.

How the woven-in fresh botanicals will dry is a bit of a gamble, but the good news is you can always remove or replace them. The orbs are also beautiful without any woven enhancement.

Alternatively, you can put a glass vase filled with flowers inside your orb to create an attractive centerpiece or table decoration.

A word of warning: My dog ran off with one of my orbs when I left it unguarded, batting and tossing it around until it was smashed to pieces. Oh well. He had fun while it lasted . . . me, not so much.

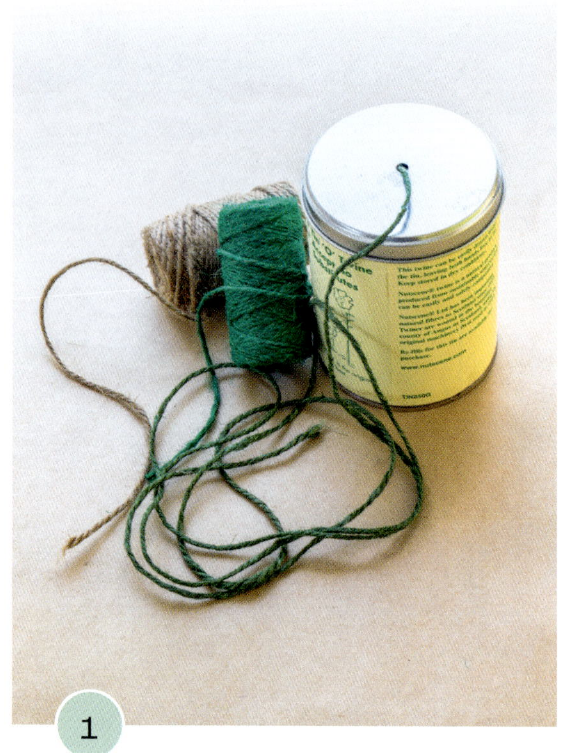

1

Get Set Up

Collect your supplies and choose your twine or string wrapping. Blow up your balloon or chosen mold to the size you want your orb.

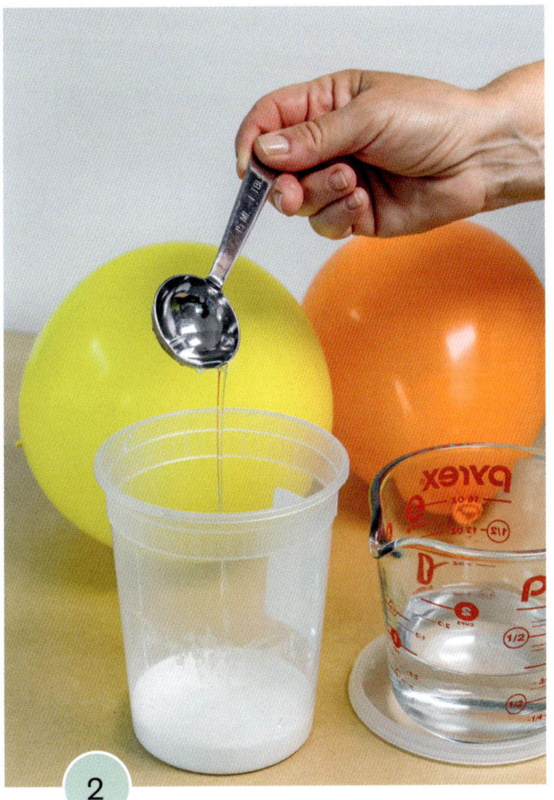

2

Mix the Glue

Mix the glue with water in a plastic container until it is about the consistency of heavy cream. The amount you need depends on the size of your orb and how densely wrapped you want it to be. About ½ cup of glue and 2 to 3 tablespoons of water will coat enough twine for a medium-sized balloon.

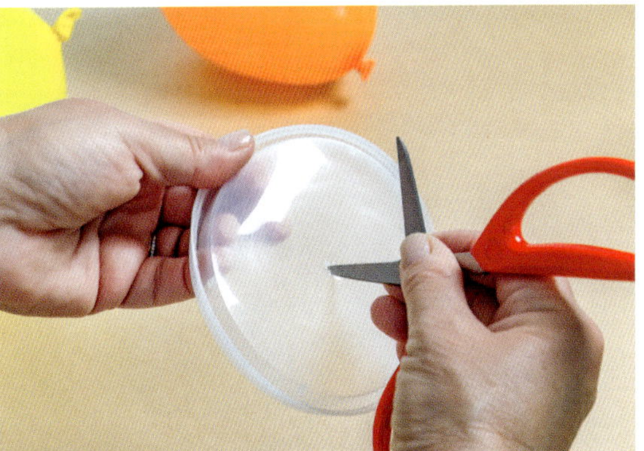

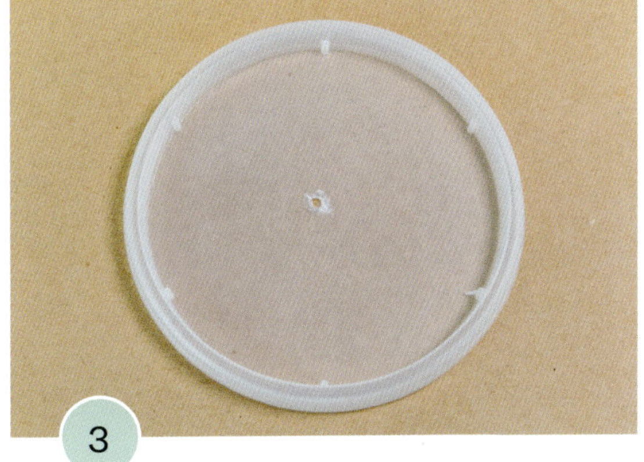

3

Prepare the Container Lid

With the tip of a knife or sharp scissors, punch a hole in the center of the lid. It helps if you pierce through the underside of the lid so that the string won't get caught on any rough spots. Ideally, make the hole big enough for the twine to easily slide through but small enough that excess glue gets wiped off as the twine is pulled up through the hole.

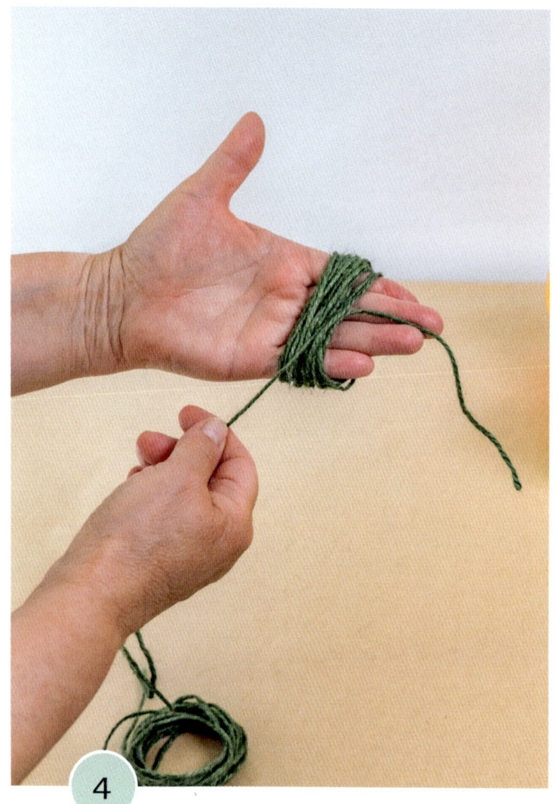

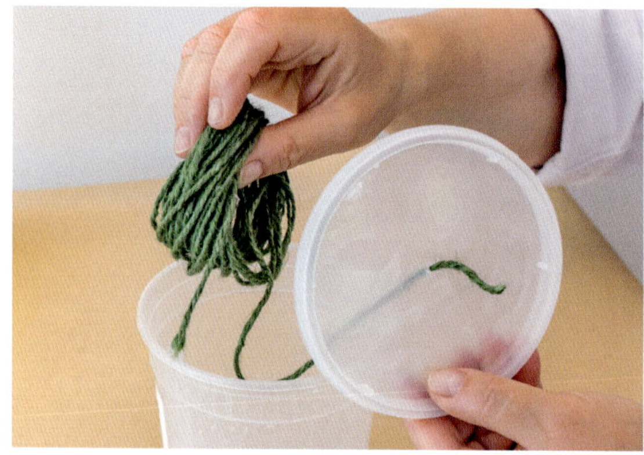

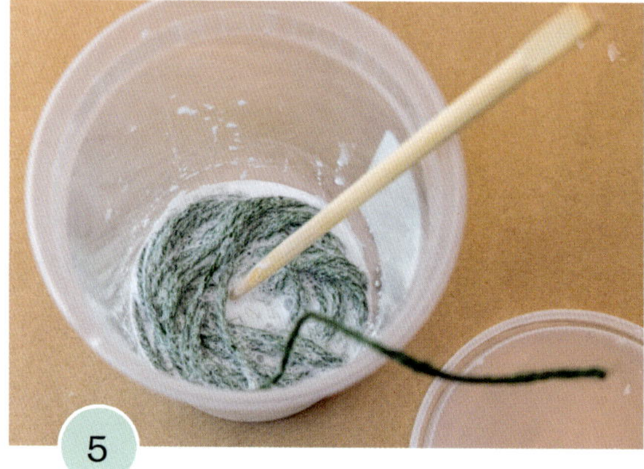

Make the Twine Bundle

Measure the twine for your project. The amount will depend on how big your mold is and how dense you want your wrapping to be. For a medium balloon, pull off about 25 feet of twine. This doesn't have to be exact; you can always add another piece. Wrap the twine around your hand to create a bundle, keeping the starting end—the one that comes from the center of the bundle—accessible.

Soak the Twine

Holding the starting end, slip it through the hole in the container lid. Then place the bundle into the glue mixture. Using the chopstick or stirrer, carefully stir and poke the twine into the glue without tangling the strands. You want the glue to cover and soak into the twine, even between the strands.

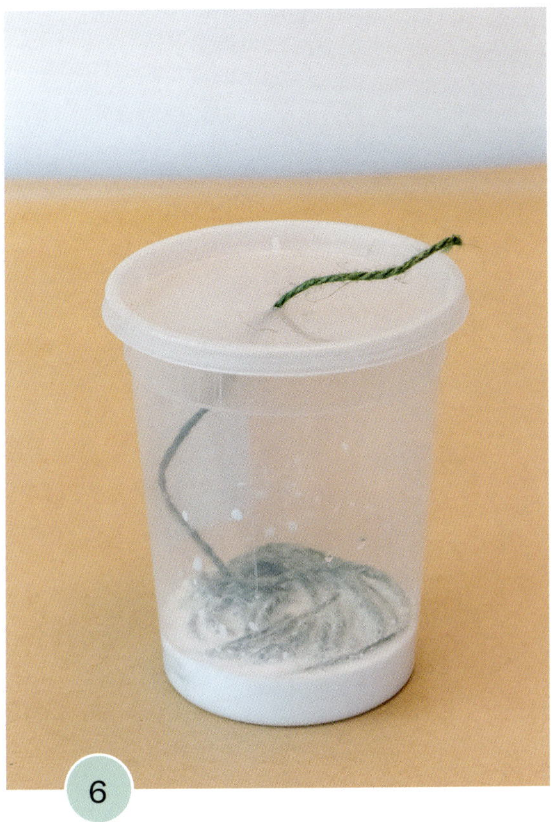

6

Seal the Container

Fasten the lid, with the twine end sticking out, onto the glue container. The twine should spool out easily.

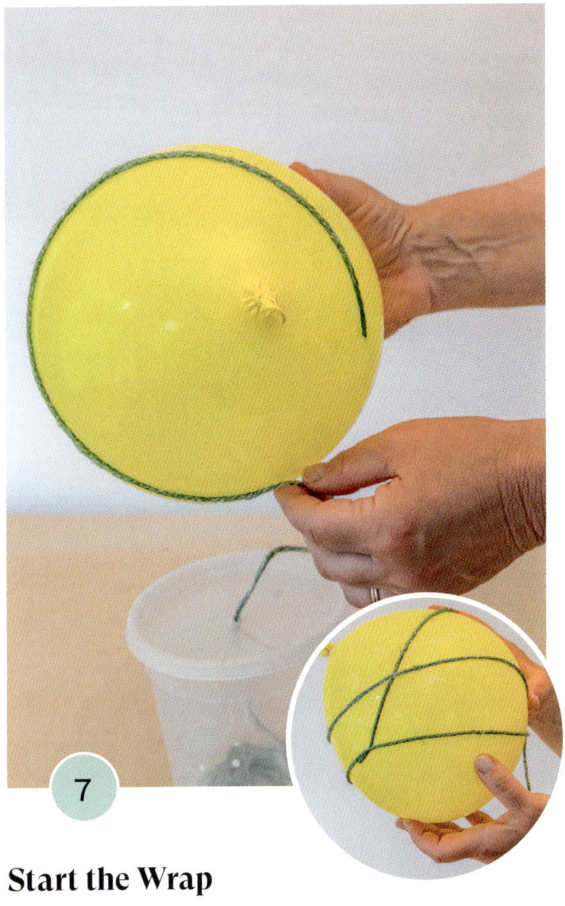

7

Start the Wrap

Now comes the goopy part. Pull out a length of twine from the container. It will be very gluey. If it is too drippy, you can wipe off some of the excess with your fingers. Wrap the twine around your mold, tucking in the starting end.

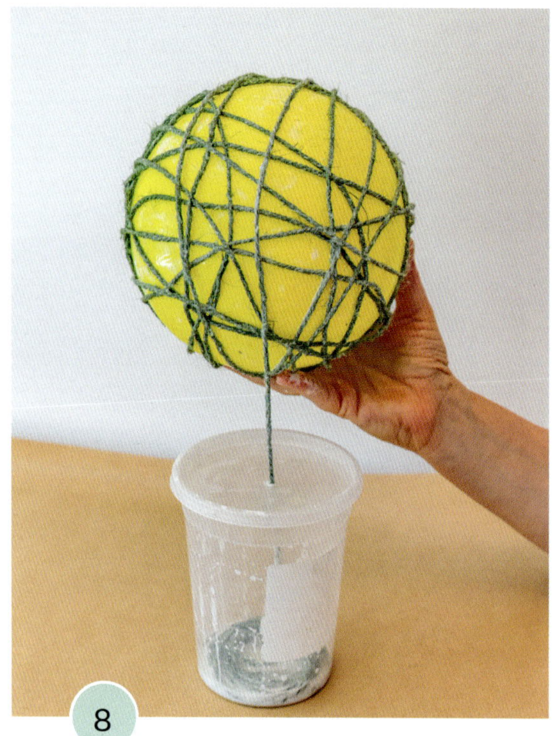

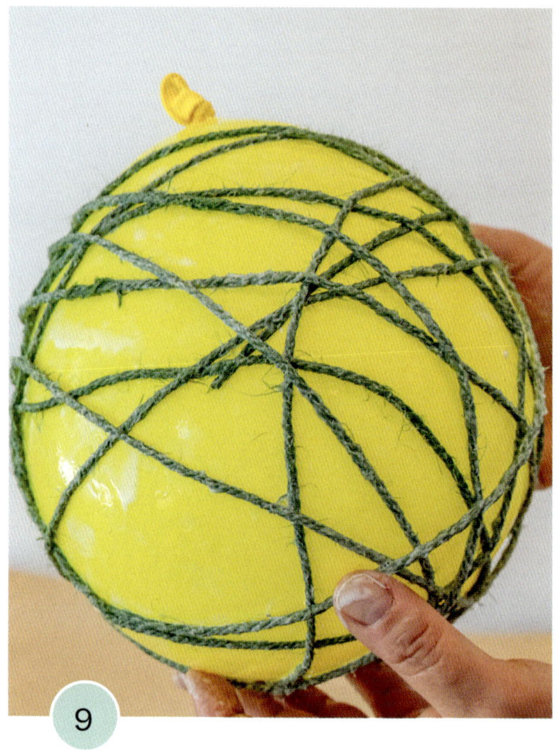

Wrap

Keep wrapping the twine around the mold, forming random patterns that are pleasing to you. Wrap it as densely as you choose while trying to keep enough tension on the twine so that it stays in contact with the mold and doesn't get too loose and floppy.

Add Another Twine Bundle, if Needed

If you run out of twine before you are done wrapping, tuck the loose end under a wrap to secure it. Wipe off your hands (baby wipes or paper towels come in handy here) and create and soak another twine bundle as described in steps 4 though 6. You may need to mix up more watered-down glue as well. Start the new gluey twine by tucking in the end under a piece of twine and continue wrapping until you are happy with how the orb looks.

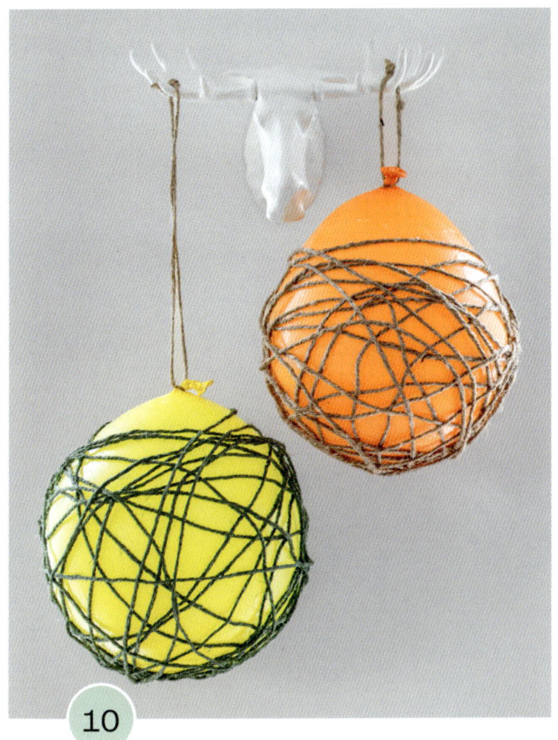

10

Dry the Orb

Tie a piece of dry twine to the end of your balloon or to a convenient place on your mold and hang it for 24 hours to dry. If you can't hang your wet orb, you can rest it on the rim of a plastic container, making sure to release it and turn it upside down after a few hours so it doesn't stick to the container and so all parts of the orb dry completely.

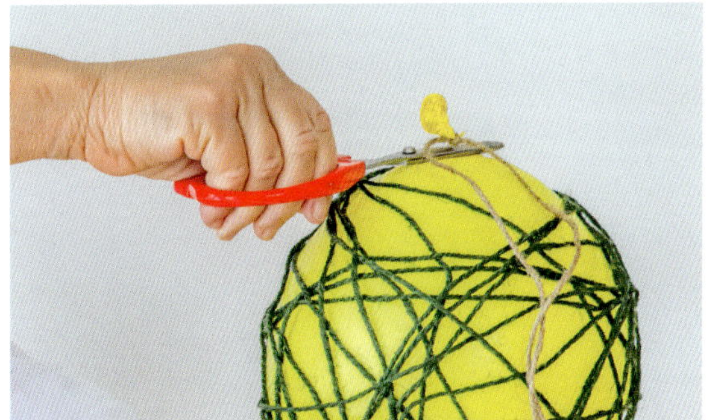

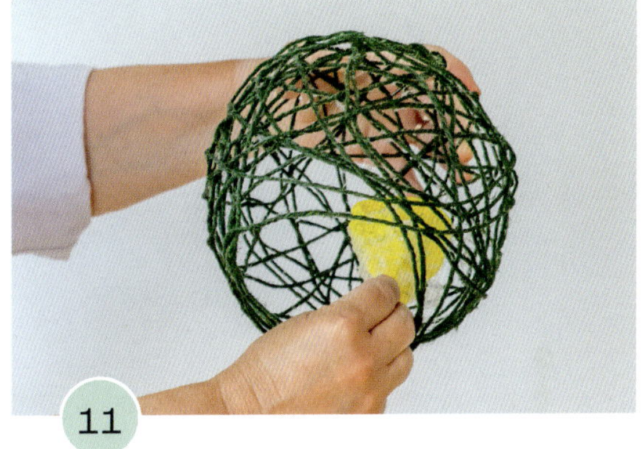

11

Free the Orb

Pop the balloon or release air from the mold. The sound of the balloon peeling off the string is delicious! You may have to gently poke and prod to release and remove the deflated mold, but it should come away and leave the orb intact. At this point, tidy up the orb with your fingers or a soft toothbrush to remove any unsightly dried glue flakes that are hanging on. This can be an easy though time-consuming process, depending on how densely your twine has been wrapped.

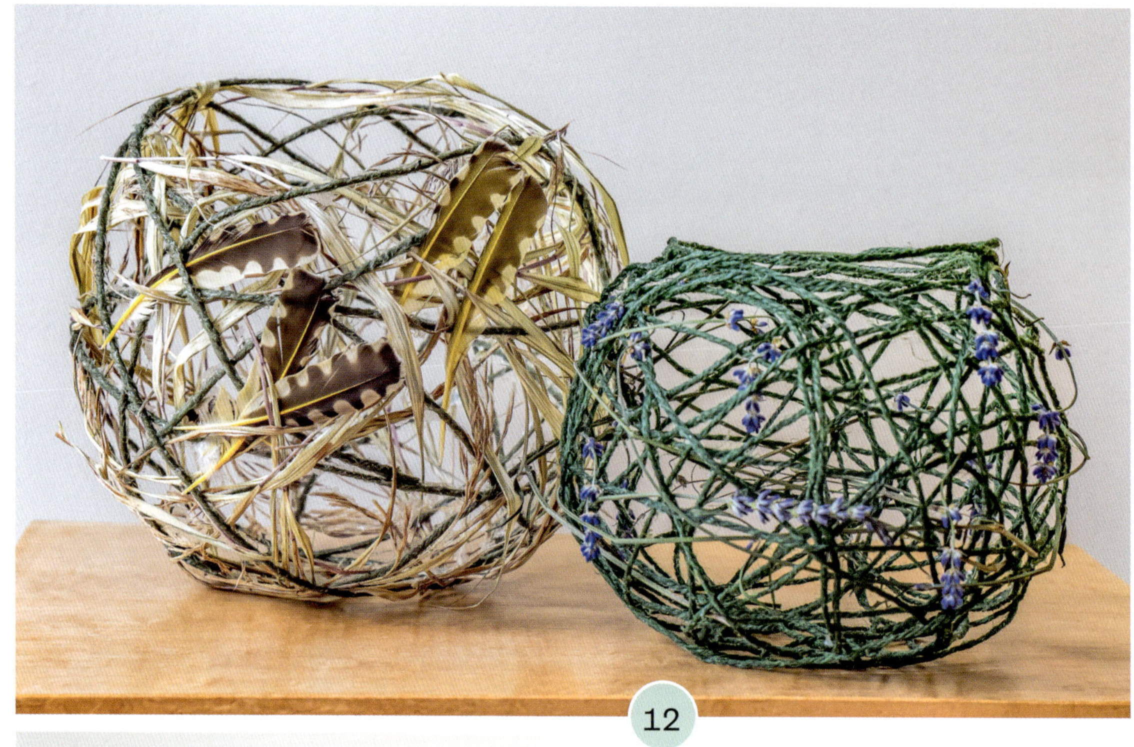

12

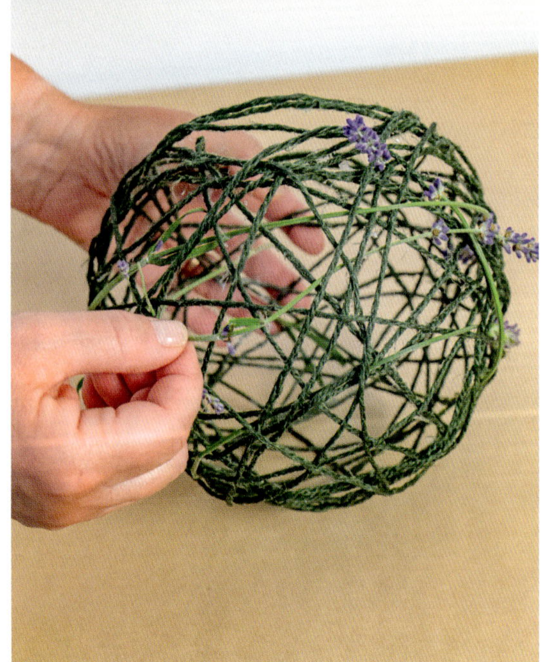

Weave and Display

Take fresh lavender sprigs or grasses and weave them between the holes in the twine to dry over time. Alternatively, decorate with other botanicals or feathers. You can also place battery-operated fairy lights in the orb. If you want to hang your orb, use fishing line or twine.

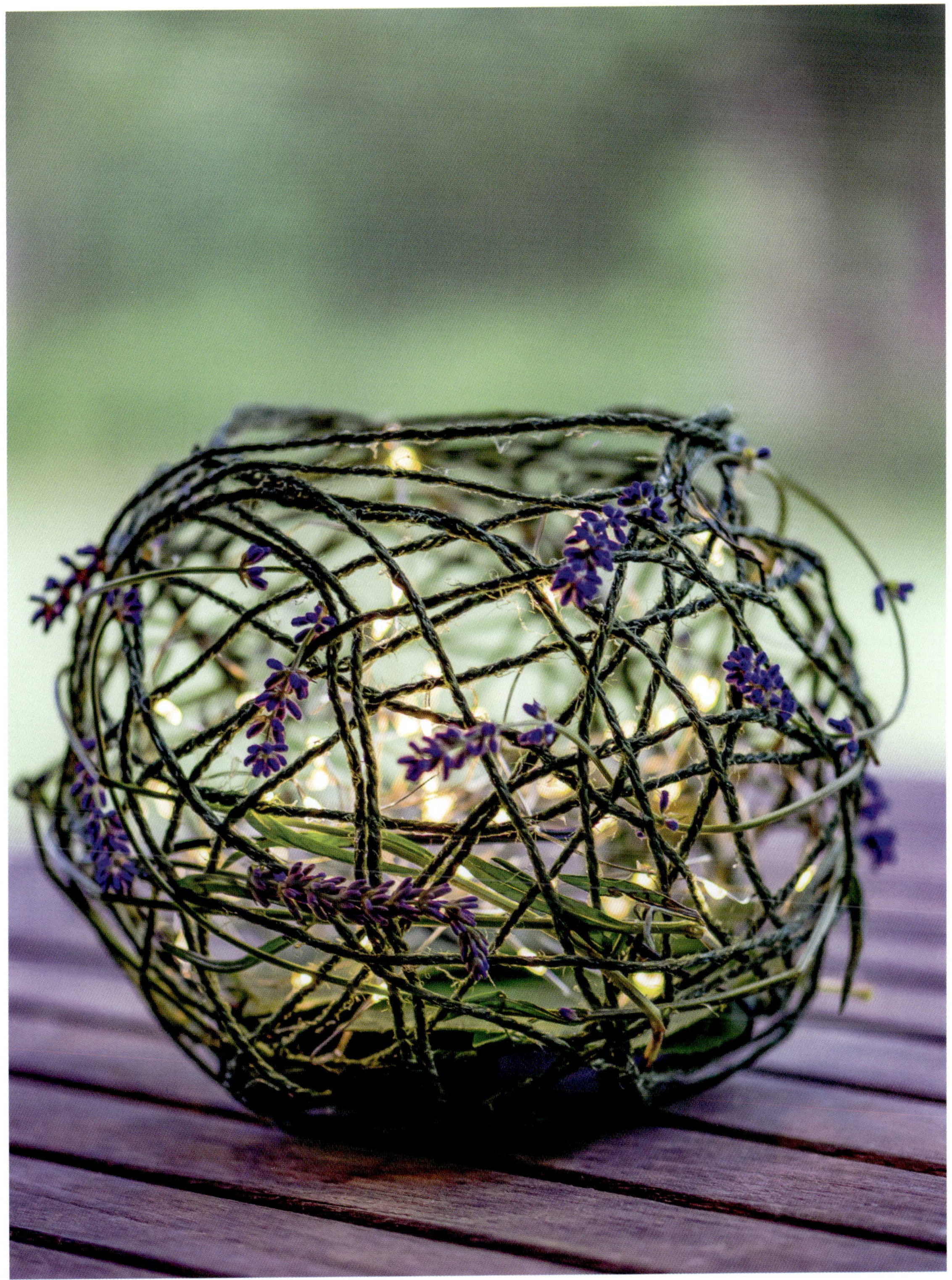

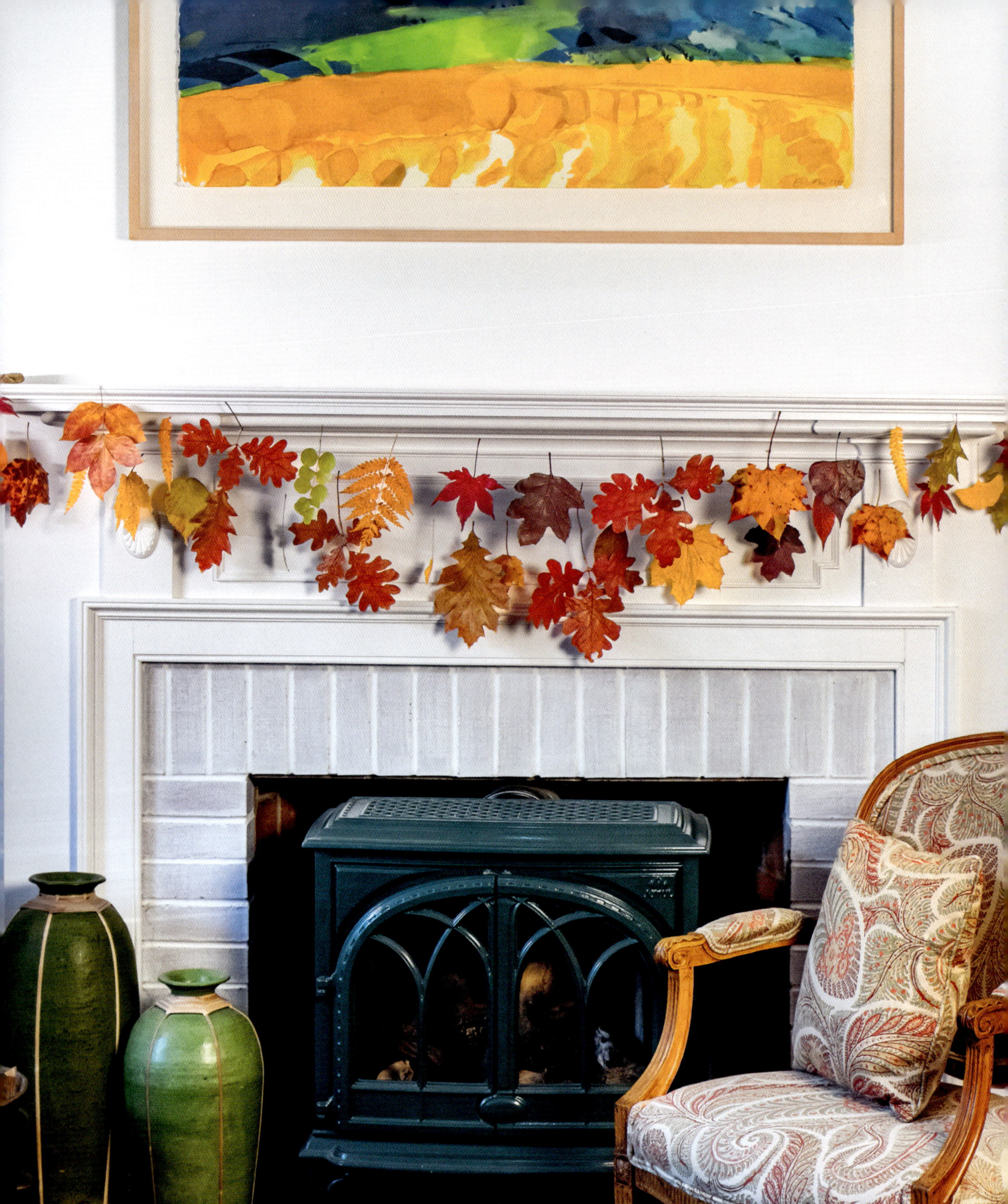

WHAT YOU NEED

- Leaves
- Double boiler or a bowl and pot
- Aluminum foil
- 1 pound beeswax (in brick or pellet form)
- Tweezers (optional)
- Waxed paper or parchment paper
- Fishing line, twine, or string
- Scissors
- Cardboard
- Tape
- Glue gun and glue sticks or a quick-drying glue
- Pushpins, temporary stick-on hooks, small nails, or painter's tape (optional)
- Fairy lights (optional)

20

Waxed-Leaf Garland

Fall is unquestionably my favorite time of year. Here in New England, there is a brief exuberance of color and radiant light before the endless dark and monochrome of winter sets in. Fall is a season that lives up to its clichés, and I am always thankful for that. An easy and gratifying way to preserve the colors and beauty of fall leaves is to coat them with melted beeswax and string them into a garland or swag.

And while making a garland or swag of waxed fall leaves is fabulous, there's no reason why you can't use any leaves at any time of year. Just look for interesting colors and shapes that complement each other. Use one variety or pick several different types of leaves, stringing them together randomly. You could also choose to create a simple repeating pattern from a few different kinds of leaves. Keep in mind that the design is as much about the negative space created between the leaves as it is the leaves themselves.

If you want the leaves to appear to float, use fishing line, which largely disappears. However, fishing line is slippery and not easy to tie. If you tie it too loosely, the leaves fall out of the knot. Tied too tight, the line will sever your stem. To reduce the difficulty of this project, you can use twine or string instead.

Alternatively, if you don't feel like stringing a garland or don't have a place to hang it, you can simply take the waxed leaves and create a tablescape with them.

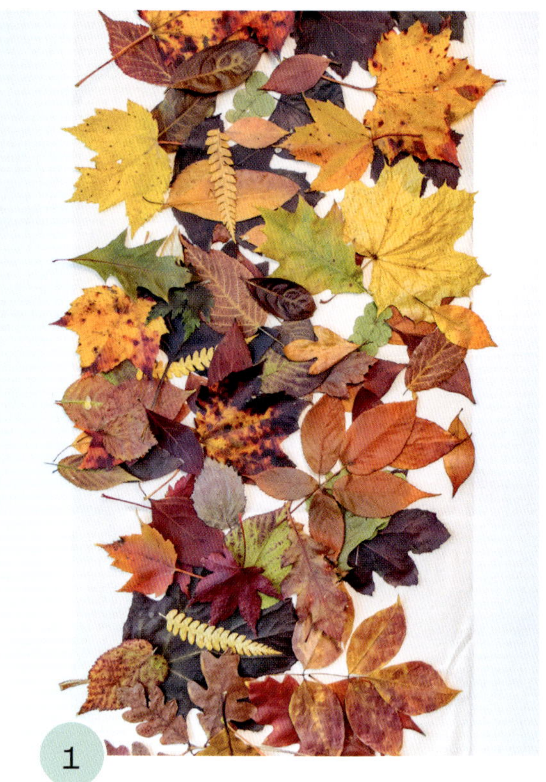

1

Select and Flatten the Leaves

Look for leaves with pleasing shapes and colors and that preferably have a long, strong stem. The perfect leaves aren't too damaged by insects and are relatively flat. To flatten them further, press them between sheets of paper or newsprint under some weight, like a pile of books, or use a flower press. The flattening process can take a few hours or overnight, depending on how flat and dry your leaves are to start with.

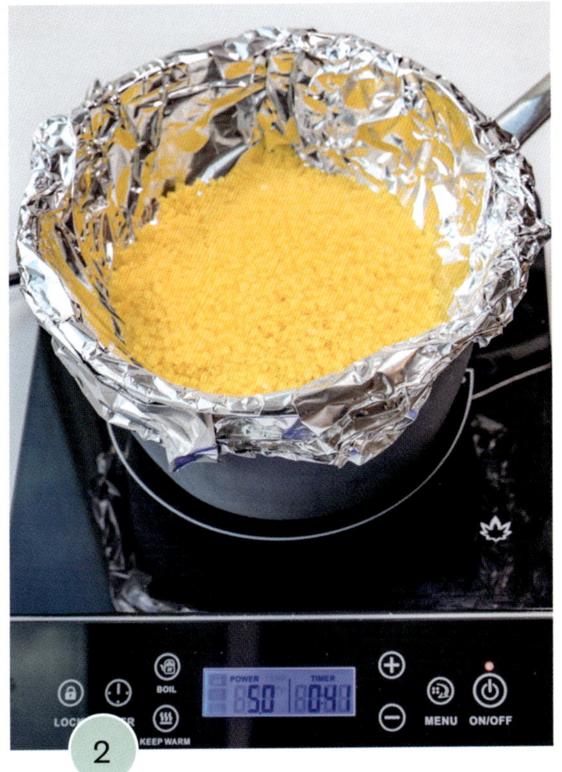

2

Melt the Wax

Pour a few inches of water in the bottom pan of the double boiler. If you don't have a double boiler, create one by resting a bowl on top of a saucepan filled with a few inches of water. The water should not touch the top pot or the bottom of the bowl. Because melted beeswax is hard to clean, protect the top pan or bowl by covering it with two layers of aluminum foil. Set the double boiler on the stovetop over low heat and melt the wax. The water should be just simmering, not boiling.

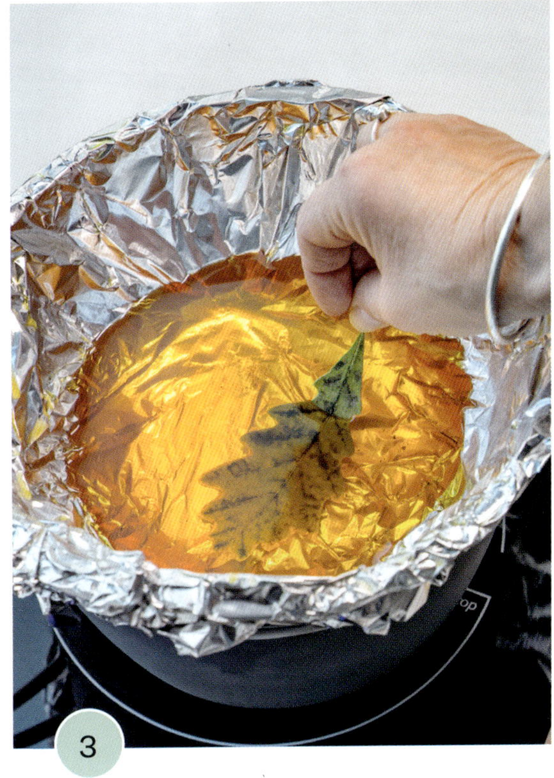

3

Dip the Leaves

Holding a leaf by the very end of the stem, slowly slide it into the wax. Pull it out as soon as it is fully submerged, and very gently shake off any excess wax. If you drop the leaf into the wax or the stem breaks, you may have to pluck it out with tweezers.

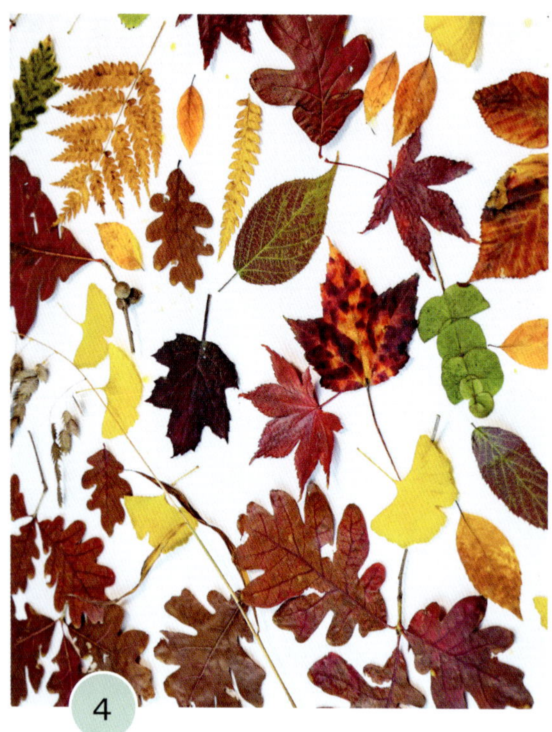

4

Dry the Leaves

Place the leaf onto waxed paper or parchment paper to dry. It is important for the leaves to dry flat. Let them dry for about an hour, or until the wax is no longer sticky.

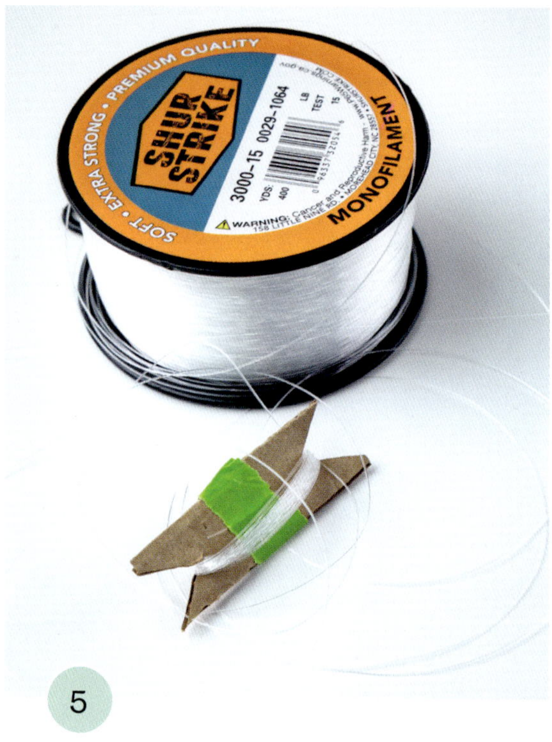

5

Make a Bobbin

Particularly if you are using fishing line, it is very helpful to create a bobbin out of cardboard to keep the cord in order. You want the bobbin to be an inch or two long and about ½ inch wide: just big enough to keep the line from becoming a mass of intractable tangles when you tie knots. If you are using corrugated cardboard, make sure the corrugation lines orient vertically so that the cardboard doesn't fold when you wind the line. Measure out how much line you need for your garland, adding a few feet extra. Then tape the first end of the line onto the bobbin and wind it up.

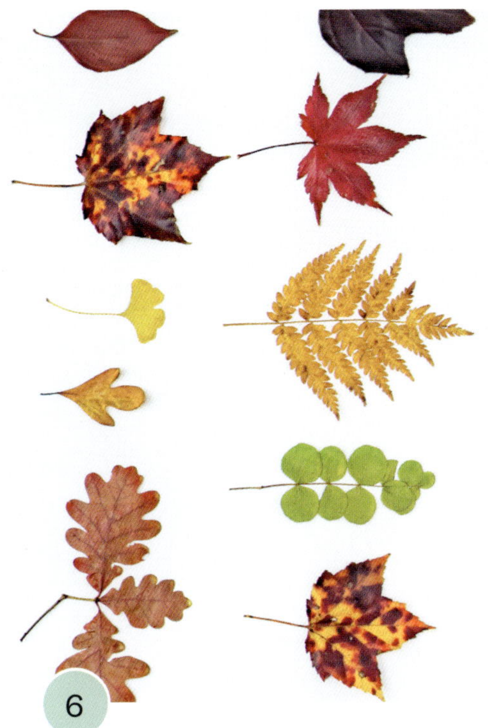
6

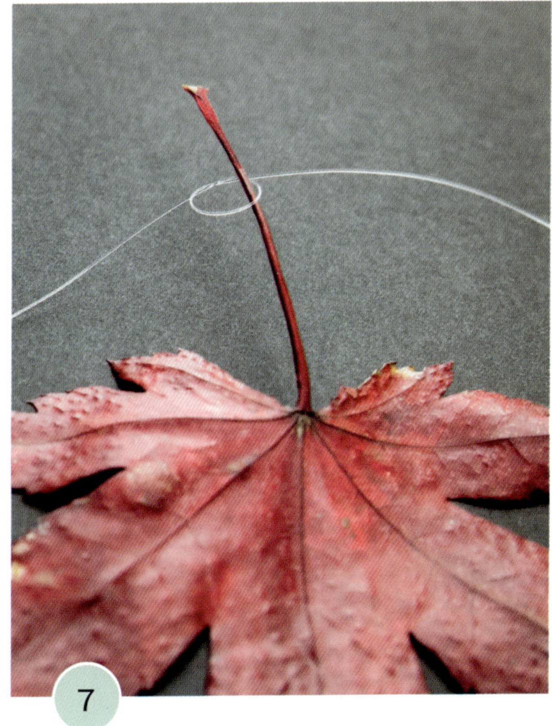
7

Lay Out the Design

Choose your leaves and lay out a design. For a swag longer than the table on which you are working, you can double or triple the rows. If you are creating a double garland, lay them both out so you will know how they will relate to each other when hung.

Tie the Leaves

This is the tricky part because you want to firmly tie your leaves without breaking the stems. Try a simple overhand knot. Keep the knot loose until the leaf is positioned and then tie it firmly.

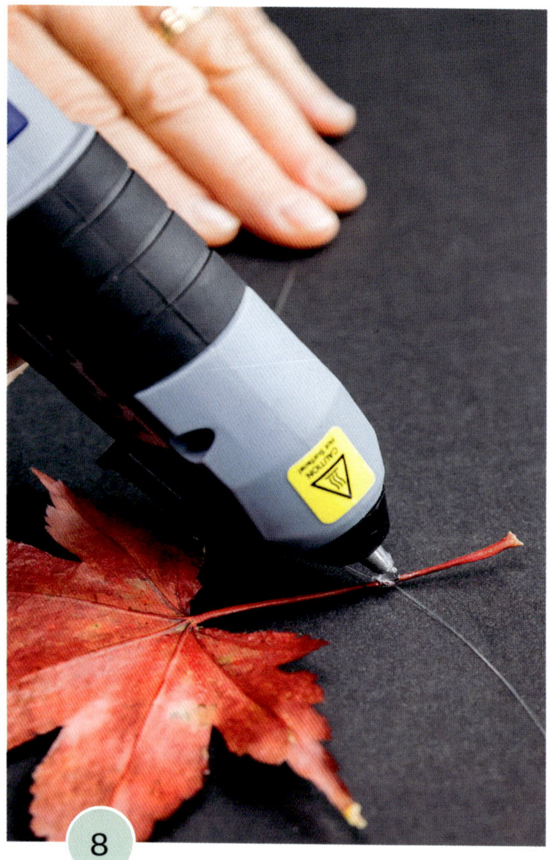

8

Glue the Stems

Even if you tie your knots tightly, leaves can fall out as you move your garland, which is irritating. Applying a small dot of glue can solve this problem. A glue gun is a great tool to use here, as the glue will dry quickly and be almost invisible. Make sure to hold the stem perpendicular to the fishing line and apply glue on the knot as well as the stem.

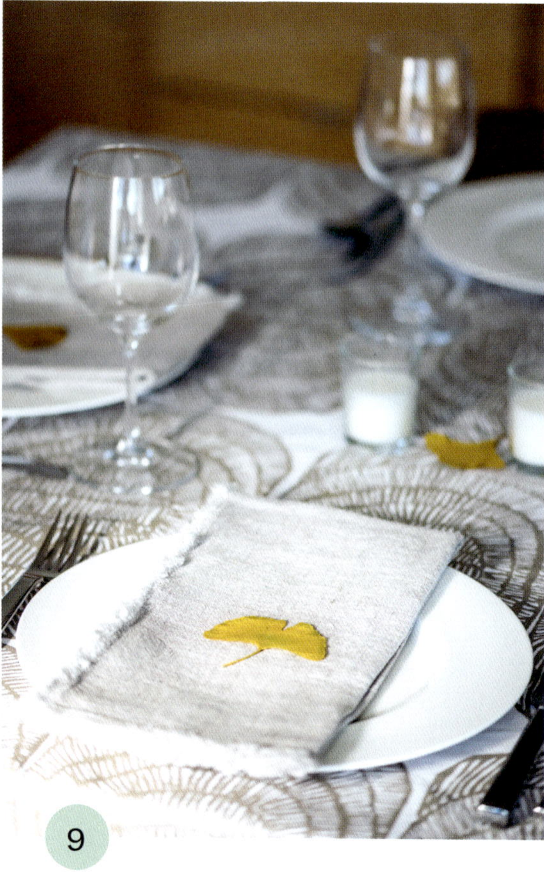

9

Hang or Tablescape

You can hang the garland by creating a loop at the end of your line and use pushpins, temporary stick-on hooks, nails, or painter's tape to secure it. For an added glow, you can string fairy lights behind or around your garland. Or skip the stringing altogether and simply lay the leaves on napkins, down the center of a table, or on a plate as a centerpiece.

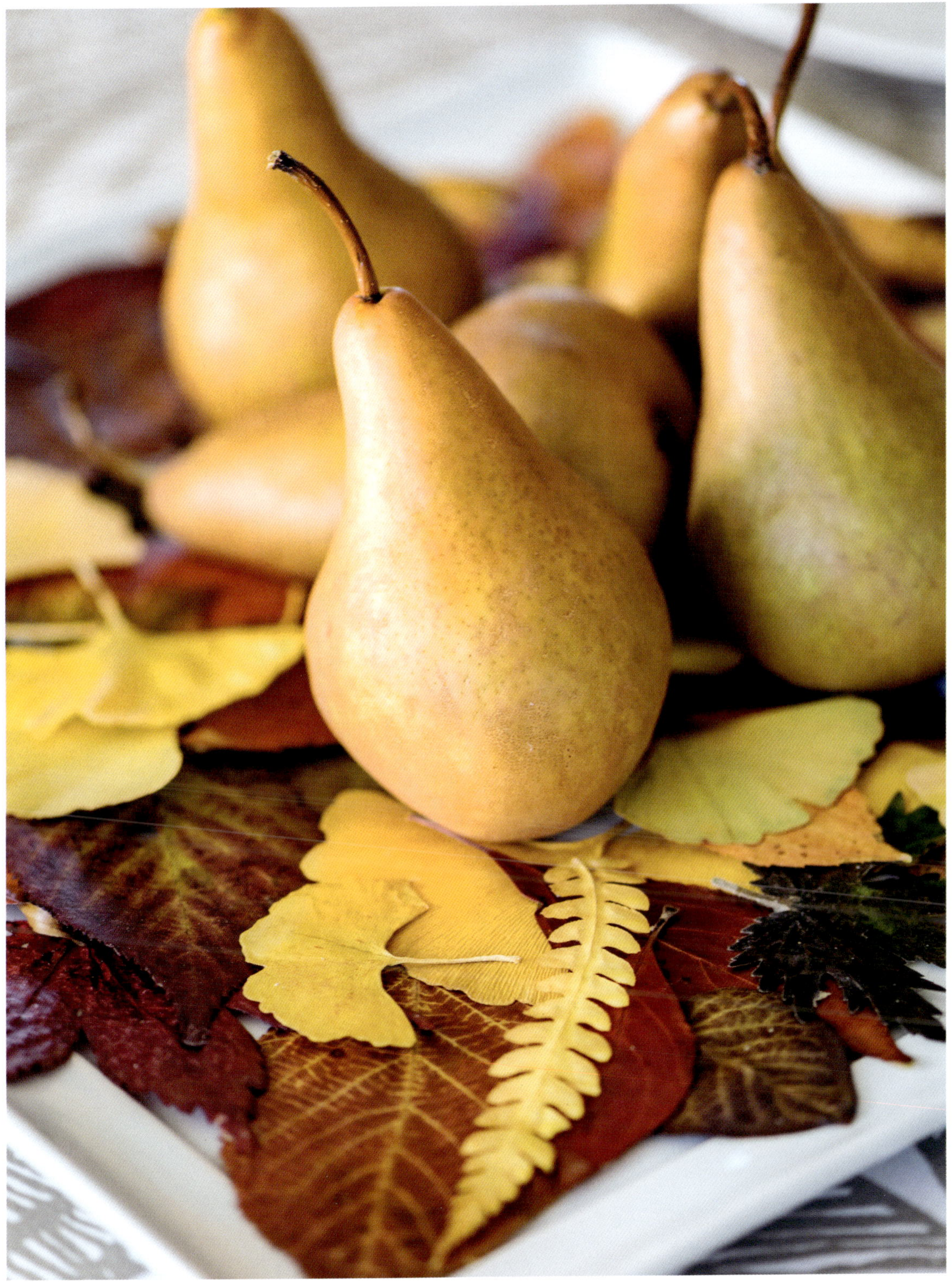

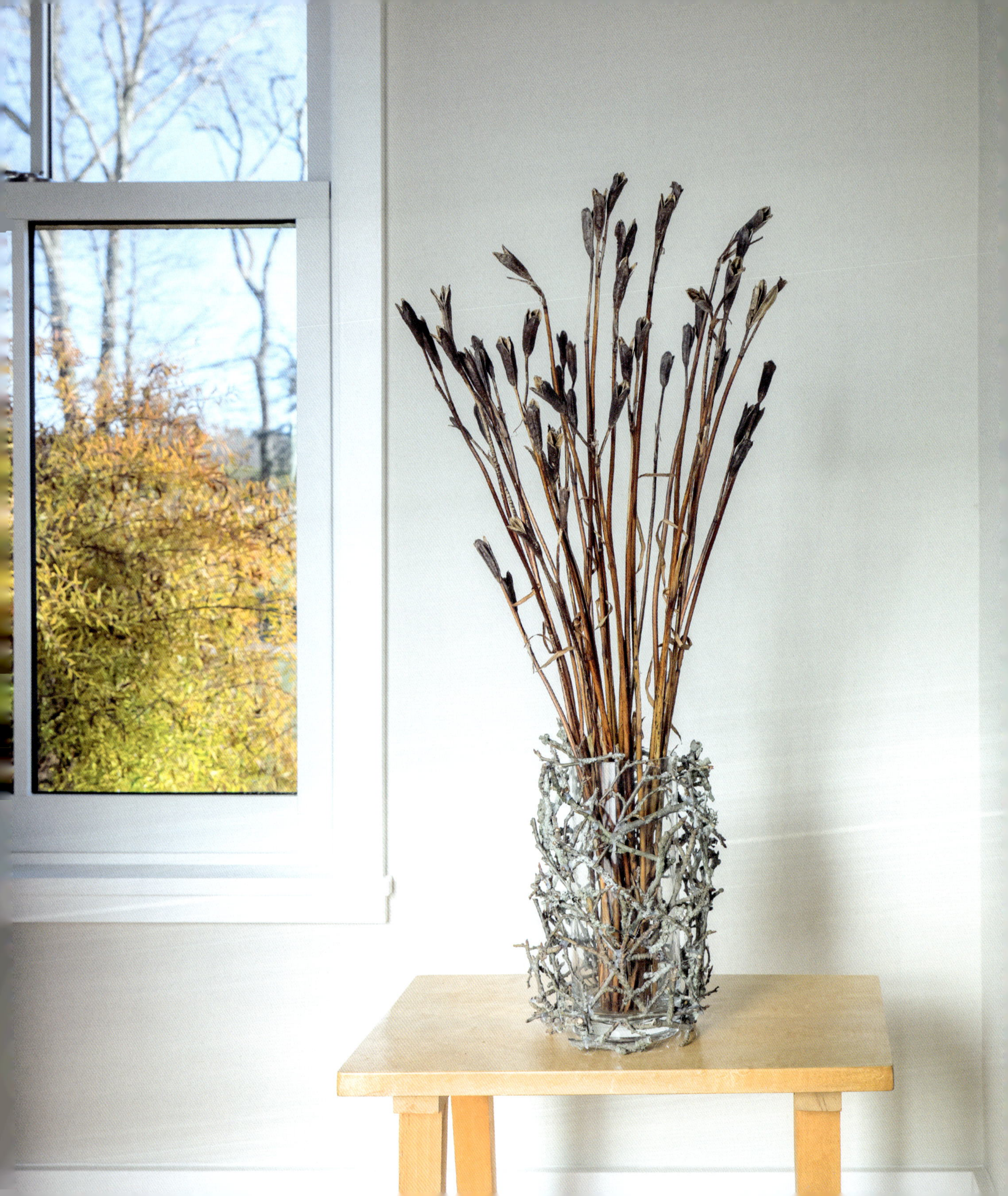

WHAT YOU NEED

- Big bunch of hardwood branches and twigs
- Straight-sided cylindrical glass vase
- Bubble pack
- Tape
- Garden clippers
- Glue gun and glue sticks
- Dull knife
- Matte acrylic spray (optional)
- Patience (not optional)

21

Twig Vase Sleeve

I'm not going to lie. Making a twig sleeve for a vase is challenging—especially attaching the first twigs. The good news is that once you get the hang of placing and gluing the twigs, and as the sleeve grows, the process gets much easier.

A twig sleeve can transform an inexpensive columnar vase into something striking. It looks elegant filled with big, lush, colorful bouquets or monochromatic, dried botanicals. Additionally, you can put a candle in the bottom of the vase or add water and a floating candle. For a different look, fill the vase with fairy lights. You can also use the sleeve on its own, without the vase, as a sculptural piece—keeping in mind that it is very lightweight and fragile.

I am lucky to have some old fruit trees in my yard with branches that are twisted and gnarly—some embroidered with beautiful lichen, moss, and algae. I love using these for organic, wild-looking results, but straighter, younger branches work well too. If you don't have trees from which you can cut branches, you can collect fallen twigs. Just make sure they aren't rotten, and check for bugs.

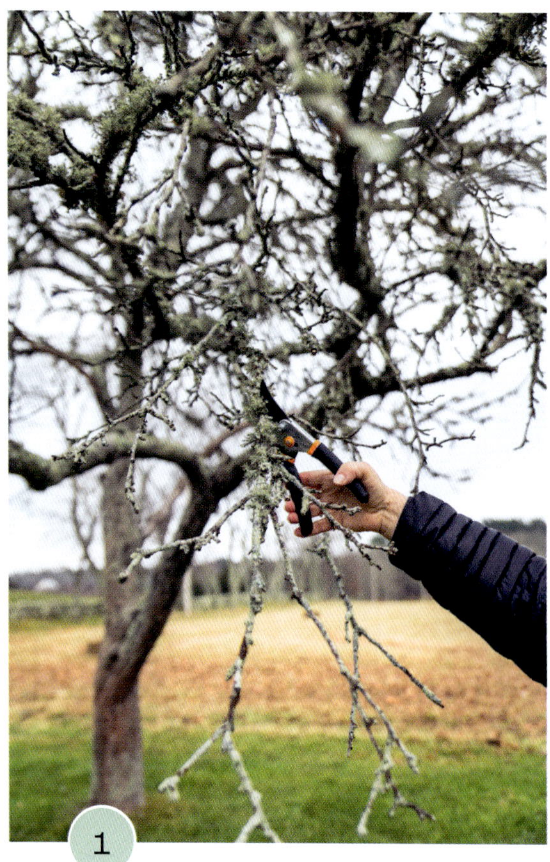

1

Cut or Forage Branches

Gather a big pile of branches and twigs—more than you can possibly use. Make sure they are hardwoods, as pine is often sticky and the sap is hard to remove from clothes and skin. I like branches with texture on the bark, but smoother branches will make sleeker and more modern sleeves.

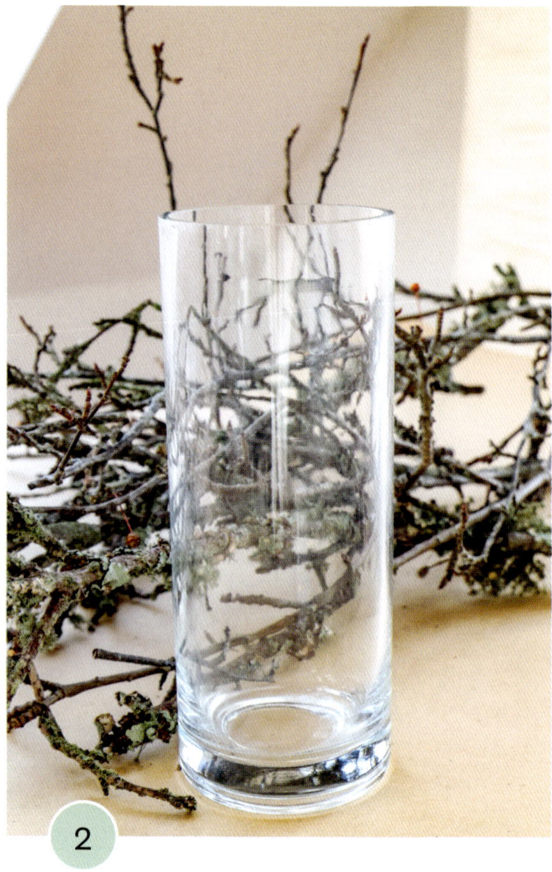

2

Wrap the Vase

Wrap the vase in a generous layer of bubble pack (at least ½ inch thick) using tape to secure it. If your bubble pack has small bubbles, wrap the vase twice; you want at least ½ inch of separation between the twigs and the vase. The wrap not only gives you space between the sleeve and vase so the vase can more easily be removed, it prevents you from inadvertently gluing twigs directly onto the vase.

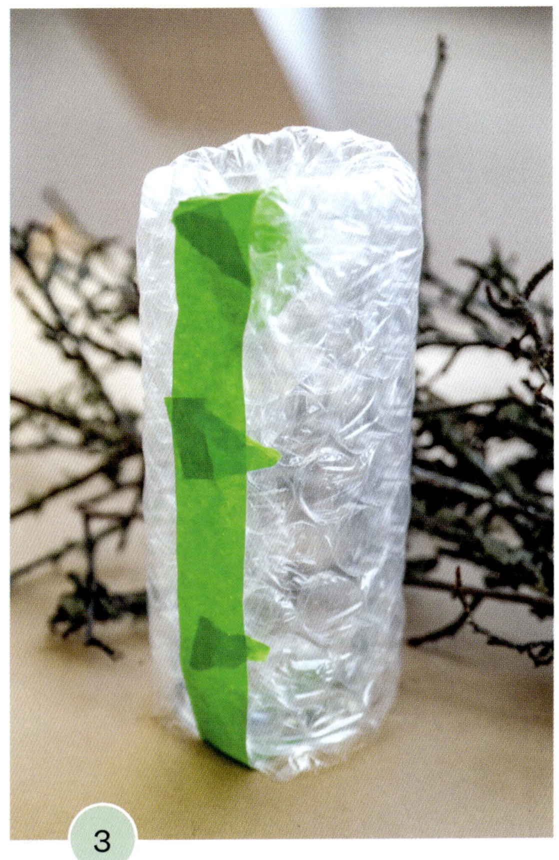

3

Cut Twigs for the Bottom Edge

Cut a few twigs that will form the bottom edge your sleeve. They should cover about half the circumference of your vase and be small enough that they don't extend beyond the sides of the wrapped vase. You want to be able to follow the curve of the vase.

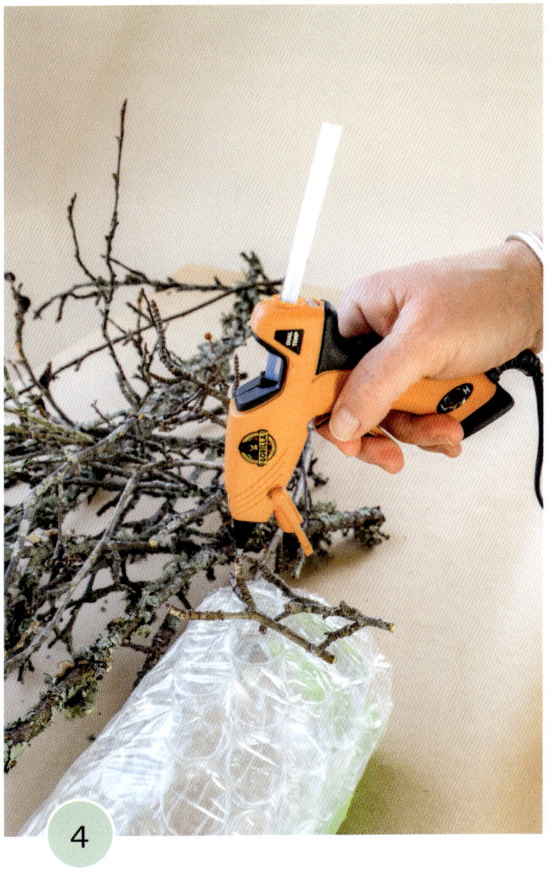

4

Lay the Vase on Its Side

Lay the vase on its side and, starting from the bottom, glue two twigs together. To give your sleeve stability, try to glue each twig in three places. Make sure the twigs are as close to the bottom edge of the vase as you can without having them extend beyond the end. It's important that the bottom edge be relatively even so that the sleeve can sit upright and straight on the table.

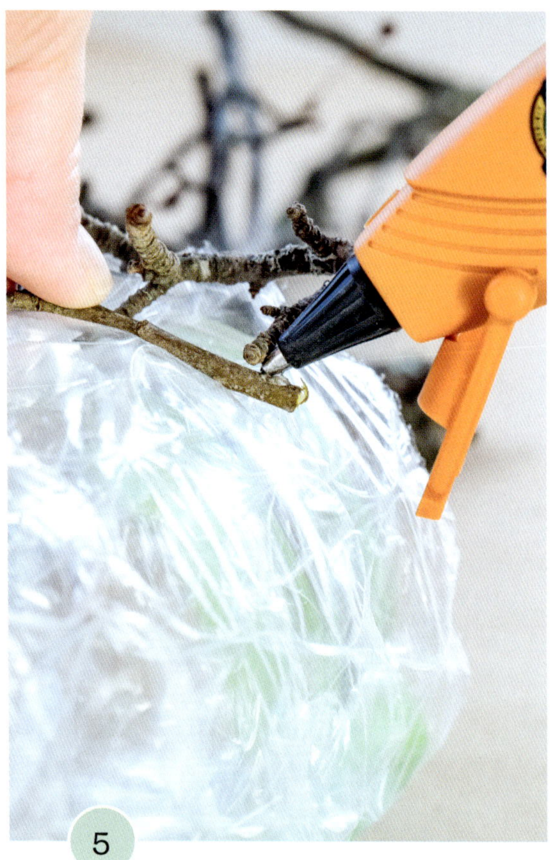

5

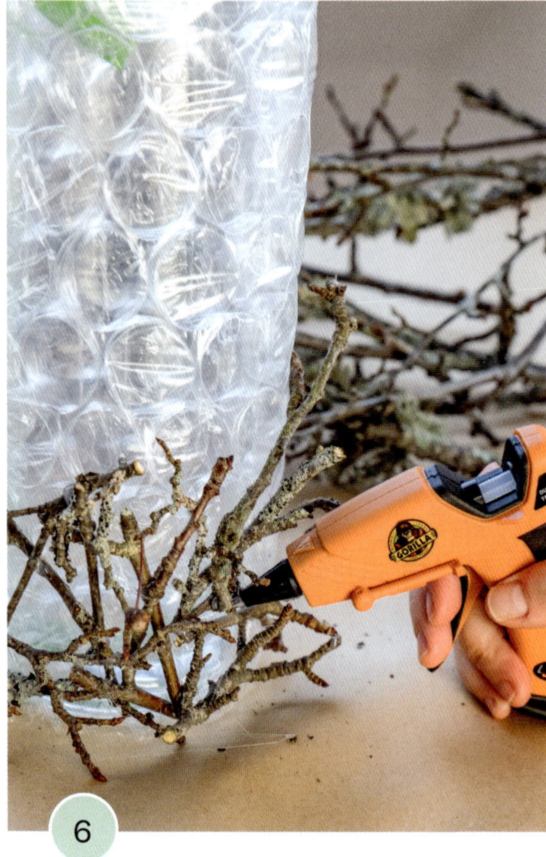

6

Glue

Aim the nozzle of your glue gun to the place where the twigs touch. Squeezing the trigger, place just enough of a blob of glue to solidly join the pieces. Hold the pieces until they are stuck together. This usually takes 15 to 30 seconds.

Add More Twigs

Adding the twigs is very much like putting together a puzzle. As you go, cut twig pieces off your branches to fit your design and then glue them together. If you want to keep the blunt ends of the twigs hidden, cut them on an angle. Cutting on an angle also creates more surface area to make gluing easier.

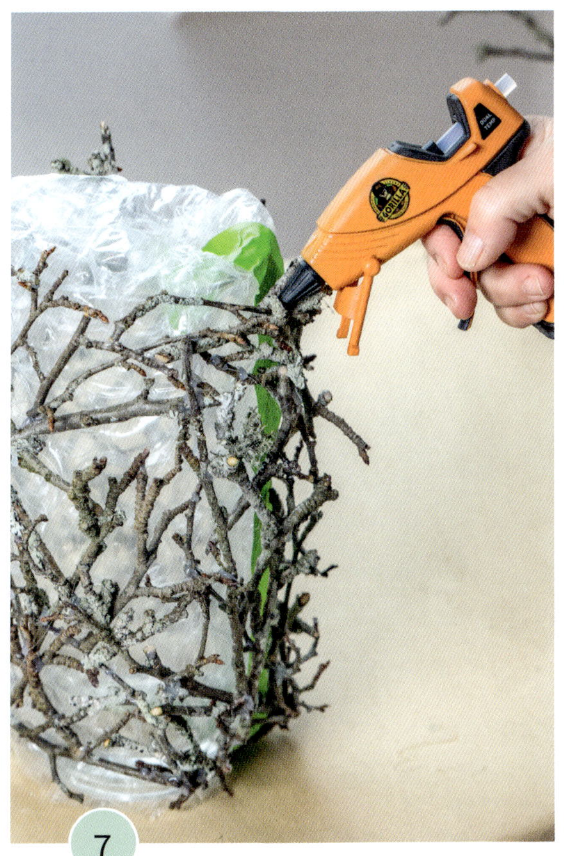

7

Build Up the Sides

Keep adding twigs until you reach the top edge of the vase. You want the twigs to be dense enough to form a pleasing pattern as well as to give the sleeve stability.

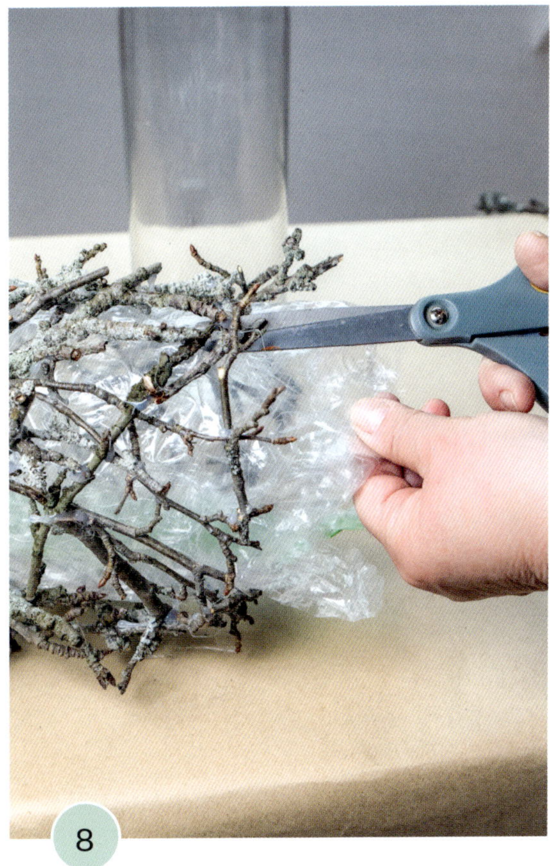

8

Remove the Vase

Remove the vase from the sleeve, then carefully peel the bubble pack off the twigs. This can be difficult, because your twig sleeve will be glued to the pack in some places. To help free it, you can pop the bubbles and cut the bubble pack and/or use a dull knife to pry the pack free from the glue.

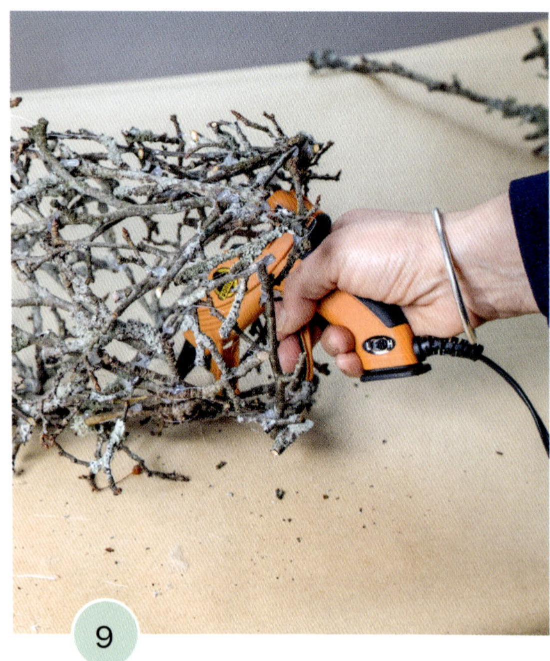

9

Reinforce the Sleeve

Once you successfully remove the vase and your sleeve is free of bubble pack, reglue any twigs that have fallen off or loosened in the process. Also check the inside of the sleeve for places that could use an extra dot of glue for reinforcement. If the sleeve doesn't sit straight, add twigs to the bottom edge to prop up the side that is lower.

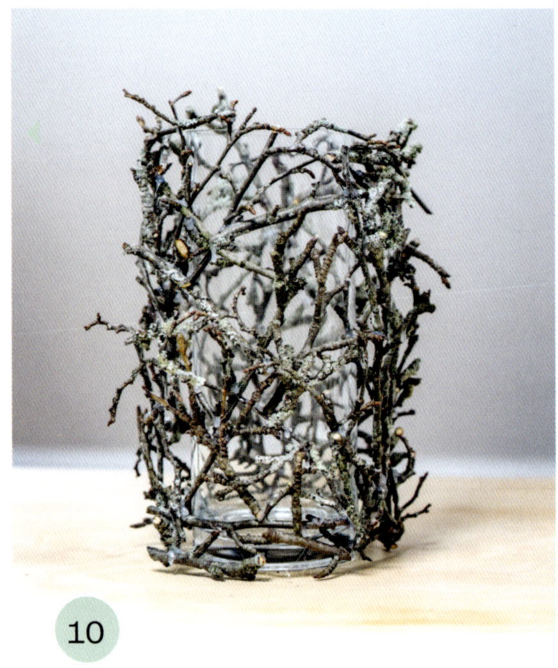

10

Remove Excess Glue

Unless you're incredibly meticulous and a glue gun expert, you will have blobs of glue and gossamer strands like spiderwebs in places you don't want them. Carefully brush or pull off the offending strands. Any glue blobs that are distracting to your design can be carefully pulled or cut off. You can always reglue pieces, if necessary. To add to the longevity of your twig sleeve and make it a bit less delicate, you can use a matte acrylic spray. Just make sure to remove the vase first.

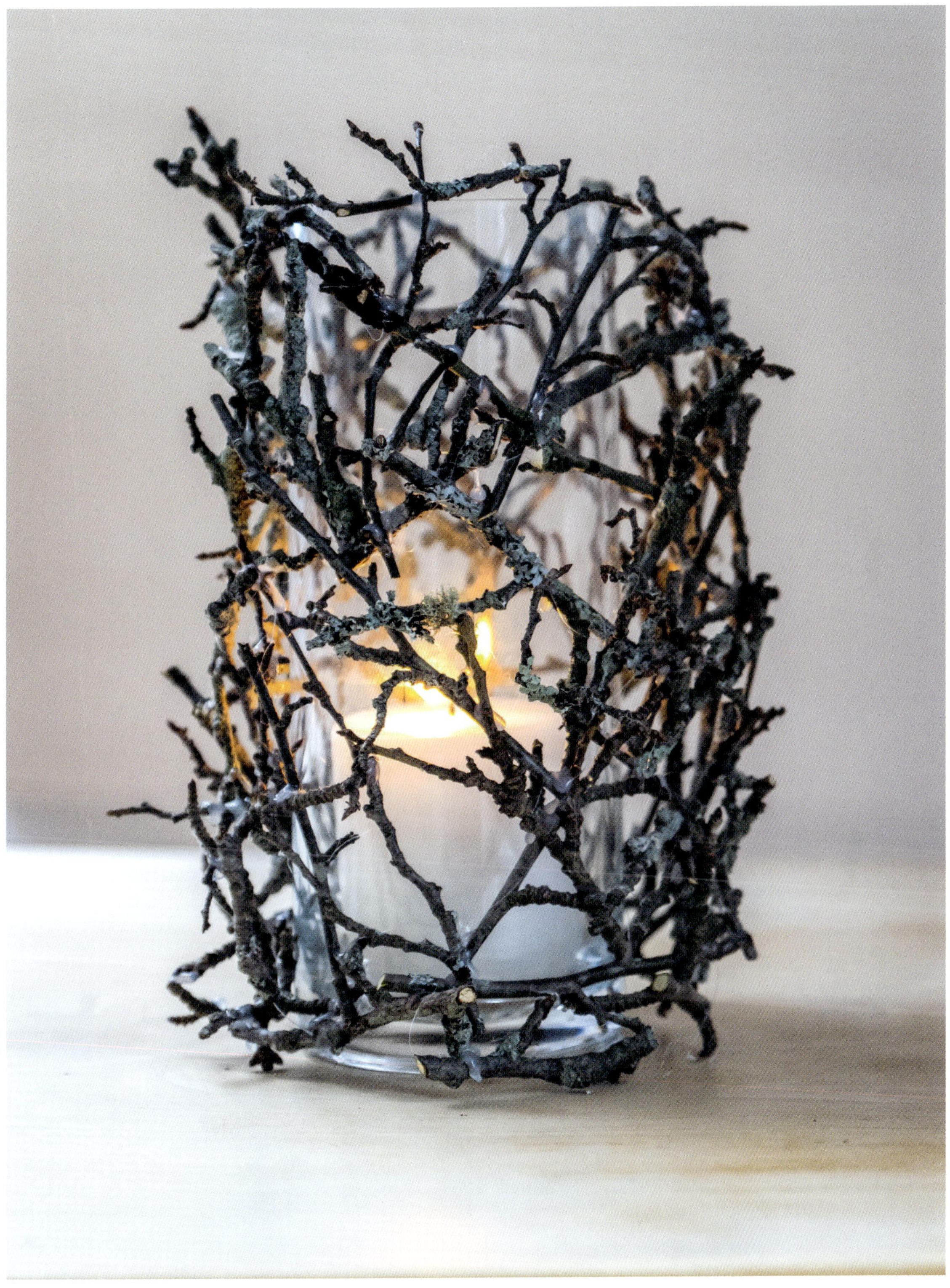

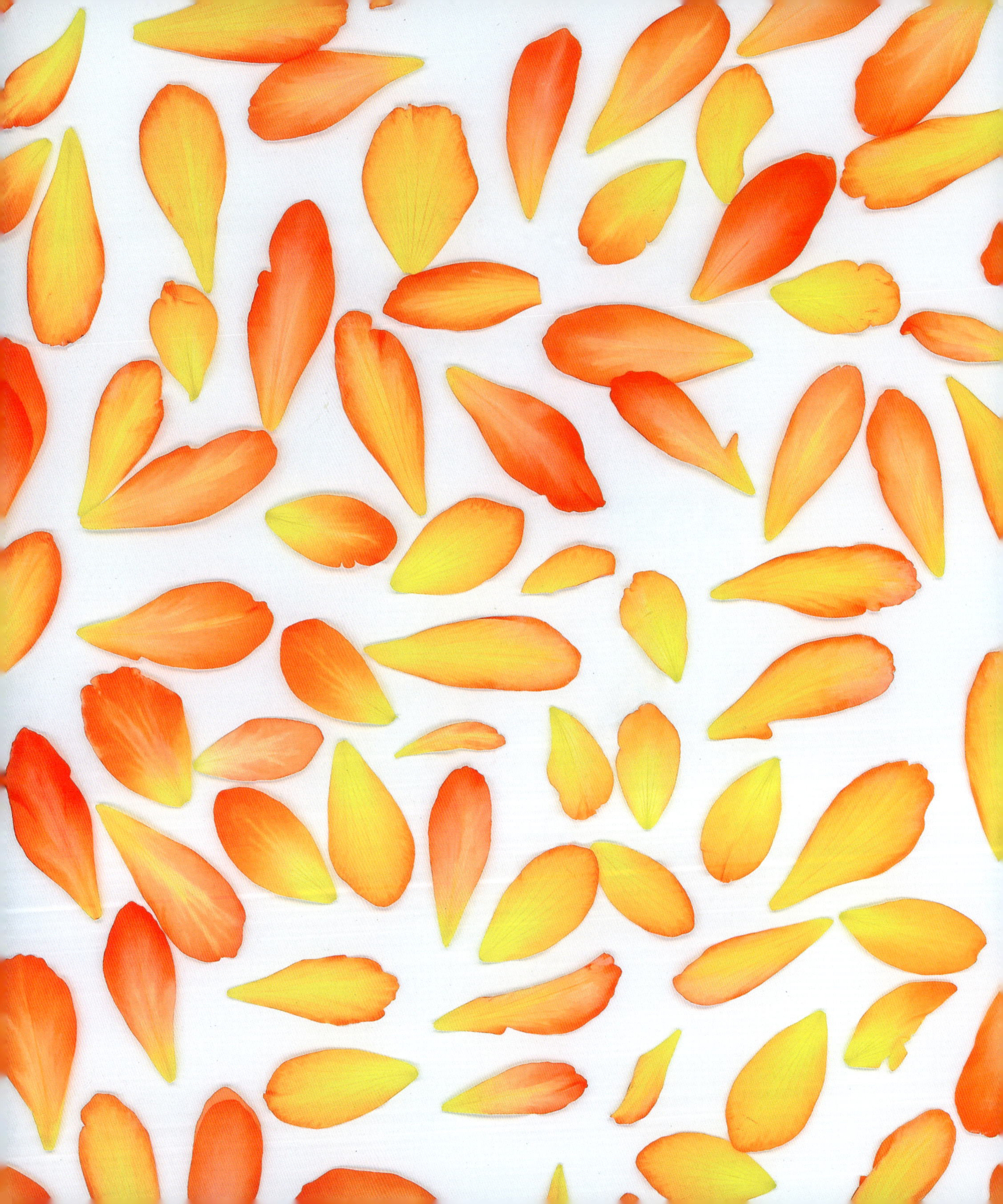

WHAT YOU NEED

- Flatbed scanner or multifunction printer
- Botanicals
- Tweezers
- Glass wipes or lint-free cloth
- Computer with photo editing software (optional)

22

Scanography

I fell in love with scanner photography, also called scanography, in 2010, when I was given a magazine assignment to photograph fall leaves. I had seen examples of scanography but had never tried it. In one of my more brazen moves, I suggested to my editor that we scan the leaves for the piece instead of photographing them. Much to my surprise, she went for the idea, even knowing I had no idea what I was doing.

In a complete panic, I called well-known scanography artist Ellen Hoverkamp, whose work I greatly admired. Thankfully, even though I was a stranger, she took my call. I will be forever grateful for her incredible generosity and patience as she explained the process in great detail. I went out and bought an inexpensive flatbed scanner, which I still use today. I believe that the fall leaf scans piece is one of the most successful photo stories I have ever done.

When creating with a scanner, I always think of the quote comparing the dancer Ginger Rogers to Fred Astaire, "Sure he was great, but don't forget that Ginger Rogers did everything he did ... backwards and in high heels." One of the challenges with scanography is that you are creating a composition that is shot from underneath, so you can only guess what the finished image will look like—sort of photography backwards in high heels. It often takes many iterations and lots of moving things around to get a worthwhile scan. This can be time-consuming because you need to clean the glass often, as pollen and pieces of botanicals make dots and smudges that you will either be stuck with in the finished image or will have to edit out.

While you can buy a flatbed scanner, you may have a perfectly good scanner built into your home printer. And while you can print a scan directly onto copier paper or photo paper, you'll get much better final images if you connect your scanner to a computer so you can edit the scanned image before printing. Your printer or scanner may have software that allows you to transfer digital files. Alternatively, some printers or scanners have a port for a thumb drive, and you can transfer your scans that way. Additionally, to make large prints or products, you may have to multiply the pixels of your image file with Photoshop or another software.

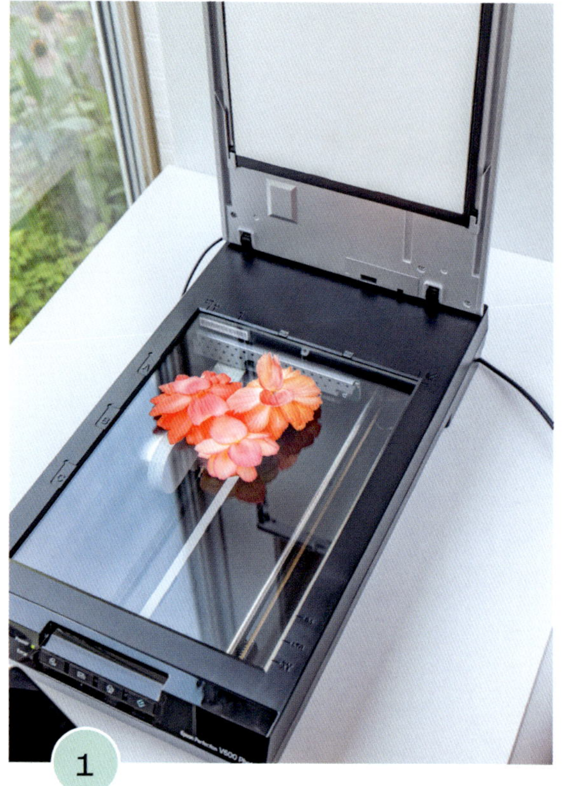

1

Set Up the Scanner

Place the scanner on a flat surface and figure out how you want to use the files it produces. If you are connecting to a computer, download the scanner software and connect the computer. Practice scanning documents or other objects before you start with delicate and ephemeral botanicals. Try scanning with the cover open and closed.

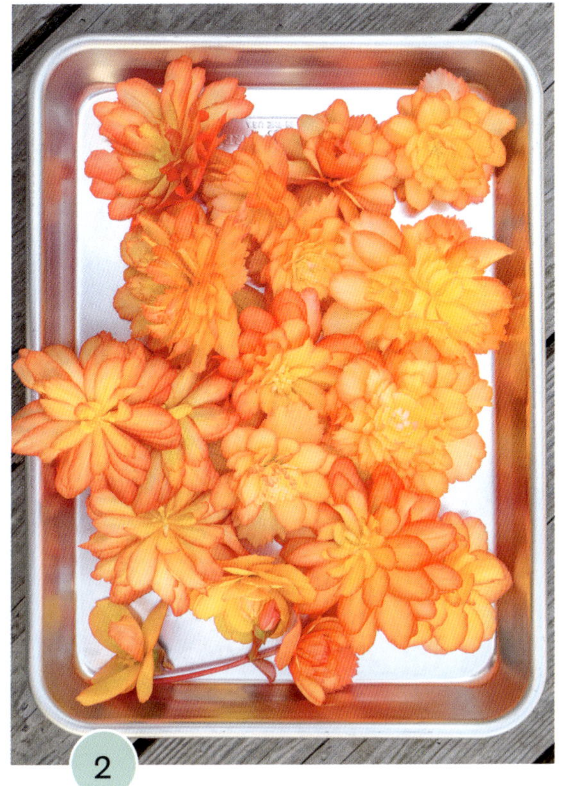

2

Select the Botanicals

Your choices are limitless. But while you can scan almost anything, coming up with a pleasing composition is the challenge. A single blossom can be stunning, as can a scanner platen (the glass bed of the scanner) filled with flowers, leaves, even fruit. Carefully inspect botanicals for any bugs or dirt, as they will show up in your scan.

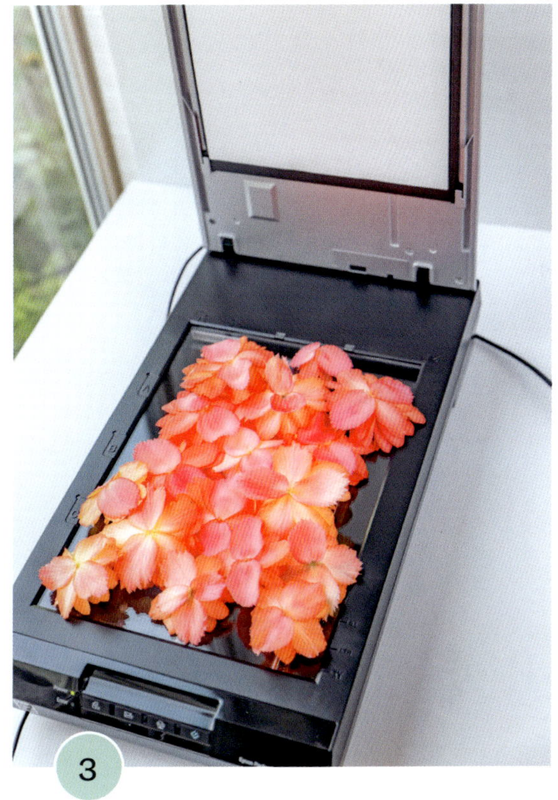

3

Place the Botanicals and Preview

Place and arrange your botanicals carefully on the scanner glass. Take a preview scan to see if you like your composition. If not, move things around, making sure to clean up any pollen or bits that have inevitably fallen. Use tweezers, a glass wipe, or a moistened lint-free cloth so as not to add fingerprints to your scan.

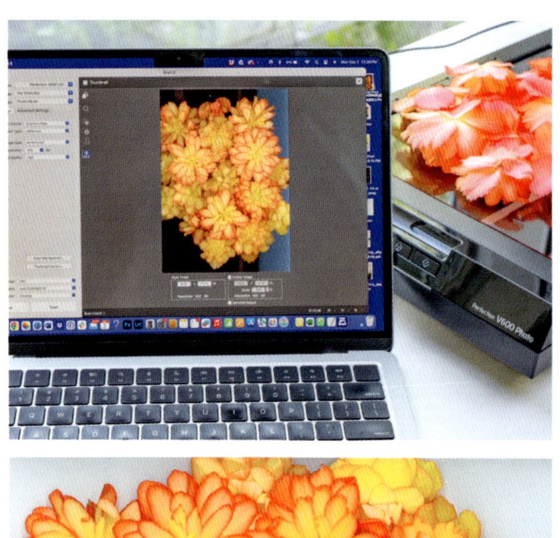

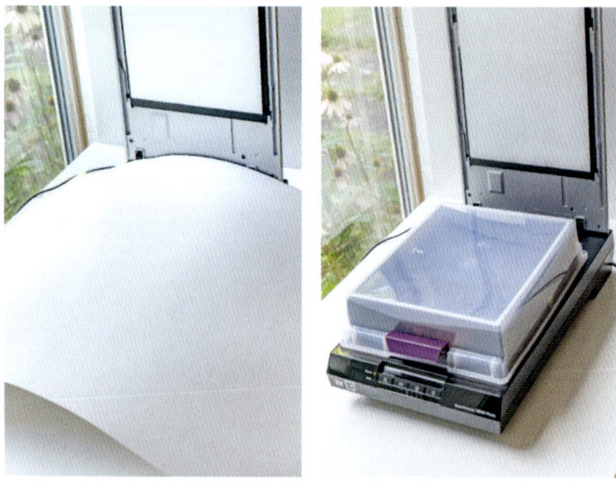

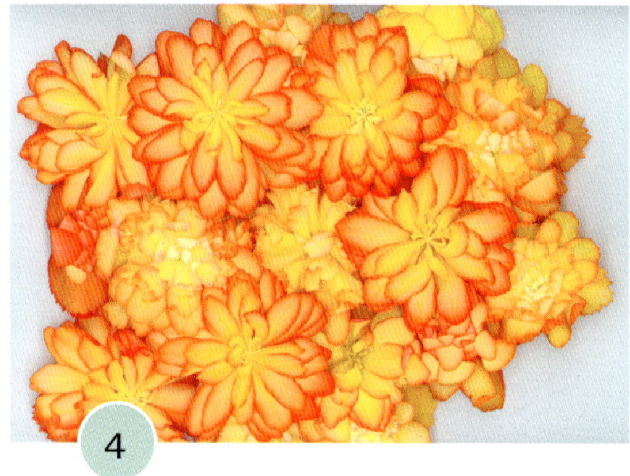

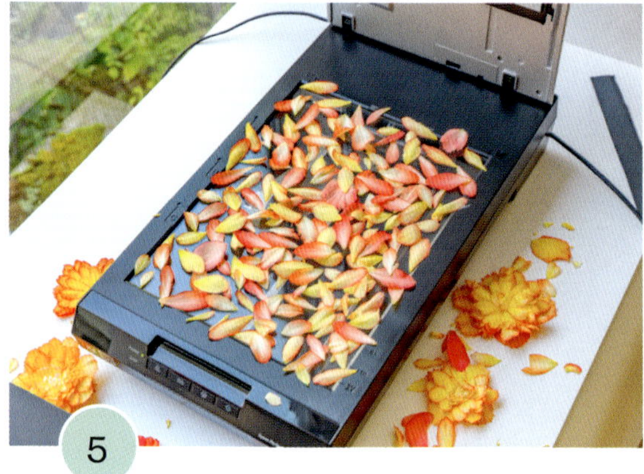

4

Scan

Once you are happy with your preview, make the actual scan.

5

Experiment

Try scanning with the top open to get a dark background, or close the scanner to get a white background. Keep in mind, though, that by closing the scanner you'll be squishing your botanicals, so you might want to experiment with this approach last. To change the background color without damaging your plants, you can create a paper tunnel. With your scanner open, take a piece of stiff paper large enough to cover the printer and bend it to form a tunnel, taping it to the sides.

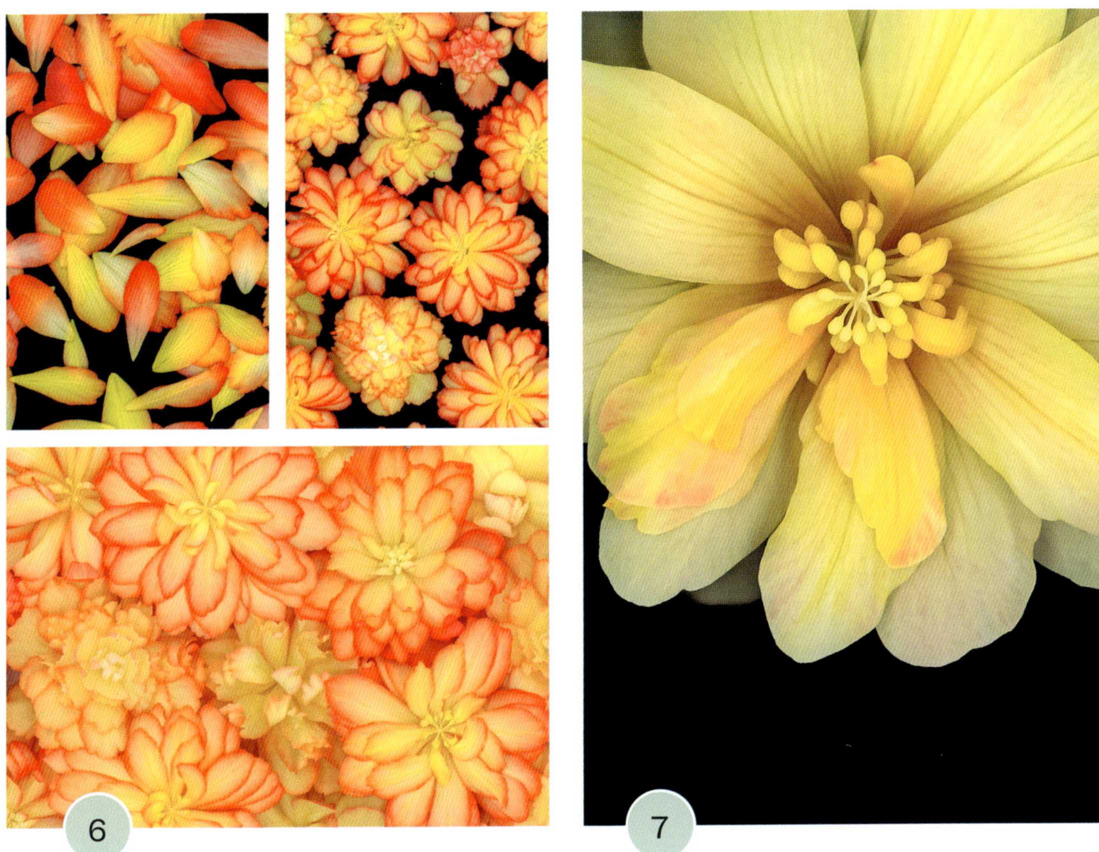

Edit (Optional)

If you choose to edit your images, the possible changes are limitless. You can simply clean up any dirt or spots that you missed or completely transform your scan, altering the colors and contrast or cropping it to a different size and shape.

Print the Images

Once you are happy with your scan, if you have a good printer, you can print your own images on photo paper. There are also lots of gorgeous fine-art papers that will work in a printer, from translucent rice paper to heavy and textured watercolor paper. Or you can send your image to a specialized company that will print your image on paper or any number of products.

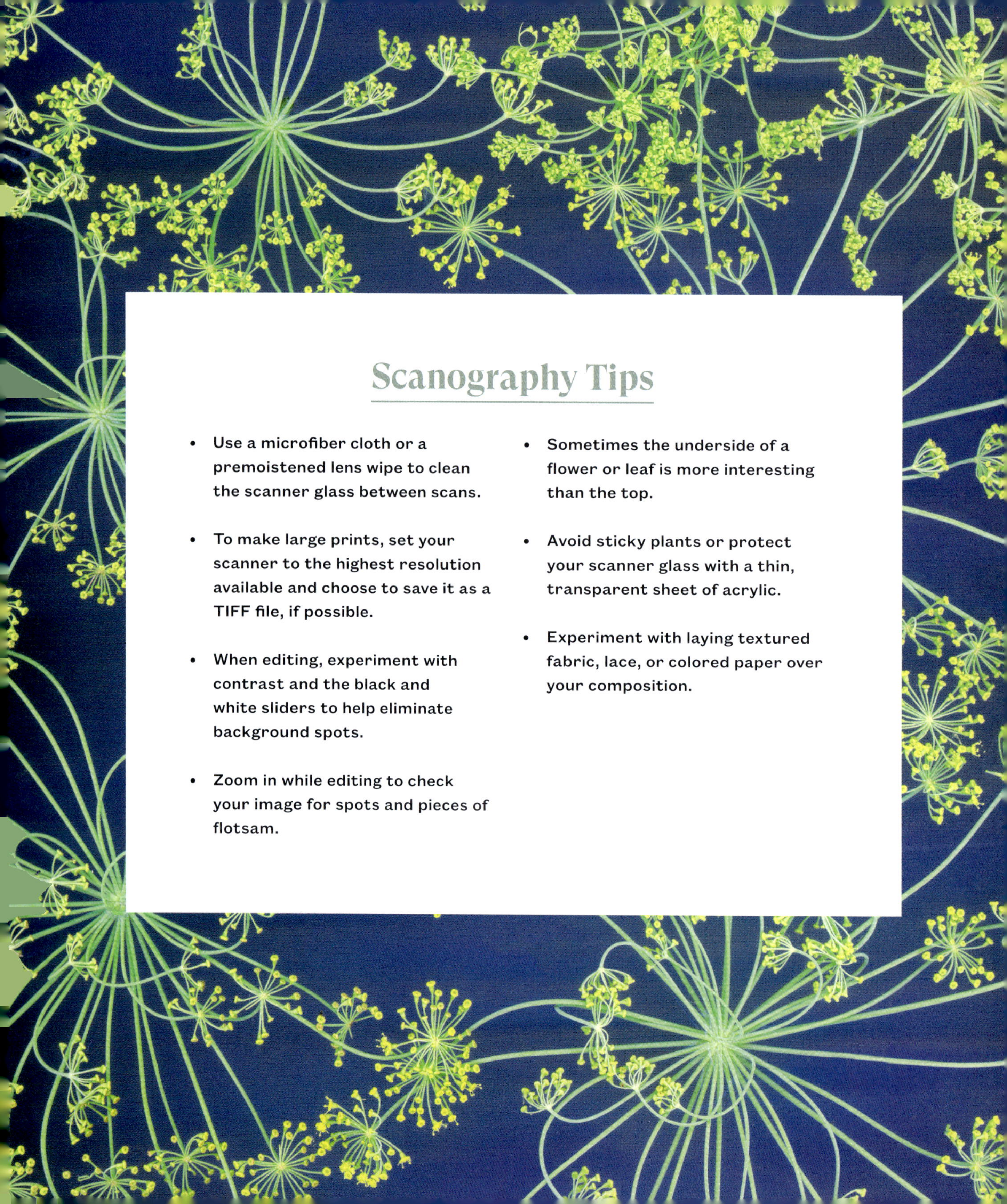

Scanography Tips

- Use a microfiber cloth or a premoistened lens wipe to clean the scanner glass between scans.
- To make large prints, set your scanner to the highest resolution available and choose to save it as a TIFF file, if possible.
- When editing, experiment with contrast and the black and white sliders to help eliminate background spots.
- Zoom in while editing to check your image for spots and pieces of flotsam.
- Sometimes the underside of a flower or leaf is more interesting than the top.
- Avoid sticky plants or protect your scanner glass with a thin, transparent sheet of acrylic.
- Experiment with laying textured fabric, lace, or colored paper over your composition.

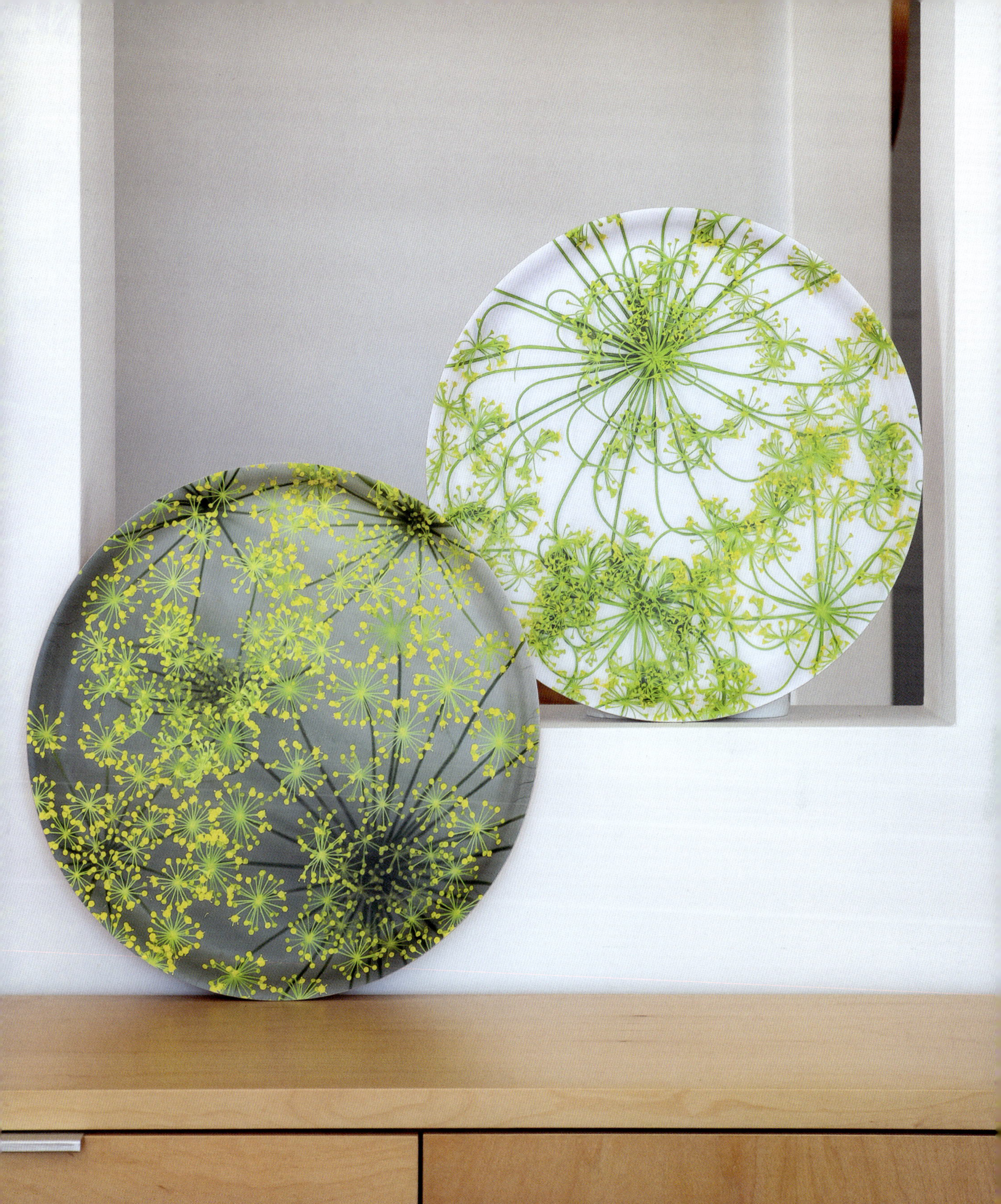

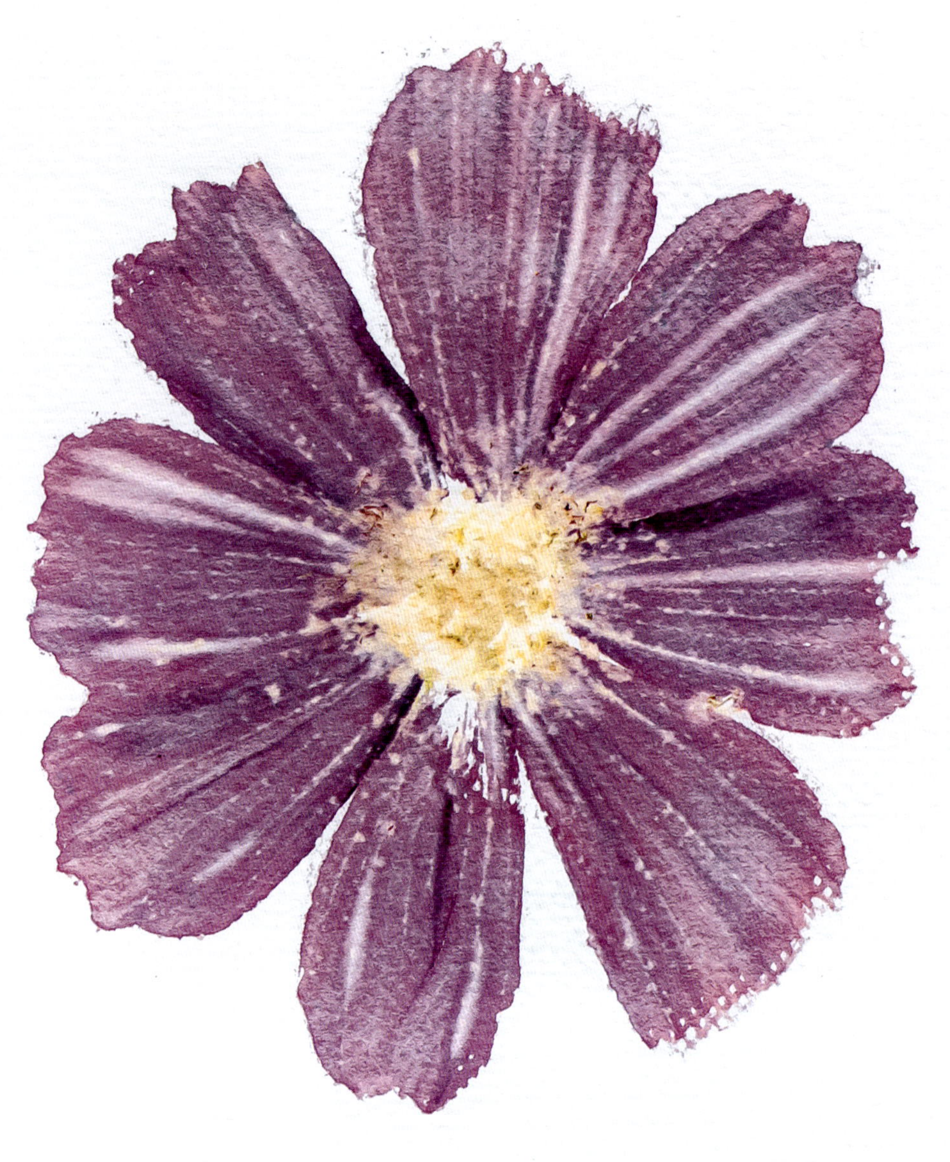

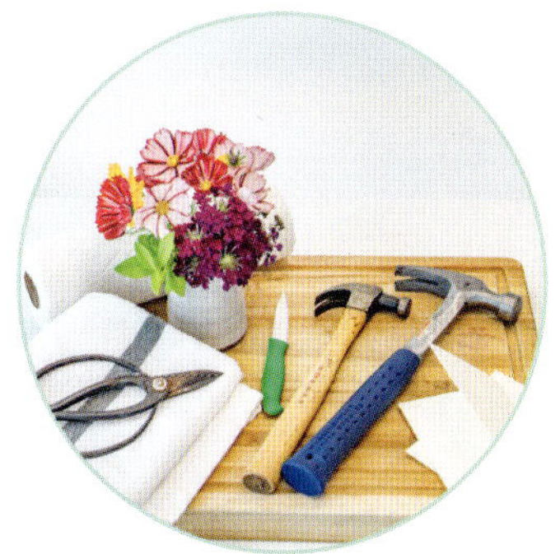

WHAT YOU NEED

- Fresh botanicals
- Sharp scissors or garden clippers
- Hammer or mallet
- Heavy paper or fabric
- Heavy cutting board or wood board
- Paper towel, plastic baggie, or lightweight smooth fabric
- Knife (optional)
- Clear acrylic fixative (optional)

23

Hammered Botanical Prints

Before my mother died, I never fully appreciated the beauty and profound importance a hand-written card can hold. I thought that cards were largely an antiquated and unnecessary relic, and because I am a terrible speller, they were excruciatingly painful to write. To my surprise, I found that the condolence cards I received contained and uniquely conveyed oceans of grief, sympathy, humor, and love in ways electronic messages simply couldn't. And while I loved the emails and texts, I could feel the time and effort people put in to writing cards, and I deeply felt the connection they had with my mom and with me. I also loved seeing people's handwriting, some of which I had never seen, and some of which had been absent from my life for decades. The writing and warmth became embossed on my heart and brain in ways that electronic messages simply couldn't match.

So I am making a pitch here for bringing back handwritten cards: short, long, handmade, or store-bought (but of course, I believe hand-made is the way to go if you can). And not just for death, but for celebration, congratulations, gratitude, or simple connection. I discovered that if you can't spell, you can write the note on a computer or your phone, spell-check it, and then handwrite it on the card.

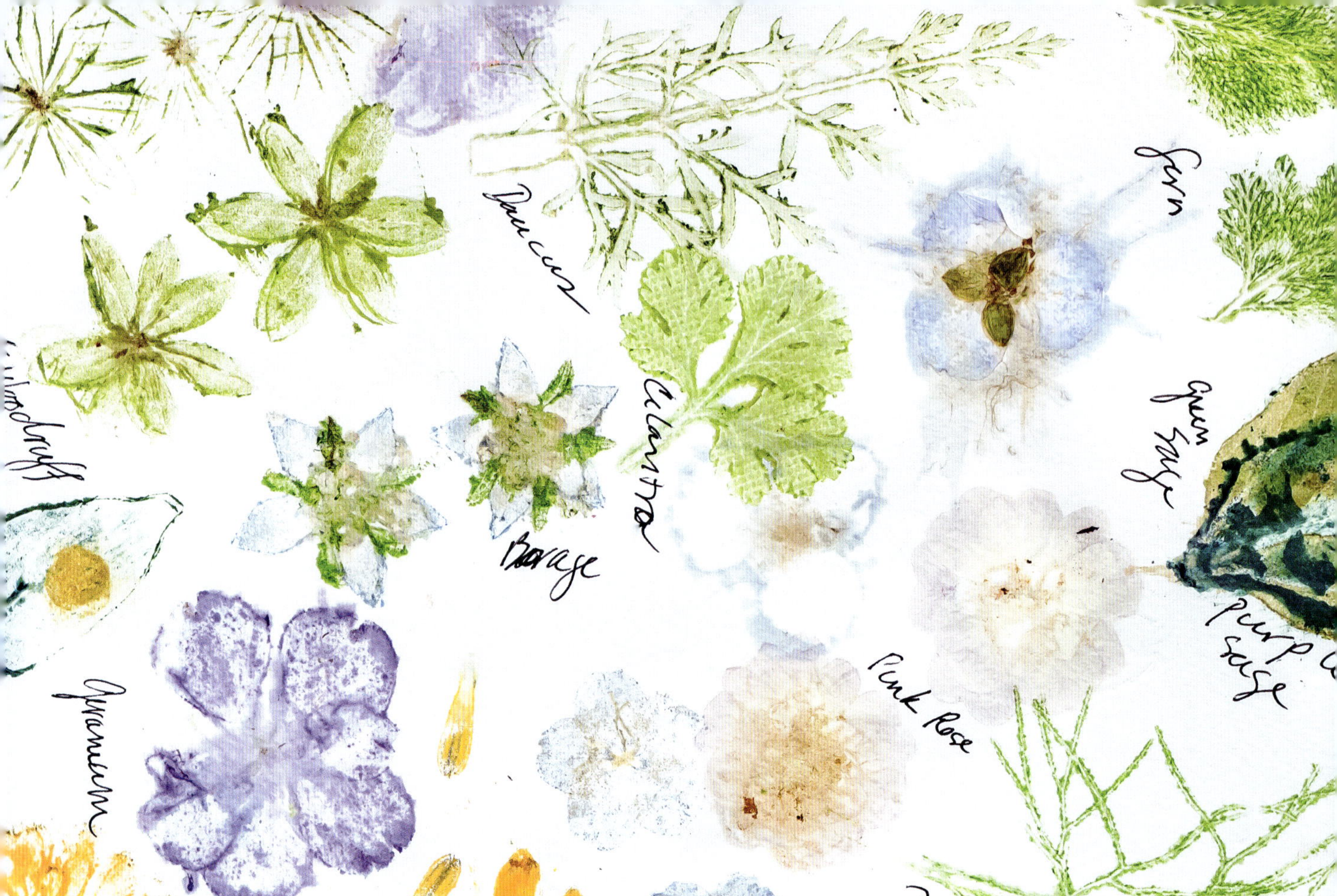

Hammering botanicals is a great way to make cards. It's noisy, satisfying, and harder than it looks to get a good impression. If you make a mistake (which I can assure you, you will), a card can often simply be cut and made smaller—excising the error. There are many variables and choices that will determine the results when hammering, including the botanicals you use, the type of hammer or mallet you choose, and the paper or fabric that receives the image. They all affect the outcome. Any hammer will work, but I like having two: a heavy one for leaves that can be smashed all over, and a smaller, lighter one that can maneuver around the center of a flower, which often needs a light touch to avoid turning your impression to mush.

For paper, choose one heavy enough to withstand being beaten with a hammer and absorbent enough that the pigment doesn't slide off. A smooth watercolor paper or even some cardstock will work well. Experiment until you find what you like.

In addition, the material you put between the hammerhead and your botanical also affects the outcome. I have tried plastic bags, toilet paper, paper towels, and several different fabrics. For most botanicals, using fabric is my favorite, but for more abstract and less defined looks, plastic works better. If you don't want to get too far into the weeds with this, a paper towel is a great all-around choice.

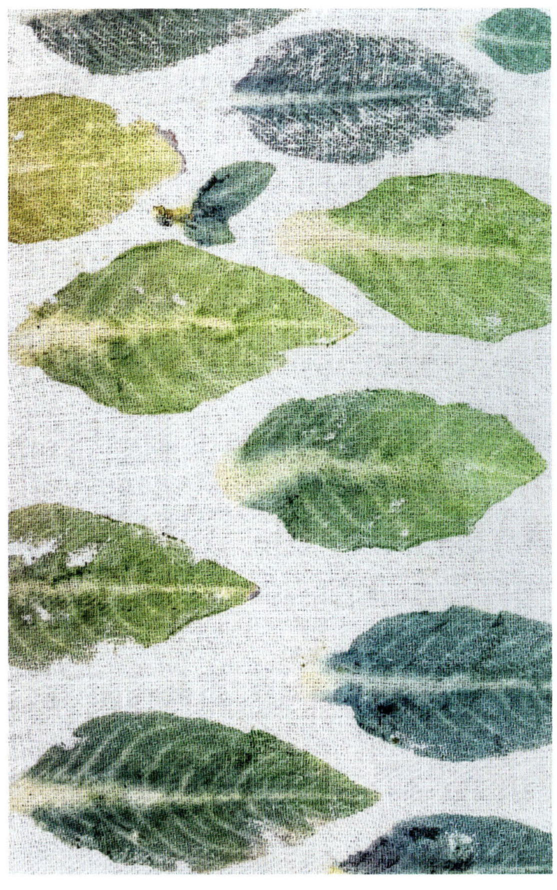

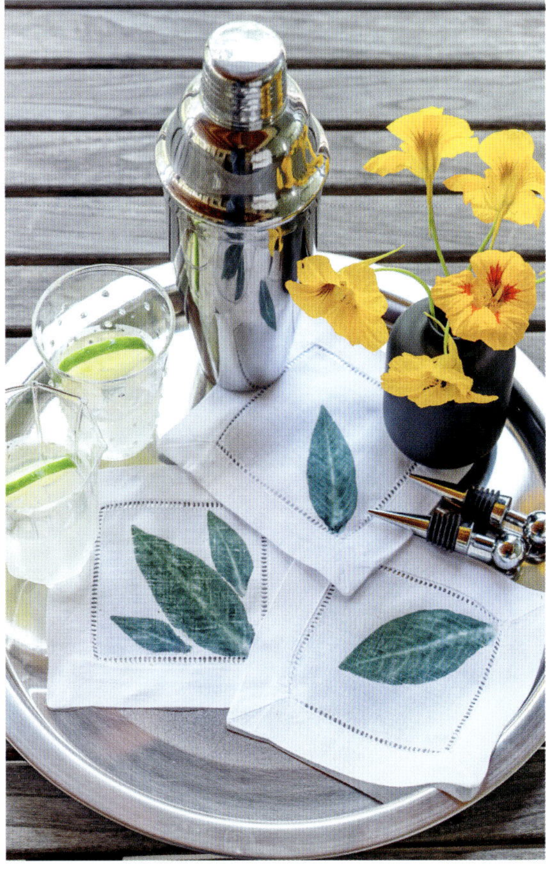

Some things to look out for when choosing botanicals: nothing too juicy (like begonias) because they tend to explode under the force of the hammer, so instead of a nice impression you are left with a messy splotch that looks more like a Rorschach test than the flower or leaf you picked. And be willing to experiment, because botanical colors can change radically when hammered. An attractive lime-and-dark-green–striped sage turns a mucky brown when hammered, as does purple basil and some coleus. Of course there are also delightful surprises, like the magenta verbena that becomes an almost midnight blue when smashed, or the dill that transforms into a sweet pale green that looks like it came from the sea.

I must also mention indigo here. I am completely smitten with Japanese indigo (*Persicaria tinctoria*). To me, it is a fascinating and magical plant. The dark green leaf, when pounded and exposed to air, transforms into a shade of blue or blue-green. I've had the best luck hammering the leaves onto smooth fabric, making sure to smash the entire leaf, but being gentle with the stem, as it can get gloppy.

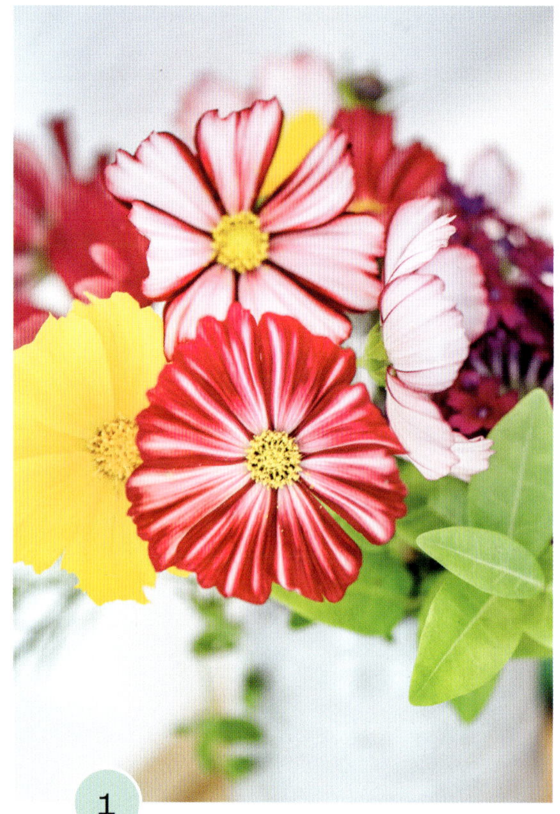

1

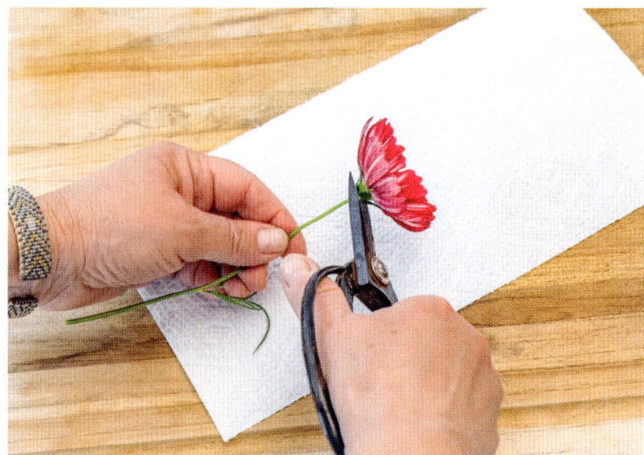

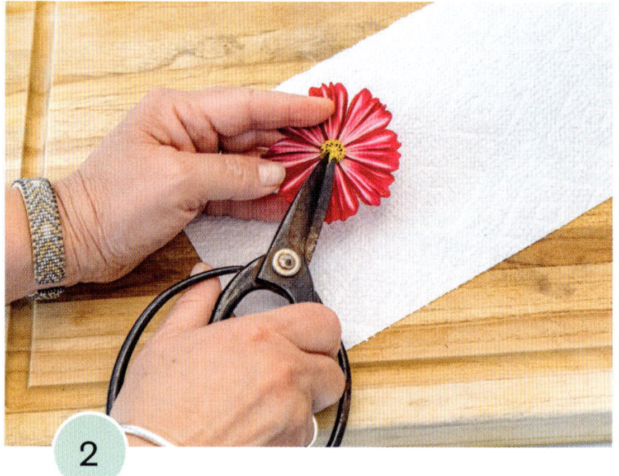

2

Select the Botanicals

The easiest botanicals to hammer are flat and not too juicy. Pansies, ferns, dill, coreopsis, and cosmos are great plants to start with. Blossoms or petals taken from geraniums, verbena, and hydrangeas can be gorgeous too. Many thin, flat leaves also make great, clean impressions.

Prepare the Botanical

Depending on your flower or leaf, you may choose to keep or cut off the stem. If you leave the stem on, be aware that some stems contain quite a bit of moisture and, if hammered too enthusiastically, can leave a wide, unattractive band. You can also trim the center of your flower to help it lie flat and prevent a muddy mess when hammered too hard.

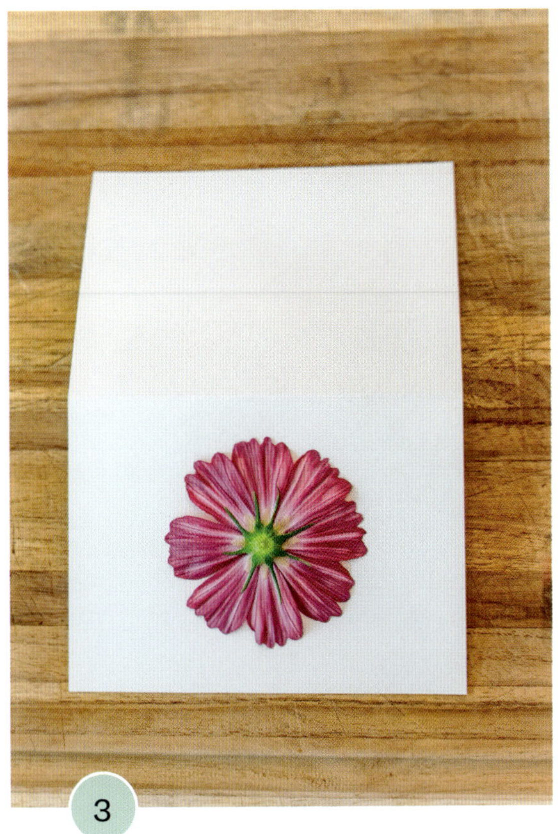

3

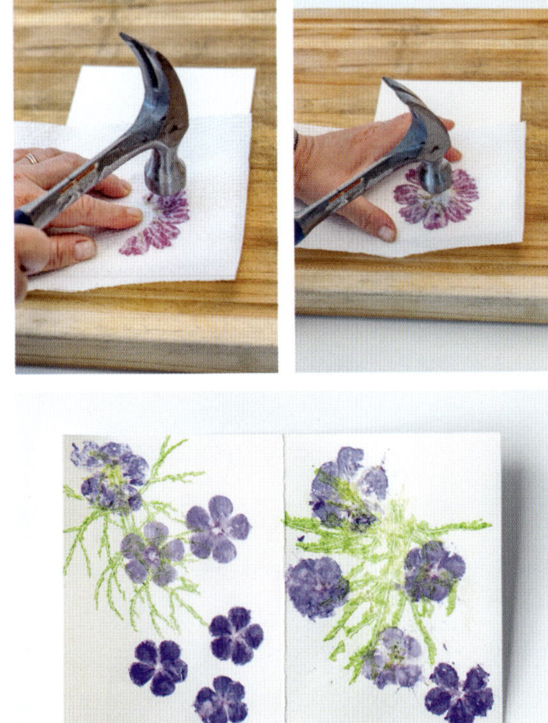

4

Place the Botanical

Set the paper (or fabric) on the cutting board. If you have a single large botanical, place it carefully where you want it on the paper, making sure that all the petals are spread and not folded. If you are making a composition with several botanicals, you can either place them one at a time and then hammer, or put them all down at once.

Place a Protective Layer and Start Whacking

Once the botanicals are in place, cover them with a clean piece of plastic, fabric, or paper towel. In the bottom image for this step, the flowers on the left were covered with paper towel, and on the right, with acetate. I like to start hammering on the outside edge and work my way in. How hard to hammer depends on the botanical and which hammer or mallet you are using. You have to really whack drier botanicals, like ferns, to leave a colorful imprint, but delicate flowers, like cosmos, require a lighter touch. The center of a flower often needs just a slight tap—hit it too hard and you will be left with an unsightly blob in the middle of your beautiful design.

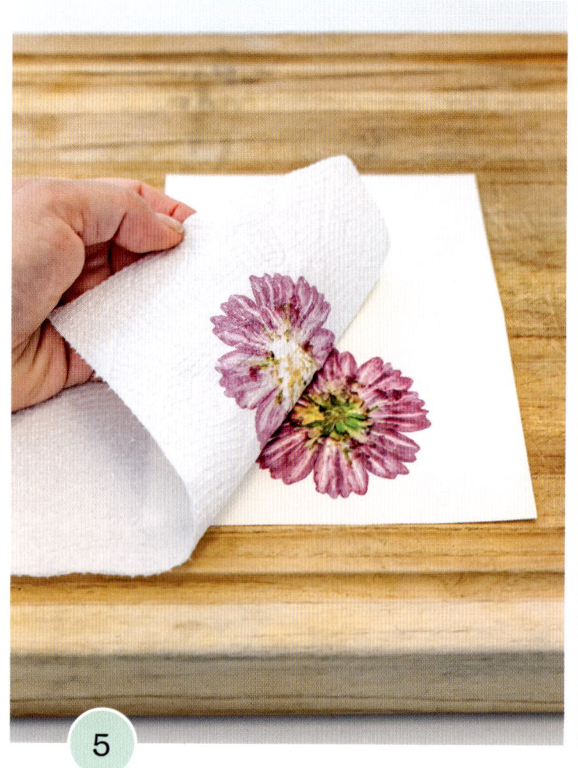

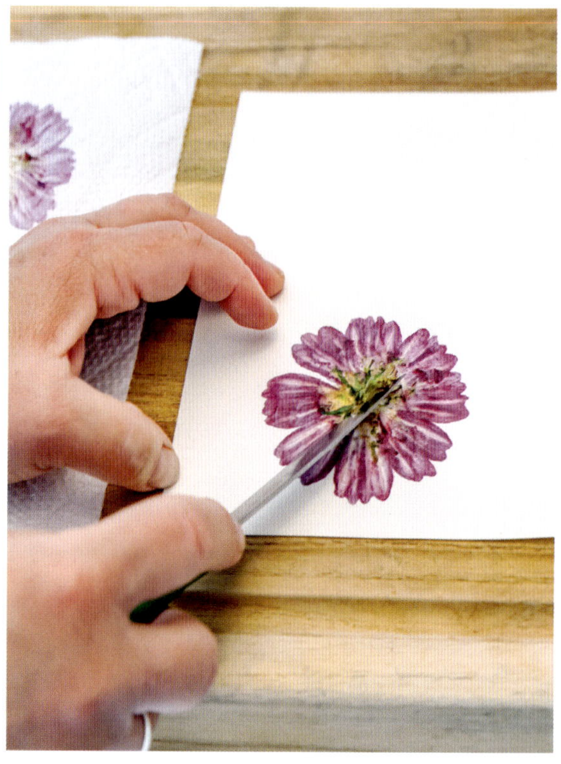

5

Remove the Protective Layer and Botanical

When you peel off the protective layer, sometimes you'll get lucky and most of the botanical will come with it. Often, however, you'll have to gently scrape off the remaining flower with your finger and/or a sharp knife. It helps to scrape from the outside in, as the scrapings, which still have a lot of color, can mark your paper. After the impression has dried, if you choose to, you can spray the card with a clear acrylic fixative, to protect it from possible smudging. If you want to make multiples, photograph or scan the finished project to make prints.

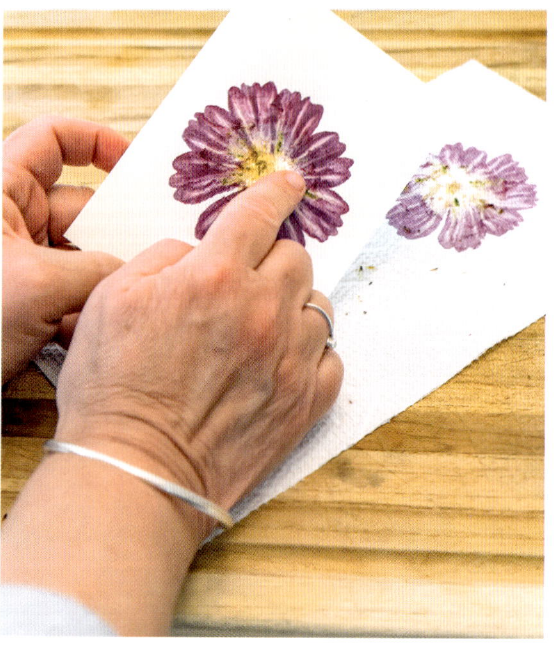

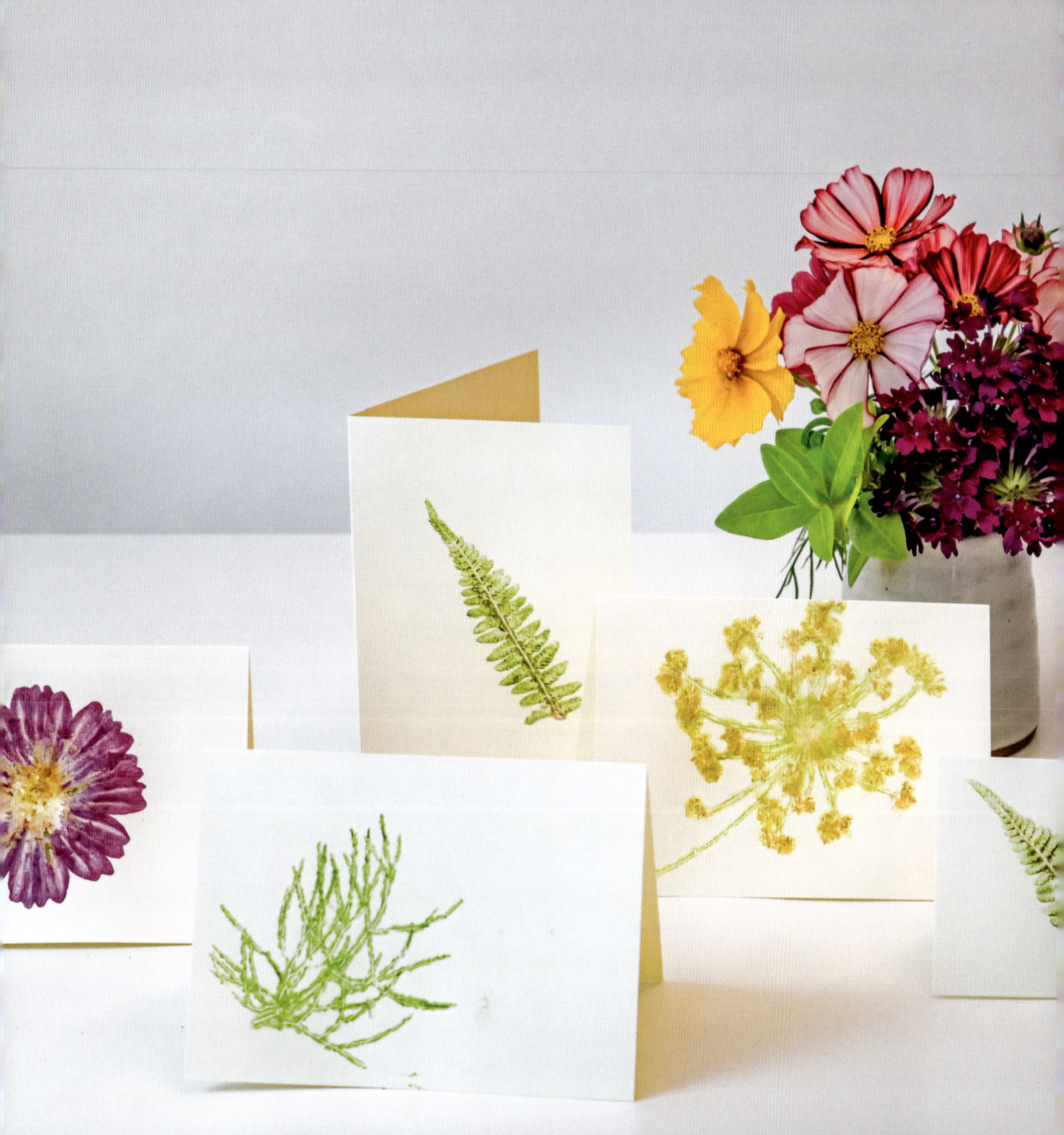

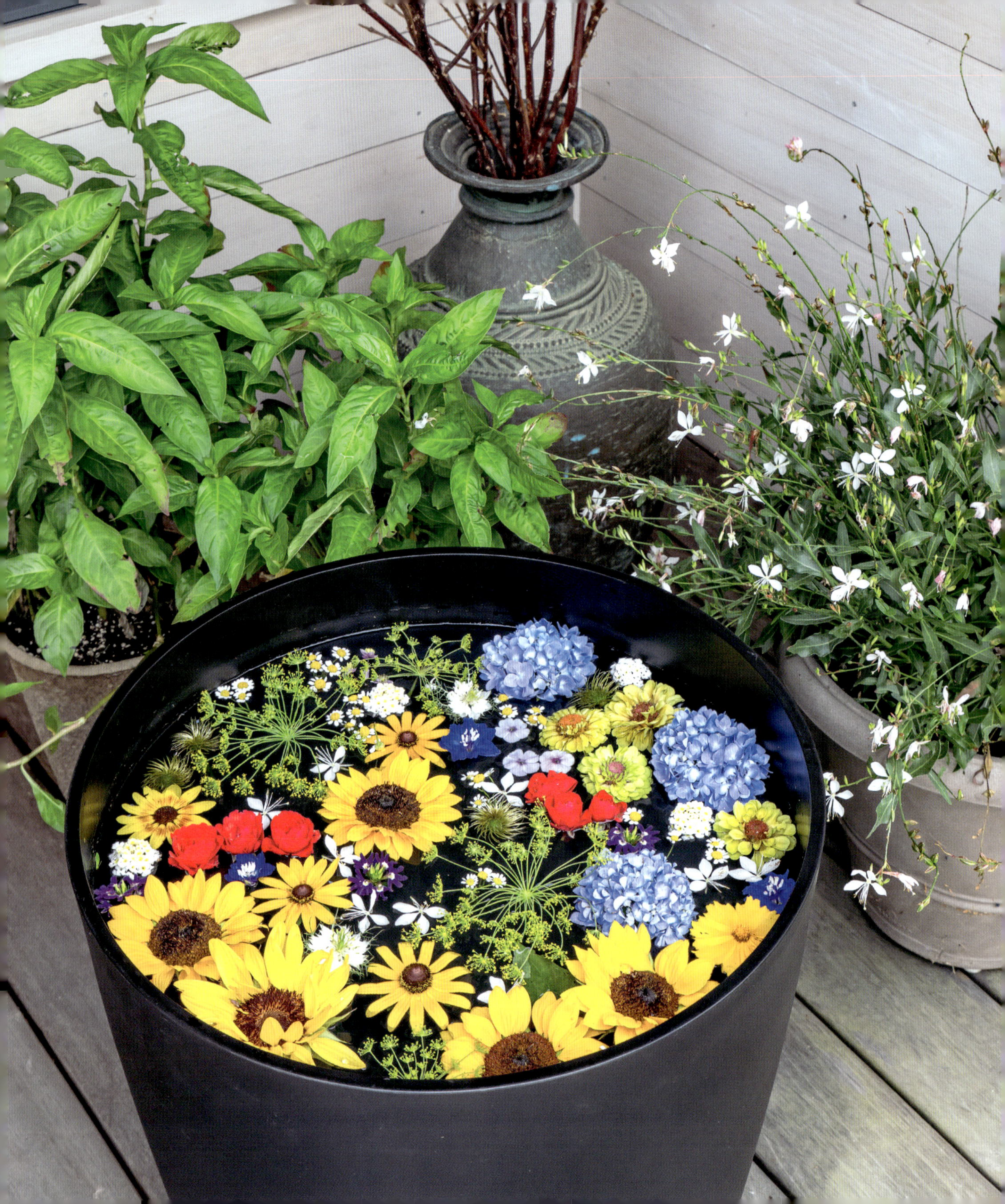

WHAT YOU NEED

- Botanicals
- Watertight vessel
- Small sharp scissors or garden clippers

24

Floating Bouquet

This may be the easiest project in the book. All you need is a water-filled bowl and some blossoms. Actually, all you need is a water-filled bowl and one spectacular blossom to make a stunning floating bouquet. A big, fat dahlia floating in an elegant vessel is my idea of heaven, as is a jam-packed riot of color and texture floating in a large planter.

Any watertight bowl, bucket, or planter will work. Glass, plastic, metal, concrete, or stone all work well. If you want to use a planter that has drainage holes, carefully cover the holes with duct tape or other waterproofing to make the container watertight. If you can, fill it with water and let it sit a few hours or overnight to make sure there are no leaks.

Photographing floating flowers is also a treat. One of my favorite ways to shoot flowers is to float them in an enormous stainless-steel bowl, where the flowers and light are reflected on the sides.

A floating bouquet is the perfect project for midsummer, when gardens are overflowing and flowers are plentiful. Most flowers will float, or partially submerge, and will last surprisingly well in water if they don't get too hot.

I find that creating a floating bouquet can be a very calming and meditative process. I like to take my time and move the flowers around in the bowl, trying different combinations. I'm often surprised by what works and what doesn't. Flowers that you would think would be harmonious sometimes don't get along at all, while some that would seem to be at odds end up forming a lovely and cooperative tapestry.

Floating bouquets can last a few days or be more ephemeral and last just a few hours, depending on the flowers and the temperature. To maximize longevity, use the freshest flowers you can find and keep your vessel out of direct sunlight.

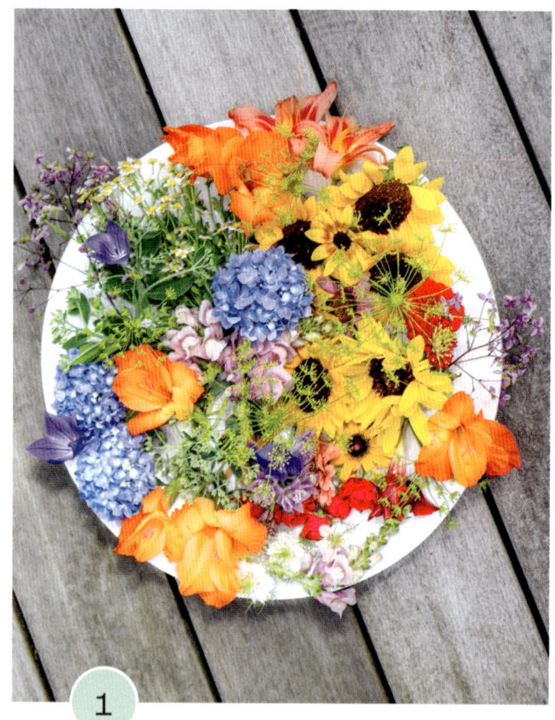

Select the Botanicals

Floating bouquets can be as minimal or lush as you choose. You can use contrasting colors and textures or even make your bouquet monochromatic.

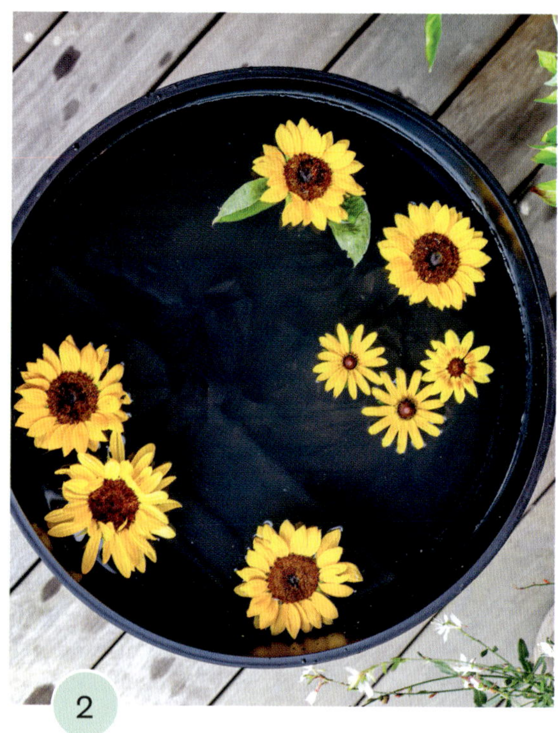

Prepare the Container and Flowers

Fill your vessel with clean, cool water and place it where you want it to be displayed. Moving the arrangement after you have carefully placed all your flowers is kind of a nightmare—not only can the vessel be incredibly heavy, but the water and flowers inevitably slosh around, no matter how careful you are, wrecking the arrangement. Once you have filled and placed your vessel, cut the stems off the flowers with sharp scissors or garden clippers. Then carefully lay the blossoms on top of the water.

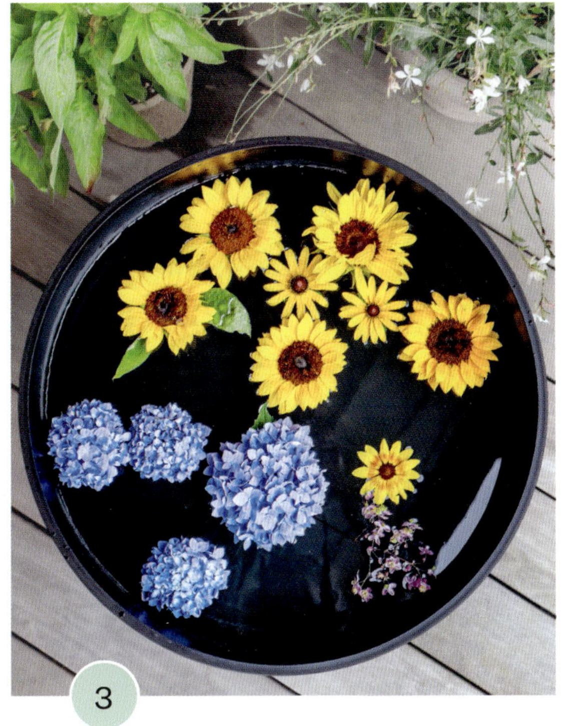

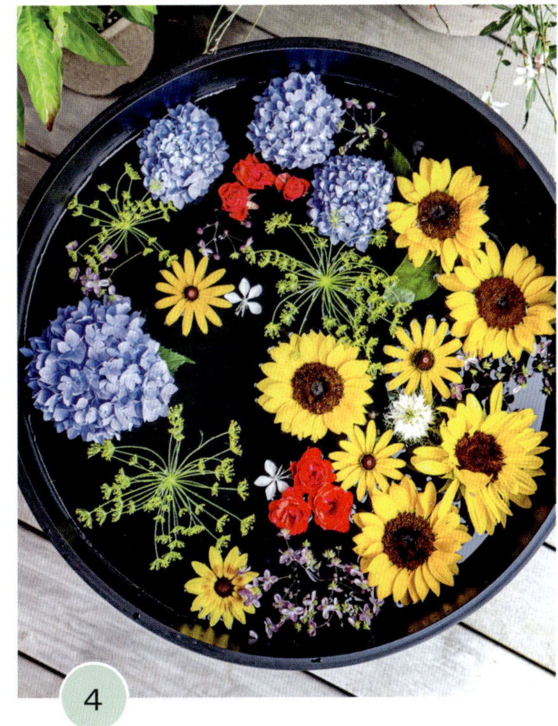

Begin Your Arrangement

The flowers will move around in the water as you place them, which is delightful and kind of hypnotic. Try placing the largest flowers first and then fill in around them. Keep in mind that the negative space between the flowers can be as visually impactful as where the botanicals are. Also, some blooms are more buoyant than others—some will partially submerge, and others will stay completely afloat. Both can work.

Add More Botanicals

Keep adding botanicals, stopping and stepping back often to notice what is working and what is not. Take some photos with your phone to see if the colors and shapes are cohesive. Don't hesitate to move the flowers around, adding and subtracting until you find an arrangement that is satisfying. You can always use any excess blooms in another arrangement.

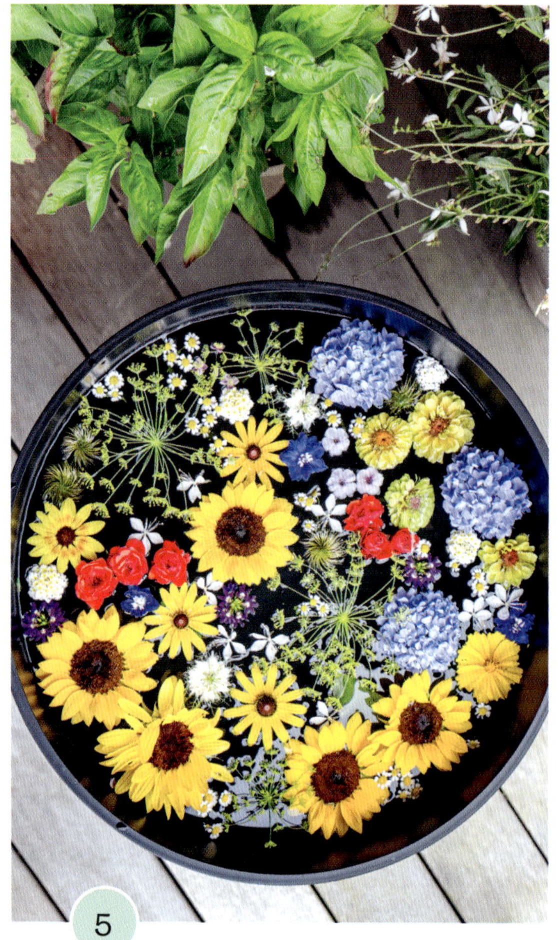

5

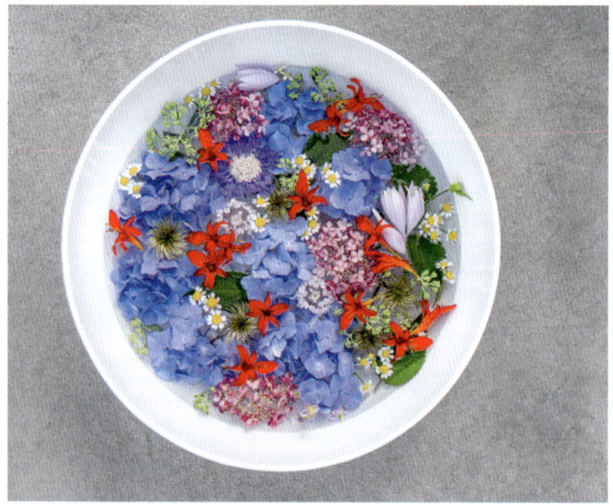

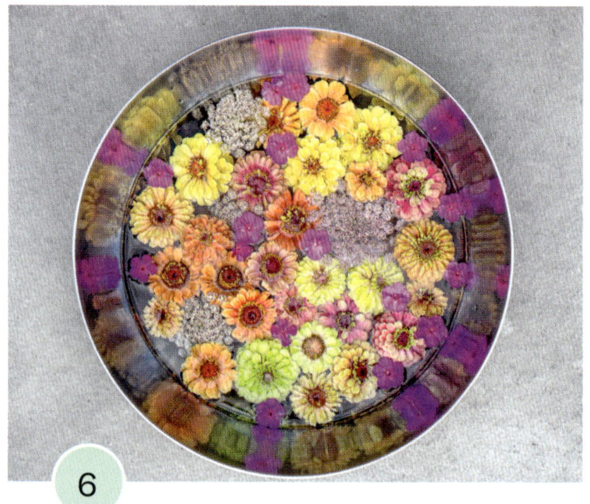

6

Add a Pop of Color

Sometimes adding a contrasting pop of color can bring together an arrangement that is either too blah or just isn't working. It's also fun to see how a few bright blossoms can change the feel of the design entirely.

Experiment

It is enormously satisfying to experiment with different flowers and different types of containers. Push yourself to come up with unusual or exciting color combinations and flower forms.

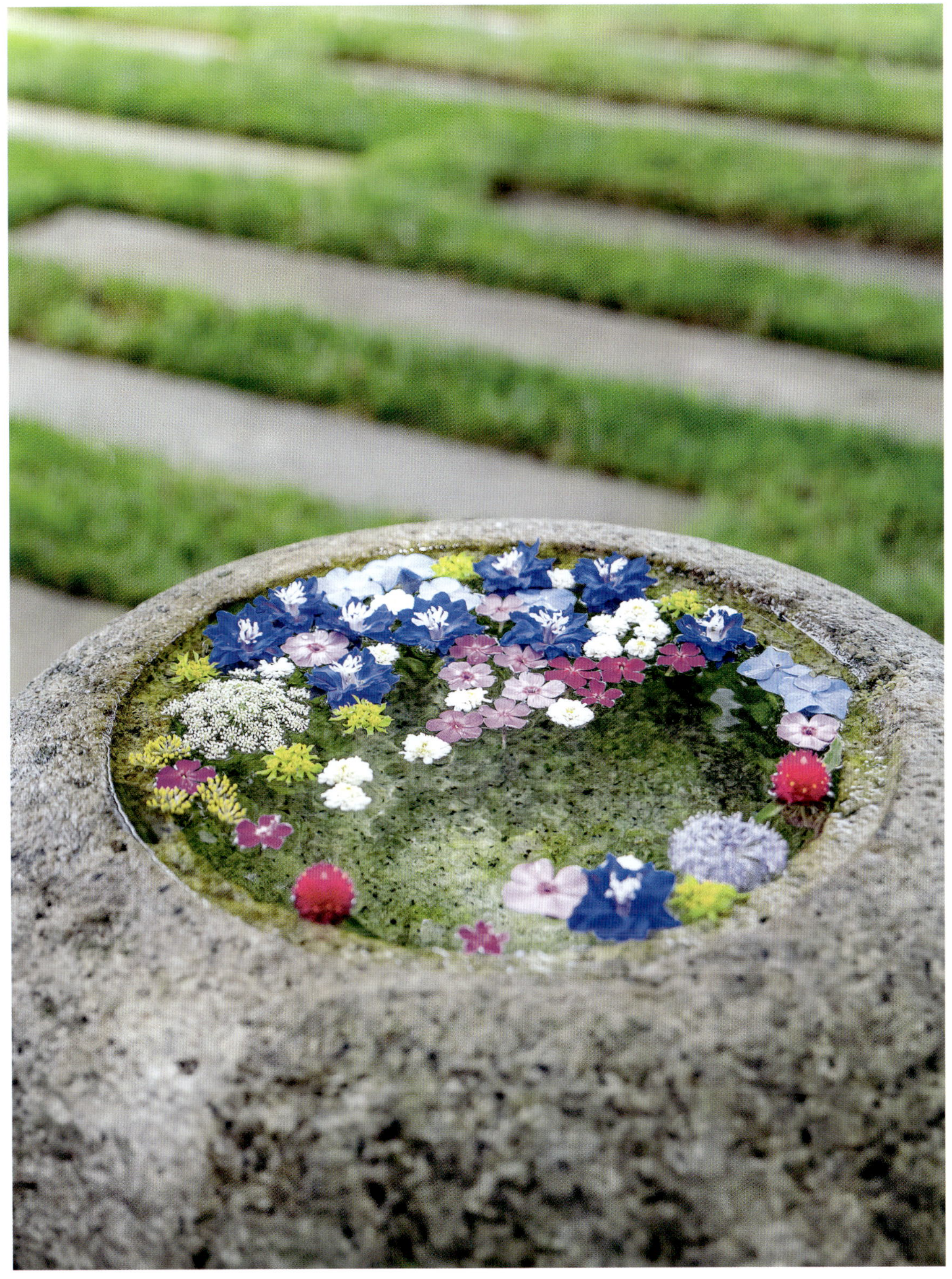

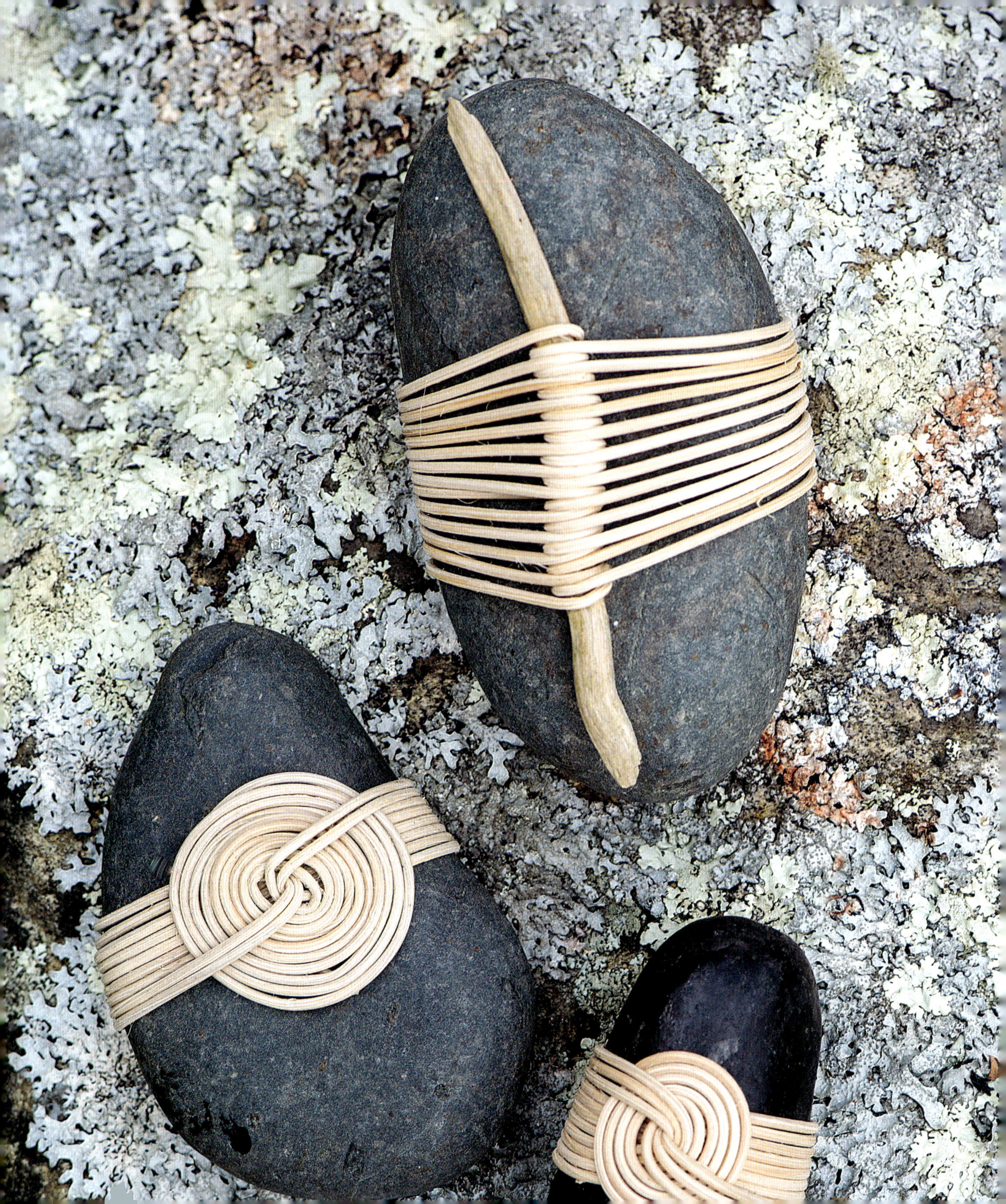

WHAT YOU NEED

- Rock
- Small round, half-round, or flat cane; raffia; twine; yarn; string; or leather cord
- Large darning needle (if using twine, yarn, or string)
- Stick
- Bowl of water
- Masking tape (optional)
- Wooden skewer, small screwdriver, awl, or lacing fid
- Sharp scissors

25

Wrapped Rocks

While some consider wrapping rocks a meditative and peaceful pursuit, I have taken to it more like a dog with a bone—rapacious, impatient, and always wanting more. I know, not very Zen of me. But I love making them. I find the process to be simultaneously hugely satisfying and enormously frustrating—it tests my patience and dexterity. However, as projects go, it is relatively quick and needs very little equipment, and while not exactly easy, it is possible to get a satisfactory piece your first time. I also love that I can create these year-round—in winter sitting in front of the woodstove, and in summer sitting on a dock with my feet in a lake with the wrapping canes soaking in the fresh water.

Interestingly, I have not been able to find any books specifically about rock wrapping, though there are lots of helpful and informative videos online, where you can get ideas and find patterns to try. According to the amazing rock wrapping artist, Karen Okino Butzbach of Shizu Designs, the process employs the "ornamental knots used in Japanese ikebana basketry" and is based on traditional Japanese craft. I have found that basketry and knotting tutorials are also good places to look for patterns.

As with many of these projects, your designs can be as simple or as complex as you choose. You can use string, yarn, raffia, leather cord, or cane. I prefer cane, as I enjoy working with it, and the results are simple and the lines are clean. You can use colorful wrappings or go monochromatic. Each has its charm. To start with, experiment by wrapping a rock with no knots or fancy embellishments. Simply wrap whatever you choose around the circumference of the rock and then tuck in the ends.

I often start a wrapped rock using a pattern that someone else has created, but in the middle I change my mind and go rogue, creating something that is very different from what I set out to do. Sometimes my version works well and sometimes it's a bomb. The good news is that if it's a bomb, I can simply start over with a new piece of wrapping.

For this how-to, I have chosen a simple design that incorporates a stick. It is fairly easy to create, and the final product is beautiful and elegant. The first part of the wrapping is the hardest. Holding the end of your wrap and wrapping a rock, while maintaining tension and holding the stick at the same time, is challenging. Keep at it. You may need to try a bunch of times before you get all the machinations to make it work, but once you do, it becomes much easier.

These stones look lovely displayed as a group in a bowl or placed singly on a shelf or table. They also make great paperweights and can be used in table settings to weigh down napkins. Large, wrapped rocks make excellent doorstops.

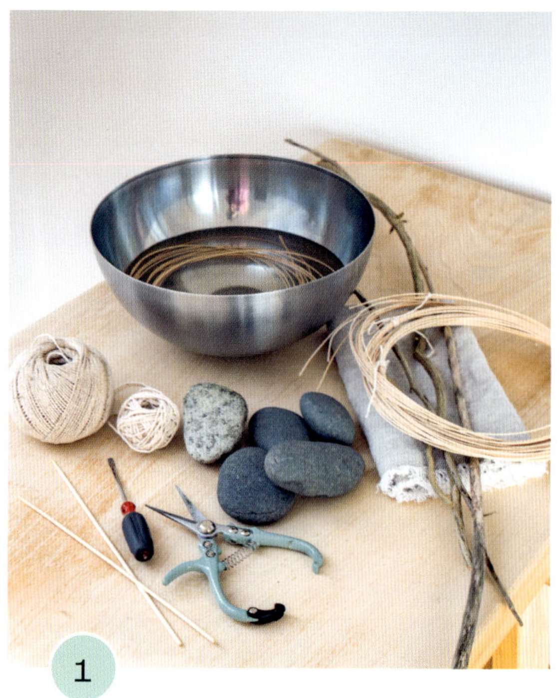

1

Choose the Rock

Your rock can be any size or shape, but for this design, I suggest you choose something that easily fits in your hand but is not too small. A rock that is oval and smooth would be a good choice. You want one with sides as straight as you can find so the wrapping doesn't easily slide off. Avoid stones with sharp edges or angles, as they can cut the caning.

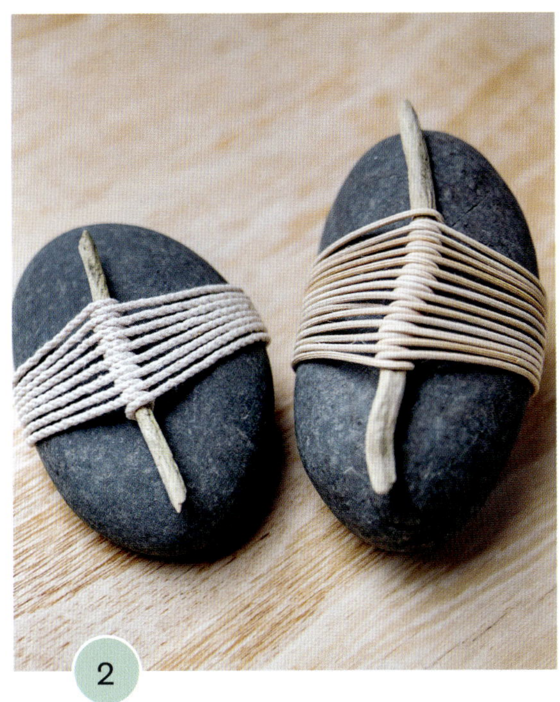

2

Choose the Wrap

Each type of wrap has its advantages. I prefer using cane for my final projects, as I like the classic look it gives. You can either use round, half-round, or flat cane. You can also use string, twine, leather lacing or yarn, which are accessible, inexpensive, and easy to use—and they don't need soaking. Because they are floppy, you will need to use a needle to create the wrap.

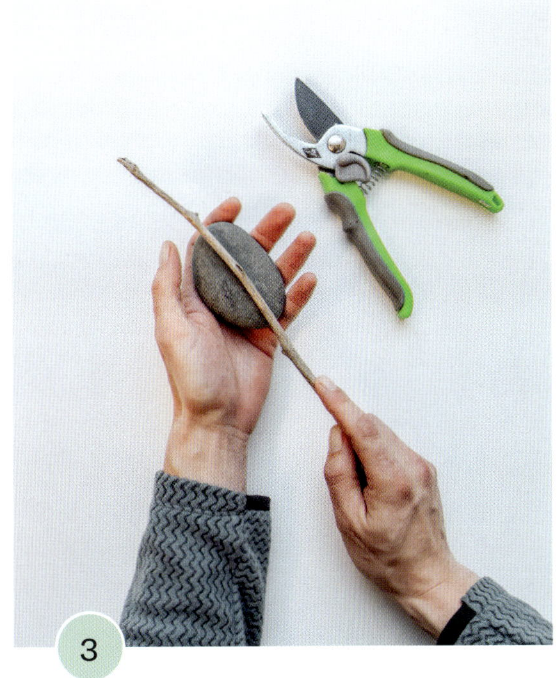

3

Choose Your Wood

Find a piece of wood that has a pleasing feel, color, and shape. I look for branches in the woods that have been smoothed and bleached by the weather but are still firm and dry.

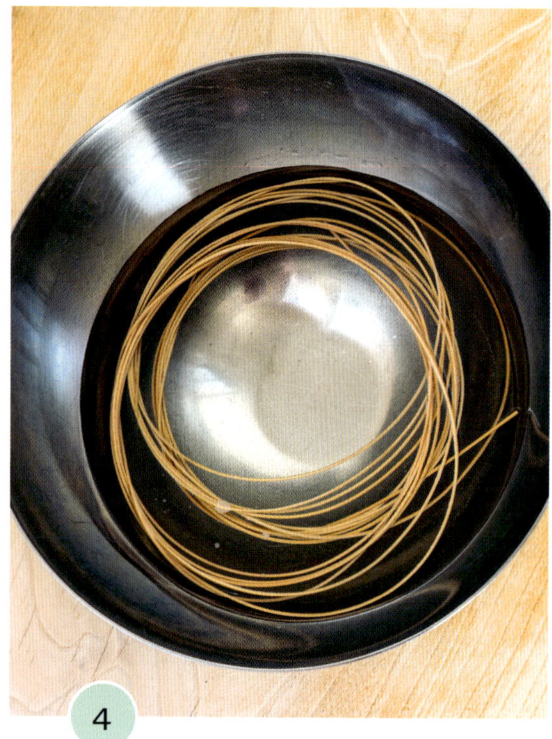

4

Soak the Cane

Soak the cane in water for about 20 minutes to make it flexible. Note that if you leave it in the water for too long, it can turn a bit gray. Put in few extra strands to soak as they sometimes break during the process, which usually means you have to start over.

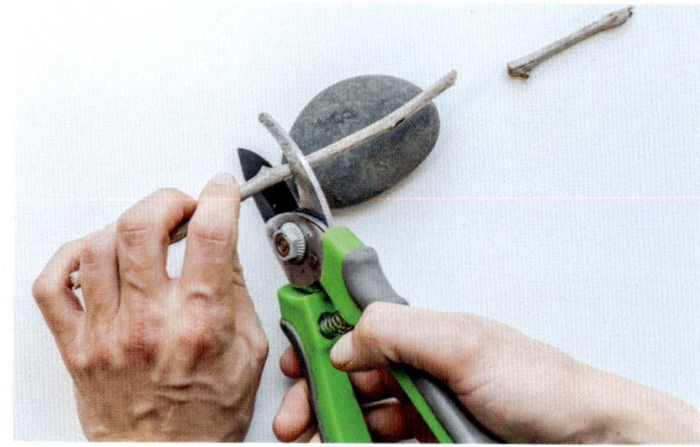

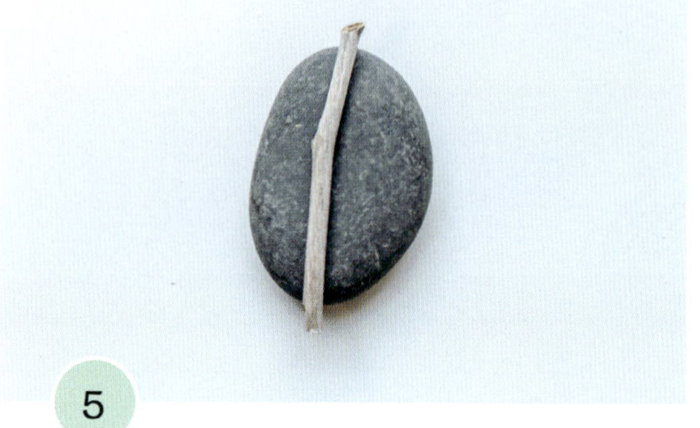

5

Fit the Stick

Cut your piece of wood to fit the rock. You can have it extend beyond the ends of the rock or aligned with the edges. I like to turn the wood against the rock to find the side that will best hug the stone before I cut the ends.

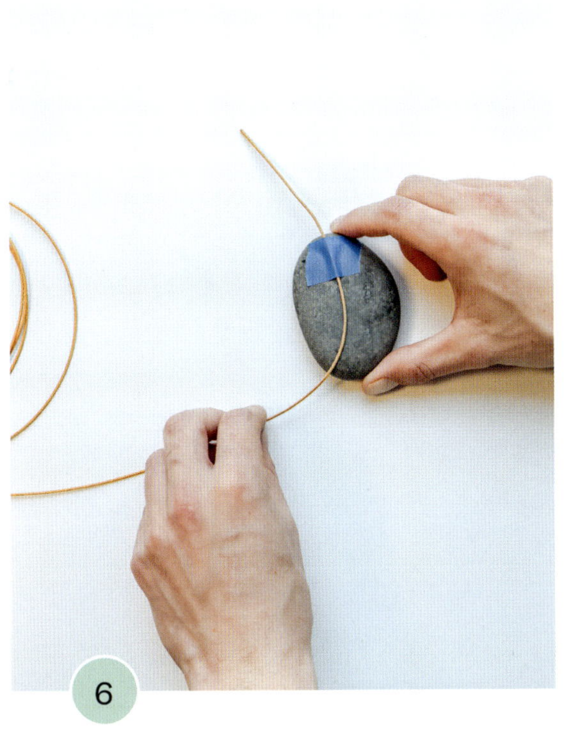
6

Start Wrapping

One end of the cane will be called the passive end, which you will keep in one place for the duration of the wrapping. The active part or end is what you work with. Start your wrap on the top back of the rock. Make sure you leave a few inches for a passive tail. You can use masking tape to secure the passive end of the wrap to the rock or use your fingers to hold it in place. About three-quarters down the rock, bend the wrap so the active part of the cane points left.

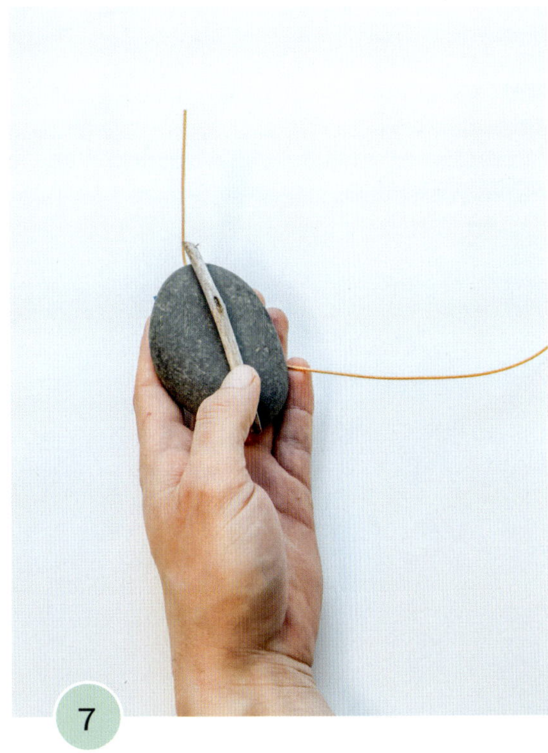
7

Form the First Loop

Holding the bent section of the cane with one hand, turn the rock over. Now the active end will be on your right. Place the stick on the rock.

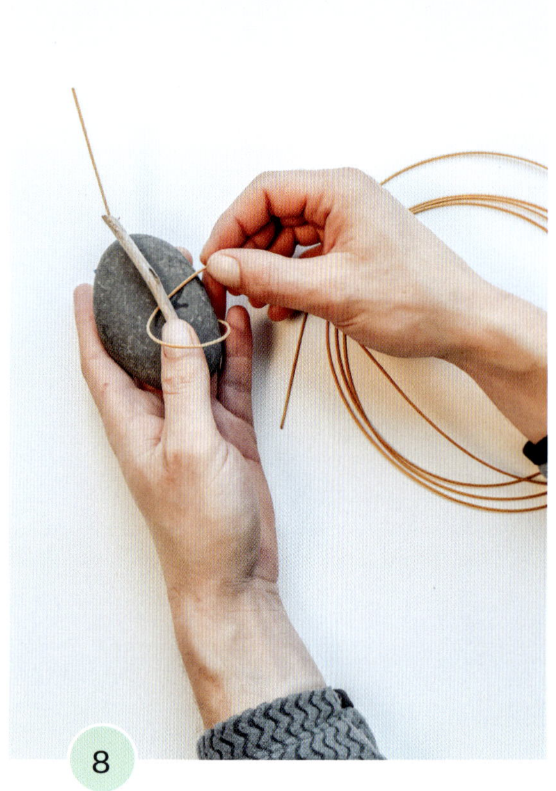

8

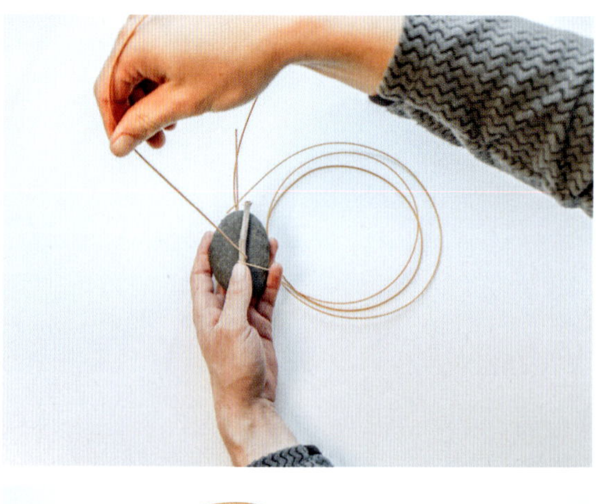

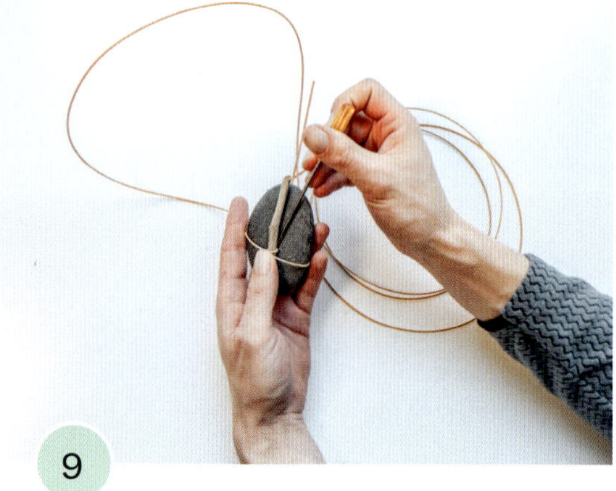

9

Wrap

Holding the stick on top of the rock, wrap the cane over the top of the stick. Loop the wrap over the stick, then under. Now the active end is pointing right. Loop the wrap over the top of the stick.

Loop

Go over the top of your stick (active end now pointing left). Even out the wrap so it is perpendicular to the stick, making sure to keep the stick secured and straight.

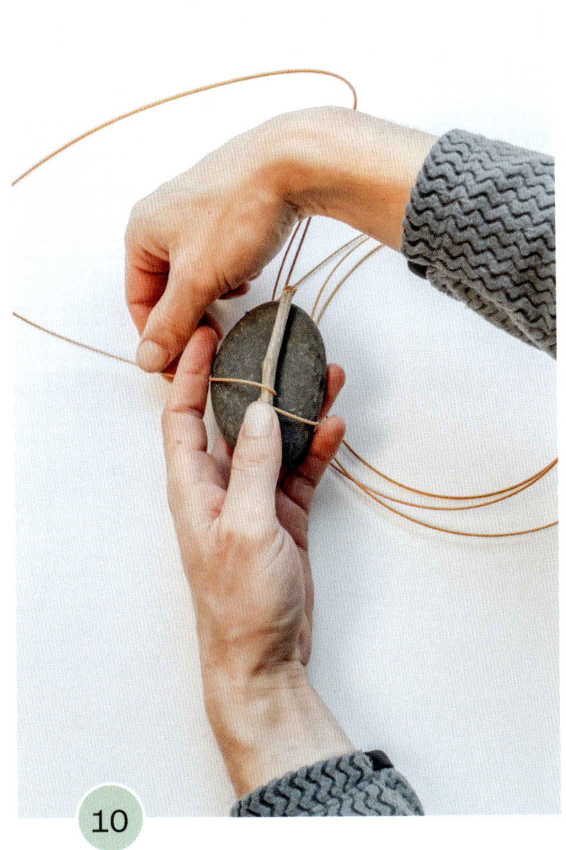

10

Wrap around the Back

While holding loop and stick, wrap the active end around the back of the rock. You want the wraps in back to go over the passive end of the cane, which will start to secure it. Also make sure to lay each wrap right above the previous wrap.

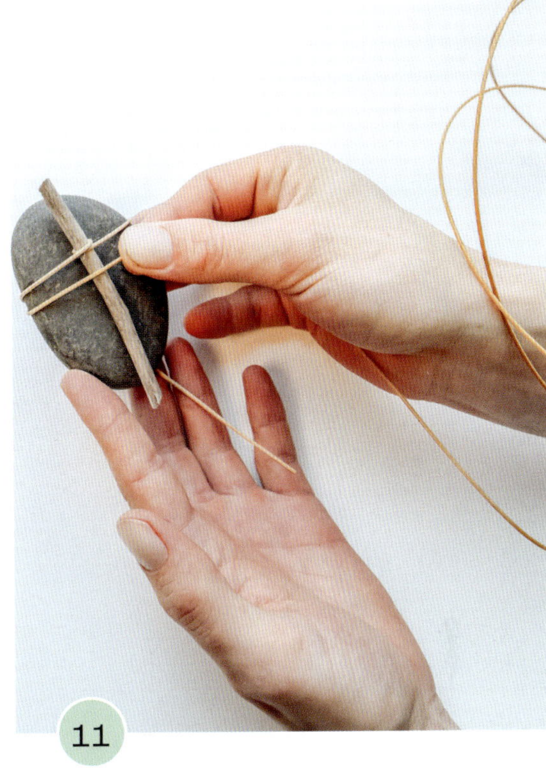

11

Repeat the Wrap

Maintaining tension, repeat the process. You want all your wraps to be evenly spaced and only overlap where they are supposed to. Keep checking both the front and back.

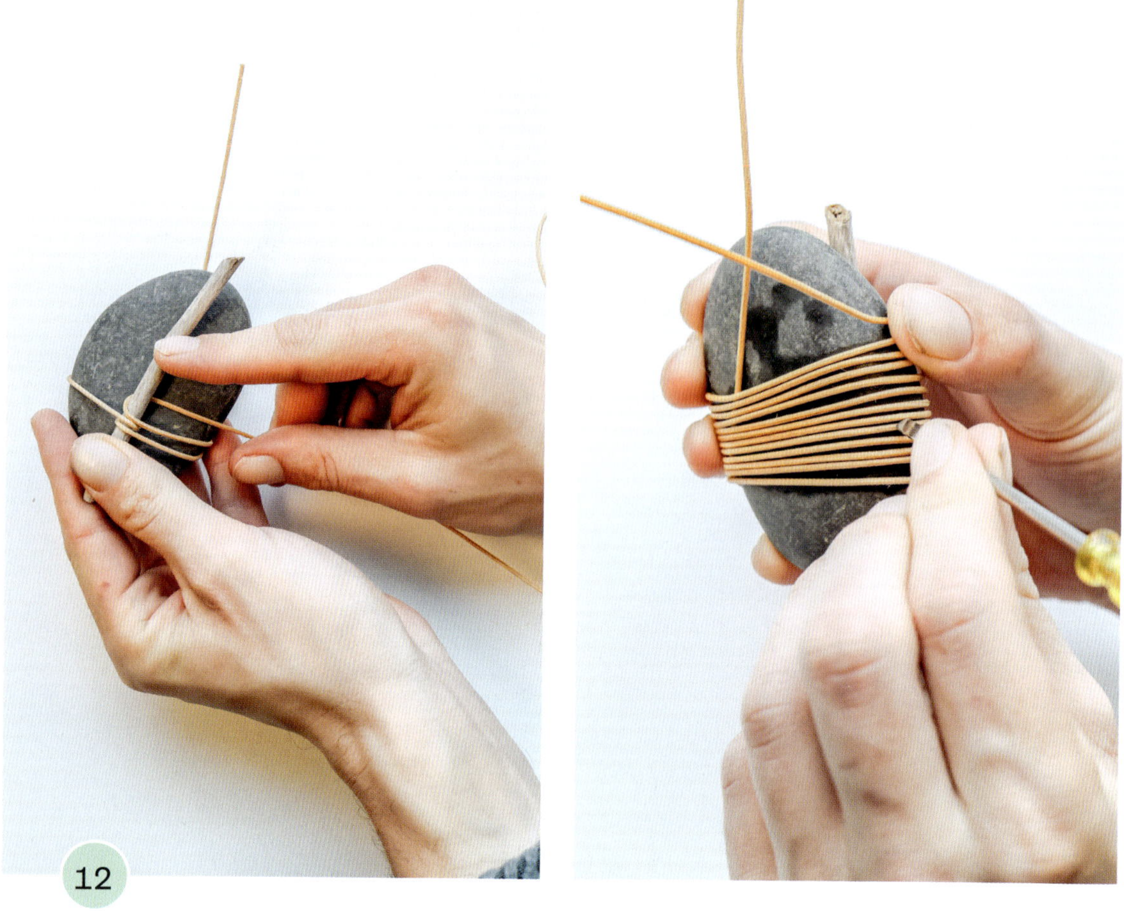

12

Straighten and Align

As you work, you can use the wooden skewer, screwdriver, awl, or lacing fid to make sure the wraps are evenly spaced and symmetrical.

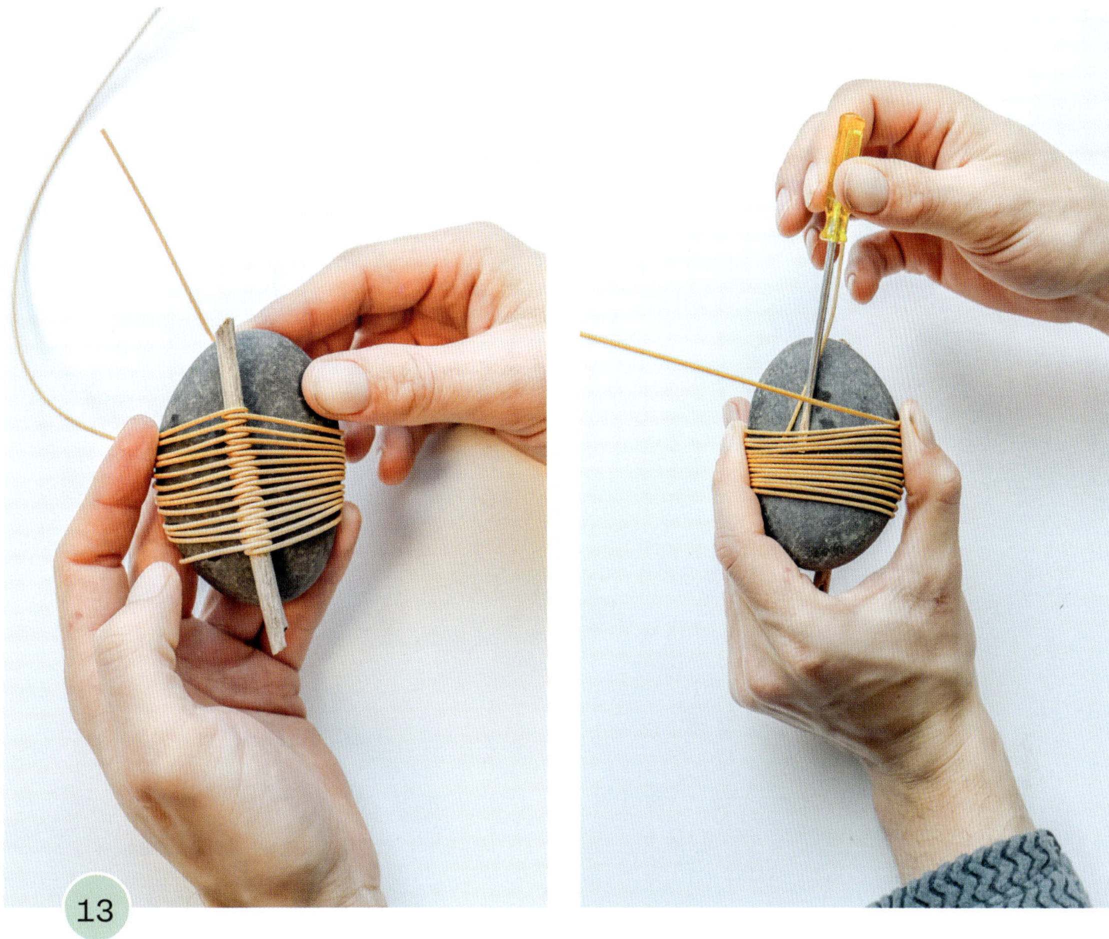

13

Finish

Once you have made as many wraps as you want, turn the stone over. Take the screwdriver or lacing fid and, while keeping tension on the active cane end, insert the tool behind all wraps on the back.

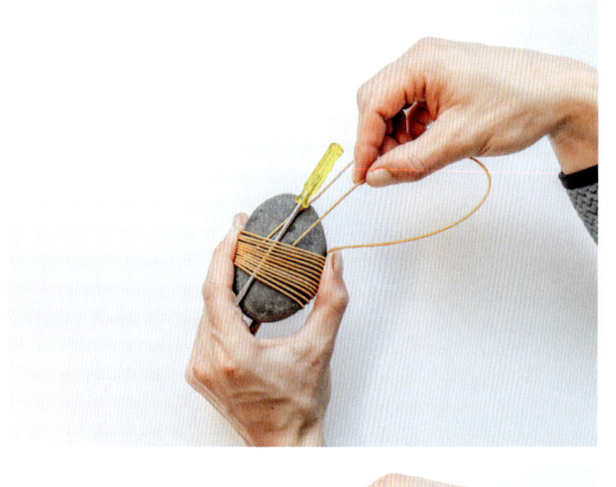

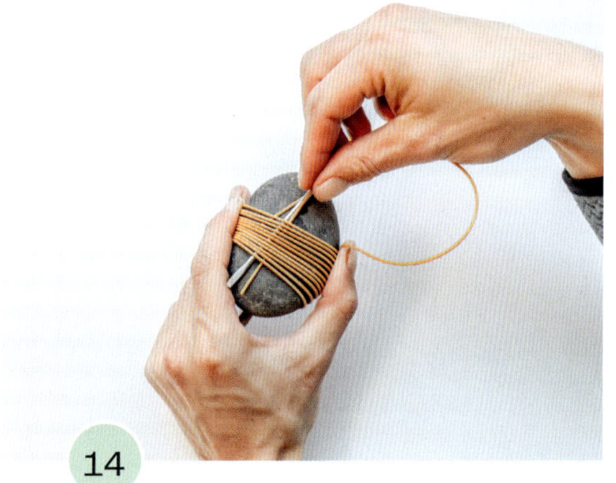

14

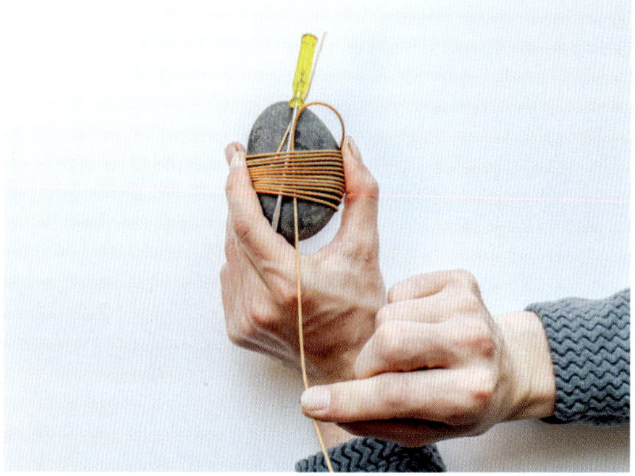

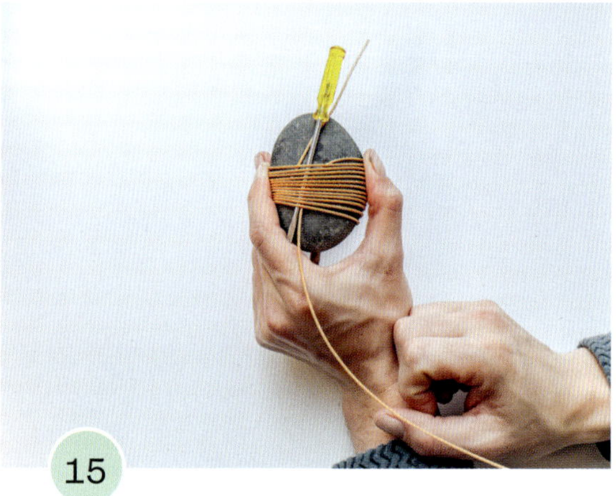

15

Tuck the End

The screwdriver or lacing fid should have enough room next to it so that you can slide the active end behind the wraps and out the bottom. If you need more room, twist the screwdriver or fid slightly to create more space.

Tighten the End

Pull the active end until it is tightly secured next to the top wrap.

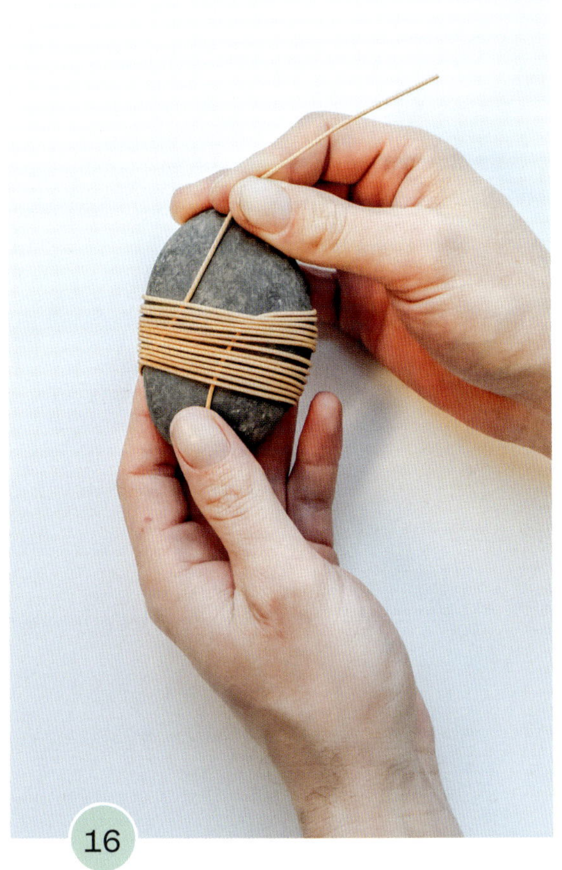

16

Pull the Ends

Remove the screwdriver or fid. Pull on both the passive and active ends until they are tight and secured.

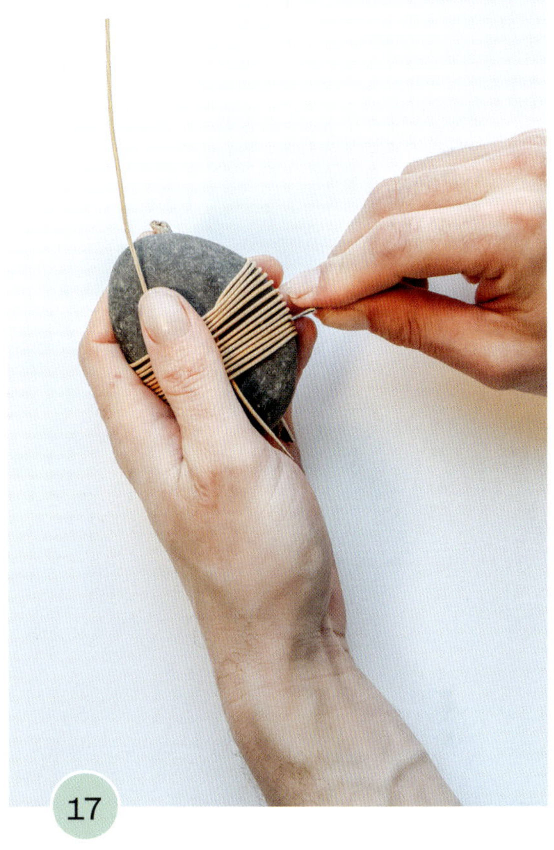

17

Double-Check the Spacing

Do a final check on the spacing of the wraps and adjust as needed.

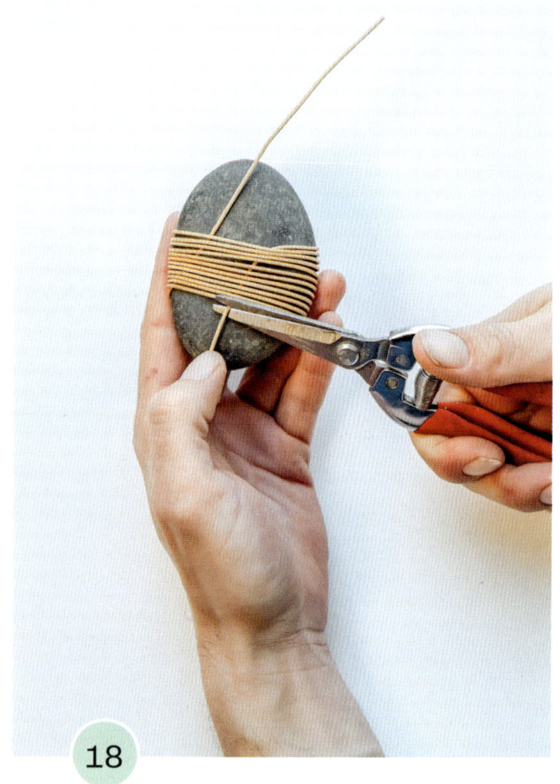

Clip the Ends

Cut the ends as close to the final wraps as you can.

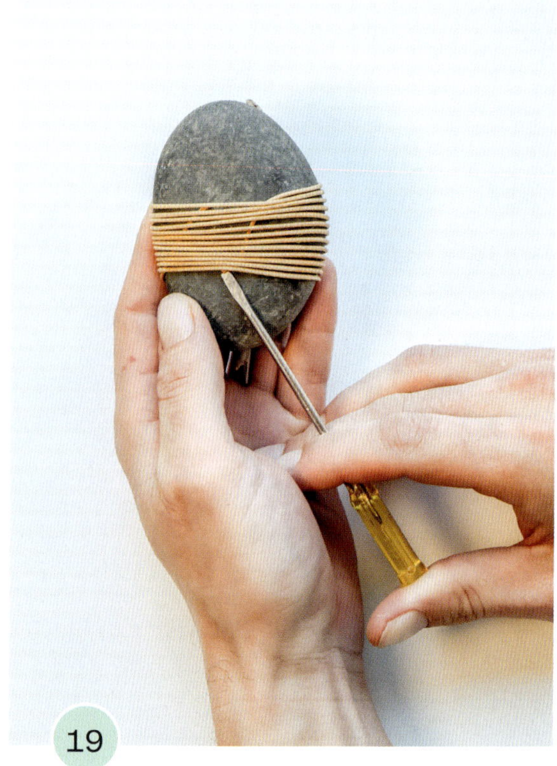

Tuck the Ends

Use your tool to push the ends just under the wraps. The cane will shrink a bit as it dries, tightening around the rock.

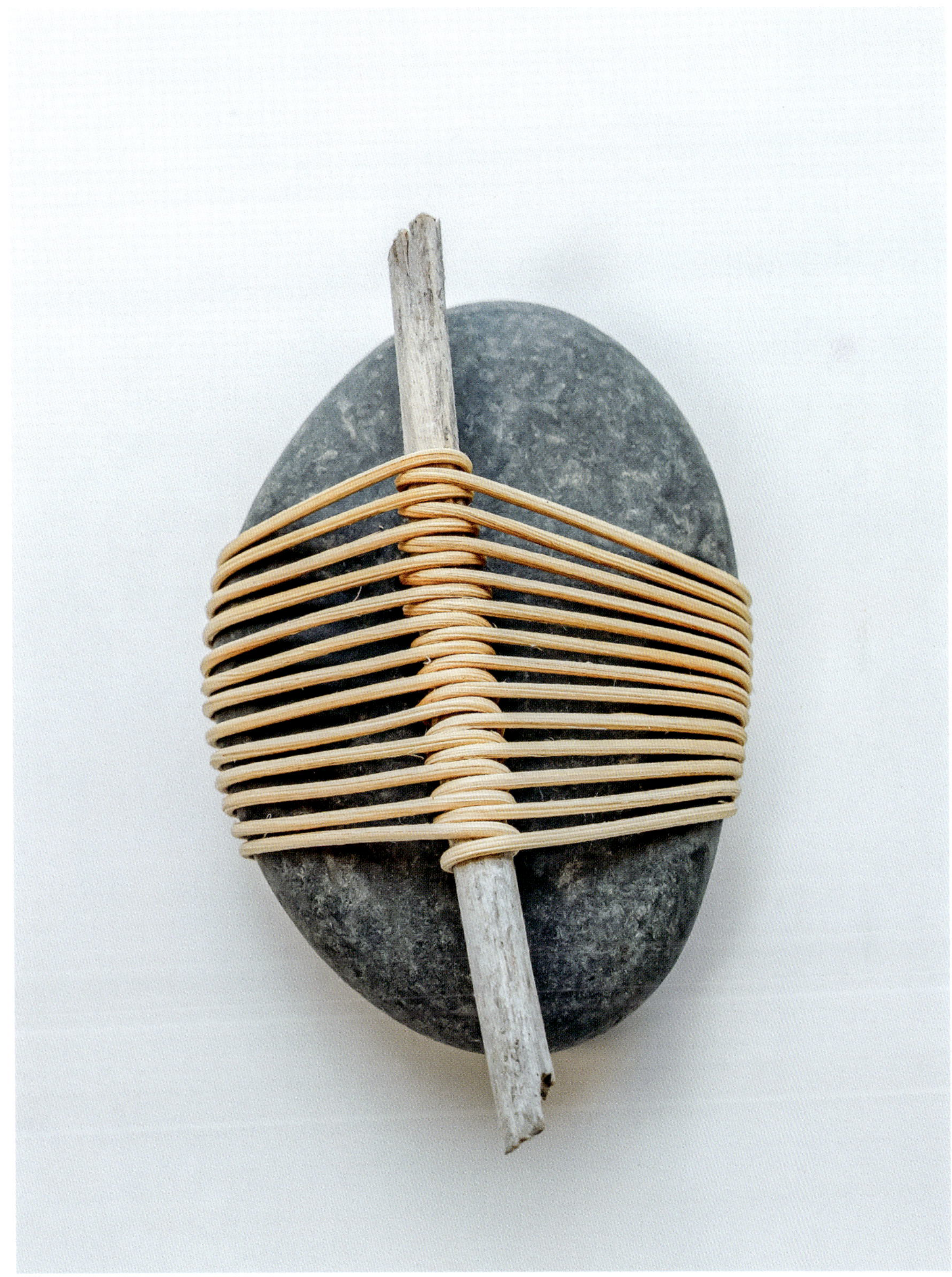

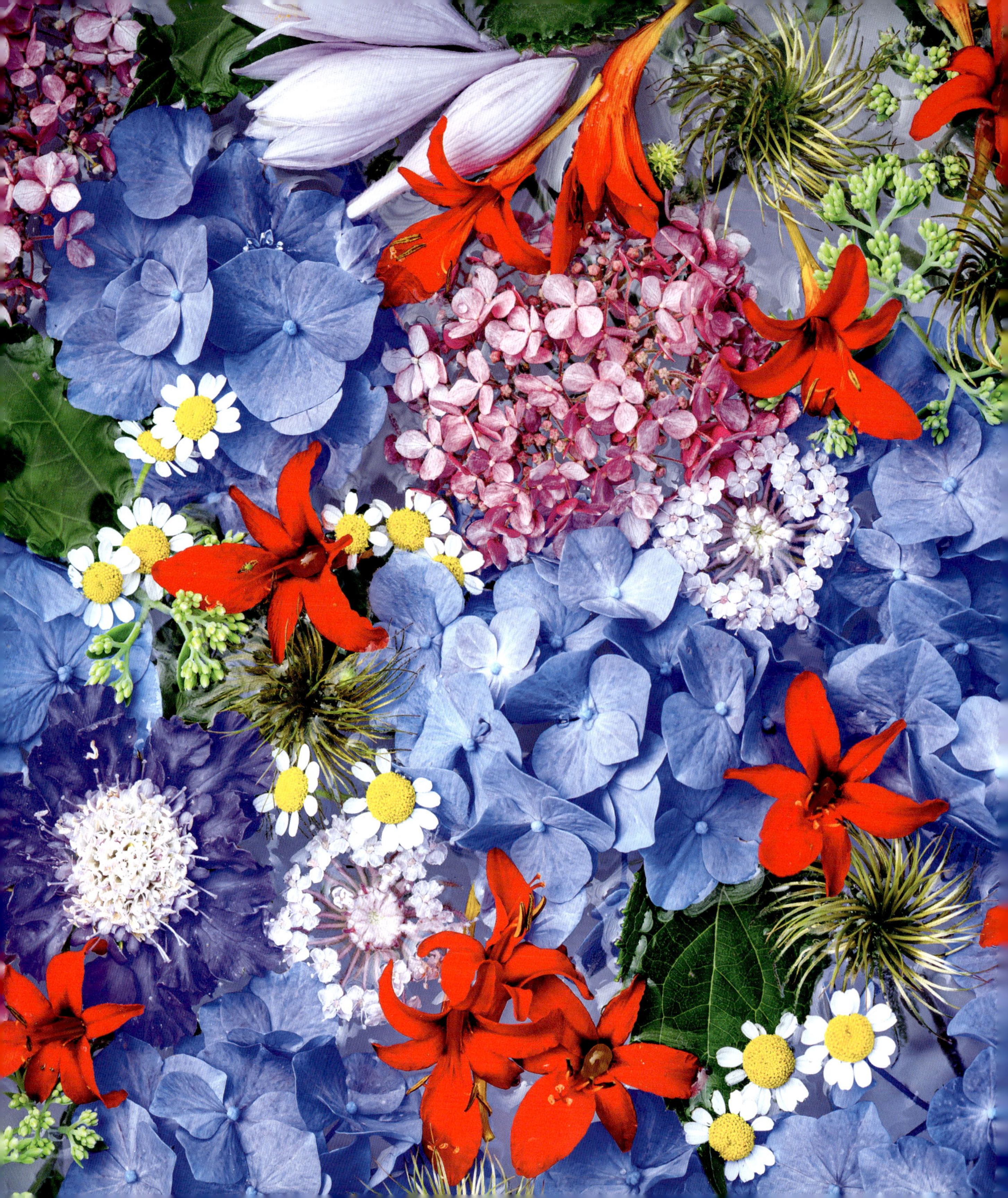

Resources

BOOKS

Ashmore, Jennie. 2019. *The Art of Pressed Flowers and Leaves: Contemporary Techniques and Designs*. London: B. T. Batsford.

Richardson, Melissa, and Amy Fielding. 2022. *The Modern Flower Press: Capturing the Beauty of Nature*. New York: Abrams.

Hoffman, Mary Jo. 2024. *STILL: The Art of Noticing*. New York: Monacelli.

Anderson, Christina Z. 2019. *Cyanotype: The Blueprint in Contemporary Practice*. New York: Routledge.

TOOLS

Bailey Ceramic Supplies
baileypottery.com
Pottery tools

C. S. Osborne & Co.
osborneleathertools.com
Lacing fid and leather tools

SEED COMPANIES

Botanical Interests
botanicalinterests.com

Grand Prismatic Seed
grandprismaticseed.com

Hudson Valley Seed Company
hudsonvalleyseed.com

Johnny's Selected Seeds
johnnyseeds.com

Renee's Garden
reneesgarden.com

ART SUPPLIES

Agawami Factory
awagami.com

Artist & Craftsman Supply
artistcraftsman.com

B&H Photo
bhphotovideo.com

Bostick & Sullivan
bostick-sullivan.com

Cyanotype Store
cyanotypestore.com

Dick Blick
dickblick.com

Freestyle Photo and Imaging
freestylephoto.com

H. H. Perkins
hhperkins.com

Photographers Formulary
photoformulary.com

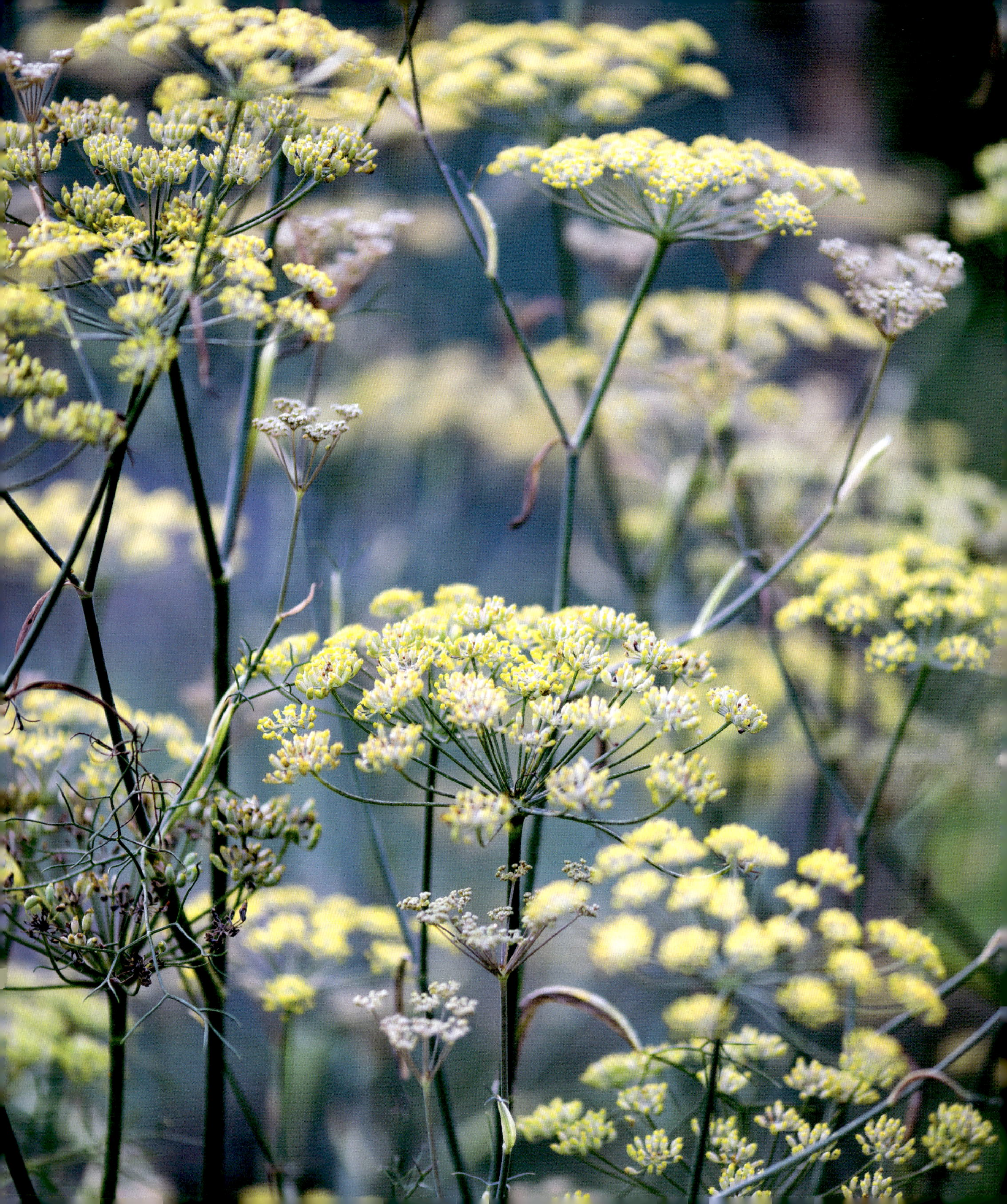

List of Useful Botanicals

Alstroemeria
Anemone
Astilbe
Azalea
Begonia
Blackberry lily
Black-eyed Susan
Borage
Calendula
Coreopsis
Cosmos
Creeping Jenny
Crocosmia
Daffodil
Dahlia
Daisy
Daucus
Delphinium
Dill
Echinacea
Fennel
Fern
Feverfew
Forget-me-not
Gaura
Geranium
Geum
Hellebore
Hydrangea
Japanese indigo
Japanese maple
Lady's mantle
Lavender
Leucojum
Lilac
Lily of the valley
Lisianthus
Marigold
Muscari
Nasturtium
Nigella
Orlaya
Pansy
Parsley (flat-leaf)
Passionflower
Peony
Phlox
Queen Anne's lace
Ranunculus
Rose
Rosemary
Scaevola
Scilla
Salvia
Sage
Sea oat
Sunflower
Sweet peas
Sweet potato vine
Sweet woodruff
Thalictrum
Tulip
Verbena
Vinca
Weigela
Zinnia

Acknowledgments

It has been a dream of mine to shoot and write a book, as books have always been one of the centers of my world. Working on this project has been a joyful experience, in large part because of the support I was lucky to have from so many people.

Big gratitude goes to my family, who all participated in this process, from literally lending their hands to endlessly looking at photos and reading drafts. Thanks also for their patience with my botanical obsessions. Special thanks to Brett for his tireless enthusiasm, infinite optimism, and helpful suggestions, as well as the endless proofing. And so much gratitude goes to my mom, who didn't get to see the book finished, but whose spirit and encouragement lives on every page.

I am deeply grateful to the team at Timber Press: Naomi Ruiz, Sarah Milholin, Makenna Goodman, Matthew Burnett, and Sara Isasi, who were supportive, creative, and smart. They helped guide and craft this book from the beginning and made the process profoundly gratifying. Thanks also to Paula Brisco for taming my unruly syntax and punctuation.

The bench of supporters for this project is very deep. Many thanks to Kathy Biberstein, Liza Bakewell, Diane Dreher, Lisa Keith, Janet McTeer, Heidi Steele, and Fiona Wilson. These are the people who told me I could in fact write and shoot a book and then supported me along the way, with long walks and talks, laughter, good advice, cocktails, and looking at oh-so-many photos.

Much gratitude to Nan Olin, Kevin O'Connor, John Spooner, Will Makris, Doug Reed, Stephen Fletcher, Michael Walden, Colleen O'Neal, Ellen Zachos, Lia Micheels, Maryann Biberstein, Cynthia Stuart, Gina Michaels, Brad Michaels and Susan Simon for their help and support.

Thanks also to Proven Winners and Pleasant View Gardens for providing many beautiful plants.

Special thanks to Liz Micheels, my oldest friend and now essential collaborator. And thanks to David, Graham, and Erik for their support that made this all possible.

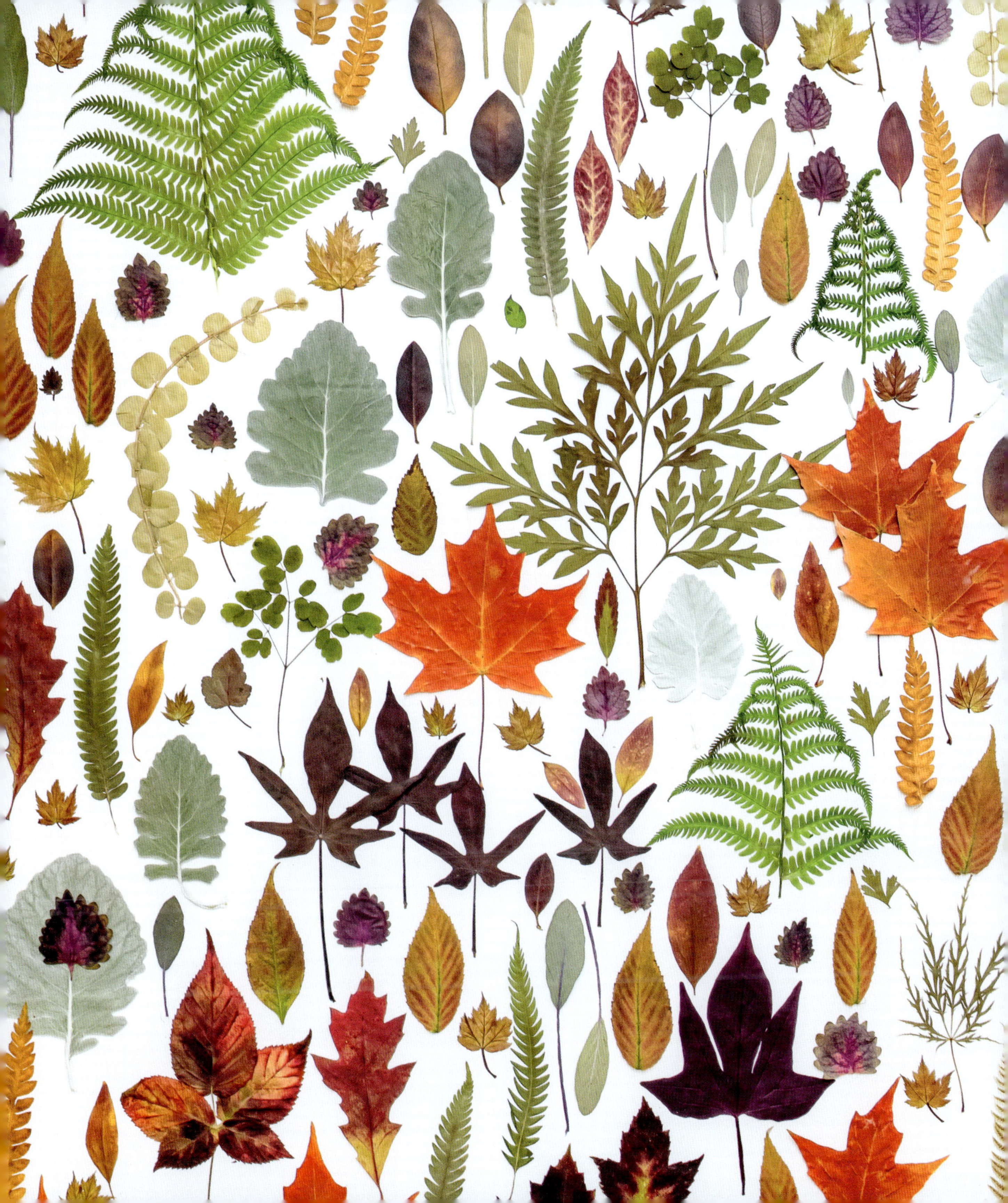

Index

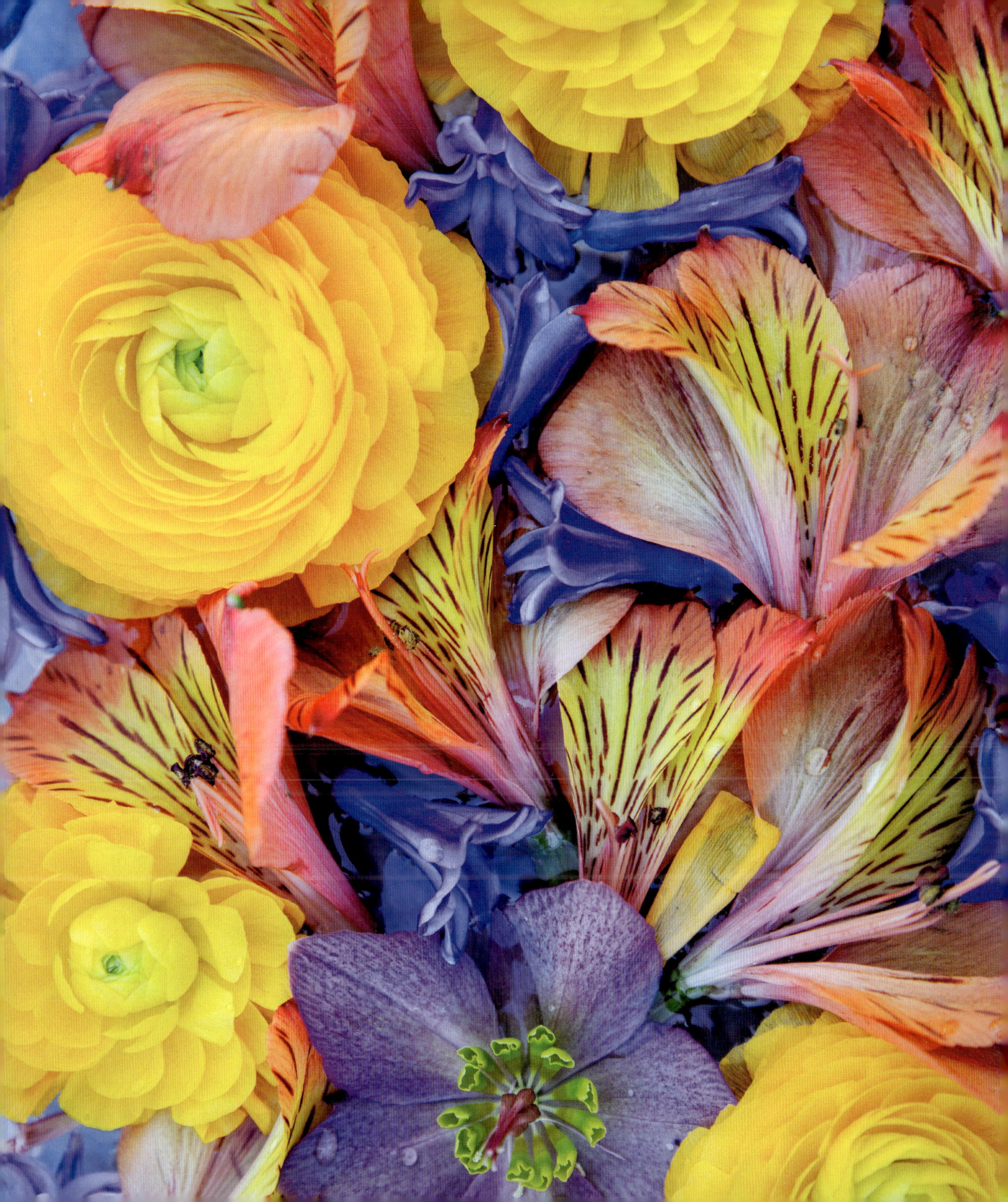